The American Profile

The American Profile

2 nd
edition

Morton Borden
Otis L. Graham, Jr.
University of California, Santa Barbara

D. C. Heath and Company
Lexington, Massachusetts   Toronto

Published simultaneously in Canada.

Printed in the United States of America.

International Standard Book Number: 0-669-84822-0

Library of Congress Catalog Card Number: 77-077540

Preface

"History is bunk," Henry Ford once announced, and our experience as teachers suggests that the sentiment is not entirely dead. Studied as a compilation of facts to be memorized and then quickly forgotten, history is painful. Twisted to serve particular causes, it is dishonest. Taught as a patriotic exercise, it is dangerous. We have tried to avoid these abuses—which does not mean we have not committed others. Students should bear in mind that the past is not fixed, and its issues are never finally settled. Our sense of the past is constantly altered by present circumstances and changed perspectives. The civil rights revolution of the mid-twentieth century has forced scholars to reexamine the history of blacks and women. The American experience in Vietnam, the debacle of Richard Nixon, the problem of environmental pollution all have led to readjustments of perspectives on history. The contemporary vantage point *will* influence written history. The challenge is to use that vantage point to add to our understanding rather than to restrict it.

We have revised the first edition of *The American Profile* to provide more detail, to incorporate some of the recent developments in scholarship, and to carry our account of events into the presidency of Jimmy Carter. The book's purpose is to evoke questions, to stimulate interest, to serve as a guide for college students who make their first tour in American history. Ideally it should be supplemented with appropriate readings from other books that treat particular subjects more exhaustively.

In this new edition we have greatly expanded the illustration and map programs and have treated more fully such topics as the colonial period, minorities, and women. Although our emphasis is on political history, we have also included relevant discussions of economic, social, cultural, ethnic, and intellectual history. In addition, commentaries at the ends of chapters provide helpful insights into the material covered in each chapter.

We wish to thank those who used the first edition and suggested ways in which it might be improved. We hope they will continue to send us their opinions. So that criticisms may be allocated properly, the first eight chapters are the responsibility of Morton Borden, the last eight of Otis L. Graham, Jr.

We owe a considerable debt to our students and colleagues at the University of California, Santa Barbara, as well as to our wives, our children, and our editors, who, for quite different reasons, urged us to complete the tasks of revision.

MORTON BORDEN

OTIS L. GRAHAM, JR.

Contents

MAPS

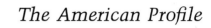

The American Profile

1

The Seventeenth Century

God or Gold

"Let us rejoice," Christopher Columbus proclaimed after his initial voyage, "as well on account of the exaltation of our faith, as on account of the increase of our temporal prosperity." The words were really a boast to mask his failure. Instead of treasure and spices Columbus had found only frightened Indians and lush vegetation. Three times more he led expeditions without ever discovering the fabled wealth of the Indies, without ever realizing that he was touching the fringes of a vast, unknown hemisphere. Nevertheless, in that one sentence Columbus combined what were to become the twin motivating forces for European expansion: the spiritual and the secular. In the coming centuries men ventured into strange lands either to enrich king and country or to escape them; either to proselytize for Christianity or to practice it undisturbed; either to earn a livelihood or to make a fortune. Some went unwillingly as prisoners or slaves, and others from a sense of adventure. But two major impulses predominated for most explorers and settlers, and who can now tell which was the stronger—God or gold?

The Iberian Empires

Portugal had been the first western European country to create an overseas empire. Before the voyages of Columbus, Portuguese mariners had ventured into the Atlantic, explored the western coast and rounded the southern tip of the African continent. By the early 1500s Portugal had established numerous trading posts in Ceylon, India, and the East Indies. Spices in Asia were cheap and plentiful, and could be easily transported because of their small bulk. In addition, prices on the European market were so high that each successful voyage yielded enormous profits. Portugal's population, however, was inadequate to colonize and defend its widely distributed commercial stations. European competitors gradually seized the most lucrative sites.

Spain's disappointment at the comparatively meager wealth of the Caribbean changed abruptly after the conquests of the Aztecs by Hernando Cortez and the Incas by Francisco Pizarro. So much gold and, especially, silver poured into Spain from the mines of Mexico and Peru that the sudden influx of wealth touched off an

A series of voyages begun in 1497 convinced Amerigo Vespucci that the newly discovered lands were not a part of Asia, as Columbus had thought, but rather a "New World." In 1507 a map showing Vespucci and the New World first used the term "America." (New York Public Library)

inflationary spiral that affected every aspect of European life. Outside the Iberian Peninsula inflation aided capitalistic development, which in turn helped to erode medieval institutions. In Spain and Portugal, paradoxically, the treasure of Asia and America served to freeze the rigid social structure of the past. Spain used its wealth to gild church altars, wasted it on courtly extravagance, and dissipated it in fighting holy wars against northern Protestants. The Iberian nations started poor—and ended poor.

Spanish Power

At first glance the Spanish empire appeared too bloated to defend itself. Buccaneers intercepted and seized Spanish galleons loaded with bullion, and carried out daring raids on Spanish colonial ports. Sir Francis Drake, on the *Golden Hynd,* brought back so much Spanish treasure in 1580 that Queen Elizabeth's portion was sufficient to pay off all England's foreign debts and to balance the national budget. Other shareholders in the venture realized a profit of 4600 percent. Some fifty years later the Dutch admiral Piet Hein captured an entire Spanish treasure fleet off the Cuban coast. The prize amounted to nearly ten million dollars.

Nevertheless, Spain was quite capable of defending its colonial possessions. The attempts made by the Dutch, the English, and the French to whittle away at the Spanish-American empire during the sixteenth century failed. Competitors established colonial posts from Florida to Canada, but none of them lasted for more than a few years. French settlers in Florida and South Carolina were slaughtered by the Spaniards. English settlers in North Carolina disappeared without a trace. To this day the fate of Sir Walter Raleigh's "Lost Colony" remains an enigma. Even the defeat of the Spanish

Armada in 1588, contrary to legend, did not signify the twilight of Spanish power. The central parts of Spain's imperial domain remained impregnable throughout the colonial era.

Not until 1607, at Jamestown, Virginia, did an English seed take permanent root in the New World. The settlement seemed totally inconsequential to the Spanish monarch. After all, the Spaniards controlled an area which stretched from Texas to Tierra del Fuego. The English, moreover, who yearned to duplicate Spanish triumphs, discovered neither gold, silver, nor precious stones. Rather, they encountered malaria and hostile tribes of Indians. In Virginia, and elsewhere on the North American continent, English explorers were frustrated in still another respect. They expected to locate a water route through the continent to the Pacific, and thus to the Orient. Sir Humphrey Gilbert had composed a *Discourse on the Northwest Passage* to prove that such a route existed. Despite repeated failures and mounting geographic evidence to the contrary, the belief and the fruitless search long persisted.

None could foresee that from such an unpropitious and unrewarding beginning the English would create a mighty empire. A small island nation, torn by religious dissent and political unrest, without colonies to provide

Foundations of English Power

John White, an artist, and Thomas Hariot, a mathematician and surveyor, were among the initial settlers (in 1585) of Sir Walter Raleigh's doomed colony at Roanoke. The Pamlico Indian village shown here appeared in Hariot's Brief and True Report of the New Found Land of Virginia, *illustrated by White's watercolors. The structure marked A is a building housing the tombs of "their kings and princes," B, the area for their "solemn prayers," C, the location for dancing and to "make merrie together," D, where they feasted, F, an outpost to guard against animals who might devour their crops. After serving as governor of Roanoke, White left for England, leaving behind his daughter and son-in-law and their child, Virginia Dare, the first white child born in the English colonies. In 1591, when he again set foot at Roanoke, the entire colony and all traces of the colonists themselves had disappeared. (Rare Book Division, New York Public Library)*

easy windfalls of bullion or spices, England nevertheless emerged as an international power to rival and then to surpass Spain. How was it possible? What were the special ingredients that contributed to this remarkable achievement?

First, after Jamestown the English literally swarmed across the Atlantic in an unprecedented mass migration. In less than four decades some seventy thousand came, not only to Plymouth and Massachusetts Bay, fanning out into New England, but also to the Chesapeake region, and to Bermuda, Barbados, and other West Indian islands. The men who ruled England were delighted. At one stroke, they reasoned, the homeland would be rid of unemployed vagabonds, incorrigible jailbirds, potential rebels, and religious malcontents like the Puritans. Ironically, the foundations of English imperial power were based in part on the work of these fugitives, who found conditions at home intolerable.

Second, overseas expansion was made possible by an extension of burgeoning capitalism in England. As the Spanish noble had wasted, the English capitalist had accumulated. The British made a virtue of necessity by extolling thrift and exalting business. Entrepreneurs who made fortunes in coal mining and iron manufacturing, in the glass and textile industries, or in trade and agriculture, invested some of their surplus capital in colonial experiments which they hoped would yield even greater profits. Of course, settlers had to be willing to make the journey across the Atlantic; but they also had to be equipped, transported, and maintained. The costs of colonization were often financed by groups of capitalists who formed joint-stock companies under royal charters.

These companies proved a poor investment for the individual speculator. In Latin America, Indians mined silver for the Spaniards; in Canada, they gathered furs for the French. In between, there was no quick way to instant wealth. The land was virtually free, but hard work and patience were necessary to make it self-sustaining and profitable. (The English colonist came to venerate productive labor and to sneer at "indolent" foreigners—a prejudice many Americans still possess.) Eventually the colonies did produce money crops: tobacco from Virginia, sugar from the West Indies, rice and indigo from Carolina, flax and wheat from Pennsylvania, and lumber and fish from New England. The colonists flourished and England as a whole prospered, but the original investor was usually wiped out.

Virginia (1607)

The history of Virginia's growth provides an excellent illustration of how a colony progressed economically while its backers failed. The company responsible for sending the first expedition to Virginia was directed by men of great wealth and distinction: financiers like Sir Thomas Smythe and Sir Ferdinando Gorges, the Earl of Warwick, the Lord Chief Justice Francis Popham, Lord Thomas de la Warr (later to become governor of Virginia), and others. In 1609 and again in 1612 their royal charter was revised to give the company more land, more authority, and the opportunity to raise more money. In addition to the considerable investments made by these men, other individuals and groups purchased smaller numbers of shares. But still more capital was needed. When the investors' confidence faltered, the company conducted a series of lotteries. Some members of Parliament complained, however, that the lotteries "do beggar" the motherland. "Let Virginia lose rather than England." King James I agreed, and the lotteries were suspended—a fatal blow to the company.

The settlers in Virginia were so ill-prepared for the hardships of the American frontier that the death rate was appalling. Within the first six months 50 percent died. Nor did this percentage decrease. A later investigation concluded that between 1607 and 1623, of some five thousand persons who emigrated to Virginia, about four thousand had perished! On one occasion, when relief ships dispatched by the company failed to arrive, settlers were reduced to eating snails, snakes, and whatever animals they could find, and one man was reported to have killed and devoured his wife. On another occasion the relief ships, commanded by Lord de la Warr, arrived just as the surviving remnants were abandoning the colony and sailing down the James River.

Supplies from England kept Virginia alive, but tobacco was its true salvation. John Rolfe, who married the Indian princess Pocahontas, grew the first crop in 1612. By importing West Indian seed and crossing it with local Indian tobacco, he obtained a strain that sold for an excellent price in England. Thereafter Virginians went tobacco mad. They planted it everywhere they thought it might grow, even on the streets of Jamestown. They grew it so exclusively, neglecting other crops, that food shortages continued. By 1618 Virginia had shipped fifty thousand pounds of tobacco to England. But whatever income accrued to the Virginia company did not meet its debts or expenses. Sir Thomas Smythe was ousted as head of the company and replaced by another financier, Sir Edwin Sandys. Sandys tried to institute a number of progressive measures—to no avail. In 1624 the company's charter was revoked and Virginia became a royal colony. By that time it had spent well over £160,000 on Virginia. No dividend was ever paid.

The Pilgrim Settlement (1620)

Before its dissolution the Virginia company had agreed to permit a group of Pilgrims to settle within its colony. Yet permission by no means signified approval of Pilgrim beliefs. The Pilgrims were regarded as an obnoxious minor sect of self-righteous religious extremists, holding views which threatened the established Anglican church as well as the monarchy. Like all the "Reformed" followers of Calvin, the Pilgrims believed they were among the elite whom God had predestined to heaven while scoffers (including Catholics, Jews, Lutherans, Anglicans, and heathen) were foredoomed to hell. Moreover, the Pilgrims refused to recognize the dictates of any higher ecclesiastical authority. Each of their congregations selected its own minister and formed its own church polity.

Persecuted in England, a number of Pilgrims had fled to Holland in 1608, where they expected to live in theological harmony with the Reformed

Dutch. After a decade they were discouraged, for they found life in an alien land hard and unpromising. Despite their labors, they were still poor. Some of their children had taken to the sea and drifted away from the true faith. Their small community seemed to be aging and disintegrating. After considerable debate and soul-searching, the majority of the Pilgrims voted to migrate to America. "It was granted the dangers were great," one of the Pilgrim leaders, William Bradford, later recorded in his *History of Plymouth Plantation*, "but not desperate; the difficulties were many, but not invincible." The Virginia company would benefit by having its lands populated and productive. The Pilgrims would benefit by an opportunity to create their own Zion in the wilderness.

Pilgrims from both Holland and England came on the *Mayflower* in 1620, though not to Virginia. Perhaps by accident, possibly by design, they decided to locate permanently at Plymouth on Cape Cod Bay. The climate there was severe. They had few supplies. Disease struck, wiping out half their members. Only a few, Miles Standish among them, were strong enough to move about and nurse the sick. Friendly Indians helped, but it was the Pilgrims' unswerving faith and determination that sustained them through the first bitter winter. By April 1621, when the *Mayflower* sailed back, no Pilgrim elected to return to England; and in October the survivors shared a thanksgiving feast with the Indians. They had mastered a hostile frontier, created a government, erected their churches—and they worshipped as they pleased—which might not have been the case in Virginia. In time the Pilgrims obtained a patent to their land. They also renegotiated and repaid their collective indebtedness to the English backers who had financed their voyage.

Statistically the number of Pilgrims was insignificant, and Plymouth was never a major colony. The Pilgrims loom large in American history, however, because of their indomitable spirit and remarkable accomplishment. William Bradford wrote, with justifiable pride: "All great and honorable actions are accompanied with great difficulties, and must be overcome with answerable courage." His words were meant as a legacy to all Americans.

Another group of Reformed Calvinists, the Puritans, had remained within the Church of England, hoping to shape its policy and alter its form to accord with their beliefs—in short, to rid Anglicanism of certain Catholic vestiges. The Stuart kings and their appointed bishops resisted these attempts. King James I stated that he would have "one doctrine, one discipline, one religion in substance and ceremony," and that it would not be contaminated by Puritan practices. Persecution of the Puritans grew increasingly severe, particularly during the reign of Charles I. To cite but one extreme example, a Puritan preacher was fined £10,000, flogged, pilloried, his ears were lopped, his nose slit, his cheeks branded "S S" (Sower of Sedition), and he was sentenced to long imprisonment. Thousands of Puritans decided to follow the Pilgrims' example and escape to America. Those who remained in

Massachusetts Bay (1630)

"We shall be as a City upon a Hill," John Winthrop, the Puritan leader, told his fellow passengers on their voyage to America, "the eyes of all people are upon us; so that if we shall deal falsely with our god in this work we have undertaken and so cause him to withdraw his present help from us, we shall be made a story and a byword through the world." The burden was great, and Winthrop's portrait reveals the gravity and dignity, the sober intelligence of a Puritan steward faced with the sacred duty of leading his people upon this great venture. The first governor of Massachusetts, Winthrop held that post, except for brief intervals, until his death in 1649. (Courtesy of the Trustees of the Boston Public Library Rare Books and Manuscripts)

England ultimately precipitated a rebellion—the Puritan Revolution—which overthrew the monarchy.

The Puritans who settled at Massachusetts Bay in 1630 were far superior to their Pilgrim neighbors in education, social status, and economic position. In numbers alone they dwarfed the Pilgrim settlement. But both shared a common purpose: to create a community dedicated to the glorification of God, at least the God which fitted their Reformed prescriptions. Puritan leaders took extensive precautions to insure the achievement of their goals.

First, by prearrangement they carried the charter of the Massachusetts Bay Company with them to Boston. The step was as audacious as it was unprecedented. It meant that control of the company could not fall into the hands of the Puritans' English enemies. King Charles I tried legal action to recover the charter, but the Puritans ignored the rulings of the royal court. He then ordered an expedition to seize the charter by force. The vessel designated to carry new officers to Massachusetts broke on launching and never sailed. For fifty years the Puritans ruled fairly unfettered by royal interference before the charter was revoked and Massachusetts became a royal colony.

Second, the Puritan elders cleverly converted the company charter into a frame of government, and so interpreted its clauses as to maintain their power. Thus, as the instrument of a commercial organization, the charter stated that all stockholders were freemen who could vote and participate in company affairs. As the constitution of a commonwealth, however, the definition was radically and illegally altered. Only members of the Puritan churches were considered freemen who could vote and participate in political affairs.

Third, the Puritans were as intolerant of dissenters as the Stuart kings were of them. Roger Williams, for example, though a famous Puritan minister,

This detail of an early print of Boston harbor clearly shows Harvard College, which first opened in 1638. By 1650 Harvard had received an official charter announcing its purpose to be "the advancement of all good literature, arts and sciences." President Henry Dunster of Harvard requested and received missionary funds to erect a special building to house Indian students (in 1654). His successor Charles Chauncy wanted more money for tutors to Indians, since "they have to deal with such nasty savages." The attempt to educate Indians failed, and the building was torn down in 1698. With this exception, Harvard prospered. As the city grew, so did the college, reflecting the Puritan emphasis upon education. (American Antiquarian Society)

was banished from Massachusetts Bay for his heretical teachings. (He became the founder of Rhode Island.) Quakers who insisted upon preaching anti-Puritan doctrines in Boston were candidates for martyrdom. Many were brutally whipped, and some of the more zealous offenders were hanged.

For all their emphasis upon religious orthodoxy, the Puritans' legacy to America was secular and practical rather than spiritual and theological. Puritans are remembered for their belief in devils, their witch trials, their Sabbath laws, and their strict moral imperatives. But their practical contributions were also great. They founded Harvard College, passed laws to establish grammar schools, and set up the first printing press in the English colonies. The earliest general treatise on medicine in North America was written by Cotton Mather, a Puritan divine. To be sure, the Puritans considered education and science as adjuncts of religion—as tools to help men read the Bible, master the catechism, train for the ministry, and understand God's arrangement of the universe. Nevertheless, the American emphasis on education is derived from these Puritan antecedents.

The Virginian dream of riches and the Puritan dream of a Biblical common-wealth were altered by the realities of frontier existence. Other Englishmen had other dreams for America, but none worked out precisely as planned. The colonies of Maryland and Carolina, owned and established by proprietors rather than by companies, represented two different blueprints for creating feudal systems. In each the ideal had to be sacrificed to the practical.

MARYLAND   Sir George Calvert—the first Lord Baltimore, renowned as an entrepreneur, courtier, and convert to Catholicism—sought land in the New World which could serve as a Catholic refuge and, at the same time, be developed into a vast medieval estate to enhance the fortunes and prestige of the Calvert family. Though he died before the royal charter for Maryland was issued in 1632, his two sons carried forward the task of colonization. The charter granted to the Calverts over ten million acres of what had been northern Virginia. Once a year the proprietors were to present to the king of England a symbolic payment of two Indian arrows, and—as specified in every charter—one-fifth of the gold and silver found within the colony. Laws were to be enacted with the advice and consent of freeholders, and could not be repugnant to the laws of England. Aside from these restrictions, the Calverts enjoyed absolute power.

They were never able to convert the Maryland wilderness into a medieval palatinate, however. Some sixty manors were created, but there were no vassals bound to lords by feudal obligations. Few Englishmen in the seventeenth century would willingly turn themselves into serfs. Emigrants who came with funds insisted upon freehold land tenure, which the Calverts granted in order to attract settlers. Emigrants without funds came as indentured servants, contracting to work a specified number of years to repay their transportation costs. When this contract was satisfactorily completed, the indentured servant was given fifty acres of land and, at the same time, all the privileges and prerogatives of other property owners.

Most servants and freeholders in Maryland were Protestant. Conflicts with Catholic settlers were inevitable in an age of pronounced religious bigotry. Yet, the Calverts ruled Maryland fairly and judiciously, and remarkably little blood was spilled. Some Jesuits, for example, who proved to be a disruptive influence, were recalled to England at the request of the Calverts. Overzealous Protestants, who wished to make Anglicanism the official religion, were thwarted by Maryland's so-called Toleration Act of 1649. The law protected the Catholic minority by guaranteeing religious freedom to all who accepted the trinitarian creed. Marylanders did attempt to overthrow the proprietary government—five times between 1660 and 1689—but their major grievances were basically economic and political, not religious. The Calverts temporarily lost political control of Maryland for several decades, but they regained power in 1715 and never relinquished it until the American Revolution.

CAROLINA   With all its problems, Maryland proved so lucrative an investment that other Englishmen decided to emulate the Calverts. Eight of the richest and most renowned Englishmen—including the Earl of Clarendon, the Duke of Albemarle, and Lord Ashley Cooper—in 1663 were granted a charter, patterned after that of Maryland, to the vast Carolina area which lay between Virginia and Florida. Here the joint proprietors envisioned a colonial society neatly balanced between feudal nobility and freemen. They planned to hold one-fifth of the land for themselves and their heirs, as seigniors exercising feudal jurisdiction over a race of hereditary tenants. Another fifth of the land would be formed into baronies. The remaining three-fifths would be apportioned among freeholders, who would pay quitrents to the proprietors. The details of their grandiose scheme were meticulously worked out in the "Fundamental Constitutions." Drafted by John Locke and adopted by the proprietory board in 1669, it was neither accepted by the Carolina colonists nor effectively enforced by the proprietors.

From the beginning there were two Carolinas, with separate governments, contrasting economies, and divergent social patterns. The northern part was settled initially by Virginians, some of whom had located around Albemarle Sound a decade before the proprietors received their charter. Without good harbors, North Carolina lacked both major ports and bustling commercial centers. In fact, it had no town until after 1700. The people were more dispersed and isolated, culturally cruder, and less affluent than those in neighboring colonies. Most settlers lived on small farms with a few slaves and grew subsistence crops and tobacco. Even after the plantation economy developed in the eighteenth century, the ratio of slaves to owners was smaller in North Carolina than anywhere else in the South.

South Carolina attracted a heterogeneous lot of emigrants, and imported so many slaves that early in its history the black and white populations were about equal in size. Charleston, named Charles Town after King Charles II, quickly became the focus of a thriving triangular trade. South Carolinians shipped their cattle, lumber, and grains for sale to Barbados; there vessels reloaded with cargoes of sugar for markets in England; and then returned to Charleston carrying English manufactured goods. Like upstate New York, South Carolina also profited by an important traffic in deer skins and furs. But the money crops, first rice and then indigo, in time came to dominate the economy of South Carolina. The owners of plantations in the coastal region became the wealthiest class in all North America. Charleston developed into a social, political, and trading center for the planters, a gay and cosmopolitan capital.

Though the "Fundamental Constitutions" were formally renounced by the proprietors, relations with the settlers scarcely improved. Carolinians regarded the proprietors as too mercenary, their government as too autocratic. Colonists in all areas of Carolina resisted the payment of quitrents, quarreled with officals over land titles, and despaired of receiving adequate military aid in fighting the Indians and Spaniards. Proprietary governors were often defied by the colonists, and sometimes forced out of office. In 1719 South Carolinians rebelled, deposed the governor, and seized the colony in the name of the king. Ten years later, having long since abandoned any dream of erecting a feudal paradise, and without realizing any profit from their venture, the proprietors sold their rights to the crown.

Pennsylvania was profoundly influenced by the theology of its founder, William Penn. The son and heir of an admiral in the royal navy, an aristocrat by birth as well as by inclination, Penn had nevertheless embraced a religion of the English lower classes. Indeed, Penn was probably the most illustrious member of that sect, the Society of Friends, disparagingly called Quakers because their leader, George Fox, had warned a hostile judge to "tremble at the word of the Lord." Quakers taught that all men were possessed of the Inner Light, the voice of God in the human soul. They believed that men needed neither books nor ceremonies nor priests to discover God, but only a pure heart and free conscience. They believed in social simplicity, religious toleration, peace, and brotherly love—tenets which antagonized the nobility, the clergy, and the military establishment of England.

To save his fellow Quakers from further persecution, Penn sought a charter from his friend, Charles II, to establish a proprietary colony for them in America. Charles was willing, but the court party was so hostile to the Quakers that he needed some excuse. One was found in an old financial debt owed by the crown to Penn's estate. The debt, which no one had ever expected would be repaid, was to be canceled in exchange for land in the New World. Penn received the charter in 1681. It was the last proprietary grant ever issued by the English government. Years later he explained that "the government at home was glad to be rid of us at so cheap a rate as a little parchment in a desert three thousand miles off."

The Holy Experiment (1681)

Quakers who came to Massachusetts Bay and insisted upon preaching heretical doctrines were publicly whipped, as depicted in this illustration by a later artist. One such Quaker, William Brent, wrote: "I further Testify, in the Fear of the Lord, and witness God, with a Pen of Trembling, That the Noise of the whip on my back, all the Imprisonments, and Banishing upon pain of Death . . . did no more affright me, through the Strength and Power of God in me, than if they had threatened to have bound a Spider's Web to my Finger." (State Street Bank and Trust Company, Boston)

Pennsylvania was a desert only in the metaphoric sense. From the beginning it prospered as thousands of immigrants, attracted by Penn's pamphlets, flocked there to benefit from the liberal land allowances he offered. Pennsylvania became one of the most ethnically and religiously diverse of the American colonies. Its toleration of non-Quaker Christian denominations and its degree of political democracy and personal freedom were scarcely equaled, except in Rhode Island. Slavery existed, but the institution was essentially repugnant to Quaker beliefs and the earliest movements for manumission originated in Pennsylvania.

Toleration, diversity, and material success did not ensure that Pennsylvanians lived in harmony. Indeed, the issues which divided colonists living in Penn's "Holy Experiment" were comparable to those which caused disturbances in the feudal experiments of Maryland and Carolina. First, the Quakers considered the heirs of William Penn too greedy in their collection of quitrents. A Quaker party attempted to thwart the proprietary governor through control of the colonial legislature. Second, Scotch-Irish settlers in the west were angered by the reluctance of the Quaker-dominated colonial legislature to appropriate funds to defend the frontier against Indian attacks. Third, the Quakers themselves eventually split into factions, as rural members found their Philadelphia brethren too wealthy and too worldly for their simple orthodox tastes.

The Quakers' concern for the whole human community, their pacifism, and their emphasis upon the right of dissent, then and in subsequent centuries, have served to stir the conscience of other citizens. No conscience is stirred without some irritation, which Americans have on occasion exhibited toward Quakers. But no other group has set a better example of democracy in action than the Quakers, a fact which Americans have recognized and of which they have proudly boasted.

Each colony was endowed with a distinctive character—a character long retained, even after statehood—which resulted from the interaction of its geographic circumstance, cultural inheritance, ethnic composition, economic structure, and religious persuasion. A strong current of competition and no little animosity ran between many of the colonies. Rhode Island, for example, which became a haven for religious dissidents and refugees, was dubbed "the latrine of New England" by Puritans. Virginians spoke disparagingly of North Carolinians as a worthless and shiftless people who wallowed in filth with their hogs. There were intercolonial squabbles over boundaries, western lands, trade, and political jurisdiction. But the impact of climate upon colonial development was decisive. Three distinct and contrasting economic sections emerged on the American mainland in the seventeenth century.

Colonial Economic Differences

NEW ENGLAND   The inhospitable climate and rocky soil severely limited the growth of commercial agriculture in New England. Farmers did adapt wheat successfully, but a fungus wiped out virtually the entire crop and destroyed its future. Thereafter New Englanders concentrated upon corn production and cultivated some other grains, as well as fruits, vegetables, dairy products, and livestock which were shipped to West Indian markets. They also harvested the ocean for fish from Cape Cod to Newfoundland. Dried and salted, seafood became a major export to the Caribbean and to southern European countries. From the forests of America an apparently inexhaustible supply of timber was available to build ships. Northern vessels began to range over the entire Atlantic. Boston and Newport became major seaport communities, competing with the trading centers of England and Holland.

MIDDLE ATLANTIC COLONIES   New York, New Jersey, Pennsylvania, and Delaware became the breadbasket of America, producing large wheat surpluses (as well as other grains), which the West Indies depended upon for survival. New York City was not yet the equal of Boston as a trading center, but it seemed to have more taverns, more drunks, and greater problems with law enforcement. A visitor reported in 1643 that one could hear eighteen different languages spoken there. In 1699 Lord Bellomont, who served as governor of New York, called it "the growingest town in America." Actually Philadelphia, settled fifty years after Boston, was destined to surpass all its competitors in the next century. The Middle Atlantic colonies were the most economically diversified and heterogeneous part of continental North America.

THE SOUTH   The plantation economy was not yet a dominant southern institution in the seventeenth century, but tobacco culture was. In terms of acreage, corn was the major crop. The leading staples for export, however, were tobacco in the upper south, rice (and later) indigo in the lower south. In 1628 some 500,000 pounds of colonial tobacco were shipped to England; by 1670 the figure was over 9,000,000 pounds; by 1700, it had risen to more than 35,000,000 pounds. During all this time, there were only sleepy hamlets south of Philadelphia for a distance of 750 miles, and no towns of any size until one reached Charleston. So in effect, each tobacco planter was his own merchant; each private dock a port of entry. Up the river systems came ships carrying slaves, supplies, household furnishings, or other goods ordered from English factories, which were unloaded directly at the plantation wharf, and then reloaded with hogsheads of tobacco to be carried to England. "Most houses are built near some landing-place," the Reverend Hugh Jones of Virginia noted, "[and] anything may be delivered to a Gentleman there from London . . . with less trouble and cost than to one living five miles in the country in England." In the South, commercial towns were not only regarded as superfluous, but as a positive danger to the interests of tobacco growers.

Life was indeed hard and tedious in New England, especially for women, and more so during the long winters when their monotonous round of drudgery could not be relieved by even such simple communal activities as husking bees and house-raisings. Moreover, the Calvinist code forbade

While the sun shone and blacks labored, gentlemen planters in Virginia could sit and smoke at leisure. The woodcut is from the label of a tobacco container, c. 1700. (The Granger Collection, New York)

Religious and Cultural Differences

wasteful idleness. But it is a mistake to portray the Puritans appareled in somber grays and blacks, as do so many popular illustrators, the lack of color somehow characterizing a dour and repressed people. As a matter of fact Puritan clothes were brightly colored, and with the passage of time the Puritans began to enjoy a variety of recreational activities. "For a Christian to use recreation," Increase Mather noted in 1688, "is very lawful, and in some cases a great duty." The distinction is that the Virginia Cavalier pursued and enjoyed his pleasures freely; personal salvation was not involved. The Puritans, though, never lost their fear that an omnipotent and wrathful God would foredoom them to an everlasting hell for frivolity.

Throughout the colonies, of course, the Sabbath was not to be defiled under penalty of law. But none could compare in rigor with New England: No work was permitted, no business transactions, no unnecessary travel, no play, and in some towns, no cooking, no bed-making, no housecleaning. The Puritan Sabbath lasted from Saturday sundown until Monday morning, and the laws were imposed upon strangers as well as natives. On one occasion the citizens of Yarmouth seriously debated whether to dig out a man trapped in a well on the Sabbath or to leave him there until Monday.

The two main problems Puritan leaders confronted in the seventeenth century were increased secularization and the struggle to maintain control of church and colony by a small elite group. On both counts it was a losing battle. Later generations of Puritans lacked the austere and primitive piety of the founders. Some theological changes were inevitable to save Puritanism from slow extinction, and would find expression in the Great Awakening of the next century. Control of church organization also slipped from their hands. The famous "Cambridge Platform" adopted in Massachusetts in 1651 provided that religious offenses would be punished by civil authorities, and that all churches within the colony would abide by common principles. But these regulations could not be enforced either in Boston or on the frontier. Churches split, new unauthorized ones formed, and each proclaimed and practiced its own doctrines.

In the tobacco colonies the settlers' social ideal was to duplicate the life-style of English country gentlemen. To some extent they were successful. Fox hunting, horse racing, balls, personal duels, heavy gambling, lavish hospitality, even dress and manners, all aped the Cavalier practices in England. As Anglicans they were not religious refugees, nor did they have theological quarrels with the established Church of England. Yet, as in so many other cases, New World conditions transformed Old World institutions. The parishes in Virginia were too large, the roads too poor, the country too crude, for the Church of England to survive its transatlantic voyage unchanged. In England the Anglican church was, by ancient tradition, hierarchically structured, with ultimate control vested in powerful bishops; the Virginia church had no bishops throughout the colonial period. In England matters of dogma were shaped, decided, and enforced by the bishops, synods, and other councils of the clerical elite; Virginia had no central ecclesiastical authority, the leading laymen of each parish more or less deciding religious matters as local circumstances dictated. In England ministers were appointed by the bishop, and not generally accountable to the parishioners; the tenure of Virginia clergymen was on a year-to-year basis at the pleasure of the vestrymen. A clergyman's salary was legally fixed at a certain number of pounds of tobacco. Thus the money value each one received depended upon both the quality of the tobacco grown in that parish and the market price it fetched. There were always more clerical vacancies in parishes that grew the cheaper and cruder "oranoco" than in those that specialized in the milder and preferred "sweet scented"; clergymen who wished to retain a "sweet scented" parish would not dare challenge the vestry.

The frontier experience was common to all colonists, and it had an overwhelming impact upon the initial settlers. "A plain soldier that can use a pickaxe and spade," John Smith commented on life in early Virginia, "is better than five knights." Military figures were esteemed for their leadership qualities. Exalted social rank meant less in a new environment in which the art of survival depended upon other talents. But it is a mistake to think the frontier touched all arrivals with the wand of equality, immediately leveling social differences and transforming class-conscious Europeans into rugged individualists. Cheap land and economic opportunity eased the climb up the social ladder to the rank of gentry. But it did not dissolve the pecking order of colonial society.

The Frontier and Inequality

Quite the contrary, the seventeenth-century colonist firmly believed in social ranking. "God almighty, in His most holy and wise providence, has so disposed of the condition of mankind, as in all times some must be rich, some poor," wrote John Winthrop, the renowned Puritan leader, "some high and eminent in power and dignity, others mean and in subjection." It was expected that the elite would govern and, in the interest of order and stability, would impose a strict code of social conduct. Colonists were expected to obey that code—and were punished if they did not. In fact, a correlation existed between one's rank and punishments received for infractions of the law. Rarely would a gentleman be whipped, though that sentence was usual for others. Josias Plastowe of Boston, for example, who was found guilty of "stealing four baskets of corn from the Indians," was ordered to "return them eight baskets, be fined £5, and hereafter to be called by the name of Josias and not Mr." His servants, however, who had participated in the theft, were severely flogged. Philip Ratliffe was fined, whipped, had his ears cut off, and banished from Boston for the crime of "uttering malicious and scandalous speeches against the government." Yet Roger Williams, the famous divine, was simply commanded to leave the colony for his "new and dangerous opinions against the authority of the magistrates." The sentence of death for capital crimes was carried out according to sex and rank in Maryland: women might be burned at the stake; lower-class men were to be hung, drawn, and quartered; and aristocrats were to be accorded a dignified beheading.

Class distinctions obtained in matters of dress, at church, at the meeting house, in education, and, in fact, in most social institutions and relations. Graduates of Harvard and Yale were listed, not alphabetically, but by their "dignities." Church seating was by rank. The Massachusetts village of Woburn assigned its pews according to "estate, office, and age." Swansea divided its inhabitants into three classes, and Saco into seven classes, for purposes of seating. Only the gentry could wear silk or lace, gold or silver girdles, slashed sleeves, embroidered capes. The authorities in Connecticut were so distressed at the practice of lower-class inhabitants wearing upper-class fashions that they enacted legislation to tax the upstarts as if their property amounted to £150. The first Virginia assembly provided for penalties against "excess in apparel." Even the Quakers, who made a fetish of plainness in "dress and address," displayed their concern by warning their Philadelphia brethren to cease wearing "long lapped sleeves, or coats gathered at the sides, or superfluous buttons, or broad ribbons about their hats, or long curled periwigs."

Internal Dissensions

One must keep in mind that neither the very rich nor the very poor came to America. The rich might invest in colonial ventures, but they had no desire to abandon their elegant estates or luxurious living standards. Less than 1 percent of those who sailed from Bristol, a major port of embarkation, were styled gentlemen. Nor did the destitute, the hopelessly impoverished, locked in a cycle of poverty for generations, have the ambition to leave the slums for the wilderness. The poor of England "live meanly," a contemporary noted, "and send their families to the parish to be relieved rather than to undertake a long journey to mend their condition." About 33 percent of those who sailed from Bristol were listed as yeomen and husbandmen, 20 percent as artisans and tradesmen, 10 percent as laborers. One of every four migrants was female. The chance to own land, to improve one's condition, to attain the rank of gentleman, and for women to marry a step or two above their status, were prime attractions. Some who came with family and furniture, cattle, domestic help, and accumulated capital had a decided advantage over those who arrived as indentured servants. But that advantage was temporary. In the new world economic position and political power were not fixed, as in England. Fortunes were to be made—and lost—in land speculations, trading with Indians, commercial enterprises, and agricultural staples. Thus, in America social mobility came into conflict with social stratification, which in turn created a number of serious internal quarrels. Some of these broadened into outright rebellions. Two uprisings were particularly noteworthy. In 1676 the rebellion of Nathaniel Bacon wracked Virginia, and in 1689 Jacob Leisler captured and ruled New York for twenty months.

BACON'S REBELLION Seventeenth-century America was marked by a struggle for power between contending elites who sought the privileges it bestowed. In Virginia the popularity of the royal governor, Sir William

Berkeley, declined as the price of tobacco fell in the 1660s. Berkeley was not to blame for the economic problems of tobacco growers, but there were other discontents for which he was responsible. No election to the House of Burgesses had been called for fourteen years; a poll tax was being levied without the consent of freeholders; the governor's clique held the key administrative posts of the colony, and profited accordingly; rumor had it that Berkeley was planning to award a monopoly on fur trading to himself and his friends. (In 1675 Berkeley had rejected Bacon's secret offer to buy from the governor a monopoly on the Indian trade.) Such favoritism offended those who were excluded from its rewards, many of whom were wealthy planters. They rallied behind Nathaniel Bacon, who was in fact a cousin of Lady Berkeley.

The immediate cause of Bacon's rebellion was Berkeley's defensive rather than offensive military policy toward Indians. (Of course, the fundamental causes were much more significant. Surely the rebellion would not have reached such serious proportions without the complex struggle for power between contending elites and the serious economic grievances of many settlers.) Berkeley agreed to build forts, but rebellious Virginians called them expensive "mousetraps," and complained that Berkeley "does not take a speedy course [to] destroy the Indians." The followers of Nathaniel Bacon "swore to be true to him," but they could not foresee the extremes to which Bacon would carry the revolution. In defiance of Berkeley's orders, Bacon raised and led a volunteer expedition of three hundred settlers against the Indians. Berkeley promptly labeled the recruits "rebels and mutineers," and sent a force that tried unsuccessfully to halt the expedition. Bacon returned in triumph—some 150 Indians were killed—and Berkeley, though angry, was forced to pardon a man he regarded as "the greatest rebel that ever was in Virginia." Meanwhile, a new House of Burgesses passed "Bacon's Laws," which provided for a vigorous campaign against the Indians, required that sheriffs be rotated in office, and forbade individuals to hold multiple offices. In effect, the House of Burgesses was now allied with Bacon. Berkeley was forced to flee, but there were still many Virginians who remained loyal to the governor. Bacon's volunteers captured Berkeley's mansion, burned Jamestown to the ground, and took an oath to resist even the royal navy.

What Bacon might have done next is unknown. Victorious against Berkeley, he died of a fever contracted while fighting at Dragon Swamp against the Pamunkey Indians, and with his death the movement collapsed. Berkeley returned and summarily ordered the hanging of 23 rebels. "That old fool," Charles II remarked, "has hanged more men in that naked country than I did for the murder of my father." Berkeley was recalled, and Charles pardoned the rebels. But it was many decades before Virginia recovered from the devastating effects of civil war.

LEISLER'S REBELLION Like Bacon, Jacob Leisler had personal reasons for resenting the colonial ruling classes. A German immigrant, he had married into a prominent Dutch family in New York and had amassed a fortune by trading in furs, wine, and tobacco. The power structure of New York, however, tried to exclude him from the fur trade by restricting the trading privilege to Albany merchants. A similar law limited the bolting of grain to millers in New York City, placing Leisler's mill, located in Suffolk County (outside the city), at a competitive disadvantage. When James II was overthrown in 1688, and the Dominion of New England fell, the ruling classes in New York declared their loyalty to James. Leisler sided with the vast majority of citizens, who wished to endorse Parliament's choice, the monarchy of William and Mary. A chance remark made by Lieutenant Governor Francis Nicholson while drunk, threatening to burn the city, touched off the revolution in 1689. Leisler, as captain of the local militia, seized the town fort, forced Nicholson to flee, and organized a provisional government.

That government functioned effectively, despite the opposition of aristocrats in New York City and Albany, and the threat of the French and their Indian allies. A legislative assembly was convened, taxes were collected, law and order was maintained, and the frontier was protected. Ironically and tragically, after this period of dedicated service, Leisler was arrested and ordered to be tried for treason by Governor Henry Sloughter, an appointee of William and Mary. The court was composed of Leisler's enemies, who had convinced the new governor that Leisler was a traitor and usurper. On May 16, 1691, Leisler and his son-in-law were hanged, cut down while alive, their bowels ripped out and burned, and their bodies quartered. A decade later the injustice was recognized, and Leisler's heirs were granted an indemnity.

English settlers never doubted that logic, right, equity, and morality were on their side in the conquest of America. They reasoned somewhat as follows:

Defeating the Indians

> The Indians were barbarians and wasteful wanderers, incapable of properly utilizing the natural resources of land and sea.
> If England did not control North America, surely the French and Spanish would—and one consequence would be the conversion of the natives to Catholicism.
> The continent was vast, thinly populated, and had enough room for both red man and white man.

If the Indians could be convinced of the benefits of a better life that would accrue to them by cooperating with the English in a true community of interest—economic prosperity, spiritual salvation, and all the blessings of civilization—then the great work of expansion could proceed in peace and harmony. But if Indians could not be convinced, then force would be justified. Early in the seventeenth century the clergyman and geographer, Richard Hakluyt, advised the Virginia company that gentle measures with the heathen were preferable but that they should rely on soldiers "to square and prepare them to our Preachers hands" if necessary. Along with the cross, settlers brought the gun.

Some Englishmen were troubled by the methods used to dispossess the Indians. Reverend John Gray in 1609 asked in a sermon, "by what right or warrant we can enter into the land of these savages, take away their rightful inheritance from them, and plant ourselves in their places." And some others recognized and respected the dignity and individuality of the Indians and treated them honorably. Nevertheless, the vast majority of settlers—and many of their descendants to the twentieth century—regarded Indians as sly, lazy, dirty, and treacherous. But who, white or Indian, was more treacherous remains highly debatable. Examples of murders and massacres, deceptions and cruelties, false promises and broken treaties abound on both sides. The Indians felt justified in their actions; once English intentions of conquest were evident, it became vital for them to fight relentlessly and mercilessly to defend their homeland by driving out the invaders. The English also felt justified; like all other racial conquerors, they believed they possessed a divine injunction, and all means were thus permissible to replace a squalid lot of nomadic primitive savages with a civilized and Christian society. The most devastating of all Indian wars erupted in New England in 1675. Led by Metacomet (or King Philip, as he was known to the Puritans), it resulted in the total annihilation of twelve Puritan villages and the partial destruction of many others. One-tenth of the adult white males were killed; the Indians also suffered heavy casualties. In fact, a higher proportion of whites and Indians died than in any other such war before or after. Many of the surviving Indians were executed or shipped off to the West Indies as slaves.

War, disease, and starvation also decimated Indian ranks. Far worse, however, was the cultural dependence that resulted from their mixing with whites. Indians were convinced that their way of life was infinitely superior. They scorned weakness, tolerated eccentricity, abhorred routine, exalted nature, considered the concept of private property to be preposterous, and took pride in their freedom from any restraints imposed by others. They viewed the white man as bound by chains of discipline, leading a monotonous existence, and endlessly laboring for material acquisitions. Nevertheless, for all their abhorrence of white man's standards, they eagerly sought articles introduced by the enemy—cotton shirts, steel needles, metal pots, as well as knives, guns, and alcohol. The surprise is not that the Indians were both defeated and corrupted but that they resisted white institutions for so long, preserved so much, and fought so obstinately against overwhelming odds.

Colonists who wrestled with the problems of Indian attacks and internal rebellions received little help or guidance from England. The motherland was preoccupied with its own disruptions, especially foreign wars and the Puritan revolution of the 1640s. As a result the colonists slowly shed their dependence upon England and developed traits of economic and political self-reliance. Self-reliance was a prelude to self-determination. In 1656 James Harrington wrote in *Oceana* that though the colonists "are yet babes" in need of a parent, they would "wean themselves . . . when they come of

The Colonists and English Mercantilism

age." The weaning process ran counter to the theories of English mercantilists, who wished the colonies to remain as permanent economic dependencies designed to build and sustain the strength of the motherland in four ways:

1. By supplying raw materials unavailable at home.
2. By providing a market for manufactured goods.
3. By serving as a dumping ground for what was thought to be excess population, thus alleviating unemployment.
4. By stimulating trade and thus adding to the royal revenues, primarily through customs duties.

As early as the first half of the seventeenth century it became apparent that the colonists did not always agree with these precepts. Dutch ships selling slaves and hardware and carrying away sugar and tobacco were welcomed in Virginia, the West Indies, and other English settlements. A series of royal decrees forbade such trade, but enforcement was difficult. So extensive was this illegal commerce that Dutch currency became a common medium of exchange in New England. Dutch merchants even extended lines of credit to planters in Barbadoes and the Leeward Islands.

With Charles I executed and Oliver Cromwell in control of the government, England took its first legislative steps to exert mercantilistic control over the colonies. In 1650 a parliamentary law prohibited foreign ships from trading with any English colonies except by special license. A 1651 act decreed that goods brought from Asia, Africa, or America to England must be transported in English ships (which included, by definition, vessels of the English colonies). With the restoration of the Stuart monarchy in 1660 still other laws were passed and administrative agencies created to define and to regulate the economic relations of England and its colonies. An act of 1660 specified that sugar, tobacco, and cotton—enumerated articles—could be sent only to England or to another English colony. That list gradually was extended to include all sorts of goods—from rice and copper ore to whale fins and coconuts. Three years later another law of Parliament declared that all but a few European goods bound for the colonial market must be sent by way of England. An act passed in 1673 imposed export duties upon enumerated articles to be paid at the colonial port. This law necessitated stationing royal customs officials in America. In 1675 a committee of the Privy Council was appointed to supervise colonial affairs. It was later replaced by a fifteen-man Board of Trade that could recommend but not make or enforce laws. Finally, in 1696 Parliament enacted a comprehensive law incorporating previous regulations and adding several new provisions. All colonial governors were to take an oath promising to uphold the Navigation Acts (as they were called). A system of vice-admiralty courts, eventually twelve in number, was established in the colonies to hear cases involving violations of the acts. By a ruling of the attorney general in 1702, jury trials in these courts were not permitted.

Large numbers of colonists ignored or violated whatever Navigation Acts they considered inconvenient. Customs officers sent out from England proved susceptible to bribes. Colonial lawyers found loopholes. Smugglers became increasingly adept. An English administrator sent to America in 1676 to reform the customs service reported: "There is no notice taken of the acts of navigation, or any other laws made in England. All nations having free liberty to come into their ports and vend their commodities. . . . [they] would make the world believe they are a free state." Increasingly the colonists came to depend upon their own elected assemblies as a line of resistance against parliamentary laws and royal decrees.

By order of the Virginia company, the first representative assembly was established at Jamestown in 1619. The acts of this assembly, the House of Burgesses, could be vetoed by the governor or set aside by either the company or the crown. Nevertheless the germ of self-government had been introduced, and when Virginia became a royal colony, the House of Burgesses remained part of the political structure. Eventually all thirteen of the colonies possessed legislative assemblies, twelve of them bicameral and one (Pennsylvania) unicameral.

Representative Government in America

Each colony had its own rules for voting and officeholding. Usually women, slaves, indentured servants, propertyless individuals, and non-Christians were excluded from the suffrage. Rhode Island was the sole colony without a religious qualification for voting. The other New England settlements—Plymouth, Massachusetts Bay, Connecticut, and New Haven—all limited the suffrage to members of an approved Calvinist church. The major prerequisite for voting in most colonies was the ownership of a minimum amount of property. The required amount ranged from as little as fifty acres (or £50 in cash) in Pennsylvania to either a working plantation or three hundred acres of undeveloped land in South Carolina. With certain exceptions, as the number of landholders increased the suffrage became more broadly based.

Gradually the colonial legislatures assumed greater prerogatives and powers, until they began to resemble the English House of Commons. Members debated without fear of arrest; they selected their own speaker; they won the right to initiate, not merely to ratify laws; and, above all, no taxes could be levied without their consent. Control of taxation gave the legislatures a degree of administrative power over public finances. They appointed public treasurers and audited the accounts of public officers. Supervision of the pursestrings gave the assemblies in turn a major voice in military and judicial matters, in Indian relations, and in ecclesiastical policies. Since some colonies were behaving like independent republics, obviously the English government could not rely on them to enforce the Navigation Acts. Their growing independence was beginning to manifest itself in other ways too. Massachusetts refused to recognize an English customs official and even arrested local agents he appointed.

In 1684 King Charles II began legal actions to revoke the Massachusetts

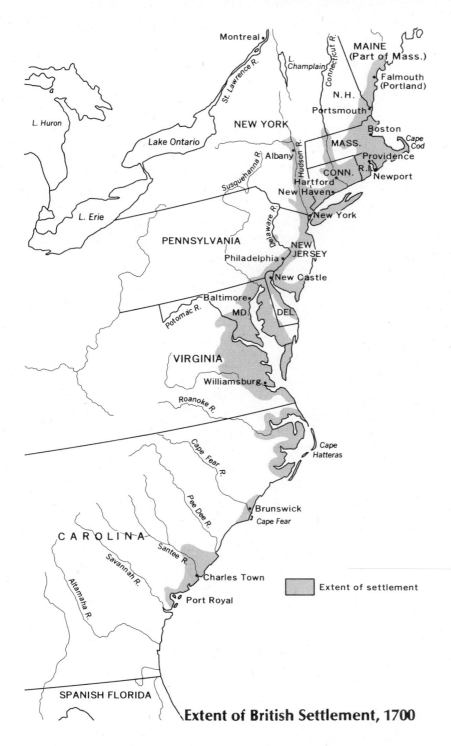

Extent of British Settlement, 1700

In 1700 the colonial population was over 250,000, and settlers had moved beyond
their coastal beachheads for the interior. In New York and New England they
followed the river valleys (notice the dark areas stretching up the Hudson and
Connecticut rivers). In Virginia they were well into the Piedmont region. Further to
the south, at Cape Fear and Charleston, they still clustered along the Atlantic
tidewater.

charter. His brother and successor, King James II, had less patience. Determined both to exert his authority immediately and to centralize the administration of the colonies under his control, in 1685 he ordered that Massachusetts and all other New England colonies be combined into one unit, to be known as the Territory and Dominion of New England. Soon thereafter the colonies of New York and East and West New Jersey were added to it. As governor of the Dominion James II appointed the able but dictatorial Sir Edmund Andros, who soon antagonized the vast majority of colonists. He abolished colonial assemblies and town meetings, levied new taxes, and issued orders to enforce the Navigation Acts. When colonists protested that their rights as Englishmen were being violated, Andros responded that they had none.

The English revolution of 1688 saved the colonists from further harassment. When news arrived that James II had been deposed, Andros was seized and imprisoned. His subordinate, Lieutenant Governor Francis Nicholson of New York, fled to England. Massachusetts did become a royal colony in 1691, with a governor appointed by the king, but its elected assembly was restored. In fact that was the major meaning of the Glorious Revolution of 1688 in America. "What had been preserved," a scholar has noted, "was the practical right of the colonists to determine very largely for themselves questions of public policy fundamentally affecting their domestic life."

COMMENTARY

By the end of the seventeenth century twelve colonies were well established on the Atlantic coast (Georgia, the last, was not settled until 1733), with a total population numbering some two hundred fifty thousand. There were jealousies between colonies and within colonies, cultural cleavages, and struggles for power. The danger of Indian attacks persisted, and foreign competitors, the French and Spanish, surrounded the colonies. In the main, however, the colonists were prosperous and secure and could take a fierce pride in their accomplishments. A "howling wilderness" had been converted to a state of civilization. The average settler had improved his material status considerably. There were indigent in America—14 percent of the adult white males were so listed in Boston in 1687—but thousands of humble origin in England had crossed the ocean and had become independent farmers, planters, artisans, merchants, and even manufacturers. Moreover, they had a voice in government far beyond what was possible at home. In 1700 none could foresee what epic changes lay over the horizon of the dawning century: a huge influx of non-English whites, and so many blacks as to alter the ethnic and racial complexion of the land; a great awakening in religion that would divide churches yet promote the idea of toleration; a contest for empire between the French and English fought in the Caribbean, in the Indian Ocean, on the Asian and European continents, and on the North American frontier.

JAMES T. ADAMS, *Provincial Society* (1927)

CHARLES M. ANDREWS, *The Colonial Period of American History* (1934)

BERNARD BAILYN, *The New England Merchants in the Seventeenth Century* (1955)

DANIEL J. BOORSTIN, *The Americans: The Colonial Experience* (1958)

JOHN B. BREBNER, *The Explorers of North America, 1492–1806* (1933)

CARL BRIDENBAUGH, *Cities in the Wilderness* (1938)

VERNER W. CRANE, *Southern Frontier* (1929)

WESLEY F. CRAVEN, *The Southern Colonies in the Seventeenth Century* (1949)

LAWRENCE H. GIPSON, *The British Empire Before the American Revolution* (1939–70)

LAWRENCE A. HARPER, *The English Navigation Laws* (1939)

DAVID HAWKE, *The Colonial Experience* (1966)

LEONARD W. LEVY, *Freedom of Speech and Press in Early American History: Legacy of Suppression* (1960)

KENNETH LOCKRIDGE, *A New England Town: the First Hundred Years* (1970)

PERRY MILLER, *The New England Mind* (1953)

EDMUND S. MORGAN, *The Puritan Dilemma* (1958)

SAMUEL E. MORISON, *Admiral of the Ocean Sea* (1942)

————, *Harvard College in the Seventeenth Century* (1936)

RICHARD B. MORRIS, *Government and Labor in Early America* (1946)

HOWARD H. PECKHAM, *The Colonial Wars* (1964)

SUMNER POWELL, *Puritan Village* (1963)

DARRETT B. RUTMAN, *Winthrop's Boston* (1965)

JAMES M. SMITH, *Seventeenth-Century America* (1959)

RAYMOND P. STEARNS, *Science in the British Colonies of America* (1970)

CARL UBBELOHDE, *The American Colonies and the British Empire* (1968)

ALDEN VAUGHAN, *New England Frontier* (1965)

WILCOMB E. WASHBURN, *The Governor and the Rebel: A History of Bacon's Rebellion* (1957)

THOMAS J. WERTENBAKER, *The First Americans* (1927)

GEORGE F. WILLISON, *Saints and Strangers* (1945)

LOUIS B. WRIGHT, *The Cultural Life of the American Colonies* (1957)

2
Colonial Society, 1700–1763

Economic Success: Facts and Myths

All observers agreed that America was a land of unparalleled economic opportunity for skilled workers, white and free of debt. "Here there are no beggars," the Maryland legislature boasted in 1699, "and they that are superannuated are reasonably well provided for." A Georgia settler reported that "industrious people live more comfortably here than in their native country." Wages were 30 to 100 percent higher than in Great Britain. Colonies competed to attract workers with special skills by offering various inducements. Particular craftsmen were exempted from labor on roads as well as from compulsory militia training. Those who could set up desired manufacturing processes were rewarded with tax exemptions for a specified number of years, or with land grants, or with interest-free loans. In 1719, for example, New York City permitted two immigrants, William Dugdale and John Serle, to use "certain lands as tenants at will" to erect a building for the making of rope. In England skilled workers were employed as journeymen or workshop foremen; in America they became capitalists. "Some from having been wool-hoppers and of as mean and meaner employment," a contemporary noted, "have there grown to become great merchants and attained to the most eminent advancements the country afforded."

There was no class struggle in America, except the struggle to climb from a lower to a higher class. Colonial history is filled with rags-to-riches accounts. William Byrd I began his family fortune by selling pots, pans, rum, and guns to the Indians. Robert Livingston utilized his position as town clerk in Albany to acquire one hundred sixty thousand acres, which led the governor to comment sarcastically: "[from] his being a little bookkeeper, he has screwed himself into one of the most considerable estates in the province." Daniel Dulany and his two brothers came to America in 1703 as indentured servants: through perseverance, ability, clever real estate speculations, and astute marriages into wealthy families, they amassed an enormous fortune. But for every celebrated success, there were hundreds of silent failures. For every Benjamin Franklin, whose rise from poverty to affluence has become part of America's legend, there were countless vagabonds or habitual drifters. For every indentured servant who acquired property and advanced economically, there were four others who either died during their term of service, became landless workers, or returned to England.

The plain fact is that life in the American colonies was not so good for some workers, either because they were unskilled or debt ridden. In the seaboard communities especially, the number of indigent rose in the eighteenth century. As Boston's population doubled, so did the number of adult white males classified as poor. The overseers of Philadelphia in 1712 complained that "the poor of this city daily are increasing" and suggested that a workhouse be established "to employ the poor and to compel vagrants to labor." All paupers in New York City by law had to wear a badge marked "in blue or red cloath." By the 1720s there was a permanent indigent population in Charleston, South Carolina.

Poorer immigrants tended to collect in cities where employment was cyclical and uncertain, depending on the vagaries of the import trade. But poverty was not confined to cities. The Marquis de Chastellux, traveling in Virginia, was shocked by the "wane looks," "ragged garments," and "miserable huts" of the rural poor. Indentured servants were so often mistreated by their masters that royal governors were instructed to have laws passed "restraining of any inhumane severity." Thousands of servants fled before their terms were completed. Court dockets were filled with complaints against the brutality of masters, whose offenses appeared to be the most flagrant in the tobacco colonies. "While it would be unfair to indict the whole planter class," Richard B. Morris concludes, "the fact remains that an impressive number of masters led drunken, dissolute lives and were brutal and sadistic toward their workmen."

Nevertheless, the belief that America was the golden land of opportunity was wholeheartedly adopted and apotheosized by eighteenth-century colonists. A single story of economic success had greater impact than all the statistics of poverty—and the success stories were more plentiful than in England or Europe, where tradition was strong, chances limited, and the class structure rigid. Half the property in Philadelphia, one writer boasted, belonged to "men whose fathers or grandfathers WORE LEATHER APRONS." Cadwallader Colden of New York wrote that "the most opulent families, in our own memory, have arisen from the lowest rank of the people."

The Elite Classes

"The rich, by the advantages of education, independence, and leisure," John Adams wrote with customary certainty, "are qualified for superior status." So it was in the colonial period. An aristocracy of great landholders and merchant princes dominated society. Colleges depended upon their endowments, artists upon their patronage, and the indigent upon their contributions. If many were generous, they also paraded their wealth in other ways. Aristocratic weddings were ostentatious affairs; their funerals expensive displays. In 1736 Governor Jonathan Belcher of Massachusetts distributed a thousand pairs of gloves to mourners in honor of his deceased wife; Peter Faneuil of Boston outdid him two years later by handing out three thousand pairs at the funeral of his uncle. The dinners of the affluent were sumptuous feasts, served on Nankin or East India china over the finest damask cloth. English nobles visiting the colonies were handsomely feted in the richest homes, and colonists vied for the attendance of the dignitaries. French officers were similarly entertained during the American Revolution. The Comte de Ségur wrote with approval that "democracy has not banished luxury."

These upper classes exercised enormous political influence, but it was never total. First of all, royal governors sent out from England, with all the jurisdiction and coercive powers of that office, frequently were at odds with the native-born aristocracy. When "King" Carter of Virginia, owner of three hundred thousand acres and a thousand slaves, wanted a minor naval position transferred from one son to another, his request was denied by the deputy governor. Royal officials were strangers in the land: they came to make or recoup fortunes lost at the gambling tables of London and to return home as quickly as possible. Haughty and disdainful of the colonial elite—at least those who resisted authority—they engaged in fierce rivalries with the leading families of America. Second, although the lower classes were largely deferential, it would be an error to overemphasize their passivity. The tenant farmers of New York, for example, rose to challenge the power of the wealthy landlords on issues of rent, tenure, land titles, and personal obligations. A historian, Milton M. Klein, finds the electorate in that colony "more articulate, more active . . . and more extensive" than had been thought. The local aristocracy did occupy a predominant political position, before as well as after the American Revolution. Nevertheless, upper-class candidates had to appeal to lower-class voters for support, and they did so in many cases by outright bribes. The price in 1761, Robert Livingston informed Abraham Yates, was forty shillings a man.

The most persistent problem throughout the colonies was the shortage of labor. Because Indians refused to work for others and would not tolerate enslavement, attempts to persuade or to force labor upon them failed. The system of indentured servants, although important to the colonial economy, was also unsatisfactory. When the period of indenture expired, replacements had to be found. "Help is scarce and hard to get, difficult to please, and uncertain," was a familiar complaint of American colonial society. Particularly in the southern colonies where plantations were developing, the necessity of a steady and cheap labor supply became imperative. Since the red man would not work and not enough white men could be hired, the solution was to enslave the blacks. The supply from Africa seemed inexhaustible; if a black man refused to work he could be chastised with an easier conscience than could a white man; if he tried to escape his color made it simple to identify him. Besides, an indentured servant cost his master on the average of £2–4 per year during his service; a slave could be purchased for £18–20 for a lifetime of service. Where slaves could be used effectively, they were cheaper than white labor, and inevitably replaced them.

The first Africans brought to Jamestown in 1619, and those transported to

Slavery in the Colonies

TO BE SOLD on board the Ship *Bance-Iſland*, on tueſday the 6th of *May* next, at *Aſhley-Ferry*; a choice cargo of about 250 fine healthy

NEGROES,

juſt arrived from the Windward & Rice Coaſt. —The utmoſt care hàs already been taken, and ſhall be continued, to keep them free from the leaſt danger of being infected with the SMALL-POX, no boat having been on board, and all other communication with people from *Charles-Town* prevented.

Auſtin, Laurens, & Appleby.

N. B. Full one Half of the above Negroes have had the SMALL-POX in their own Country.

In the British West Indies, contrary to the mainland colonies, the slave population failed to reproduce itself by natural increase in the eighteenth century. Brutal treatment and poor living conditions led many slave women to the common practices of infanticide and abortion. In addition, periodic devastating epidemics of infectious diseases swept the islands. So notorious were the epidemics that—as this advertisement in Charleston, South Carolina, indicates—the slaves to be sold were described as "healthy" and "free from the least danger of being infected with the SMALL-POX." (Library of Congress)

the colonies over the next several decades, were treated as servants rather than as slaves. According to Christian dogma only heathens could be enslaved, and many blacks were baptized. Those who completed their period of indenture were granted the stipulated amount of free land. By the middle of the seventeenth century, however, economic necessity overcame religious scruples. Blacks were imported either without indenture or as "personal servants." In 1664 slavery was legitimized in Maryland by an act of the legislature that secured the title of their white masters. Three years later the Virginia assembly declared blacks to be slaves by virtue of their color. In time every colony adopted slave codes. The fact that many blacks had accepted Christianity became immaterial. "Baptism," the Virginia legislature decided, "does not alter the condition of the person as to his bondage or freedom." There was also a racist edge to the slave system, as written in colonial laws prohibiting miscegenation. An early Virginia statute declared that any "christian" who "shall commit fornication with a negro man or woman, he or she so offending" shall pay double the usual fine. In 1691 the colony banned all interracial liaisons, denouncing "that abominable mixture."

Not until the eighteenth century, however, were slaves brought to the New World in large numbers. In 1700 there were no more than twenty-five thousand slaves in the mainland colonies, less than 10 percent of the total population. By 1760 over three hundred thousand made up 20 percent of the population. Their sectional distribution was highly concentrated from Maryland southward:

	Total Population, 1760	Black Population, 1760
New England	500,000	13,000
Middle colonies	400,000	30,000
Southern colonies	700,000	300,000
Total	1,600,000	343,000

The institution never took a strong hold in the North, primarily for economic reasons. Slavery was most profitable in large-scale enterprises that required a considerable amount of unskilled gang labor. It was not suited to household industries, commerce, or small farming operations, all of which flourished in the North. The capital investment for a slave was simply too great since his productivity could not be fully utilized during the long northern winters when farm work was minimal. In the South, on the other hand, slavery thrived because it proved vital to the commercialized agriculture of the plantation system, which required a large and stable labor supply

1

The four scenes depicted here show blacks being (1) captured in Africa, (2) transported to the coast—a march often of hundreds of miles, during which many perished, (3) flogged and loaded on ships, and (4) chained in the holds during the trans-Atlantic journey. The death rate of blacks during the ocean crossing was probably over 10 percent—but it was higher still for the white sailors. The slaves were treated like cattle; the sailors like outcasts. If sailors died they did not have to be paid. Finally, while disease was rampant, many blacks had developed a resistance to African fevers which whites had not. The fact that so many whites died became the most effective argument of those who wished to suppress the trade. (American Antiquarian Society)

2

3

4

to produce crops for export. One foreman could readily oversee the daily work of dozens of slaves. They could not leave after a few years, as did white servants. And while the initial capital investment to purchase slaves was heavy, planters who could afford slaves and large landholdings profited accordingly. All other variables being equal—soil fertility, transportation costs, and market prices—profits were greater on larger farms that could be worked more efficiently.

One can easily understand how apologists for slavery could argue that everyone benefited from the institution. The expanding southern plantation economy received the labor supply it required. The New England merchants gained a fair share of the slave trade, which returned lucrative profits. The African was exposed to Western culture, and his soul was saved by conversion to Christianity. A critic, on the other hand, could point to the slave insurrections as an index of their misery and to repressive laws as eloquent testimony of the whites' fears. Slavery may have created a leisure class of whites, giving them the time and wealth to build beautiful mansions, to educate their children abroad, to cultivate social graces, and to acquire the qualities of leadership that America needed. But slavery also had degrading effects upon whites as well as on blacks. Whites considered the black man as inferior, a species of property, certainly not as a constituent member of society. They did not expect him to participate in the American dream of material success and personal liberty. Consequently, the southern white often developed traits of callousness, ruthlessness, and profligacy. A Quaker visitor to Virginia in 1746, John Woolman, recognized the evil: "I saw in these southern provinces so many vices and corruptions increased by this trade and way of life, that it appeared to me as a dark gloominess hanging over the land."

If blacks were considered unassimilable, whites were not, regardless of their religion or country of origin. This does not mean that all whites were immediately and universally welcome in America. The impoverished Sephardic Jews who arrived in New Amsterdam in 1654 were harshly received by the Dutch leader, Peter Stuyvesant. A Boston mob prevented the debarkation of a shipload of Scotch-Irish immigrants from Belfast and Londonderry. On another occasion the Puritans of Worcester, Massachusetts, destroyed the Presbyterian church of Scotch-Irish settlers. These examples of intolerance did not halt the influx of non-English whites, however, who were found in every colony as early as the seventeenth century. A few Poles and Italians were residents of Virginia even before it became a royal colony. The Bronx, one of New York's boroughs, received its name from Jonas Bronck, a Dane. Germans were flocking into Pennsylvania. Swedish settlers colonized the Delaware region. French Huguenots, though heavily concentrated in South Carolina, penetrated the entire seaboard. Scots and Welsh, Irish, Finns, and Swiss all added to the pluralism of white America. Nevertheless, until the eighteenth century, in terms of sheer numbers rather than variety, the non-English stock was not substantial enough to alter the basically English character of the colonies.

Ethnic Variety in America

Peter Stuyvesant, the fiery governor of New Netherland—pictured above railing at his burgomeisters—did not want any Jewish settlers in his colony. When a group of twenty-three impoverished Jews arrived in New Amsterdam in 1654 from Brazil, Stuyvesant asked the Dutch West India Company for permission to order their departure. "The deceitful race, such hateful enemies and blasphemers of the name of Christ," he warned, should "be not allowed further to infect and trouble this new colony." In spite of Peter Stuyvesant, the Jews stayed in New Netherland. The earliest laws of that colony, copying those of Europe, forbade Jews from citizenship, from owning property, from guild membership, from retail trades, and from holding public religious services. But in time the laws were either abrogated or ignored. (Courtesy of the Boston Public Library, Print Department)

In the 1700s, however, hundreds of thousands of non-English immigrants swarmed across the Atlantic. By the time of the Revolution, fully half the population south of New England was non-English. This massive migration profoundly changed colonial life. First, English ethnic homogeneity was decisively broken. Second, military defense against the French and Spanish, as well as the Indians, was enhanced as these colonials poured into the backcountry. Third, many brought with them a feeling of hostility toward Anglicanism, toward parliamentary rule, and toward political authority of any kind. Fourth, despite the cultural isolation some sects were determined to maintain, a considerable degree of assimilation and amalgamation took place. If America has not been quite the melting pot of legend, still few lived as did the Pennsylvania Amish, neither relating to nor being influenced by the New World. Except for the Germans, and even for many of them, aloofness gradually gave way to fusions, and intermarriage with other stocks was common. "I could point out to you," wrote Hector St. John de Crève-coeur, author of *Letters from an American Farmer*, "a man whose grand-father was an Englishman, whose wife was Dutch, whose son married a French woman, and whose present four sons have now four wives of different nations." Only in America, said Crèvecoeur, have "individuals of all nations . . . melted into a new race of men . . . which you will find in no other country."

Numerically the two most important non-English groups in America were the Germans and Scotch-Irish, far different from one another in religion and temperament but similar in their hunger for land. "Both these sets [of people]," reported James Logan, "frequently sit down on any spot of vacant land they can find, without asking questions." They were destined to meet on the American frontier acting as a protective buffer between the Indians and the seaboard settlements.

THE GERMANS So many Germans crowded into Pennsylvania, according to Benjamin Franklin, that "unless the stream of importation could be turned from this to other colonies . . . they will soon outnumber us, [and] all the advantages we have, will in my opinion, be not able to preserve our language, and even our government will become precarious." The overflow of German colonists traveled by way of Lancaster down into the Shenandoah Valley, settling the western regions of Maryland, Virginia, and the Carolinas. They usually colonized by their denominational persuasions—pietistic sects from the Rhineland, such as the Dunkers and River Brethren, New Mooners, and Mennonites; others from the Palatinate, usually poorer and chiefly Lutherans; and Moravians, who had fled first from Austria to Saxony, becoming the founders of "Wachovia" in North Carolina. As a group they were industrious and thrifty, their well-tended farms easily recognized and frequently commended. "A German farm," Benjamin Rush noted, "may be distinguished from the farms of other citizens by . . . a general appearance of plenty and neatness in everything that belongs to them." A cautious people, both passive and pacific by nature, the Germans were not interested in politics or esteemed as Indian fighters. Yet they made solid contributions in the conquest of the West. German gunsmiths in Lancaster developed the long Pennsylvania rifle, forerunner of the Kentucky rifle, the indispensable companion of the frontiersmen. With this weapon, more quickly and quietly reloaded than the cumbersome European guns, a skilled marksman could snuff a candle at fifty yards and behead a turkey at eighty yards. Germans also developed the sturdy Conestoga wagons, usually blue-colored and covered with stretched canvas, the forerunner of the prairie schooners known to every western pioneer in the nineteenth century.

Eighteenth-century German settlers in Pennsylvania made the Conestoga Valley famous for its wagons and its horses. The heavy, broad-wheeled covered wagons came to symbolize the whole westward movement of Americans. The Conestoga horses, bred from English stock, were renowned as the finest draft animals of the colonial period. (The Bettmann Archive)

THE SCOTCH-IRISH "Men who emigrate are, from the nature of the circumstances," wrote Arthur Young, who was thinking of the Scotch-Irish, "the most active, hardy, daring, bold and resolute spirits, and probably the most mischievous." Not to be confused with either the Scots (who rarely settled the frontier) or the Irish (who were Catholic), the Scotch-Irish should more properly be called Ulster Scots: people of Scottish descent who had been residents of northern Ireland since the early seventeenth century. Accustomed to border wars in Ireland, tough and pugnacious, they tried at first to live among the inhabitants of Massachusetts, assuming—incorrectly—that their conservative Presbyterianism would mix well with Puritanism. Cotton Mather considered their residence another "formidable attempt of Satan and his Sons to unsettle us." When they found the best coastal lands occupied, streams of Scotch-Irish went to the frontiers of America: New Hampshire, Vermont, the far reaches of Maine, up the Hudson River into northern New York, across the Appalachians to western Pennsylvania, down the Shenandoah Valley, into the hinterlands of Georgia. Though fiercely defensive of their own rights, the Scotch-Irish had few qualms about possessing slaves, and none at all about dispossessing Indians. They fought Indian battles and political battles with equal zeal. Above all, the Scotch-Irish were people of fortitude, ready to endure enormous hardships in the wilderness to attain personal freedom. They represented the best and worst of American yeomanry: practical and humorless, independent and dogmatic, courageous and mercenary, and many of these qualities could be found in the long roster of distinguished statesmen descended from Scotch-Irish stock.

Religion in America

"One can make a good living here, and all live in peace," wrote a young Jewish housewife from Petersburg, Virginia, to her parents in Germany. "Anyone can do what he wants. There is a blessing here: Jew and Gentile are as one." Her words were extravagant. Religious prejudice has never vanished; it has always been a contrapuntal theme of American development. But an unusual idea began to emerge in the eighteenth century, imperfectly realized to be sure and frequently violated, that religious persuasions were personal matters, to be left untrammeled by government. This new idea of religious liberty was fed by three sources: one practical, one theological, and one philosophical.

THE PRACTICAL REASON: RELIGIOUS DIVERSITY The first American colonists carried with them the germs of prejudice. Toleration was a rare concept, championed by a few exotics and eccentrics such as Roger Williams. The very idea of toleration was considered heretical to those who were certain they fought for the Lord, and all other religions served the Devil. "To allow and maintain full and free toleration of religion to all men," said Edward Winslow in 1645, "would make us odious."

What made America different from Europe was the profusion of faiths, for with ethnic variety went religious diversity. The multiplicity of creeds served to checkmate each other and made it difficult for colonial founders to establish and maintain rigorous church-state systems. The ideal held by both Puritans and Anglicans, imitating European practice, was religious conformity. They certainly had no intention of permitting dissenters the free practice of heretical notions. But settlers were needed in every part of America, especially on the frontiers. Religious principles had to give way to economic interests. Four colonies—Rhode Island, Pennsylvania, Delaware, and New Jersey—had no state church. In five others—New York, Maryland, the Carolinas, and Georgia—the established church was too weak to impose its will upon dissenters. The rulers of South Carolina, for example, passed laws in 1704 excluding all non-Anglicans from the legislature, and creating an ecclesiastical court. An uproar ensued since Anglicans were far outnumbered by dissenters, and these acts were annulled by Parliament. Anglicanism was strongest in Virginia, as persecuted Baptists and Presbyterians could testify, yet it was disestablished after the American Revolution. Even in Massachusetts and Connecticut, though rather grudgingly, a degree of religious liberty prevailed despite the intentions of Puritan leaders. This was partly the result of pressure from England, where Protestant dissenters had finally cracked the wall of Anglican authority in 1689. Thus, the Royal Charter of Massachusetts in 1691 guaranteed that "there shall be liberty of conscience allowed, in the worship of God, to all Christians (except Papists)." With so many Quakers, Baptists, and Anglicans settled within its borders, Massachusetts Puritans were forced to compromise still further by the 1730s, permitting some dissenters to pay taxes to the church of their choice.

THE THEOLOGICAL REASON: THE GREAT AWAKENING Bursts of religious enthusiasm periodically swept through many congregations in the colonial period. An epidemic or other natural calamity, for example, would often bring frightened souls before the altar in large numbers. When fear receded, so did the religious fervor of the communicants. Particular ministers became adept at stirring audiences with evangelistic sermons. Jonathan Edwards, the pastor at Northampton, Massachusetts, sparked a revival movement in the 1730s of such proportions, he reported, that "scarcely a single person in the whole town was left unconcerned about the great things of the eternal world." Usually it was a matter of time before the level of enthusiasm waned, and the revival quietly passed away. At Northampton several residents who became despondent because they thought their souls were endangered, including Edwards' uncle, committed suicide. That ended the Northampton revival.

The Great Awakening of 1740–1741 thus did not break unexpectedly upon an unsuspecting people. Many were already attuned to religious emotional stimuli, having experienced previous "mini-revivals." Nevertheless, despite some successful preaching, there had been numerous complaints of religious lassitude. Too many stayed away from church. Too many attended without a sense of commitment. Too many sermons were tedious, stylized, and repetitive. Too many churchmen were content to stress tradi-

Preaching in fields, since the doors of churches were closed to him, George Whitefield drew huge crowds both in the colonies and in England. Even some of the skeptics reacted favorably. Benjamin Franklin listened to one of his sermons in 1740 and noted: "I perceived he intended to finish with a collection, and I silently resolved that he should get nothing from me. I had in my pocket a handful of copper money, three or four silver dollars, and five pistoles in gold. As he proceeded I began to soften and concluded to give the copper. Another stroke of his oratory made me ashamed of that and determined me to give the silver; and he finished so admirably that I emptied my pocket wholly into the collector's dish, gold and all." (Courtesy, Museum of Fine Arts, Boston)

tion, form, and proper standards while the spiritual core was moribund. Samuel Blair noted the "dead formality" of church life in Pennsylvania. Jonathan Edwards commented that people "do not so much need to have their heads stored as to have their hearts touched." Edwards brought theological distinction to the Great Awakening. His brilliant expositions defended the Calvinist doctrines of human depravity and predestination. Man was indeed a sinful creature, without redemption, Edwards taught, unless God chose to touch him with religious fire in the form of a "saving" experience. The foremost preacher of the Great Awakening, however, was George Whitefield, whose sermons were "scaled down to the comprehension of twelve-year olds." Renowned in Britain, Whitefield became more so in America, preaching to enormous crowds in all parts of the country. Some listeners "were struck pale as Death," a contemporary wrote, "others wringing their hands, others lying on the ground, others sinking into the arms of their friends, and most lifting up their eyes toward heaven, and crying out to GOD." Whitefield himself reported that "the groans and outcries of the wounded were such that my voice could not be heard."

The Great Awakening was divisive. More conservative clerics deplored its excessive emotional displays. To men like Charles Chauncy, pastor of the First Church in Boston, individual salvation could not be achieved through an orgasm of religious frenzy. A person so touched "mistakes the workings of his own passion for divine communication, and fancies himself immediately inspired by the spirit of God," wrote Chauncy, "when all the while, he is under no other influence than that of an overheated imagination." Others complained that the mingling of the sexes at revival meetings—and most of the converts were young—led to sexual immorality.

Many congregations split over the issue of revivalism. Departing members, known as "New Lights" (Congregationalists) or "New Sides" (Presbyterians), formed their own churches or joined the Baptists. Villages, neighborhoods, even some families became fragmented. Yet these schisms, while bitter, were less significant than the deeper ecumenical effects of the Great Awakening upon American Protestantism. Revivalism may have been anti-intellectual, but it forced a degree of sober introspection and reformulation that shattered the old molds of religious thought. Seventeenth-century sects had been narrow and intolerant, each jealously guarding the keys to heaven for its own membership. Now sects vanished and denominations began to sprout, less arrogant, less exclusive, and each following its own form of worship while recognizing the validity of others, for all promoted a common faith. The result of the Great Awakening was a multiplicity of churches within a community where hitherto an established church had dominated. Now a variety, with different beliefs and principles, competed for members. Thus despite its controversies and schisms, the Great Awakening, according to one scholar, "ended by establishing more firmly than ever the plurality of forces that made increased toleration, and finally full religious liberty, the most amenable solution for civic life."

THE PHILOSOPHICAL REASON: DEISM Religious revivals were only of psychological interest to intellectuals who worshipped at a different shrine: science. Just as pietistic evangelists never doubted divine revelation and trusted in "no creed but the Bible," so Enlightenment thinkers were equally certain that human reason was the sole gateway to truth and knowledge. The findings of Galileo, Kepler, Descartes, Sir Isaac Newton, and others had unlocked the secrets of planetary movement, revealed the workings of gravity, and reduced motion itself to a formula. Eighteenth-century philosophers believed that the universe and all it contained was a giant mechanism, governed by immutable laws that could be discovered by man. Some clergymen saw no conflict between science and scripture. The Newtonian universe was easily incorporated and bonded to their theology. Was not God's existence confirmed by the order of the universe, proven by the empirical evidence of science? Yet others found religion and science incompatible. At a later date Thomas Paine wrote that he could not see how science and Christianity could be "held together in the same mind." God to the rationalists was not an omnipotent and wrathful deity to whom one prayed but a master mechanic; not a Trinitarian miracle worker in the human image but a God of nature who had created an ordered and structured world yet did not interfere with its operation.

Such beliefs, called Deism, circulated mainly among the educated. Some Deists, like Paine, were distinctly anticlerical, but most were men of moderation and practicality. They found Christian teaching, stripped of its superstitions, an admirable ethical code for society to emulate. Thomas Jefferson was profoundly influenced by Joseph Priestley's *An History of the Corruptions of Christianity*. Yet he attended church and advised his grandson to read the Bible as one would read Tacitus or Livy—with critical detachment and moral purpose. In other hands Deism became a form of skepticism, a step toward atheism, but to Jefferson natural law, moral law, and religious law were complementary.

Since Deists believed in no one church yet saw merit in all, they championed religious liberty. Moreover, as Enlightenment intellectuals they concluded that freedom of conscience was a natural right that was not subject to the demand or will of government. Thus, for a brief historical moment, two forces with opposite thrusts—a pietistic movement with faith in divine revelation experienced through emotion and a philosophical movement with confidence in human reason—combined to effect the same ends. Both united in opposition to a shared enemy: the world of tradition and authority. Thomas Jefferson's Declaration of Independence was the ultimate fruit of Enlightenment philosophy in America. But, as J. M. Bumsted and John E. Van de Wetering have recently noted, "it was the revival which had first involved colonial Americans on a grand scale in confrontation politics. . . . The Great Awakening produced a general political polarization in matters of intellectual principle."

Political Ideas

The Great Awakening and the growth of rationalism, added to the ethnic variety of the population and combined with the colonial practice in local self-government, served to nourish a sense of freedom and political liberty. Loyalty to Britain was still strong, however. The Union Jack was displayed everywhere. Toasts to the health and long life of the monarchy were common. Benjamin Franklin recalled that before 1763 the colonials "had not only a respect, but an affection, for Great Britain, for its laws, its customs and manners, and even a fondness for its fashions." Yet the colonials gradually were becoming conscious of their separate identity. Third- and fourth-generation inhabitants spoke differently and thought differently from the English. A sense of continental community began to emerge. Thus, although the colonials expressed their loyalty to Britain, they were aware of being different, quick to defend their rights and privileges, and receptive to writers whose ideas corroborated their experience in self-determination. Colonials read John Locke's writings with approval, especially his *Two Treatises of Civil Government* (1690), which helped to destroy the theory of the divine right of kings. To Locke the purpose of government was to protect the natural rights of people: life, liberty, and property. When government fulfilled this purpose, it should be obeyed; when it did not, when in fact it violated natural rights, the people might rebel and establish a new government that would. Even more influential than Locke upon the colonial mind was "Cato," a pseudonym for the writings of two British journalists, John Trenchard and Thomas Gordon. "No one can spend any time in the newspapers, library inventories, and pamphlets of colonial America," Clinton Rossiter concludes, "without realizing that *Cato's Letters* (1733–55) rather than Locke's *Civil Government* was the most popular, quotable, esteemed source of political ideas in the colonial period." Trenchard and Gordon advanced bold concepts of intellectual and political liberty, at the core of which was their emphasis upon freedom of expression. Their most famous essay, "Of Freedom of Speech; That the Same Is Inseparable from Public Liberty," was quoted in every colonial newspaper from Boston to Savannah. Trenchard and Gordon stressed the self-aggrandizing tendency of the monarchy, the manipulations and corruptions of the British government, and the threats these posed to constitutional rights. Power and liberty were constantly at odds, and free men must be vigilant lest their rulers seize too much of the former at the expense of the latter.

The lessons of Locke and "Cato" were well digested across the ocean. The colonists regarded natural rights and constitutional rights as primary and complementary. Their loyalty to Britain was firm but not blind, and they were prepared to protest vigorously at the first signs of tyranny.

For more than a century, Englishmen periodically had expressed their concern about the potential of colonial independence. Lord Cornbury, the renowned pervert who served as governor of New York, wrote: "If once they [the colonists] can see they can clothe themselves without the help of England, they—who are already not very fond of submitting to government—would soon think of putting into execution designs they have long harbored in their breasts." In 1736 Sir Robert Brown complained to the Earl of Egmont "that there was a spirit in all the colonies to throw off their dependency on the Crown of England." Such fears were voiced with greater frequency by the middle of the eighteenth century, and with good reason. In all but the newest settlements (Georgia and Nova Scotia), the colonies had achieved substantial control over their own affairs. One scholar refers to them as "pockets of approximate independence" within the British empire. Although no one marched in rebellion and the traditional symbols of loyalty were honored, a rash of warnings from royal governors indicated that Britain and its colonies were on a political collision course. "The assembly," wrote William Shirley, governor of Massachusetts, in 1748, "seems to have left scarcely any part of His Majesty's prerogative untouched, and they have gone to great lengths towards getting the government, military as well as civil, into their hands." The governor of New York, George Clinton, agreed. It was "high time," he informed his superiors in England, "to put a stop to these perpetually growing encroachments of the assemblies."

The signs that Britain intended to do just that were obvious. Lord Halifax, president of the Board of Trade, "systematically set about the task of shoring up imperial authority in the colonies." A packet-boat system was inaugurated to regularize communications with the colonies. A tax system upon the colonies was urged. Governors were ordered to direct their correspondence to the Board of Trade rather than to the secretary of state. Moreover, governors were enjoined to follow their instructions to the letter and to veto any colonial bills that were contradictory to those instructions. In one case, the House of Commons censured the colony of Jamaica for its violations of Board of Trade directives. The changed attitude of the British government,

Shift in British Policy

beginning in 1748, stirred the colonists to protest. The era of imperial neglect and permissiveness was over. A new era of coercion was beginning, but it was soon interrupted by a major war between Britain and France. Colonial help was needed. The Privy Council suggested that "in the present situation of affairs, when peace, unanimity, and a good understanding" were vital to military success against France, the royal governors should not press the colonies by attempting to tighten imperial controls.

The climactic showdown between France and Britain followed a series of wars for domination of North America: King William's War (1689–1697), Queen Anne's War (1701–1713), and King George's War (1744–1748). As part of a continuous struggle with Britain, France had sent a succession of explorers, settlers, Jesuit missionaries, and troops to carve out an American empire. Canada was a costly experiment; it had a sparse population and was far weaker than the strong, stable, solidly occupied English colonies. "We must not flatter ourselves that our colonies can compete in wealth with the

The Seven Years' War Begins

European Possessions in North America, 1754

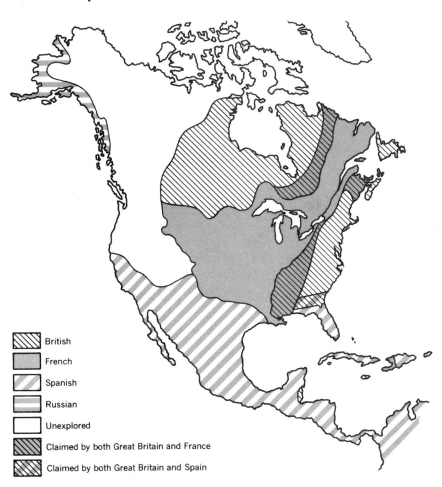

British

French

Spanish

Russian

Unexplored

Claimed by both Great Britain and France

Claimed by both Great Britain and Spain

From 1607, when Britain first established a precarious toehold in Virginia, her possessions in North America gradually increased. By ousting the Dutch from New Netherland, checking French and Spanish expansion, and commercially penetrating the West Indies, Britain sought to protect and enlarge her empire. By 1754 European possessions were as the map indicates, but that same year contention between Britain and France for control of the Ohio Valley caused war once again.

adjoining English," the governor of Canada wrote in 1750. But if France could control the Mississippi valley, linking Canada and Louisiana, thereby surrounding the British and confining them east of the Appalachians, they would control the continent. The fur trade and all internal trade would be totally theirs. In time French agricultural communities would dot the Ohio and Mississippi valleys, replacing the unruly and independent *coureurs de bois*. The savages would be subjugated. Anglo-Saxon expansion would be stopped. Of course, precisely the same aggressive strategy was adopted by the British. Colonial land speculators were encouraged to stake out tracts in the Ohio valley, "inasmuch as nothing can more effectively tend to defeat the dangerous designs of the French."

In 1752 a new governor of Canada, the Marquis Duquesne de Menneville, ordered the construction of a string of forts along the upper reaches of the Ohio River (in what is now western Pennsylvania). Virginians responded by sending a small expedition headed by a young militia officer, Lieutenant Colonel George Washington. An initial and inconclusive skirmish took place in July 1754. Twelve French soldiers died, including the French commander, but their forces were too strong to be dislodged, and Washington was obliged to retreat. The following year the British returned to the wilderness with an army of regulars, aided by colonials, and headed by a seasoned veteran, General Edward Braddock. Their mission was to capture Fort Duquesne (Pittsburgh) and then to march on the other French strong-holds at Venango, Le Boeuf, and Presque Isle. Eight miles below Fort Duquesne on the Monongahela River, they were attacked by the French and Indians. George Washington bitterly reported its outcome to Governor Robert Dinwiddie. "The regulars," he wrote,

> . . . were immediately struck with such a deadly panic, that nothing but confusion and disobedience of orders prevailed amongst them. . . . The Virginia companies behaved like men and died like soldiers. . . . The das- tardly behavior of the English soldiers exposed all those who were inclined to do their duty to almost certain death; and at length, despite every effort to the contrary, broke and ran as sheep before the hounds, leaving the Artillery, Ammunition, Provisions, and every individual thing we had with us a prey to the enemy. . . . The General [Braddock] was wounded behind in the shoulder, and into the breast, of which he died three days after. . . . I luckily escaped without a wound though I had four bullets through my coat and two horses shot under me.

It was a crushing defeat. French and Indian losses numbered fewer than sixty. The British suffered 977 killed or wounded (of a total force of 1,495).

Two years later the minor French and Indian War widened into the Seven Years' War. France, Austria, Sweden, several of the German states and, later, Spain opposed Britain and Prussia in a conflict of global dimensions. In Calcutta, Manila, and Minorca, on the continent of Europe, on the Indian Ocean and the Caribbean, and on the North American frontier at places like Fort Niagara, Crown Point, Oswego, and the Shenandoah valley, the strug-

George Washington was only twenty-one on his first official mission into western Pennsylvania during the winter of 1753. In that ordeal, some "French Indians" fired upon his party; he nearly drowned crossing a freezing river on a log raft; and "the cold was so extremely severe," he wrote, that a companion "had all his fingers and some of his toes frozen." The artist captures Washington's youth, the rugged terrain, and the bitter cold of the journey. On a second trip, in 1754, Washington's small force fought a short battle with the French. Then, in 1755, as a volunteer with General Braddock's army, he witnessed total defeat by the French. "I have been on the losing order ever since I entered the service," Washington complained. In those years he aspired to military fame, and displayed an unbecoming aggressiveness for promotion and recognition. (American Antiquarian Society)

gle for empire continued. The British appeared to be losing in the early years, much to the distress of colonial Calvinists who feared the spread of Catholicism. "God indeed is remarkably frowning upon us everywhere," Reverend Jonathan Edwards wrote in 1756. "God is making us, with all our superiority in numbers, to become the object of our enemies' almost continual triumphs and insults. . . . And in Europe things don't go much better."

When William Pitt became prime minister, the fortunes of war changed in Britain's favor. "I know that I can save England," he is alleged to have said, "and that nobody else can." Instead of sending troops to the European continent Pitt concentrated Britain's army and navy forces in the American theater. One by one in 1758 the French strongholds fell: Fort Louisbourg on the Atlantic coast, Fort Frontenac at the mouth of Lake Ontario, and Fort Duquesne, which was renamed in Pitt's honor. The last victory was particularly satisfying to George Washington, who participated in its capture. Then came 1759, often called Britain's "wonderful year" for the long succession of global triumphs. The French were crushed in India and ousted from Guadaloupe in the Caribbean. Hanoverian forces, subsidized by Britain, almost totally destroyed a French army at the battle of Minden in western Germany. A French fleet bound for Canada was defeated by Admiral Hawke at Quiberon Bay. On the American frontier the French abandoned Forts Ticonderoga and Crown Point to the advancing troops of General Jeffrey Amherst. Another expedition was victorious at Fort Niagara. The climax came with General James Wolfe's remarkable capture of Quebec.

The British Triumph

The gateway city to Canada, located on a steep granite cliff fronting on the St. Lawrence River, Quebec was a most formidable target. All summer long Wolfe's repeated sorties had failed, while the French, under the Marquis de Montcalm, hoped to hold out until the Canadian winter forced the British to leave. With courage born of desperation, Wolfe decided to attempt a final maneuver. Ships and men were rowed upstream and then, on a dark night, drifted down in silence to Anse au Foulon (now known as Wolfe's cove), a mile from Quebec, where a narrow trail zigzagged up the rock cliff. "The difficulty of gaining the top of the hill is scarcely credible," Admiral Charles Saunders reported. "It was very steep in its ascent, and high, and had no path where two could go abreast, but they were obliged to pull themselves up by the stumps and boughs of trees." By dawn a British army of 4,800 stood on the Plains of Abraham, arrayed for battle against a French force of comparable size. Montcalm accepted the challenge of an open-field engagement. On the morning of September 13, 1759, under a withering and accurate fire at close range—an English historian called it the "most perfect volley ever fired on a battlefield"—the French broke and fled. Both generals were mortally wounded, Montcalm in retreat, Wolfe dying in the happy knowledge of an impending victory.

The war dragged on four more years before a peace treaty was signed in Paris. But in America the fighting was over when Montreal collapsed after Quebec, and the French governor surrendered the whole of Canada in 1760.

The bells pealed, great bonfires were set in celebration in Philadelphia, Boston, and New York, and some colonials envisioned the beginning of a mighty British empire in America, "in numbers little inferior perhaps to the greatest in Europe, and in felicity to none." Cities "rising on every hill," predicted Jonathan Mayhew in 1759, ". . . happy fields and villages . . . and religion professed and practiced throughout this spacious kingdom in far greater purity and perfection than since the times of the apostles." Benjamin Franklin agreed. "The future grandeur and stability of the British empire lie in America," he declared in 1760, "[where foundations exist] broad and strong enough to support the greatest political structure human wisdom ever yet erected." Yet victory could not mask the signs of strain that had been present between Britain and its colonies throughout the war years. Consider the following four examples.

Signs of Colonial Discontent

THE ALBANY PLAN In 1754 a conference of colonial leaders meeting in Albany discussed the necessity of forming a political federation. Colonial cooperation was vital because of the French threat. Governor William Shirley of Massachusetts stated that "there is no time to be lost; the French seem to have advanced further toward making themselves masters of this Continent within the past five or six years than they have done ever since the first beginnings of that settlement." The conference adopted a plan of union worked out by Benjamin Franklin, which provided for a president-general appointed by the king, and a grand council elected by the colonial assemblies. Power between them would be both divided and shared. The president, with the council's advice, could negotiate treaties and declare war; the council, though subject to the president's veto, could regulate the Indian trade and pass tax laws. Not a single colony accepted Franklin's plan. They would not relinquish their taxing power to any other sovereignty, and they were not willing to delegate to Britain the degree of control the plan authorized. Nor was the plan well received by the British government, which chose to ignore it. Franklin put the matter succinctly: "The Assemblies thought there was too much *prerogative* in it, and in England it was judged to have too much of the *democratic*." Obviously there existed radically different views of the locus and degree of political authority within the empire.

LOUDOUN'S EMBARGO OF 1757 Colonials may have hated and feared the French, but many had no qualms about turning a profit by trading illegally with the enemy during the war. Before his death General Braddock wrote that the people of New York and Pennsylvania "are reported to be most notoriously guilty of supplying the French with provisions." A number of merchants—how many it is impossible to say—continued to smuggle goods to and from the French West Indies. "This dangerous and ignominious trade," Pitt called it, "was subversive of all law, and highly subversive of the honor and well-being of this Kingdom." In 1757 Lord Loudoun, commander in chief of British forces in North America, imposed an embargo upon colonial shipping from Virginia northward. An uproar of public protest ensued. The Massachusetts legislature voted to end Loudoun's embargo in that colony. The governor of Virginia, Robert Dinwiddie, told the general that he could not enforce the law since the people "are unanimous in their opinion of the absolute necessity of taking off the embargo." The Pennsylvania legislature remonstrated with the sharpest words of all: "A people cannot be said to be free, nor in the possession of their rights and properties, when their Rulers shall by their sole authority even during the sitting of their assemblies, stop the circulation of their commerce, discourage the labor and industry of the people, and reduce the province to the greatest distress."

Loudoun's embargo was impolitic. "He tried to ignore over a half-century of colonial political experience," Alan Rogers notes. "Among other things, this led colonials to look to their local assemblies for relief rather than to the home government which they knew would always support the generals."

WRITS OF ASSISTANCE Colonial smuggling continued, and in 1760 customs collectors in Massachusetts applied to the Superior Court for writs of assistance: an old practice by which customs officers, aided by the local police, could enter any premises in search of evidence of illegal importation. Writs of assistance were authorized by an act of Parliament but had to be reissued whenever a new sovereign came to the throne of England. Thus, when George III became king new writs had to be obtained. Massachusetts merchants decided to challenge the legality of the writs and hired James

Otis, a Boston attorney, to argue their case. His speech to the court in 1761 is lost to posterity, but observers reported upon its brilliance, as well as its impact. "Otis was a flame of fire!" John Adams later wrote. "American independence was then and there born." Otis argued that the parliamentary act authorizing writs of assistance was contrary to the British constitution, as well as to natural law. Parliament could not infringe upon either, and it was therefore the duty of the courts to declare the law void. Otis lost his case, but in the next decade more and more colonials adopted the logic of his position against parliamentary supremacy.

THE PARSON'S CAUSE   Clergy of the established Anglican church of Virginia traditionally received their salary by the market value of a fixed amount of tobacco (customarily sixteen thousand pounds). A drought in the late 1750s seriously affected tobacco production, caused a shortage, and raised its price. Planters were reluctant to pay the clergy this inflated rate, and they peruaded the assembly to pass the Two-Penny Act in 1758, by which the value of tobacco was set at two pence per pound (rather than the market value, which was three times higher). In time the king, acting through the Privy Council, disallowed the act and censured the governor for signing it. Several parsons sued to recover back wages lost because of the act, and in one such suit in 1763 Patrick Henry defended the parish against its rector. His speech to the jury accused the clergy of being lazy, rapacious, mercenary men, who would "snatch from the hearth of their honest parishioner the last hoecake, from the widow and her orphan child their last milch cow!" They "ought to be considered as enemies of the community," Henry continued, "and very justly deserve to be punished with signal severity." As for the king who disallowed the Two-Penny Act, he had "degenerated into a tyrant, and forfeits all rights to his subjects' obedience." The jury awarded the parson one penny in damages. Henry's name became known throughout the colonies.

Thus, while colonial patriotism to the motherland received an enormous spur from the victory at Quebec, still it was limited, fragile, grounded in self-interest, and laced by a thousand jealousies. Colonials resented the necessity of quartering troops in their homes. They complained about the practice of impressment. There was open antagonism between the militia and regular army. They bridled at the cultural condescensions of English visitors. " 'Tis true we in America are little inferior things in comparison of you great folks in London," James Logan of Pennsylvania noted sarcastically. In 1759 an English vicar traveling through Virginia reported that the people were "haughty and jealous of their liberties, impatient of restraint, and can scarcely bear the thought of being controlled by any superior power."

By the peace treaty signed in Paris in 1763, Britain allowed France to retain possession of its Caribbean islands, invaluable for their production of sugar. But on the North American continent, except for the islands of St. Pierre and Miquelon off the Canadian coast, France lost everything. Britain acquired

The Burden of Empire

Canada and all French lands east of the Mississippi; Spain, France's ally in the war, received New Orleans and all French lands west of the Mississippi as a consolation for giving up the Floridas to Britain.

Many British voices criticized the peace settlement. Britons believed that the West Indian islands were more valuable than the "frozen acres" of Canada and that Britain had selected the wrong prize. Caribbean islands were easier to defend, cheaper to maintain, and quicker to yield a profit. Moreover, without the threat of the French in Canada, it was predicted, the British colonies would soon make manifest their tendency to independence. "You are happy in the cession of Canada," a French diplomat wrote to an English acquaintance, "we, perhaps, ought to think ourselves happy that you have acquired it. Delivered from a neighbor whom they have always feared, your other colonies will soon discover that they stand no longer in need of your protection. You will call on them to contribute toward supporting the burden which they have helped to bring on you; they will answer you by shaking off all dependence." Ten years later, when the colonies were in fact in the throes of rebellion, the governor of Massachusetts, Thomas Hutchinson, noted that had Canada "remained to the French, none of the spirit of opposition would have yet appeared."

The new empire with its thousands of square miles of wilderness imposed a weight of responsibility and new problems that would test the abilities of British statesmen: What policies should be evolved concerning the western lands and the Indians? How should Canada, with its French population, be administered? What defensive measures would be necessary to protect the empire? How much would the costs of empire amount to, and who would pay them? These expenses had to be added to an already astronomical national debt, the accumulated costs of four major British wars in seventy years. British taxpayers wanted relief from their intolerable obligations, not additions to them.

COMMENTARY

Beginning in 1763 the British government attempted to solve its imperial problems—raising money, governing Canada, distributing land, regulating commerce, guarding the frontiers, dealing with Indians, dispensing justice—by enacting a series of laws it considered just and equitable. The colonists opposed the laws, however, and their dissent mounted and culminated in revolution. A colonial society, becoming conscious of its separate identity and quick to defend its rights, began to reexamine its position within the British empire. The colonists had shared common experiences and common characteristics: ethnic and religious diversity, economic opportunity, rapid growth, the menace of Indian attacks, the development of local self-government. What they lacked was a unity, a spirit of cooperation, a national impulse, and this was provided by the impact of British legislation. By 1776 they rebelled as "one people" who found it necessary, in the words of the Declaration of Independence, "to dissolve the political bands which have connected them with another."

BERNARD BAILYN, *Education in the Forming of American Society* (1960)

T. H. BREEN, *The Character of the Good Ruler* (1970)

ROBERT E. BROWN and B. KATHERINE BROWN, *Virginia, 1705–1786: Democracy or Aristocracy?* (1964)

PHILIP A. BRUCE, *The Virginia Plutarch* (1929)

J. M. BUMSTED and JOHN E. VAN DE WETERING, *What Must I Do To Be Saved?* (1976)

LAWRENCE A. CREMIN, *American Education: The Colonial Experience* (1970)

PHILIP CURTIN, *The Atlantic Slave Trade* (1969)

CARL DEGLER, *Neither Black Nor White* (1971)

JOHN I. FALCONER and PERCY BIDWELL, *History of Agriculture in the Northern United States* (1941)

WESLEY GEWEHR, *The Great Awakening in Virginia* (1930)

PAUL GOODMAN, *Essays in American Colonial History* (1967)

L. C. GRAY, *History of Agriculture in the Southern United States* (1958)

LORENZO GREENE, *The Negro in Colonial New England* (1942)

RICHARD HOFSTADTER, *America at 1750* (1971)

WINTHROP JORDAN, *White over Black* (1968)

MICHAEL KRAUS, *The Atlantic Civilization* (1949)

J. G. LEYBURN, *The Scotch-Irish* (1962)

SIDNEY MEAD, *The Lively Experiment* (1963)

PERRY MILLER, *The American Puritans* (1956)

———, *Jonathan Edwards* (1949)

EDMUND S. MORGAN, *The Puritan Family* (1966)

GERALD W. MULLIN, *Flight and Rebellion* (1972)

GARY B. NASH, *Class and Society in Early America* (1970)

———, *Red, White and Black* (1974)

ALAN ROGERS, *Empire and Liberty* (1974)

CLINTON ROSSITER, *Seedtime of the Republic* (1953)

M. EUGENE SIRMANS, *Colonial South Carolina* (1966)

CHARLES SYDNOR, *Gentlemen Freeholders* (1952)

THOMAS J. WERTENBAKER, *The Old South* (1942)

———, *Patrician and Plebeian in Virginia* (1958)

THOMAS G. WRIGHT, *Literary Culture in Early New England* (1966)

MICHAEL ZUCKERMAN, *Peaceable Kingdoms* (1970)

3

Empire and Revolution, 1763–1789

Pontiac's Rebellion

The defeat of the French did not mean that their Indian allies also surrendered. Quite the contrary; the western tribes became more belligerent as British colonials began to encroach even more upon their lands. On the southern frontier bloody clashes mounted in ferocity from 1761 to 1763. The British tried to obtain the support of the Cherokees and Choctaws against the Creeks but without success. The Creeks, on the other hand, tried but failed to forge an alliance of southern tribes. On the northern frontier the Senecas took the lead in fighting the British. General Jeffrey Amherst, commander in the West, violated a treaty by giving lands belonging to the Senecas to his soldiers. (It was Amherst who thought of decimating Indian tribes by infecting them with smallpox. A few blankets carrying the germ, he suggested, would do the trick.) With the French removed, Indians had to sell their furs to British traders, at British forts, and they were cheated outrageously. Moreover the British refused to supply the Indians with traditional gifts. Poverty stricken after the war and short of food, they asked for aid. Amherst responded that they would have to shift for themselves. Apart from a long list of grievances, the Indians were goaded to war by the preachings of a Delaware prophet, Naolin. He traveled from tribe to tribe, claiming to speak the revealed words of the Master of Life, warning Indians to give up "the customs you have adopted since the white people came among us." He called for a cultural rebirth of Indian values and a commitment to revolutionary resistance. "Wherefore do you suffer the whites to dwell upon your lands?" Naolin asked. "Drive them away; wage war against them. I love them not. They know me not. They are my enemies, they are your brothers' enemies."

An Ottawa chief, Pontiac, took up the message. "It is important for us, my brothers, that we exterminate from our lands this nation which seeks only to destroy us." One by one different tribes—the Delawares, Chippewas, Shawnees, Miamis, Potawatomis, Hurons, and so forth—joined the fray in 1763. And one by one, across the entire Northwest, the forts at Sandusky, Presque Isle, St. Joseph, Le Boeuf, and Venango fell to the Indians in a matter of weeks. Pontiac's rebellion aimed at driving the British back across the Appalachians, and it almost worked. More than two thousand soldiers and settlers were killed. Shawnees drove deep into Virginia, and Delawares swept up the Monongahela River. But the Indians could not capture the three main forts at Detroit, Pittsburgh, and Niagara. Colonel Henry Bouquet instituted effective guerrilla operations against Indian villages, burning them, and destroying their crops. His victory at Bushy Run (near Pittsburgh) was decisive. The siege at Detroit was lifted by another British expedition. At a peace conference Pontiac accepted "the King of England for my Father, in presence of all the Nations now assembled." His despair and bitterness, however, were apparent in his private remarks: "I myself will never be a friend to the English. I shall now become a wanderer in the woods; and if they come to seek me there, while I have an arrow left, I will shoot at them." Pontiac's remarkable rebellion was over. But many Indians felt as he did, and the pacification of the West was only temporary.

Pontiac's rebellion spurred the British government to announce a new policy that had been brewing for some time in the minds of politicians concerned about the American West. Previously western settlement had been encouraged. So long as the French were competitors, the British wanted their colonials to move into the lands beyond the Appalachians. By 1763 it seemed more beneficial to keep them out. After all, the British now controlled the fur trade, and land settlements would reduce the enormous profitability of that trade. Moreover, it would be proportionately more difficult to govern colonials as they became dispersed throughout the West. Finally, to permit western migration would serve only to ignite a new round of Indian wars. Thus, in October 1763, as a temporary measure, the king issued a proclamation reserving all land from the Appalachians to the Mississippi, and from the Florida border to fifty degrees north latitude, to the Indians. In effect, it put the West under military control, closed to settlers and speculators, and open to traders only under careful regulation.

Proclamation of 1763

The proclamation accomplished none of its intended purposes. First, it had some loopholes. It permitted soldiers who had fought against the French to occupy western lands. Second, it was difficult to enforce, and squatters poured through the mountain passes in defiance. Even George Washington advised fellow speculators to ignore its restrictions and to mark out their western land claims "in order to keep others from settling them." The British government never repudiated the idea of the proclamation, but it was obviously unpopular, impractical, and expensive to administer. As ministers in charge of American affairs changed, so British policy vacillated. The Earl of Shelburne proposed the gradual formation of new colonies in the West. The Earl of Hillsborough preferred to impose permanent restraints. Colonial land speculators and fur traders, with conflicting desires, continued to pressure the government for solutions that would favor their interests. Neither side was wholly satisfied. A number of treaties negotiated with Indian tribes opened new lands to settlement. Most notable was the 1768 Treaty of Fort Stanwix (New York), which moved the proclamation line into the Ohio valley. As late as 1772 Lord Hillsborough noted his distrust of that treaty and its consequences: "Every day discovers more and more the fatal

policy of departing from the line prescribed by the Proclamation of 1763. . . . Instead of being attended with advantage to this Kingdom and security to the Colonies . . . [it] will most probably have the effect to produce a general Indian war."

No laws or proclamations could have stopped the sweep of population into the Mississippi valley. To the extent that Britain tried, western lands remained a cause for irritation between the colonial governments and Parliament. Nor would the problem lessen. By 1774, because of further British legislation, it would in fact become an important contributing factor to the American Revolution.

Land was cheap and abundant in America, but much hard work went into clearing the forests and preparing the land for crops. By the late eighteenth century the typical family farm in the North was about one hundred acres, divided into woodland, pasturage, and fields. (The Bettmann Archive)

Sugar and Stamps

Since the Seven Years' War increased the British national debt by some £130,000,000, and the colonials benefited from the defeat of France, and since the expense of maintaining garrisons against Indian attacks was also to their benefit, the British government believed it was only just and reasonable for America to contribute to the costs of empire. How might it be done? There was no central colonial government to act as a tax collector. To tax each colony individually opened the problem of proportion, which none could agree upon. George Grenville, chancellor of the exchequer, concluded that the best device was to raise money by customs duties and stamp taxes. Thus, at his urging, Parliament passed the Sugar Act (1764) and the Stamp Act (1765).

The Sugar Act increased the duties on a variety of goods—sugar, indigo, coffee, wine—but lowered by one-half the tariff on foreign molasses (used in the making of rum). Grenville hoped that the reduced costs would remove

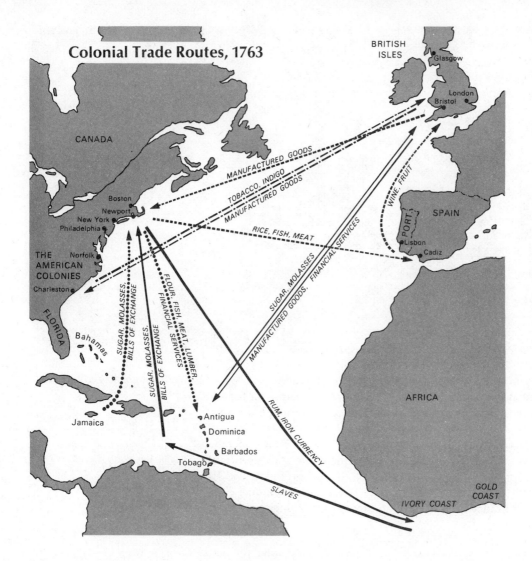

Colonial Trade Routes, 1763

Foreign trade was the key to economic prosperity for the American colonies. Frequently, as the map indicates, it took a "triangular" form. What the colonies made in trade with the West Indies and southern Europe—the two most lucrative avenues of colonial commerce—was used to compensate for their unfavorable balance of trade with England. British regulations after 1763, especially the capricious and arbitrary enforcement provisions, seemed to threaten colonial mercantile interests.

the inducement to smuggle. To be certain of this result, the Sugar Act provided for strict enforcement. A new vice-admiralty court was established at Halifax, which heard smuggling cases without the traditional trial by jury. (Later three more courts were added, at Boston, Philadelphia, and Charleston.) The burden of proof was on the accused. Even if acquitted, he had to pay court costs. If convicted, he might lose both his vessel and cargo, which would be sold and the proceeds distributed in equal shares to the crown, the governor, and the informant. In a sense the act worked. It raised nearly 90 percent of the total revenues collected in America. But colonials dreaded the admiralty court system with its potential for corruption and its treatment of Americans as second-class citizens.

The Stamp Act required the payment of a tax on all kinds of legal documents—contracts, ships' papers, mortgages, college diplomas, land deeds, licenses, judicial writs—as well as on playing cards, pamphlets, newspapers, even newspaper advertisements. A donation to a school? The tax was £2. A lawyer's license to practice? The tax was £10. An almanac? The tax was four pence per copy. The tax had to be paid in sterling, not paper currency, which meant in effect that the actual cost was considerably greater to the taxpayer. Moreover, the law provided that violators could be tried in the hated admiralty courts. Grenville defended the Stamp Act on practical and political grounds. First, the money collected would be spent in America, especially to cover the cost of military garrisons which ran to £350,000 annually. Second, though the tax was internal—the first so levied by Parliament—the colonists were virtually represented in Parliament. Every member of that body, it was argued, represented the interests of the entire empire. After all, many citizens in Britain without the franchise were subject to similar taxes.

A number of prominent colonials rushed to become stamp distributors, since each received an 8 percent commission: George Mercer of Virginia, Jared Ingersoll of Connecticut, Andrew Oliver of Massachusetts. Benjamin Franklin, then in London, advised a friend to become the stamp distributor in Pennsylvania:

> A firm Loyalty to the Crown and faithful adherence to the government of this nation, which is the safety as well as the honor of the colonies to be connected with, will always be the wisest course for you and I to take, whatever may be the madness of the populace or their blind leaders, who can only bring themselves and country into trouble, and draw on greater burdens by acts of rebellious tendency.

Franklin had miscalculated. He did not foresee the depth of feeling or the unanimity of sentiment the Stamp Act would evoke. Although the Sugar Act directly affected only shippers and importers, the Stamp Act touched all classes, including the most articulate: lawyers, editors, printers, and dissenting preachers, as well as artisans and shopkeepers.

The colonists responded with words and acts, the former to persuade and the latter to coerce Britain into withdrawing the legislation. The Sons of Liberty in Boston, urged on by the merchants, burned admiralty court records and sacked the home of Lieutenant Governor Thomas Hutchinson. "Some of the principal ringleaders in the late riots," Hutchinson complained, "walk the streets with impunity; no officers dare attack them, no

The Stamp Act Congress

attorney general prosecute them, and no judge sit upon them." Boston was not the only scene of revolutionary activity. In New York City a mob forced the lieutenant governor to flee for safety. A garrison officer had threatened "to cram the Stamp Act down the people's throats." They gutted his residence. In Charleston a mob would not be appeased until the governor promised that stamp taxes would not be imposed. Everywhere stamp distributors were burned in effigy; frightened by threats of physical violence, they quickly resigned their commissions. Merchants in Philadelphia, New York, and Boston agreed to boycott British goods. Colonial legislatures passed resolutions of protest, and royal officials and their supporters were intimidated by vigilante organizations. "The flame is spread through all the continent," the governor of Virginia wrote, "and one colony supports another in their disobedience to superior powers." Nowhere could the Stamp Act be enforced.

The colonists maintained that they were not revolutionaries but good citizens upholding the traditional rights of Englishmen. By natural rights, by historic practice, and by the fundamental law of England, taxation without representation was a tyranny that they were bound to resist. Patrick Henry told the Virginia assembly that it possessed "the only and sole and exclusive right and power to lay taxes," and the assembly responded by passing a set of resolutions to that effect. So did the assemblies of other colonies, just as explicitly. Finally, in October, delegates from nine colonies met in New York at the famous Stamp Act Congress, which affirmed this position once again:

> That the people of these Colonies are not, and from their local circumstances cannot be, represented in the House of Commons in Great Britain;
> That the only Representatives of the people of these Colonies, are persons chosen therein by themselves, and that no taxes ever have been, or can be constitutionally imposed on them, but by their respective legislatures.

The Stamp Act Congress was an intercolonial meeting of officially appointed delegates initiated by the Americans themselves. Although their strongest emotional ties were local, they were beginning to realize that they must act in unity. Christopher Gadsden of South Carolina told the delegates "there ought to be no New England man, no New Yorker, known on this continent, but all of us Americans." That message would become more impelling with every passing year.

In effect, what the colonists were postulating was a federal empire in which authority was divisible. Parliament could legislate for the colonies, but it could not tax them. The distinction seemed theoretically clear. Its application, even if the British accepted the definition, would be difficult.

The colonial position had its champions in Parliament. It was Colonel Isaac Barré who first labeled the Americans "sons of liberty" in a fiery speech before the House of Commons. William Pitt became enormously popular in the colonies because of his words: "The Americans have been

The British Response

wronged! They have been driven to madness by injustice! Will you punish them for the madness you have occasioned? No! Let this country be the first to resume its prudence and temper." But men like Barré and Pitt were in a distinct minority, and one doubts whether their arguments had much effect on Parliament. More important was the fact of colonial solidarity; the British realized that the Stamp Act could not be enforced against such firm and united opposition. Moreover, the colonial boycott injured British merchants, who then pressed petitions on Parliament calling for the repeal of the Grenville duties. After Grenville fell from power the tariff on molasses was reduced even further, and the Stamp Act was repealed by a vote of 275 to 167 in the House of Commons. The colonists had gained every point except one, for along with the repeal of the Stamp Act was passed the Declaratory Act (1766), which stated that Parliament had absolute authority to legislate for the colonies "in all cases whatsoever."

Parliament had lost a skirmish but had refused to concede the battle. Only one of the conflicting views of empire could ultimately prevail: either the British government had to agree to a division of power, or the colonists had to accept the sovereignty of Parliament.

CURRENCY   British merchants complained that some colonists were paying their debts in depreciated paper rather than sterling. To correct this abuse, Parliament passed the Currency Act in 1764, which prohibited the colonies from issuing bills of credit as legal tender; moreover, it mandated that bills of credit already issued were to be retired from circulation. The Currency Act was not a departure from previous practice, but it was resented nonetheless. Benjamin Franklin declared the currency problem to be a major cause of discontent. The scarcity of specie, added to the normal postwar economic contractions, hurt colonial debtors, who now had to pay their taxes and other obligations to the British in hard currency. Of all British legislation, one scholar concludes, "currency restriction probably had the profoundest economic impact on the colonies and posed the greatest threat to their domestic economic arrangements."

Other Colonial Discontents

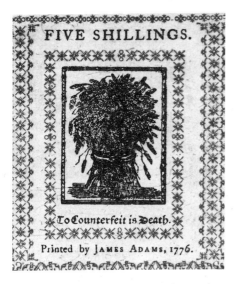

In 1773 Parliament relaxed the provisions of the Currency Act of 1764, permitting colonials once again to issue paper money. By that time other divisive problems had developed and revolutionary sentiment continued to mount. Paper money was common in the revolutionary period— samples are shown here— and the Continental Congress issued some 200 million dollars' worth by 1779. Citizens had little faith in it, and came to describe any item without value as "not worth a Continental." (American Antiquarian Society)

TROOPS Contrary to colonial expectations, British troops were not removed at the close of the Seven Years' War. Their presence served as a constant irritant to Americans. Two quartering acts (1765–1766) required the colonial governments to furnish housing and other necessities for the soldiers. Georgia at first refused to comply; but when the British troops were withdrawn and the colony was exposed to Indian attacks, the Georgia assembly voted the necessary funds. New York, site of the headquarters of the British army, was more adamant. The New York legislature, reflecting its changes in composition, refused all but the scantiest appropriations in 1766, approved expenditures for military housing in 1767, reversed itself in 1768, and yielded again at the close of 1769. So heated were the relations between British redcoats and the New York Sons of Liberty that several serious clashes and even riots took place. When royal troops were moved to Massachusetts, the New Englanders inherited New York's problems. In 1770, a more famous incident occurred in Boston. A file of redcoats, their pride stung because of a beating British soldiers had received in a street fight several days before and taunted by the jeers of a crowd, fired on the colonists without warning. Five citizens died in the Boston Massacre, an event that stirred the Americans deeply. Many colonists who had not yet become convinced of British perfidy changed their minds when the disagreements were expressed not in ink but in blood.

News of the repeal of the Stamp Act had been greeted with unrestrained joy in the colonies, but it was short-lived. A new chancellor of the exchequer, Charles Townshend, acting in part on the basis of inaccurate information provided by Benjamin Franklin, offered another way for the colonists to pay a share of imperial expenses. Franklin, appearing before Parliament in the previous year, had unintentionally misrepresented the colonial position by testifying that their opposition was to internal taxes only. Townshend's scheme, which Parliament adopted in 1767, was to enact tariffs on colonial imports of certain British products—tea, paints, lead, paper, and glass—and to reorganize the collection of customs to minimize corruption. How could there be any objections? Did not Parliament have the right to regulate commerce within the empire? The House of Commons, convinced that Townshend's plan would effectively increase revenues, simultaneously passed a law reducing the tax obligations of British landowners.

The Townshend Duties

  By 1770 the British government again was ready to concede. The use of force had served only to provoke the colonists to further exhibitions of defiance. The attempt to extract revenue led to further denials of parliamentary authority. John Dickinson's pamphlet, *Letters from a Farmer in Pennsylvania,* which was widely read, reiterated the American position: the colonies were unrepresented in Parliament and therefore Parliament could not pass legislation for the purpose of obtaining revenue, even in the guise of the Townshend duties. Other voices, using the same argument, questioned the right of Parliament to keep a standing army in the colonies and to deny jury trials. The British government was persuaded to retreat not by the logic of these arguments, but by a realistic appraisal of economic facts. Colonial boycotts of British goods were so effective that imports had declined some 40 percent. The Townshend duties had failed to reap the desired harvest (as many had predicted). On the very day of the Boston Massacre, Lord North requested a repeal of almost all the Townshend duties, which Parliament later passed. Tea was the only product specifically excepted. Moreover, the Quartering Act was permitted to lapse. The colonists had gained another substantial victory. But once again the British insisted on the principle that Parliament's acts could not be limited and were the supreme law of the empire.

Political consistency was not a virtue of the colonists. With the partial repeal of the Townshend duties, relations with the mother country improved. As long as parliamentary legislation did not pinch American pockets too much, there were few murmurs of protest. The tariffs on sugar and molasses continued to be collected. After 1770 the tariff on tea was paid. Both were clearly for the purpose of revenue. But since American merchants were prospering, what reason was there to sustain the fight for abstract principles? These merchants wished to maintain the new status quo, and leadership of the anti-British movement devolved on more radical men.

Samuel Adams

Samuel Adams, one of the earliest revolutionaries to think in terms of total independence, stoked the fires of American discontent. His cousin John successfully defended the British soldiers tried for the Boston Massacre by winning them only a token punishment for manslaughter. But Samuel used the episode as a valuable propaganda weapon, pouring out a stream of inflammatory material. When Britain agreed to pay the salaries of royal governors and judges to free them from their economic dependence on the colonial legislatures, Adams aroused his fellow Americans to the danger. Perhaps his most valuable contribution to the cause of independence was the organization of the Committees of Correspondence. These committees, formed in towns throughout and even outside Massachusetts, could work quickly and in unity by interchanging letters to establish a common policy against Britain. By spreading propaganda, they could also influence public opinion to subscribe to their radical viewpoint. Still, Adams could not have accomplished so much had it not been for two factors. First, many people were receptive to his propaganda. Second, the British—after a period of relative quiescence—committed another major blunder.

Tea Act

The Tea Act (1773) was regarded by a large majority in Parliament as the mildest and most equitable law possible. Its provisions permitted the British East India Company to sell tea directly to American merchants, instead of by auction in London; and to forego paying custom duties in Britain. The only tax on the tea would be the nominal three-penny duty collected in the colonies. In effect, the Tea Act gave the British East India Company a monopoly of the American tea business. The anticipated results were to be mutually beneficial. Colonial tea drinkers could purchase the product at a

lower price since it did not have to pass through Britain. In fact, they could purchase it cheaper than they could smuggle tea. Furthermore, the East India Company, a huge corporation by eighteenth-century standards, would be rescued from near bankruptcy by the profits from tea sales on the American market. The purposes of the Tea Act were indeed meritorious. For that reason its consequences were not foreseen by the responsible British ministers.

The Tea Act contained a greater threat to the profits of American merchants than any mere tax. By giving the East India Company import and marketing privileges, colonial competitors feared they would be driven out of business. If the monopoly took effect, predicted the merchants, the East India Company would raise the price of tea. If Parliament could grant a virtual monopoly in one product, they argued, it could do the same with others. The scare was convincing enough to Americans, who took up the cries of "Monopoly" and "Tyranny" in every major port. Nowhere did they permit the tea to be sold. In most cases cargoes were simply returned to Britain. In Charleston the tea was unloaded and left to rot in a damp warehouse. In Boston some fifty men "dressed like Mohawks, of very grotesque appearance," boarded the company's ships and tossed 342 tea chests overboard. Although bands in America still played "God Save the King," George III and the British ministers regarded the Boston Tea Party as something less than a patriotic act.

Events now moved rapidly, almost inexorably, toward revolution. The number of colonial supporters in the House of Commons dwindled to a handful. Even some of those who had been counted as friends of the American cause were angered by the Boston Tea Party. Lord Dartmouth

While hundreds of Bostonians watched, other citizens lightly disguised as Indians threw about 90,000 pounds of tea, valued at £10,000, into the harbor on the night of December 16, 1773. "This destruction of the tea," John Adams commented, "is so bold, so daring, so firm, intrepid, and inflexible, and it must have so important consequences, and so lasting, that I cannot but consider it as an epoch in history." (American Antiquarian Society)

Coercive Acts

called it an "outrageous madness." Colonel Barré spoke in favor of punishing Boston. By substantial majorities Parliament in 1774 passed a number of punitive measures against Massachusetts, usually referred to as the "Coercive" or "Intolerable" acts.

One bill closed the port of Boston until the East India Company was reimbursed for its losses.

A second prohibited town meetings convened without the governor's approval. The capital of the colony was removed to Salem.

A third provided that British officials charged with capital offenses committed in support of the crown would be tried in Nova Scotia or in England.

A fourth gave the king sole power to appoint the Governor's Council. The King or governor now had the right to appoint many local officials who had hitherto been elected.

A fifth was a new quartering act, requiring housing for the troops that were to arrive in Boston with the new governor, General Thomas Gage.

With incredibly bad timing, Parliament also passed the Quebec Act in 1774, further exacerbating the western issue. For French Canadians it was a piece of enlightened statesmanship; for Protestant Americans it opened alarming potentials for Catholic dominance. By this legislation the old Northwest was annexed to the province of Quebec. French Catholics who lived there were to enjoy religious freedom. Anglo-Americans who lived there would be unrepresented, since Quebec had no legislative assembly. Worst of all, the Quebec Act automatically canceled the western land claims that several colonies derived from their original charters. John Jay prophesied that if the act was permitted to stand, the number of Canadian Catholics would multiply, an inquisition would be imposed, and the Protestant colonies would be reduced to slavery.

Meanwhile the military occupation and coercion of Boston served to unite further Americans of every class and section. Other cities offered their wharf facilities to Boston merchants. Collections were taken and sent to indigent Bostonians. Illegal town meetings were convoked. Radical resolutions were adopted. Nonimportation and nonconsumption of British products were resumed. Committees of Correspondence seconded a call for a colonial congress "to deliberate and determine on wise and proper measures . . . for the restoration of union and harmony between Great Britain and America, which is most ardently desired by all good men."

The "good men" assembled at the first Continental Congress in Philadelphia in September 1774 represented a wide variety of political persuasions. John Adams characterized them as "one-third Tories, another Whigs, and the rest Mongrels." Some proposed to raise an army at once, attack the British forces under General Gage, and expel them from Boston. This position was much too extreme for most. The conservative end of the spectrum recommended

The Continental Congress

patience and reconciliation. John Dickinson believed that "procrastination is preservation." Edmund Pendleton thought there was danger in the ceaseless talk about colonial "rights." Joseph Galloway proposed a new version of Franklin's old plan of union: a president-general appointed by the king and a colonial grand council to share power with Parliament, each to have a veto power over legislation. But it had little chance since more radical members, led by John and Samuel Adams, Patrick Henry, Richard Henry Lee, and Christopher Gadsden, controlled the congress.

The radicals had previously pushed through an endorsement of the Suffolk County, Massachusetts, resolutions, which declared that "no obedience was due to either or any part of the recent acts of Parliament." The "Declaration of Rights" that the Continental Congress adopted went even further. It enumerated a long list of infringements and violations of colonial rights, including the Sugar Act, Stamp Act, Quartering Act, Tea Act, Quebec Act, and all the Coercive Acts. These rights, stated the declaration, were guaranteed "by the immutable laws of nature, the principles of the English Constitution, and the several charters or compacts." Now, in 1774, after a decade of attempting to construct an operative definition of their place in the British empire and being driven by parliamentary legislation to ever more radical positions, the leaders of the Continental Congress entirely repudiated Parliament's authority over them. However, to indicate their willingness to compromise in the "mutual interest of both countries," they promised to accept bona fide parliamentary regulation of external commerce.

The Continental Congress in effect was America's first national government. It assumed the power of legislation. It claimed to speak for all the colonies (except Georgia, which was unrepresented). And before adjourning, it agreed to reconvene unless colonial grievances were redressed by the British government.

Even if Lord North had wanted to adopt a pacific policy, neither King George nor a majority of the cabinet had any intention of appeasing the rebels—for Massachusetts was declared to be in a state of rebellion—and hostile action soon followed. At the beginning it took the form of economic sanctions. By the New England Restraining Act (1775), which prohibited New Englanders from trading with any other country except Britain and the West Indies, and which also barred them from the Newfoundland fisheries, Parliament tried to coerce the colonists into obedience. Later these provisions were extended to five other colonies. The Americans reciprocated in kind. They created the intercolonial Continental (or American) Association, by which trade with Britain was gradually closed. No British goods were to be imported or consumed; no American products were to be exported to Britain. Home manufactures, especially that of woolen goods, was encouraged. Some loopholes existed, but the association's system of inspection proved remarkably effective. For example, New York's imports of British goods fell from a value of £437,000 in 1774 to £1,228 in 1775. The ill feeling grew and began to assume a distinctly military character. When General Gage called for

War Begins

twenty thousand more troops, British ministers were shocked. They assured one another that the colonists could not stand against seasoned veterans, that only one or two battles would bring America to terms. The colonists began to mount cannons, cache arms, enlist officers, and train volunteers. Many read and took heart from Charles Lee's pamphlet, which concluded that the Americans could defeat the British and any mercenaries brought from Europe. Given the temper of both sides, one match could ignite the entire continent.

That match was struck in the early morning of April 19, 1775, on the village green at Lexington, Massachusetts. Coming up the road from Boston to arrest rebel leaders and to search out hidden arms, an advance guard of British soldiers was met by some seventy minutemen and militia. The colonists had been alerted at midnight by Paul Revere. Samuel Adams and John Hancock had fled certain capture, and the minutemen stood ready to block the British. Who fired the first shot is uncertain—scholars disagree— yet the initial battle of the American Revolution was an unfortunate beginning for the patriots. Eight Americans were killed and ten wounded, while only one redcoat suffered a slight injury. But the day was far from over. On the British went to Concord where the colonists, warned by Dr. Samuel Prescott, had had time to remove most of its military supplies. An inconclusive skirmish occurred there at North Bridge, which forced the British to fall back into the village. That afternoon the sixteen-mile march back to Boston proved disastrous for the British. All along the route hundreds of colonial sharpshooters harried the royal troops, firing from behind trees and stone walls and barns with devastating effect. Gage wisely dispatched twelve hundred men as a relief force to protect the retreating troops. Before the regulars found safety at Charlestown, there were 273 British and 95 American casualties. Who, asked Thomas Paine, could now talk of reconciliation with murderers?

Thomas Paine

More than a year elapsed between the battle of Lexington and adoption of the Declaration of Independence. During this period a series of military and political events made independence inevitable. The rebels fought at Bunker Hill. George Washington was appointed commander-in-chief of the American forces. Fort Ticonderoga on Lake Champlain was taken by New Englanders led by Benedict Arnold. An invasion of Canada was launched but failed to achieve any of its key objectives. Some colonies expelled their royal governors; other permitted them to flee. All colonies began to undergo a constitutional metamorphosis into sovereign states. Still, many rebels did not consider themselves traitors. Although they felt that Parliament had no authority over them, they recognized fidelity to the king. In other words, by 1774–75 Americans had worked out a definition of their relationship to the empire, which other dominions would not achieve for over a century: that of a completely sovereign nation, linked to the mother country only by the mutual recognition of a common monarch.

The person most responsible for breaking that final link was Thomas

Paine. A recent immigrant, he had been in the colonies less than two years when he wrote and anonymously published the pamphlet *Common Sense* (January 1776). Its reception was phenomenal. In three months over 120,000 copies were distributed, and several times that figure were eventually sold. Some contemporaries claimed that the British prosecution of the war, not Paine's pamphlet, was the determining factor in the break with England. John Adams later, and typically, asserted that Paine offered no new arguments. True enough. But if words and ideas can influence public opinion, Paine's pamphlet was crucial.

"Can ye give to prostitution its former innocence?" asked Paine. "Neither can ye reconcile Britain and America." He maintained that the colonies gained nothing by being part of the empire, except involvement in Europe's wars. American food, wrote Paine, "will always have a market while eating is the custom in Europe." He condemned those who argued for friendship with Britain: "Whatever may be your rank or title in life, you have the heart of a coward." Like most other great revolutionaries, he was acutely conscious of history: "Now is the seedtime of continental union, faith and honor. The least fracture now will be like a name engraved with the point of a pin on the tender rind of a young oak; the wound would enlarge with the tree, and posterity read it in full grown characters." He excoriated George III, declared it against all reason for an island to govern a continent, and penned an eternal apostrophe to American freedom:

Of Quaker stock from East Anglia, the self-educated son of a poor corset-maker, Thomas Paine unleashed a masterpiece of propaganda with Common Sense. *It was recognized by some as a work of "original genius," and none can doubt its catalytic action on the revolutionary movement. (American Antiquarian Society)*

> O! Ye that love mankind! Ye that dare oppose not only the tyranny but the tyrant, stand forth! Every Freedom hath been hunted round the globe. Asia and Africa have long expelled her. Europe regards her like a stranger, and England hath given her warning to depart. O! Receive the fugitive, and prepare in time an asylum for mankind.

Independence

The second Continental Congress, like the first, had its conservative and radical wings. The final attempt of the conservatives to reunite the colonies to Britain, the "Olive Branch Petition," was written by John Dickinson. George III rejected it. Thereafter Congress was spurred to declaring independence by the influence of Paine's pamphlet, by the recommendations of George Washington and other officers, and by the authorizations of several states. Richard Henry Lee introduced a resolution calling for independence on June 7, and Congress approved it on July 2. However, a committee of five had been appointed to draft a more formal declaration, which Congress voted on July 4, 1776.

The Declaration of Independence combined philosophical statement, political tract, and legal brief. Written primarily by Thomas Jefferson, it reflected the belief in natural law held by most educated Anglo-Americans. Derived mainly from John Locke, this philosophy can be summarized as follows. First, all men are equally entitled to certain inherent and immutable rights, among the most important of which are "life, liberty, and the pursuit of happiness." Second, government is purposely created by men who contract together to safeguard these rights. Third, when government no longer fulfils this function—when, in fact, government is oppressive and destroys human freedom—then as a last resort the people have a right to revolution. Further, the declaration expressed an extreme of colonial federalist theory, denying that Parliament had ever had power over the colonists and claiming that allegiance had been due solely to the king. Finally, the declaration cited a long list of abuses directly attributed to the king, thus providing justification for revolt. "With a firm reliance on the Protection of Divine Providence," Jefferson concluded, "we mutually pledge to each other our Lives, our Fortunes and our sacred Honor." The fifty-six representatives of thirteen colonies then signed their names.

Perhaps 30 to 35 percent of all colonists remained Loyalists, concentrating mainly in New York City and its vicinity, portions of New Jersey and Maryland, Philadelphia and southeastern Pennsylvania, the Mohawk Valley, the southern part of Delaware, western Carolina, and Georgia. Rebels could be found everywhere, but their main strength centered in New England and Virginia. Generally the Revolution did not divide the colonists along class lines. Merchants and artisans, farmers and frontiersmen, as well as lawyers and speculators, belonged to both sides. Why did some people remain loyal and others rebel? The answer is as complex as each local experience, as enigmatical as the personalities involved.

Causes of Revolution

Two complementary tendencies should be noted. First, by the middle of the eighteenth century the American colonies had reached a level of economic growth that was in some ways either very competitive with Britain's or seemed circumscribed by British regulations. When the colonies were an infant economy, participation in the British empire had seemed an asset; as a burgeoning giant of unlimited potential, they looked upon the same participation as restricting. Thus, a major cause of the Revolution was economic. Second, along with economic growth, the belief had gradually developed that the destiny of America was distinct from that of Britain and the rest of the Old World. Americans did not want their country to repeat the unhappy European pattern of kings, standing armies, wars, and established churches. For decades the colonies had elected their own assemblies and appointed their own courts, and the characteristics of self-reliance and political independence had become deeply ingrained. Even had there been no revolution against Britain, the impulse toward democracy would have continued and would have caused serious internal conflicts between established authorities and liberal aspirants. The struggle with Britain provided a focus for demands for political freedom. Thus, a major cause of the Revolution was political. The economic and political causes were closely linked. Property and liberty were synonymous to most colonists. British taxes therefore seemed as much a deprivation of liberty as a loss of property.

George III was not the tyrant pictured by the rebels; nor was he guilty of the offenses Jefferson submitted "to a candid world." From a British point of view the acts of Parliament were neither unconstitutional nor unreasonable. But they were unwise. The ultimate failure of the king and Parliament stemmed from their rigidity and provincialism, their hopeless misunderstanding of the colonial mentality. In thirteen years they had repeatedly demonstrated their inability to solve the problems of empire.

They could solve the problems of war no better. The British expected a quick *The Long War* victory, but the Revolution did not end until the Battle of Yorktown in 1781, and a final peace treaty between the parties was not signed until 1783.

The British miscalculated by ignoring the effects of European politics. French agents had urged the colonists to independence, and after 1776 French economic and military aid was extended, though unofficially. The astonishing defeat of "Gentleman Johnny" Burgoyne at Saratoga late in 1777 convinced the French to ally with the Americans by an open declaration of war against Britain. In 1778 France and America signed a treaty of alliance in which, among other stipulations, each party pledged not to make a separate peace with Britain and to continue fighting until American independence was assured. The following year Spain entered on the American side. Other northern European nations joined together in the anti-British "League of Armed Neutrality." British possessions in the Caribbean and the Mediterranean became vulnerable. Final victory was achieved with the aid of the French navy. At the Yorktown peninsula, where General Cornwallis was surrounded by American and French troops, the French fleet under Admiral De Grasse blocked the British navy from coming to the rescue. Cornwallis had no option but surrender.

If victory was due, in part, to French help and British miscalculation, the major architect of the American success was George Washington. Sometimes he moved so slowly, so cautiously, that his competence was questioned. A few critics suggested that he be replaced by General Horatio Gates. Nothing came of the idea, fortunately for the patriots' cause. The essence of Washington's strategy was to adhere to a defensive position. Yorktown was the result of six years of patience and fortitude. When officers quarreled over rank and honors, when state governments were tardy or remiss in supplying food, clothing, and troop quotas, when men deserted, when currency became hopelessly inflated, when French naval support seemed an infinity away—Washington resisted the "apostles of rash offensives." The ultimate defeat of the British army came about by his prolonged reluctance to risk a major battle at poor odds. "In strategy, as in land speculation," according to one of his biographers, Douglas S. Freeman, "Washington habitually was a bargain hunter. He always sought the largest gain for the least gore."

Three fears dominated the peace negotiations: Spain feared the colonies' *The Peace Treaty* westward expansion and wanted them contained; America feared that the French supported Spain's policy; Britain feared a Franco-American alliance.

The American representatives in Paris—Benjamin Franklin, John Jay, and John Adams—were under instructions to cooperate with the French. They soon suspected, however, that the French minister of foreign affairs, the Comte de Vergennes, was intent on pleasing the Spaniards. Various proposals were made which would have divested the United States of large land areas they claimed east of the Mississippi. The Americans therefore violated their instructions and met secretly with British representatives. The latter were pleased to drive a wedge between the former allies, and a peace treaty was arranged. Although the Americans did not receive Canada, as they had requested, the terms were generous. The treaty secured the trans-Appalachian area as far as the Mississippi, and it even preserved American fishing privileges off Nova Scotia and Newfoundland. "The day is now come when the sun will raise on America never to set," commented one rebel on hearing of the peace. "I look forward with pleasure to the happy days that our children will see."

The United States was the first revolutionary country to win independence, the first modern nation to reject monarchy, the first to predicate its government on the equality of mankind. Could the country live up to these high ideals? American visionaries foresaw a nation without prejudice, free from corruption, seeking not domination but peace. Cynics sneered at the attempt, and others alternated between hope and despair. Could Americans put their vision into practice? Sectional and economic rivalries had to be surmounted. Could the colonies control the conflicting pluralisms and exist together as one people? Americans were still largely locally oriented. Could they learn to think in terms of continental interests? Their heritage was revolutionary. Could they practice moderation? Radicals and conservatives disagreed on the nature of the central government. Could they discover the magic balance between liberty and order? Could they make federalism work? The French and British had failed to solve the problems of empire. Could the Americans do any better?

The beginning was inauspicious. As early as 1776 Americans were aware of the need for a permanent central government to replace the Revolutionary Continental Congress. John Dickinson composed a draft of a constitution that was debated and considerably altered, yet five years elapsed before the Articles of Confederation were ratified. The delay was caused by an issue that had plagued Britain: the problem of western lands. Certain "landed" states, on the basis of their original colonial charters, claimed possession of territories between the Appalachians and the Mississippi. Other "landless" states, lacking such claims, demanded that these lands be given up voluntarily and ceded to the central government.

The Articles of Confederation

Virginia was the last (and the largest) of the "landed" states to refuse to cede its territory. Maryland was the last of the "landless" states to withhold approval of the Articles because of Virginia's obstinacy. Maryland's argument ran somewhat as follows: states without western lands would be dwarfed in size, wealth, and influence by mighty colossi like Virginia. Virginia could derive much of its income from the sale of western lands, but states without lands would have to rely entirely on taxes for revenue. Therefore, people would flock to the "landed" states, and the "landless" states would be even worse off. Besides, the western lands should be considered as spoils of war, the common possession of all Americans, and should be administered in their behalf by Congress under the Articles of Confederation.

Western Land Claims and Cessions, 1776-1802

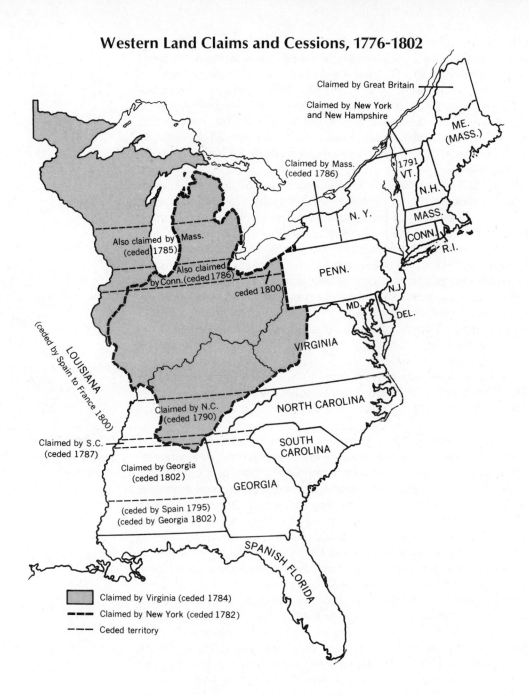

Claimed by Great Britain

Claimed by New York and New Hampshire

Claimed by Mass. (ceded 1786)

1791 VT.

ME. (MASS.)

N.H.

N. Y.

MASS.

CONN.

R.I.

Also claimed by Mass. (ceded 1785)

Also claimed by Conn. (ceded 1786)

ceded 1800

PENN.

N.J.

MD.

DEL.

VIRGINIA

LOUISIANA (ceded by Spain to France 1800)

Claimed by N.C. (ceded 1790)

NORTH CAROLINA

Claimed by S.C. (ceded 1787)

SOUTH CAROLINA

Claimed by Georgia (ceded 1802)

GEORGIA

(ceded by Spain 1795) (ceded by Georgia 1802)

SPANISH FLORIDA

Claimed by Virginia (ceded 1784)

Claimed by New York (ceded 1782)

Ceded territory

In 1776, six states claimed to control western lands because their royal charters had granted sea-to-sea boundaries, and New York argued that it had jurisdiction over all Iroquois lands. Not until 1802 did the federal government gain complete possession of the area between the Appalachians and the Mississippi.

This patriotic argument, however, was presented by groups of land speculators—including some of the most prominent revolutionary leaders of the middle Atlantic states—who acted from less laudable motives. They had formed companies, invested capital, and purchased large tracts from the Indians. Virginia refused to confirm the validity of their titles. (Why should Virginia do so? After all, Virginia had its own land speculators.) If the Articles of Confederation provided for national control of the West, Congress might prove more amenable to the non-Virginian speculators' interests.

Virginians were well aware of the baser reasons for Maryland's dissent. But the need for unity in the war effort, a threat of British invasion, and the gradual recognition that the principle of national control of the West was right, persuaded them to yield. The land northwest of the Ohio was ceded in January 1781, with two stipulations: that it ultimately be formed into states with "rights of sovereignty, freedom, and independence as the other States" and that previous purchases of lands within the ceded territory from the Indians be considered invalid. Within two months Maryland ratified, and the Articles of Confederation became effective.

Despite this unpromising start and the continued bickerings and briberies of rival land speculators, one of the enduring achievements of the Articles was the western legislation. The precedents established constituted the most progressive and successful colonial policy of any nation in modern history. The major features derived from the liberal and farsighted thinking of Thomas Jefferson. The Ordinance of 1784, for example, reflected his belief that the western territories should be self-governing and, when they reached a certain stage of growth, should be admitted to the Union as partners with the original thirteen states. The famous Northwest Ordinance of 1787 was, in a sense, less democratic, since it placed the territories under more rigid controls of the national Congress. But the Ordinance of 1787 did contain another democratic concept first advanced by Jefferson, which the law of 1784 had omitted: the prohibition of slavery in the Northwest Territory.

The Articles' accomplishments in other areas were less noteworthy, if only because Congress lacked coercive authority. Critics repeatedly pointed out the system's weaknesses. Congressional taxation could operate only by means of voluntary levies upon the states. If states neglected or only partly met their obligations, Congress was powerless. When Congress negotiated treaties, the states could and did ignore them. Britain barred all trade with its West Indian possessions to American ships or ships manned by American seamen; it placed heavy duties on imported American products and at the same time dumped huge quantities of goods in America without fear of economic reprisal. Massachusetts attempted to place a duty on British goods, but other states did not, and the loss of business forced Massachusetts to repeal the law.

Still other weaknesses of the Articles were readily apparent. Contrary to the provisions of the treaty of 1783, the British controlled and refused to abandon their northwest military posts. The Spaniards temporarily closed the port of New Orleans to Americans, a great hardship to westerners who

Strengths and Weaknesses of the Articles

floated their produce down the Mississippi for sale on the New Orleans market. Some members of Congress would have officially sanctioned the closure of New Orleans in return for a favorable commercial agreement with Spain, and the proposed Jay-Gardoqui Treaty was only narrowly defeated.

Critics of the Articles could point to a languishing economy, a depreciated currency, a burgeoning debt, a divided people, an impotent government, and national humiliation. Surely the Revolution should have resulted in something better. Unless the Articles were strengthened quickly, they felt, the result would be anarchy, financial chaos, even civil war.

Many of the economic problems facing the country, defenders of the Articles contended, resulted not from the form of government but from normal postwar economic dislocations. A recession was natural. New markets had to be found, and Americans were aggressively finding them. As commerce in the Caribbean was curtailed, trade in the Pacific was opened. The first American ship reached Canton in 1784 with a cargo of ginseng (an herb prized by the Chinese as an aphrodisiac) and exchanged it for tea. Another ship in that same year was the first to carry the American flag to St. Petersburg, Russia. True enough, the defenders argued, states had not met congressional appropriations, but only because they were at times unrealistically high. Revolutionary war debts remained vexatious, but some states— through land sales, paper money issues, and redemptions of state obligations at market value—were paying off their state debts and even assuming part of their national debt. They felt that time alone would cure many of the young nation's economic headaches.

To endow the Articles with unlimited power to regulate taxes and commerce, it was claimed, would amount to an admission that the Revolution had been fought in vain. Why free America from the despotism of the British government only to create a similar despotism in the United States? The Articles were based on the idea of cooperation among, not coercion of, its members. With the states supreme and Congress merely their agent, a national tyranny could never develop. No European country threatened invasion, despite nonpayment of debts. All the states lived in peace. The prediction of civil discord was looked on simply as the bugbear of a few pessimistic and overanxious creditors.

Annapolis Convention

All the logic of the defenders of the Articles could not erase one stubborn fact: the perennial shortage of funds in the national treasury. Money could be raised by territorial land sales, but the process was slow and uncertain and the revenue insufficient; or by a tariff, but that required the approval of all the states, which was never received; or by levies upon the states, which increasingly yielded less, since many of the states had their own financial problems. In 1786 New Jersey flatly refused to pay any part of the national requisition.

At the instigation of Virginia, a convention was held in Annapolis to draft a uniform code of commercial regulations. Although all the states had been invited, only five sent delegates. Moreover, the authority of several delegates was hampered by instructions imposed on them by their respective states.

Alexander Hamilton, James Madison, and John Dickinson, perhaps by prearrangement, argued that the issue of commercial regulations could not be separated from other vital questions and that fundamental changes in the Articles could hardly be decided by five states. Convinced, and despairing of achieving any reforms at Annapolis, the delegates agreed to adjourn, recommending a general convention to meet in Philadelphia in May 1787 for the purpose of revising the Articles of Confederation to render them "adequate to the exigencies of the Union."

There was little reason to anticipate a successful convention at Philadelphia. Indeed, there was reason to doubt that it would meet at all. Many states were apathetic, and some were hostile to the idea. Congress passed the recommendation to a committee of three, who referred it to a committee of thirteen, which was never appointed. Then came the news of a revolution in Massachusetts that—more than any other factor—gave life to the proposal.

The farmers of western Massachusetts had no particular love for Boston and the state government. In addition to other iniquities, Boston was crowded with money-hungry lawyers. And, being a litigious people, Americans found the services of lawyers frequently necessary. Court procedures were slow. Costs were outrageously high. The wealthy lawyers had a considerable influence on the government. With other creditors, they had urged the state legislature to pass tax laws unbearable to the farmers. The income from these taxes was used to pay off the holders of state debts, not at the depreciated market value of the bonds but at par. For these reasons the farmers rebelled. Of their many leaders, a former Revolutionary war captain, Daniel Shays, became known as the prime mover of the insurrection.

Local conventions were held. Petitions of grievance were drafted. Mobs of armed men stopped county courts from meeting at Concord, Taunton, Great Barrington, and Springfield. By September 1786 the Massachusetts government was inoperative west of Boston.

The state legislature had already enacted laws to lower taxes and modernize the court system. Now, at Governor James Bowdoin's request, other

Shays's Rebellion

Farmers in western Massachusetts who were losing their farms through mortgage foreclosures and tax delinquencies rose in rebellion under the leadership of Daniel Shays. The farmers demanded cheap paper money, lighter taxes, and a suspension of mortgage foreclosures. Pictured is an engraving of Shays's insurgents preparing to attack troops defending a courthouse in Springfield. (From Springfield 1636–1886, *by Mason Green)*

corrective legislation was passed to quench the discontent. But, like a fire out of control, the rebellion continued without reason or purpose. Although their grievances had been redressed, the insurgents still marched and drilled. Since they were paid, why should they go home? Their leaders schemed and wondered what to do next. But before they found an answer, the Bostonians raised an army by private subscription that marched to Springfield and on January 25, 1787, scattered Daniel Shays's forces with one volley.

Like many other rebellions, this one was misinterpreted by most contemporaries. Shays's forces were viewed as levelers, determined to hang every creditor and dedicated to spreading anarchy. The tale grew with the telling, and the result was salutary: state after state decided to send delegates to Philadelphia for the national convention.

Drafting the United States Constitution was the work of an entire summer. Although the delegates met in secret, news of their proceedings leaked out in various ways. Defenders of the Articles grew alarmed at the reports. First, the delegates had violated their states' instructions, which authorized them only to suggest changes in the Articles of Confederation. Instead, they committed the revolutionary act of deciding to compose an entirely new document. Second, it was rumored that the new Constitution would be a drastic change from the Articles, providing for what many considered a dangerous redistribution of sovereignty. Yet little could be done either for or against the document until it was actually finished and submitted. Meanwhile George Washington's presence as presiding officer of the convention served to allay the doubts of many Americans.

The Philadelphia Convention

Solutions to the problems of the Articles were not easy, for each question suggested another more difficult one. The delegates were determined to build the new Constitution on a firm foundation, but they were irresolute as to means. Conflicts between sectional interests, conflicts between those who favored greater or lesser national power, and even each individual's contradictory beliefs had to be resolved. Decisions were made, reversed, reintroduced, changed, settled, unmade again, and modified until the very last days of the convention.

For example, the founding fathers' political heritage was based on the belief that government's power derived solely from the people. But they were equally certain that the people could not be fully trusted. As Shays's Rebellion had illustrated, the majority could be as tyrannous as an individual. A New England minister expressed the dilemma as follows: "Let it stand as a principle that government originates from the people; but let the people be taught . . . that they are not able to govern themselves." How did one fashion a government that would solve the dilemma? Practical questions also divided the delegates. Small states were apprehensive of the big states' powers. Northerners raised the question of slavery. Southerners feared that an export tariff might be inflicted. How was representation to be fairly apportioned? And taxes? Each point required time-consuming discussions. Most crucial, however, was the problem of how to give the government coercive strength. To vest it with the bald power to punish states for non-compliance with national laws would be unwise. The Constitution would never be ratified with such a provision. The states were too jealous of their sovereign prerogatives. Still, without it, the rest of the document would be worthless.

The Constitution was preeminently a document of compromise reflecting a balancing of conflicting interests. Small states obtained equal representation in the upper house. Large states obtained representation based on population in the lower house. Three-fifths of the slaves were to be counted for purposes of representation and taxation. The African slave trade was allowed to continue for twenty years. Congress could pass uniform commercial regulations but could never tax exports. Money bills had to originate in the lower house. Treaties had to receive the consent of two-thirds of the upper house.

The Federal Constitution

The people were represented in the House of Representatives but were screened from too much participation in government in other ways: by an electoral college, responsible for the final selection of a president; by a Supreme Court, which had the power to strike down state laws yet was independent of the popular will; and by the Senate, which was to be appointed by state governments. The Articles had not contained such devices to check popular rule. In fact, under the Articles there was no separate executive or judiciary branch of government. But it does not necessarily follow that the Articles were a more democratic form of government than that provided for by the Constitution. The Articles were essentially a league of sovereign states in which the people had no direct voice and in which the central government had no power of coercion. It could be considered more democratic only if the state governments represented the people better than the federal government did. This was not the case in many states. The Constitution, despite its distrust of the people, proceeded solely from them. Thus it solved the problem of coercion. By its own express declaration, the Constitution was the supreme law of the land, to which all public officials swore an oath of support and which operated directly upon every citizen. In short, it created a new and superior sovereignty. The Constitution did not begin with the words "We the states," but rather "We the people." The distinction was crucial.

The Constitution challenged traditional concepts of government, best expressed in the writings of Montesquieu. It was an axiom of political philosophy that a republic could not exist over a large territory. History had shown that only in small contiguous regions could republicanism flourish; large areas required an emperor or military chief to control the people by force. When a small democratic state enlarged its boundaries (the Roman Republic's expansion was frequently cited), the government inevitably became despotic. Thus, the Constitution was a bold experiment. No one realized this fact more than James Madison, sometimes regarded as its chief creator. All governments, said Madison, are prone to the machinations of selfish men and special interests. Although republics may exist in smaller areas, in such countries it is easier for a faction to gain control and rule tyrannically. In a nation as large as the United States, with so many diverse interests—northern, southern, and western, landed, mercantile, and financial—he felt that it would be difficult for any one faction to seize and maintain control. The Constitution, therefore, by recognizing that human beings are in part dominated and directed by the passion for power, particularly economic power, turns evil into good by balancing faction against faction and requiring a national consensus on each issue.

Of the fifty-five delegates assembled in Philadelphia, thirty-nine signed the finished document. Few who signed considered it a perfect frame of government. All concurred, however, that the alternative was "anarchy and convulsion." The Constitution was submitted for ratification to special popular conventions, not to the state legislatures. The move was wise and proper for two reasons. First, many of the state legislatures would have been hostile. Second, the Constitution was a compact not of the states but of the people of the states. The founding fathers concluded that the Constitution could become operative if it was ratified by the people of nine states.

Proponents of the Constitution called themselves "Federalists" and labeled their opponents "anti-Federalists." The latter objected to these terms as inappropriate and misleading and suggested that they would be more accurate if reversed. But they gained acceptance through wide repetition. The debate over the Constitution was waged primarily in the newspapers before and during the conventions in each state. Most of the journals were Federalist, and the anti-Federalists complained that they did not receive fair treatment; that the Federalists were pushing the Constitution to a vote too quickly and without the possibility of qualifying or conditional ratification; and that objections to it were so widespread that a second national convention should be called to consider them.

The Anti-Federalist Argument

The anti-Federalists were at a disadvantage because they were unorganized and because they had no constructive alternative to offer except to retain the Confederation. Some, but by no means all, of their criticisms were:

1. The Constitution lacked a bill of rights.
2. Coercive authority would destroy individual liberty.
3. The form of the Constitution was federal, yet the effect was national. It would create a "consolidated" system. State sovereignty would be insignificant in contrast to national sovereignty.
4. The taxing power would bring down squads of collectors to harass the people.
5. The president would become an elected despot.
6. The Senate was too aristocratic.
7. There was no provision for future national conventions to review the basic law of the land periodically.
8. A standing army in peacetime was unnecessary and dangerous. It would be used as an engine of oppression.

9. The ratio of representatives to population in the lower house was too small; elections of representatives should be held annually.
10. The national courts would have the power of judicial review.

The anti-Federalists drew a picture of the supporters of the Constitution as propertied aristocrats, rich merchants, and men of great wealth motivated by the desire to protect their own economic interests. Even George Washington came under attack. "Notwithstanding he wielded the sword in defense of liberty," wrote one anti-Federalist, "yet at the same time [he] was, and is to this day, living upon the labors of several hundreds of miserable Africans; and some of them very likely, descended from parents who, in point of property and dignity in their own country, might cope with any man in America." The anti-Federalists portrayed themselves as simple agrarians, sturdy yeomen voicing the sentiment of the masses.

Acceptance of the Constitution

New Hampshire was the ninth state to ratify the Constitution in June 1788. Federalists in many regions heralded the event with fireworks, parades, and

Delaware, New Jersey, and Georgia each ratified the Constitution without a single dissenting vote. In Connecticut it passed by an overwhelming majority, 128 to 40; and in Pennsylvania by 46 to 23. Massachusetts was the sixth state to ratify by a vote of 187 to 168; followed by Maryland, 63 to 11; South Carolina, 149 to 73; and New Hampshire, 57 to 46. Technically the Constitution could have gone into effect at this point, but no one believed it could be successful without the approval of New York and Virginia. Virginia was the tenth state to ratify, 89 to 79, and New York then followed by the narrow margin of 30 to 27. As each state ratified there were usually ceremonies marked by grand parades, the shooting of cannon, public dinners, and the inevitable patriotic speeches. Shown here is a contemporary drawing of the celebration in New York, with one of the floats labeled "Hamilton." (Culver Pictures)

inspiring speeches. But some believed the celebrations were premature. Without the participation of Virginia or New York, neither of which had yet acted, the experiment could hardly hope to succeed.

The anti-Federalists in Virginia were championed by the popular Patrick Henry, an orator of incomparable ability, and by the highly respected George Mason, author of the Virginia Declaration of Rights. The Federalist phalanx was led by men of equal talent: Madison, George Wythe, and John Marshall. George Washington did not attend the ratifying convention in Richmond, but his endorsement of the Constitution helped the Federalist cause immeasurably. Both sides claimed the vote of Thomas Jefferson, who was in France. Everyone expected Governor Edmund Randolph to come forward as an anti-Federalist leader, since along with Mason, he had refused to sign the Constitution in Philadelphia. But he switched to the Federalist position. Virginia ratified by the narrow margin of eighty-nine to seventy-nine.

The news was relayed to Poughkeepsie—site of the New York ratifying convention—as soon as possible, for the Federalists there needed support. The governor of New York, George Clinton, was firmly opposed to the Constitution, and a majority of the convention seemed to agree with him. Alexander Hamilton had done everything possible to change the minds of the delegates. With Madison and John Jay, he had coauthored *The Federalist,* a series of brilliant essays explaining and defending the Constitution, which appeared in the New York press. Hamilton spoke publicly and "politicked" privately. He reasoned, cajoled, and threatened. Together with the impact of Virginia's decision, his efforts were barely enough: New York ratified on July 26, 1788, by a vote of thirty to twenty-seven. Sixteen months later North Carolina entered the Union, followed by Rhode Island in May 1790.

COMMENTARY

America's hopes for the future were laced with fears. The problems were formidable. Britain had failed to solve them. The Articles had failed. Another collapse might result in fragmentation and even civil war. Europe appeared indifferent and Britain scornful. Both Federalists and anti-Federalists believed that America, the first to throw off the shackles of the Old World, was the last refuge of liberty. "Be of good cheer," Gouverneur Morris advised Hamilton. "My religion steps in where my understanding falters and I feel faith as I lose confidence. Things will yet go right but when and how I dare not predict."

America as yet had little culture of its own— no painters to match Goya, no composers like Mozart, no legal philosophers to equal Blackstone, no sculptors as accomplished as Thorvalsen. Nor did America possess an established church, a titled aristocracy, a large standing army, or a monarchical government. The Americans had jettisoned the institutional machinery of European authoritarianism to test, for the first time in history, the possibility of a working democracy. But that democracy did not mean to include several million defeated Indians or enslaved blacks. The United States was in fact "a bold, sublime experiment" to see whether white men could live harmoniously in a society founded on liberty and equality.

THOMAS P. ABERNETHY, *Western Lands and the American Revolution* (1937)

JOHN R. ALDEN, *The American Revolution* (1954)

CLARENCE W. ALVORD, *The Mississippi Valley in British Politics* (1917)

BERNARD BAILYN, *The Ordeal of Thomas Hutchinson* (1974)

———, *Ideological Origins of the American Revolution* (1967)

———, *The Origins of American Politics* (1968)

CHARLES A. BEARD, *An Economic Interpretation of the Constitution of the United States* (1913)

CARL BECKER, *The Declaration of Independence* (1958)

MORTON and PENN BORDEN, *The American Tory* (1972)

ROBERT E. BROWN, *Middle-Class Democracy and the Revolution in Massachusetts* (1955)

EDMUND C. BURNETT, *The Continental Congress* (1941)

OLIVER M. DICKERSON, *The Navigation Acts and the American Revolution* (1951)

ELISHA P. DOUGLASS, *Rebels and Democrats* (1955)

MAX FARRAND, *The Framing of the Constitution of the United States* (1913)

DOUGLAS S. FREEMAN, *George Washington* (1948–57)

MERRILL JENSEN, *The Articles of Confederation: An Interpretation of the Social-Constitutional History of the American Revolution* (1940)

———, *The New Nation: A History of the United States During the Confederation* (1950)

BERNARD KNOLLENBERG, *Origin of the American Revolution, 1759–1766* (rev. ed. 1965)

STEPHEN G. KURTZ and JAMES H. HUTSON, *Essays on the American Revolution* (1973)

LEONARD W. LABAREE, *Royal Government in America: A Study of the British Colonial System Before 1783* (1958)

LEONARD W. LEVY, *Essays on the Making of the Constitution* (1969)

PAULINE MAIER, *From Resistance to Revolution* (1972)

JACKSON T. MAIN, *Political Parties Before the Constitution* (1973)

———, *The Social Structure of Revolutionary America* (1965)

FORREST MCDONALD, *Formation of the American Republic, 1776–1790* (1965)

JOHN C. MILLER, *Sam Adams* (1936)

———, *Triumph of Freedom: 1775–1783* (1948)

LYNN MONTROSS, *The Reluctant Rebels* (1950)

EDMUND S. MORGAN, *Birth of the Republic: 1763–1789* (1956)

RICHARD B. MORRIS, *The Peacemakers* (1965)

CLINTON ROSSITER, *1787: The Grand Convention* (1966)

MAX SAVELLE, *Seeds of Liberty* (1948)

ARTHUR M. SCHLESINGER, *Colonial Merchants and the American Revolution, 1763–1776* (1918)

JOHN SHY, *Toward Lexington* (1965)

CHARLES WARREN, *The Making of the Constitution* (1937)

GORDON S. WOOD, *The Creation of the American Republic* (1969)

ESMOND WRIGHT, *Fabric of Freedom: 1763–1800* (1961)

4

Problems of a New Nation, 1789–1800

Twentieth-century African and Asian nations emerging from colonial status to independence have problems the United States did not face in 1789: a lack of trained personnel, overpopulation, immense poverty, linguistic conflicts, tribal warfare, even foreign invasion. By comparison the new American nation was rapidly recovering from the dislocations of the Revolutionary period. Its economic potential was vast. Its geographical isolation afforded security. Its British ancestry and colonial experience had prepared it for the rigors of self-government. And its political leadership was magnificent. No other period of American history contained such an array: George Washington, John Adams, Alexander Hamilton, Thomas Jefferson, James Madison, and many others invested their political quarrels with philosophical dignity.

WASHINGTON   As commander in chief of the Revolutionary armies and again at the Constitutional Convention in Philadelphia, Washington had served the nation well. Though he longed to remain at his home in Mount Vernon, he accepted the presidency in 1789 out of a sense of duty. He was not an original thinker, a daring innovator, or an administrative reformer, but he was dedicated, incorruptible, and the one person that Americans venerated. "If the President can be preserved a few years," wrote Jefferson in 1790, "till habits of authority and obedience can be established generally, we have nothing to fear." By serving as chief executive for eight years, by rejecting opportunities to convert the government into a constitutional monarchy or a military regime, and by avoiding foreign wars and stifling domestic insurrections, Washington contributed the one ingredient indispensable to the success of the infant republic: time.

HAMILTON   Hamilton would have preferred a constitution with different provisions. He nevertheless signed the document, supported its ratification at the New York convention, and defended its contents in *The Federalist,* which he wrote with James Madison and John Jay. Hamilton had no particular affection for local and state interests. He thought only in national terms, and throughout the 1790s he labored to strengthen the central government. Critics accused him and his Federalist supporters of authoritarian inclinations. But Washington trusted Hamilton, valued his opinions, and appointed him America's first secretary of the treasury. Hamilton performed brilliantly in that post. His recommendations, implemented by Congress, provided economic stability for the new government by restoring public credit.

MADISON More than any other man, Madison deserves to be called the "Father of the Constitution." After 1789 he sat in the lower house and was instrumental in devising the Bill of Rights. But Madison's constitutional creations, when put into operation, did not function as he thought they would. Parts of Hamilton's financial program upset him. Their effect, he thought, would be to enrich speculators at the expense of honest taxpayers and to increase federal powers at the expense of states' rights. If the Constitution could be so perverted, Madison concluded, perhaps Hamilton's real aim for America was monarchy. Thus, he attempted to block the Hamiltonian system by working to form a party of opposition, the Democratic-Republicans. By choosing a peaceful and legitimate means of dissent—ballots, not blood—Madison added a vital dimension to the development of American democracy.

The Constitution did not provide for a presidential cabinet—the word is not mentioned. But George Washington called upon the advice of department heads regularly and by 1793 the term "cabinet" came into fairly common usage. Depicted here, from left to right, are Washington, Secretary of War Henry Knox, Secretary of Treasury Alexander Hamilton, Secretary of State Thomas Jefferson, and Attorney General Edmund Randolph. Not shown, though Washington also consulted them, were James Madison, a member of the House of Representatives, and Vice President John Adams. (Library of Congress)

ADAMS   Although he served the public long and faithfully, Adams felt both unappreciated and misunderstood. Many interpreted his love of titles and fancy dress, and his concept of the aristocrat's role in society, as a veiled admiration of monarchy. When Adams suggested that Washington be called "His Majesty, the President," a wag responded by labeling Adams "His Rotundity." Actually Adams's political position was between those of Hamilton and Jefferson. As the second president he proved to be a leader of remarkable fortitude, one who placed country before party. He contributed the lesson of moderation when America was wracked by political dissension.

JEFFERSON   He conceived of America as a unique experiment, destined for greatness as long as it faced westward and avoided European infection. When Jefferson served as George Washington's secretary of state, the French minister commented: "Jefferson . . . is an American, and as such, he cannot sincerely be our friend. An American is the born enemy of all the peoples of Europe." The Federalists pictured Jefferson as a doctrinaire radical, an impractical and abstract theorist, even worse, a philosopher of revolution. Nothing could have been further from the truth. To Jefferson, the right of revolution was the last resort of an oppressed people. Where legal and political means of redress were open, revolution was unnecessary. Certainly Jefferson was idealistic and introspective, but he was also eminently practical. "I can never fear that things will go far wrong," he once wrote, "where common sense has fair play." Jefferson's sacrifice of theoretical opinions to commonsense solutions became an essential part of the American political process.

While these five political leaders labored to make the Constitution a success, tens of thousands of westward-bound Americans paid scant attention. Their interest was not government but land—fertile, cheap, available in large quantities, and occupied only by Indians. Shortly before the Revolution the royal governor of Virginia, Lord Dunmore, had commented that Americans "forever imagine the lands further off are still better than those upon which they are already settled." In 1700 colonials were still huddled along the coast, and the wilderness was considered a menacing barrier. By 1800 the frontier was an exciting opportunity, attracting Yankees and foreigners, pioneers and speculators. Halted temporarily by the Revolutionary War, the westward march resumed after independence, and ever-increasing numbers joined it. "The woods are full of new settlers," wrote an observer in upstate New York. "Axes are resounding, and the trees literally falling about us as we pass." A traveler in Albany in 1797 counted five hundred wagons on the western road in a single day. And this was a small stream compared to the torrent of migrants who, in sun or in snow, by wagon or by foot, passed through the Cumberland Gap. By the close of the century Tennessee numbered close to eighty thousand people and Kentucky more than two hundred twenty thousand.

Many easterners either dismissed the West as an uncivilized place inhab-

The American West

ited by the disorderly or romanticized it as an agrarian paradise where democratic virtues reigned. Some, like Gouverneur Morris, feared its potential. He warned that "if the western people get power into their hands, they will ruin the Atlantic interests." Others gloried in its promise. Philip Freneau visualized a West of "empires, kingdoms, powers and states." George Washington thought the West in time would become a "second land of promise" for "the poor, the needy, and oppressed of the earth." Americans in the eighteenth century had turned from the ocean to the interior, had pierced the Appalachian barrier, and had begun the colonization of the continent. The West as a region was born, set apart from the seaboard by different agricultural methods, racial compositions, political loyalties, and social standards. Frontiersmen, no matter where they came from, shared certain values and exhibited certain common traits. "In the heart of the continent," writes Daniel J. Boorstin, "arose a new *homo Americanus* more easily identified by his mobility than by his habitat. He began to dominate the scene in the years between the American Revolution and the Civil War."

The West was a state of mind that reproduced itself throughout American history on every successive frontier. First, the westerner was proud to the point of arrogance of his skills and accomplishments. Some urban easterners were patronizing or scornful of the crude and uneducated westerner, but the westerner was equally contemptuous of eastern greenhorns to whom he felt distinctly superior. Second, the westerner resented eastern economic and political control of the nation. To many westerners the tax collector was an agent of oppression and the territorial judge an unwelcome representative of a distant power. Third, the westerner was more democratic than the easterner in a social sense. He judged individuals by their performance, not by their origins or status—a refreshing though disconcerting experience to travelers. Fourth, the westerner was as litigious as were his eastern forebears, but he was impatient with bureaucracies, legal complexities, and the slow operations of government. Often, and of necessity, he fashioned his own law: simple, quick, informal, and majoritarian. Fifth, the westerner was incurably optimistic, a community booster, who saw not the present scraggly village but the future great city. Enterprising publishers started newspapers in which they heralded the coming economic greatness. A press, ink, type, and paper were hauled over the mountains from Philadelphia to start the *Pittsburgh Gazette* in 1786, when that village had no more than three hundred inhabitants. In 1789 the first issue of the *Kentucky Gazette* was printed in a log cabin in Lexington. Cincinnati had its *Centinel of the North-Western Territory* as early as 1793, when Indians still menaced local settlers. The paper offered a bounty for "every scalp, having the right ear appendant," of Indians killed in the vicinity of the town.

Campaigns Against the Indians

George Washington considered himself scrupulously fair in his dealings with Indians. "Brothers," he told one tribe, "you do well to wish to learn our arts and ways of life, and above all the religion of Jesus Christ. These will make you a greater and happier people than you are." To Washington, and most other whites, Indians were either good or bad, depending on whether they were friendly or hostile, which largely depended on whether they honored treaties abdicating their lands to settlers. Friendly Indians, Washington promised, would receive the protection of Congress. Hostile Indians would be suppressed by force.

After the American Revolution tribes of Indians ravaged settlements throughout the old Northwest. Urged on by the British and undeterred by previous defeats, Shawnees, Miamis, and Kickapoos plundered boats on the Wabash and Ohio rivers and crossed over into Kentucky to continue their raids. Frontiersmen called upon George Rogers Clark to lead a punitive expedition in 1786, but the magic of his name was not enough—the expedition failed, Clark's militiamen first rebelling and then retreating in disorder. The Indians, more determined than ever, announced that all prior treaties with the white men were repudiated and that henceforth "the Ohio shall be the boundary between them and the Big Knives." Such was the situation when George Washington was sworn in as America's first president.

THE FIRST INDIAN CAMPAIGN Without hesitation Washington used his powers as commander in chief to order a military campaign against the Indians. He selected General Josiah Harmar in 1790 to lead some fifteen hundred men from the vicinity of Cincinnati into the Maumee Valley to crush all opposition. The Indians were forewarned, however, and faded into the forests; Harmar's men searched in vain for the main tribes. Then, while marching south, Harmar hoped to surprise the Indians by sending a detachment of troops doubling back to the Maumee. The tribes waited in ambush, and the detachment was badly mauled; their losses totaled 183 dead and 31 wounded. A court of inquiry vindicated Harmar's actions as "honorable" and meriting "high approbation." He then resigned from the army.

THE SECOND INDIAN CAMPAIGN The second commander Washington chose was Major General Arthur St. Clair, who was instructed to build a fortification at Miami Village (Fort Wayne, Indiana), and then to "seek the enemy" and "endeavor by all possible means to strike them with great severity." Washington personally warned St. Clair to beware of Indian deceptions and to be alert to sudden attacks and ambushes, but he proved as incompetent as his predecessor. On November 4, 1791, St. Clair camped with fourteen hundred men near the site of Harmar's defeat, without adequate guards posted and with tents pitched haphazardly. Throughout the night Indians led by Chief Little Turtle slipped into the camp. They completely surrounded the soldiers and then at dawn fell upon their victims; 632 men were killed and 264 wounded. The rest of the troops fled, leaving behind their cannon and strewing the forest paths with abandoned arms. The troops had spent ten days marching into Maumee country; their retreat to safety, covering the same ground, took twenty-four hours. St. Clair, Washington roared, allowed his army "to be cut to pieces, hacked, butchered, tomahawked. He is worse than a murderer! How can he answer to his country?" Yet an investigation absolved St. Clair of blame. He then resigned his commission, but was retained as governor of the Northwest Territory.

THE THIRD INDIAN CAMPAIGN   The confidence of the Indians soared. Settlers left their homes and sought the refuge of frontier posts at Marietta and Cincinnati. Several officers sent to negotiate with belligerent Indians were murdered. Several previously neutral tribes decided to join the belligerents. Spanish agents in the Southwest, hoping to capitalize on these disasters, began to incite the Creeks to attack American outposts. The British did the same in the Northwest, fueling the fires of Indian expectations by promising them aid. A new British fort was constructed in 1794 at Fort Miami (near Toledo), clearly within American territory.

Meanwhile, the third commander Washington picked, Major General ''Mad Anthony'' Wayne, thoroughly trained and properly equipped his soldiers. He was determined not to repeat the blunders of Harmar and St. Clair. During the winter of 1793–1794 Wayne built Fort Greenville, and he remained there drilling and disciplining his men in preparation for a spring offensive. Indian warriors were also gathering, 2,000 strong, waiting for the Americans, convinced that with British aid victory would be theirs. Chief Little Turtle saw the uselessness of resisting Wayne's army, but his counsel to seek peace was rejected. Thus on August 20, 1794, in the Battle of Fallen Timbers, a fight lasting no more than two hours, the Indians were decisively beaten. Only fifty were killed, but their spirit was shattered when the British commander at Fort Miami refused to help them. Wayne dictated the terms of the treaty; signed by the Indians in 1795 it brought peace to the Northwest for a generation and opened a new stretch of territory for American expansion.

Indians continued to fight in the nineteenth century, but their delaying actions could not stem the flow of white settlers. ''If we want it,'' wrote

Disheartened and defeated, the Indian chiefs readily accepted the terms of peace dictated by General Anthony Wayne in 1795. One of Wayne's soldiers is assumed to have painted this scene of the meeting at which the Treaty of Greenville was signed. (Chicago Historical Society)

Thomas Hutchins, referring to the West, "I warrant it will soon be ours." Indians were invisible men to those who dreamed of America's continental destiny. As Wayne opened the Northwest, the New England poet Timothy Dwight rhapsodized on the blessings of western expansion in *Greenfield Hill:*

> All hail, thou western world! by heaven design'd
> Th' example bright, to renovate mankind.
> Soon shall thy sons across the mainland roam;
> And claim, on far Pacific shores, their home;
> Their rule, religion, manners, arts, convey,
> And spread their freedom to the Asian sea.

Except for the Quakers, few Americans were much concerned with the issue of slavery until the American Revolution. Before that time the colonial conscience had remained largely dormant. But coincident with arguments against parliamentary despotism and revolutionary appeals to natural rights, the institution of slavery came under attack. "It always appeared a most iniquitous scheme to me," Abigail Adams told her husband John, "to fight ourselves for what we are daily robbing and plundering from those who have as good a right to freedom as we have." Black leaders such as Prince Hall, Benjamin Banneker, Absalom Jones, and Richard Allen petitioned both the state and federal governments to outlaw slavery. Critics pointed out that slavery was cruel, un-Christian, and contradictory to the commitment made in the Declaration of Independence. Such arguments were effective in the northern states where slavery was not crucial to the economy; blacks made up only 4 percent of the total population there, and even that small number was viewed as a threat to free white labor. In 1775 the first manumission society was organized in Pennsylvania, and in 1780 the Quaker state passed the first law providing for the gradual emancipation of slaves. A Massachusetts slave, Quork Walker, won his freedom in 1781 by a court order on the ground that the state constitution declared that "all men are born free and equal." New York enacted a freedom law in 1799, New Jersey in 1804. Slowly—but not without a struggle and not for many decades— the North became free.

Slavery in the south was morally and philosophically disturbing to many leaders of the Revolutionary generation. Patrick Henry declared his "abhorrence of slavery," as did George Washington. "Were it not then, that I am principled against selling negroes, as you would do cattle in the market," Washington commented in 1794, "I would not, in twelve months from this date, be possessed of one. I shall be happily mistaken, if they are not found to be a very troublesome species of property 'ere many years pass over our heads." The Marquis de Chastellux, traveling in the Chesapeake region, reported that people "seem grieved at having slaves, and are constantly talking about abolishing slavery, and of seeking other means of exploiting their lands." Between 1782 and 1790 individual owners in Vir-

Slavery: North and South

Benjamin Bannaker's
PENNSYLVANIA, DELAWARE, MARY-
LAND, AND VIRGINIA
ALMANAC,
FOR THE
YEAR of our LORD 1795;
Being the Third after Leap-Year.

BANNAKER.

PHILADELPHIA:
Printed for WILLIAM GIBBONS, Cherry Street

"History must record," wrote Moncure D. Conway in 1863, "that the most original scientific intellect which the South has yet produced was that of the pure African, Benjamin Banneker." Free-born and self-taught, Banneker's annual almanacs were published from the 1790s until his death in 1804. Thomas Jefferson, who received one of Banneker's almanacs, responded with these words: "Nobody wishes more than I do to see such proofs as you exhibit, that nature has given to our black brethren talents equal to those of the other colors of man, and that the appearance of a want of them is owing merely to the degraded condition of their existence both in Africa and America. I can add with truth that nobody wishes more ardently to see a good system commenced for raising the condition both of their body and mind to what it ought to be, as fast as the imbecility of their present existence, and other circumstances which cannot be neglected, will admit." (American Antiquarian Society)

ginia manumitted some ten thousand blacks. Nevertheless, no southern state enacted legislation providing for emancipation. The proslavery forces were too strong, and the economic costs of compensated emancipation would have been prohibitive. In 1790 the value of slave property was approximately one hundred forty million dollars (seven hundred thousand slaves at an average value of two hundred dollars each), nearly double the entire Revolutionary war debt. The freed blacks, it was assumed, would have to be resettled elsewhere at an additional cost of several hundred million dollars. "Among the Romans," wrote Thomas Jefferson, who had mulled over the idea, "emancipation required but one effort. The slave, when made free, might mix with, without staining the blood of his master. But with us a second is necessary, unknown to history. When freed he is to be removed beyond the reach of mixture." Thus abolition would be too expensive; it would upset the southern economy and its social system; and it would leave the problem of large numbers of freed blacks, a disturbing idea to whites in both the North and South. In a few decades more the invention and wide application of the cotton gin spurred the slave system to further growth. As the price of slaves rose, the number of personal manumissions declined. From being a necessary evil, slavery to southerners became a positive good.

Thomas Jefferson regarded slaves as human rather than a species of property, and he found slavery antithetical to the American principles of liberty and equality. As a young lawyer he had once argued for a black's freedom on the ground that "under the law of nature all men are born free." Though a slave owner himself, Jefferson had written a "vehement philippic against negro slavery" in the Declaration of Independence, John Adams noted; but the section was deleted because several from the deep South objected to it. Nevertheless, when Jefferson said "the people," he had in mind whites, not blacks. When he spoke of American expansion across the continent, he meant by white Anglo-Saxons.

A Racist Society

Most whites were racists who did not consider blacks to be constituent members of society. In fact, one might say that the American celebration of individual rights rested on a sense of supremacy over blacks. "It is not only the slave who is beneath his master," the Marquis de Chastellux observed, "it is the Negro who is beneath the white man. No act of enfranchisement can efface this unfortunate distinction." Blacks were judged to be an inferior, alien element, and the ultimate solution of the problem was to settle them elsewhere. Jefferson proposed recolonizing blacks in Africa or in the West Indies—"drawing off this part of our population, most advantageously for themselves, as well as for us." The prevailing attitude was expressed by a North Carolinian, J. C. Galloway: "It is impossible for us to be happy, if, after manumission, they are to remain among us."

For blacks, many Americans believed, the alternative to freedom was rebellion—an alarming prospect. When the black slaves in Santo Domingo rebelled against their masters in 1791 and a brutal slaughter ensued, the American government responded on racial grounds. Alexander Hamilton—a founding member of the New York Manumission Society—did not hesitate to commit forty thousand dollars of federal funds to crush the uprising without first consulting the president. Washington gave his belated approval, ordered Secretary of War Henry Knox to send arms and ammunition, and informed the French ambassador that the United States would "render every aid in their power to . . . quell the alarming insurrection of the Negroes in Hispaniola." "Lamentable!" Washington told a friend, "to see such a spirit of revolt among the blacks. Where it will stop, is difficult to say."

A few Federalists were quick to point out that the Santo Domingo nightmare stemmed from the radical ideas broadcast by the French Revolution. "That malignant philosophy," John Marshall wrote to his wife, "which . . . can coolly and deliberately pursue, through oceans of blood, abstract systems for the attainment of some fancied untried good, were gathered in the French West Indies." Jefferson was sympathetic to the white French aristocrats who fled to the American continent. Their situation "cried aloud for pity and charity," and he urged the Virginia legislature to be "liberal" in its help. But he was also scornful of them. He suggested, rather sarcastically, that the monied aristocrats might be distributed among the Indians "who would teach them lessons of liberty and equality." Jefferson saw the Santo Domingo revolt as a frightening harbinger of what might happen in America unless slavery was abolished—"bloody scenes which our children certainly, and possibly ourselves (south of the Potomac), [will] have to wade through." His friend John Breckenridge put the matter succinctly: "I am against slavery. I hope the time is not far distant when not a slave will exist in this union. I fear our slaves will produce another Santo Domingo."

Opportunities for fundamental social reform in America are rare, and even more rarely are they seized. They are present usually during times of mass economic crisis or emotional stress. The best chance to abolish slavery peacefully came during the postrevolutionary period; the institution was temporarily languishing, natural law philosophy was strong, and the Santo Domingo revolt had spurred numerous antislavery voices. But the moment was missed, never to reoccur. To northerners, the revolt confirmed the wisdom of their having freed the slaves. Southerners refused to follow that course. Instead of reform, they chose repression.

The legislators who assembled in New York City in 1789 were troubled by Indian wars and the potential for black insurrections. But their main concern was to fashion laws under which three million white inhabitants could exist harmoniously. State jealousies, sectional interests, and economic rivalries had to be surmounted. The Constitution, all agreed, must not suffer the same fate as the Articles. When the first Congress met there were three vital tasks to be accomplished.

The First Congress

First, the promise of enacting a bill of rights had to be fulfilled. At Philadelphia the founding fathers had purposely omitted a bill of rights from the Constitution as too confining in scope. A later government might construe such a bill too narrowly, assuming any rights not guaranteed therein to be logically excluded. Alexander Hamilton had argued that "aphorisms" about popular rights "sound much better in a treatise on ethics than in a constitution of government." But the people remained unconvinced, and Federalists made the incorporation of a bill of rights a campaign pledge—to be fulfilled after ratification. In 1787 and 1788 more than two hundred proposed amendments had been suggested by state conventions. James Madison took on the job of whittling these down to a manageable number. Largely as a result of his labors twelve amendments were passed by Congress in September 1789. Ten were approved by the required three-fourths of the states by December 1791. The first eight guaranteed the fundamental freedoms of speech, press, religion, assembly, and petition, from congressional encroachment; protected the people in their right to bear arms and to have a "speedy and public" jury trial; and forbade unreasonable searches and seizures of people and property, the quartering of troops, excessive bail or fines, and cruel and unusual punishments. The ninth amendment declared that these enumerated rights "shall not be construed to deny or disparage others retained by the people." And the tenth reassured the state governments by affirming that "powers not delegated to the United States by the Constitution, nor prohibited by it to the States, are reserved to the States respectively, or to the people."

The second task of the first Congress was to create the federal judiciary. The Constitution merely said there shall be "one Supreme Court" and "inferior Courts as Congress may from time to time ordain and establish." Nothing was specified about the number of justices, or the number of courts, or the procedure for judicial review. These were controversial issues. Some members of Congress wished to limit the extent and authority of federal courts, leaving the enforcement of national laws to the state judiciaries. Others feared the consequences of such an arrangement. Through the efforts of Senator Oliver Ellsworth of Connecticut, a bill was drafted that established the basic structure of the federal judicial system. The Judiciary Act of 1789 provided for a Supreme Court consisting of a chief justice and five associate justices, three circuit courts for the three sections of the nation, and thirteen district courts of one judge each. Attached to each district court were marshalls and deputies to serve as federal police. The Judiciary Act also authorized the position of an attorney general. (Washington appointed his friend, Edmund Randolph, to this post.) Section 25 of the act, one of its most important provisions, gave the federal courts the right to review decisions of state courts on appeal in all cases that involved the Constitution or national laws. Section 25 spelled out what the Constitution implied: that the federal courts might—indeed, were obligated to—strike down any state laws or reverse the decisions of any state courts that conflicted with the supreme law of the land.

A third imperative of the new government was to raise money. Funds were needed for day-to-day expenses as well as to reduce the Revolutionary war debt. On July 4, 1789, Congress enacted America's first tariff law, which imposed customs duties averaging 5 percent *ad valorem*. For a few products, such as cloth and steel, whose domestic manufacture Congress wished to encourage, the duty was set at fifty percent. Two weeks later Congress placed a tonnage duty on all shipping, with lower rates for American vessels. The tariff and tonnage measures solved the immediate need of obtaining revenues for governmental operating expenses, but there still was not enough money to pay the war debt. The total value of merchandise imported into the United States amounted to twenty-three million dollars in 1790. The war debt alone stood at fifty-two million dollars, a monstrous sum for that day. Some recommended meeting the debt by direct taxes, printing more money, selling western lands, or paying creditors a fraction of the debt; these measures would permit the new government to begin its operations without an inherited financial burden. There were objections to each suggestion, however, and Congress turned the problem over to Secretary of the Treasury Alexander Hamilton. He was asked to prepare a report on the best ways to restore public credit.

Hamilton submitted a series of reports to Congress in 1790–1791. Summarized and simplified, his major proposals were as follows:

1. The national government would pay its Revolutionary war debt, both principal and interest, by means of funding; that is, the government would take on a new debt by selling bonds, and the money collected would be used to pay the old debt.
2. The national government would also assume the Revolutionary war debts of the states. The combined national and state indebtedness totaled about seventy-nine million dollars.
3. A system of excise taxes would be enacted to supplement tariff revenues. These funds would be used to meet the interest payments and part of the principal of the new debt.
4. A sinking fund would also be created to buy the new bonds whenever their market value fell below their par value.
5. A semipublic Bank of the United States would be chartered by Congress.
6. Manufacturing would be stimulated by a protective tariff, by government subsidies, by awards for inventions, by quality controls, and by encouraging foreign artisans to emigrate to the United States.

The Revolutionary war debt, Hamilton argued, "was the price of liberty." Its prompt payment was not only morally indisputable but economically indispensable if the credit of the country was to be maintained. Equally important to Hamilton was the new debt. He did not think that the Constitution would endure if it depended upon the goodwill and shaky nationalism of the population. "All communities," he once noted, "divide themselves into the few and the many. The first are rich and well-born, the other the mass of the people. The voice of the people has been said to be the voice of God; and however generally this maxim has been quoted and believed, it is not true in fact. The people . . . seldom judge or determine right." For government to survive it had to be supported by the rich, the able, the well born—synonymous terms to Hamilton. If the rich and powerful were given an economic stake in the government, he felt, their loyalty would be ensured. By selling government bonds and bank stock—which only the wealthy could afford—the purchasers would be committed to support the federal government out of the strongest motive: economic self-interest. The new public debt, he hoped, would be a blessing, acting to bind the Union together.

Hamilton's use of the debt as a base for national economic development has a twentieth-century ring, which eighteenth-century farmers and planters could not appreciate. His logic seemed twisted to those who regarded any kind of debt—private or public—to be bad. Those who opposed his program did not wish to repudiate their obligations. What they objected to was enriching speculators, assuming state debts, and establishing a national bank. "A *money impulse,* and not the *public good,* is operating on Congress," John Taylor of Virginia warned. The debates became heated.

The first division occurred when James Madison, Hamilton's old ally and coauthor of *The Federalist,* objected to the projected method of payments. He did not doubt that the debts of the Revolution should be paid—but to whom? Many patriots who had invested their savings in the Revolutionary cause or who had earned bonds by service in the army were forced during the recession years of the 1780s to part with them at a fraction of their face value. Should not the original purchaser receive a share of the payment, instead of giving it all to "unconscionable speculators"? Why should the greedy profit at the expense of the patriotic? Was it not more equitable, more just, to give the original purchaser *and* the current holder of the Revolutionary debt proportions of the payment? Hamilton thought not. Madison's proposal, he explained, "would tend to dissolve all social obligations—to render all rights precarious and to introduce a general dissoluteness and corruption of morals." The morals of a good many members of Congress were already corrupted by the fact that they were speculating in these securities, and Madison's motion was defeated by a vote of thirty-six to thirteen. An angry poet commented:

> A soldier's pay are rags and fame,
> A wooden leg—a deathless name.
> To specs, both *in* and *out* of Cong
> The four and six per cents belong!

Congressional nerves next began to fray over the issue of the assumption of state debts by the national government. Those in favor generally represented states with heavy indebtedness, such as Massachusetts, New York, and South Carolina; they alternately pleaded for and demanded its enactment. South Carolina, said one of its representatives, "was no more able to grapple with her enormous debt, than a boy of twelve years of age is able to grapple with a giant." Those opposed represented states with little or no indebtedness, among them Maryland, North Carolina, and Georgia; they obstinately refused to have the national government absorb these obligations. "I trust we shall not run ourselves enormously into debt, and mortgage ourselves and our children," argued a congressman from Georgia, "to give scope to the abilities of any Minister on earth." The Virginia delegates also argued against assumption, contending that their constituents would be doubly penalized by the measure. Virginia had lowered its considerable debt by some 40 percent using land warrants and depreciated currency. Could not Massachusetts do the same? Why turn to the national government for relief? Why should Virginians be taxed to pay the debts of other—mainly northern—states? After a lengthy and acrimonious debate, assumption was defeated in April 1790 by a vote of thirty-one to twenty-nine.

For all the laments of the losers—many of whom had been speculating in state securities—assumption was not really vital to prosperity. But it was essential to Hamilton's scheme of enlarging and consolidating national power. By assuming state debts the national government could eventually dominate the country's revenue sources. The political consequences of assumption were so significant to Hamilton that he sought some means by which the congressional decision might be reversed. Ultimately he reached an understanding with Jefferson and Madison. Hamilton promised to have his supporters vote in favor of permanently relocating the national capital in the South, after a decade in Philadelphia; the Virginians promised to use their influence to change several opposing votes on assumption. Moreover, the assumption measure would be redrafted to include a partial allowance for states that had already paid a large part of their debts. The arrangement was concluded and assumption passed. "Of all the errors of my political life," Jefferson later remarked, this bargain "has occasioned me the deepest regret."

The sharpest sectional division Congress experienced was precipitated by Hamilton's proposal to have the federal government charter a Bank of the United States. Northern congressmen, repeating the arguments in Hamilton's report, stressed the invaluable contributions a national bank could make: it would loan money to the government during emergencies; it would provide a sound and extensive currency; and it would stimulate business by increasing the fluid capital necessary for economic expansion. Southern congressmen viewed the bank as an unmitigated evil: it would benefit capitalist and mercantile classes at the expense of agrarian interests; a financial monopoly, it would be capable of controlling and corrupting every operation of the government; and it was, as James Madison emphasized, patently unconstitutional since Congress had no authority to charter a corporation. The Banking Act passed thirty-nine to twenty. Of the majority, thirty-three votes were northern and only six southern; of the minority, nineteen votes were southern and only one northern. The arguments of his three fellow Virginians—Madison, Randolph, and Jefferson—failed to convince Washington, and on February 25, 1791, he signed the act.

The Bank of the United States was housed in Carpenters' Hall, Philadelphia, from 1791 to 1797; then it moved into the handsome neoclassic building designed by Samuel Blodget, whose architectural style other banks soon copied. (Library of Congress)

With one exception, the Report on Manufactures, every part of Hamilton's program was approved by Congress and endorsed by Washington. The Report on Manufactures was greeted with indifference, even hostility. Later generations hailed it as a brilliant exposition of policy for an industrial America, but in the 1790s few statesmen possessed Hamilton's vision. The high protective tariff it proposed seemed equally detrimental to the economic interests of southern planters and northern merchants. Nevertheless, Hamilton had succeeded in turning old devalued bonds into sound marketable securities, in restoring the credit of a nation verging on bankruptcy, and in providing America with a banking system vital to its prosperity. In later years Daniel Webster spoke of Hamilton's achievements with customary rhetoric: "He smote the rock of national resources and abundant streams of revenue gushed forth; he touched the dead corpse of public credit and it sprang upon its feet."

Results of Hamilton's Program: Economic Stability and Rebellion

Hamilton's programs were accomplished at the price of considerable dissension, however. Because they were aimed at enhancing the authority of the national government, they evoked strong opposition. As early as December 1790, Patrick Henry drafted a remonstrance for the Virginia legislature warning that the assumption of state debts would "produce one or other of two evils, the prostration of agriculture at the feet of commerce, or a change in the present form of federal government fatal to the existence of American liberty." Hamilton responded that the remonstrance was "the first symptom of a spirit which must either be killed, or will kill the Constitution of the United States." But the symptoms persisted. By 1792 the tone of debates over government policies and the national mood appeared reminiscent of 1776. Washington was openly criticized. "The President," declared a senator from Pennsylvania, "has become in the hands of Hamilton, the dish-cloth of every dirty speculator, as his name goes to wipe away blame and silence all murmuring." The *National Gazette* commented ominously that "another revolution must and will be brought about in favor of the people."

What actually led to a rebellion was not funding, assumption, or the Bank but a lesser part of Hamilton's program: an excise tax on distilled spirits. The nation, he said, could not rely solely on tariff measures, and he was reluctant to suggest a direct tax on land. Thus, despite the traditional hostility of Americans to excise taxes, it seemed the most equitable means of raising the additional funds to pay the debt. Some scholars also suspect that Hamilton realized that an excise would foment trouble in the western regions and that he relished the idea of giving the central government an opportunity to use its yet untested powers of enforcement.

Westerners did indeed consume a good deal of whiskey. One congressman boasted that his constituents "have been long in the habit of getting drunk, and they will get drunk in defiance of . . . all the excise duties Congress might be weak or wicked enough to impose." But farmers also used whiskey for medicine and currency. It was easier to ship whiskey than grain across the Alleghenies for sale in eastern markets. After the tax passed in 1791, discontent centered in Washington County, Pennsylvania. The farmers there refused to pay the tax and intimidated those who did; collectors were harassed; a few extremists threatened to secede from Pennsylvania and the Union. Having listened to contradictory opinions from his cabinet—Hamilton, of course, insisted that force must be used— Washington in 1794 ordered the militia of four states assembled to march into western Pennsylvania and suppress the "armed banditti." Led by Washington, with Hamilton at his side, twelve thousand six hundred troops made the long trek west, only to find that the alleged rebellion had evaporated. Twenty rag-tag prisoners were taken. Two were convicted of treason, and though Hamilton wished a maximum punishment imposed, both were pardoned by Washington. Thus ended the whiskey rebellion. "An insurrection was announced and proclaimed and armed against," was Jefferson's sardonic comment, "but could never be found."

The whiskey rebellion was an obvious sign of the deep sectional and economic rivalries in the country that had been aroused by Hamilton's policies. Revolutionary conditions prevailed. Political leaders were aware of the possibilities of disunion. Given the inflammable temper of America during Washington's administrations, one well-placed match might have ignited an insurrectionary blaze which would have gutted the central government. But Madison and Jefferson cautioned their followers that they must neither rebel nor secede. Even under the next administration of John Adams, and despite greater provocations, they followed a conservative, pragmatic, and democratic course. For America the age of blood had passed, replaced by that of ink. Revolutionary tactics were unnecessary when disagreements could be peacefully settled within the confines of the Constitution. Instead of revolutionary barricades, the device of political parties developed as a mechanism for change.

Growth of Political Parties

The founding fathers had understood factions, but, ironically, they had not envisioned the growth of political parties. In 1789 Americans abhorred parties; they considered them tools of unscrupulous politicians that served only to divide the people. "If I could not go to heaven but with a party," Jefferson said, "I would not go there at all." Washington warned the people "against the baneful effects of the spirit of party" in his farewell address. Nevertheless, parties developed. By the close of the century there were two national organizations, the Democratic-Republicans and the Federalists. Political campaigning became acceptable in most regions. Voters were asked to support party tickets. Candidates who had previously boasted of their independence now stressed their partisan loyalties. There were even signs that Americans were beginning to appreciate the role of parties in representative government. "Perhaps," Jefferson wrote in 1798, "party division is necessary to induce each other to watch and relate to the people the proceedings of the other."

Thus, the two-party system developed outside the Constitution, primarily in response to two events: Hamilton's financial program and the French Revolution. One issue touched the pocketbooks, and the other the loyalties of all Americans.

In addition to the disagreement over financial legislation, hostility between the Federalists and their Democratic-Republican opponents was increased by their divergent attitudes toward the French Revolution. In 1789, when news of a revolution in France was announced, virtually all Americans were overwhelmingly sympathetic to its cause. But by 1793, as the revolutionaries turned to violence, conservatives in the United States became increasingly hostile to the methods and principles being adopted.

FEDERALIST POSITION   Federalists stressed the "reign of terror" that swept across France and took hundreds of lives. They lamented the death of Louis XVI, the monarch who had supported America's liberation from Britain. They argued that the French had used specious mottoes, "liberty, equality, and fraternity," as magic sounds to seize property, destroy religion, abandon republicanism, and instigate wars. What nonsense to compare the American and the French revolutions, they thought. "Ours," said John Adams, "was resistance to innovation; theirs was innovation itself." The Federalists preferred to follow the British example of order and stability based on a balance between aristocratic rule and democratic privilege.

REPUBLICAN POSITION   Republicans were certain that the French were fighting for the same goals Americans had sought in 1776: the overthrow of monarchy and the establishment of republicanism. The French and Americans were revolutionary brothers, rejecting the past and seeking human freedom. The Declaration of Rights, like the Declaration of Independence, was a commitment to liberty and human equality. The bloodshed from the revolution was unfortunate. "But rather than it should have failed," wrote Jefferson, "I would have seen half the earth desolated; were there but an Adam and an Eve left in every country, and left free, it would be better than

Thomas Carlyle described the Parisian mobs marching in June 1791 as "gleaming Pike-forests, which bristled fateful in the early sun." This woodcut shows one pike spearing a simulated "heart of the aristocracy." Americans followed the events of the French Revolution with the keenest interest, agreeing with Jefferson that a nation cannot advance from "despotism to liberty in a feather bed." (The Bettmann Archive)

as it now is." Britain, to Republicans, was still the stepmother country, home of the obsolete common law, an oppressive monarchy, and an entrenched, arrogant aristocracy.

The French declaration of war on Britain in February 1793 posed an immediate problem for Washington's administration. Morally, many Americans considered it simple justice to assist the French. "Remember," a New York paper told its readers, "who stood between you and the clanking chains of British ministerial despotism." Legally the United States was bound by the Treaty of 1778 to help defend the French West Indies. Involvement, however, would mean war with Britain, and many Americans considered such a course the ultimate calamity. Washington sought the advice of his cabinet, and they unanimously—though for different reasons—recommended a policy of neutrality. A presidential proclamation of neutrality was issued in April and confirmed by an act of Congress the following year.

Involvement or Neutrality?

Few, however, could set aside their personal biases. When the first minister sent to the United States by the French Republic, Edmond Genet, arrived in Charleston, he was accorded an enthusiastic reception. His stopovers during the journey to Philadelphia rang with constant ovations, and at the capital itself zealous Francophiles received him with patriotic speeches and testimonial dinners. But President Washington was displeased with Genet's actions. At Charleston the minister had commissioned privateers to capture British ships and had conspired with George Rogers Clark to attack Spanish territory. When he continued similar activities in Philadelphia, even after the neutrality proclamation, and defied Washington by courting public favor, the president's displeasure turned to monumental anger. "Is the minister of the French republic to set the acts of this government at defiance *with impunity?*" he raged, "and then threaten the executive with an appeal to the people? What must the world think of such conduct, and of the government of the United States in submitting to it?"

Jefferson realized that Genet had become a liability to the Republican party. The entire cabinet decided that the French minister must be recalled. At the same time the French asked the United States to recall its minister, Gouverneur Morris, because of his royalist sympathies and intrigues. Morris returned, but Genet, believing that he would be guillotined, remained in the United States. He eventually married the daughter of Governor George Clinton and settled in the Hudson Valley where he lived as a rich country gentleman.

Washington attempted to stop the deterioration of French-American relations by appointing James Monroe, a strong sympathizer with the revolutionary cause, as the minister to France. But the Treaty of Commerce and Amity, which John Jay, the new minister to Britain, had negotiated in 1794 was interpreted by the French as an Anglo-American alliance. The "cold war" with France deepened and eventually culminated in an undeclared naval war.

Jay's Treaty

Jay's Treaty was not an alliance, but American critics considered it a disgraceful and humiliating surrender to British power. The only major gain for the United States was Britain's agreement to evacuate its northwest posts. Even this was hardly a concession; the land had belonged to the United States since 1783. British subjects were given permission to continue fur-trading activities with Indian tribes in American territory. Britain also obtained an agreement from the United States government to pay pre-Revolutionary war debts American citizens owed to British merchants; however, Britain refused to pay for the slaves it had seized from Americans during the war. Most important, Jay abandoned the American position that "free ships make free goods" and accepted the British rule that enemy cargoes on neutral vessels were liable to seizure. Another provision allowed American merchants to trade with the British West Indies but only in ships of less than seventy tons carrying capacity; in exchange the United States would prohibit for the next ten years the export of sugar, coffee, cotton, or cacao in American vessels. This legal entry to the British West Indian market was so qualified that the American government struck it from the treaty.

Washington's decision to recommend ratification of Jay's Treaty, with all its obvious defects, has been applauded by most scholars. The only alternative seemed to be a war with Britain; but the United States was not prepared militarily, and the conflict would have wrecked Hamilton's financial system and depressed the economy. Appeasement bought time; war would have been a catastrophe. Moreover, Jay's Treaty—together with that signed by Pinckney with Spain the following year—secured the frontier and opened the Mississippi River to American trade.

The Democratic-Republicans tried to block the ratification of Jay's Treaty in the Senate. Failing, they continued their opposition in the lower house. Not until May 1, 1796, by a vote of fifty-one to forty-eight, did Congress appropriate the funds necessary to implement the treaty. During this period of bitter partisanship Washington was subjected to vilification in newspapers, pamphlets, and speeches. One rabid Democratic-Republican wished Washington's "hand had been cut off when his glory was at its height, before he blasted all his laurels." A Virginian offered a toast to the "speedy death of General Washington." Little wonder that the president did not wish a third term or that his farewell address deplored the development of political parties and advised America to steer clear of permanent foreign entanglements. Although he was still revered by most Americans, Washington was happy to escape further political abuse by retiring to Mount Vernon. "The President is fortunate to get off just as the bubble is bursting," wrote Jefferson in 1797, "leaving others to hold the bag."

President John Adams did not have Washington's prestige and charismatic authority; he also lacked a first-rate cabinet; and he had won the presidency over Jefferson by a scant three electoral votes. Moreover he faced the problems of a divided people and aggravated relations with the French. American ships were being seized and their cargoes confiscated. American sailors found by the French aboard British ships—whether or not they had

John Adams Replaces Washington

been impressed—were threatened with hanging. The American minister sent to France to replace Monroe, Charles C. Pinckney, was insulted and ordered to leave the country.

Despite the bellicose attitude of the French, Adams chose to continue negotiating. But, lest his policy fail, he also advised Congress to prepare for war.

John Marshall of Virginia and Elbridge Gerry of Massachusetts were selected to join Pinckney in a bipartisan delegation that Adams hoped would "by its dignity . . . satisfy France." For months Americans waited anxiously for news. Would the French attitude change? Could a satisfactory accommodation of grievances be arranged? Or would the United States go to war? "The mind of Congress as well as the rest of the world," an observer noted, "seems suspended as to the measures our nation should adopt in relation to France, upon the expectation of intelligence to be received from our Commissioners." Finally, in March 1798, Congress requested and Adams released the diplomatic papers. They told of a complex attempt at international blackmail. Instead of being officially received by the French foreign minister, Talleyrand, the Americans were greeted by his agents (labeled X, Y, and Z), who first demanded a large personal bribe, then a substantial "loan" for the French government and a public apology from President Adams for allegedly anti-French remarks. When the three Americans answered "no; no; not a six-pence," negotiations ceased. Here, said Adams, was "proof as strong as Holy Writ" of French perfidy.

The XYZ Affair

The American people agreed. A wave of anti-Gallic sentiment swept the country. Addresses and testimonials supporting the administration flooded in. The Federalist party seemed rejuvenated. Federalists had always been respected; but now, for the first time, they experienced the heady sensation of popularity. The Republicans, on the other hand, were "confounded," one Federalist gleefully reported, "and the trimmers dropped off from the party like wind-falls from an apple tree in September." Joseph Hopkinson's patriotic composition "Hail Columbia" became an immediate success. When John Marshall returned from France he was greeted with the same wild acclaim Genet had enjoyed a few years earlier. Adams was so moved by the emotional display that he proclaimed a day of "Public Humiliation, Fasting and Prayer throughout the United States."

Before the XYZ revelations Congress had taken a largely defensive military posture, appropriating funds to fortify harbors, prohibiting the export of arms and ammunition, authorizing the equipment of three frigates, and increasing the number of revenue cutters. But since there was no American navy to speak of, French corsairs boldly attacked American shipping as far north as Long Island Sound. Marine insurance for vessels trading in the Caribbean rose an astronomical 33 percent of the value of the ship and its cargo. The United States appeared weak and vulnerable, certainly no match for a mighty European power such as France.

The Undeclared Naval War

News of the XYZ incident prompted Congress to enact positive military measures. In June 1798 all commercial relations with France were suspended. In July, Congress authorized the capture of armed vessels sailing under the French flag and also nullified all treaties with France. The army was strengthened, the militia was increased, taxes were raised, and, most important, the navy enlarged. "It is gratifying to behold the military spirit which prevails," a Federalist wrote. "When such a spirit exists our country cannot be in danger." In all but name, America was at war.

Britain agreed to protect American transatlantic shipping, thus freeing the United States navy to clear the Caribbean of French warships and privateers. The task was accomplished quickly and effectively, and American merchant vessels soon sailed the Caribbean in reasonable safety. Before the quasi-war was ended by the Convention of 1800, the previously untested American navy had vanquished the French in eight of its nine engagements. To many Americans this feat redeemed national honor and strengthened national confidence.

The fever of the XYZ affair might have been sustained and the naval victories utilized to the advantage of the Federalists. But in their anxiety to maintain power they blundered—and lost it.

The Alien and Sedition Acts

The Federalists believed that the Republicans were carriers of dangerous revolutionary doctrines, that their criticisms of the government were tantamount to treason, and that they had to be suppressed if the United States was to be saved from anarchy. Particularly disturbing was the presence both of aliens and immigrants from England and Ireland, and of French Jacobins, who propagated radical ideas and invariably joined the Republican party. Between May and July 1798 the Federalist-dominated Congress enacted a series of alien and sedition laws designed to silence such political opposition.

1. The Naturalization Act extended the residence requirement for citizenship from five to fourteen years.
2. The Alien Act gave the president authority to banish any foreigner whom he thought "dangerous to the peace and safety of the United States."
3. The Alien Enemies Act permitted the president to arrest and expel any aliens of a nation with which the United States was officially at war.
4. The Sedition Act made it a crime to say or write anything "false, scandalous, and malicious" about the president or Congress. The act specified that the truth could not be considered seditious. Since most judges were Federalists, however, the safeguard proved worthless. Dissent was equated with disloyalty. Conformity was equated with patriotism. "He that is not for us," concluded an administration newspaper, "is against us."

The effect was quite the opposite of what the Federalists intended. Jefferson believed the Alien and Sedition Acts were a crucial test: if the American people could be duped into accepting such repressive measures, there was little hope for democracy. The task of the Republican party was to employ every legal means to stop what Jefferson sincerely thought to be a first step toward monarchy. As a tactical response Jefferson and Madison authored, respectively, the Kentucky and Virginia Resolutions, which declared that the Alien and Sedition Acts violated state sovereignty and were therefore "void and of no force." As a practical response the two leaders attempted to alert public opinion to the dangers of authoritarian government. Hundreds of petitions of protest poured into Congress from Republicans in all sections of the country. When Republican editors were jailed under the Sedition Act, other Republican papers were started.

The unity of the Republican party, badly splintered by the XYZ furor, was restored. "The Alien and Sedition Acts," wrote Jefferson, "have . . . operated as powerful sedatives of the XYZ inflammation." The Federalists had handed Jefferson a significant domestic issue that diverted attention from his defense of France and that he could use effectively in the presidential campaign of 1800.

The New Mission

The long friendship of Adams and Jefferson, strained by political quarrels during the Washington administration, was shattered by the Alien and Sedition Acts, the XYZ affair, and the naval war with France. Adams had contributed to the public hysteria by his bellicose addresses in 1798. He had not requested Congress to declare war, although Federalist extremists had exerted pressures on him to make such a recommendation. Moderate Federalists, including Alexander Hamilton, were content to keep the ill feeling against France brewing without an official declaration of hostilities. Either way, so long as the public recognized France to be the national enemy, so the Federalists reasoned, the continuation of their political control was guaranteed.

Adams's position, however, had quietly shifted from hawk to dove. In February 1799 he announced the appointment of a new diplomatic mission to France. The entire country, reported his wife Abigail, reacted "like a flock of frightened pigeons." The Republicans were elated, the Federalists divided. Some approved, others were stunned, puzzled, mortified, or incensed. Hamilton's followers, their eyes on the ballot box, considered the peace mission "embarrassing and ruinous" to the Federalist cause. Adams had placed his country before his party. He had performed a sacrificial political act, paving the way for Republican victory in the next election, but he never regretted his action. "I desire no other inscription over my gravestone," Adams later wrote, "than: 'Here lies John Adams, who took upon himself the responsibility for peace with France in the year 1800.' "

The Election of 1800

Despite divisions in the Federalist party during the election (Hamilton campaigned openly for Charles C. Pinckney), the peace mission was popular and Adams was only narrowly defeated. But the result was complicated by a tied electoral vote between the Republican candidates, Jefferson and Aaron Burr. By constitutional provision, a choice between the two fell to the House of Representatives.

Hamilton exerted all his diminishing influence to persuade Federalists to support Jefferson as the lesser of two evils. The Federalists, however, would not heed his advice and voted unanimously for Burr. Jefferson, they reasoned, would systematically destroy the structure they had labored to build over the past decade; Burr, they felt intuitively, was a self-seeking politician with whom they could bargain. The Republicans in Congress just as adamantly supported Jefferson. "We are resolved," wrote a Virginia Republican, "never to yield." After thirty-five ballots neither party had obtained the necessary plurality. What would happen if the deadlock continued and no choice were made? Without a constitutionally elected president by inauguration day, the Constitution would perish, many thought. Political passions soared. Attempts to bribe members of Congress were rumored. The governor of Pennsylvania threatened to march on Washington with militia if the Federalists thwarted the majority's will. Finally a few moderate Federalists broke with their party, casting blank ballots and thereby giving the presidency to Jefferson. The precedent of a legal opposition obtaining power by persuasion and not revolution—a prime condition for successful popular government—was established.

Federalists were convinced that Thomas Jefferson worshipped at an "Altar to Gallic Despotism," as this 1800 cartoon illustrates. Only the American eagle appears to keep Jefferson from burning the Constitution at the altar. "To Mazzei" refers to a notorious letter Jefferson wrote to his Italian friend, Philip Mazzei, in 1796, criticizing George Washington. (American Antiquarian Society)

THE PROVIDENTIAL DETECTION

COMMENTARY

For years the Federalists had predicted anarchic consequences if Jefferson were elected. He would restore state power at the expense of national authority. He would ally the United States to France. America would suffer all the excesses of revolutionary change. All the constructive gains of the twelve years of Federalist rule would be dissipated. Hamilton's financial system, which had so invigorated American economic growth, would be dismantled and destroyed. To the Federalists, the Virginia radical was the political devil incarnate; he could be expected to attack the Bank, the military, the judiciary, commercial interests, even organized religion. Jefferson was feared, honestly feared, by almost all Federalists. They doubted whether the Constitution could continue its successful course under such a president.

SUGGESTED READING

LELAND BALDWIN, Whiskey Rebels (1939)
CHARLES BEARD, Economic Origins of Jeffersonian Democracy (1915)
SAMUEL F. BEMIS, Jay's Treaty: A Study in Commerce and Diplomacy (1923)
DANIEL J. BOORSTIN, The Americans: The National Experience (1965)
MORTON BORDEN, The Federalism of James A. Bayard (1954)
————, Parties and Politics in the Early Republic, 1789–1815 (1967)
JULIAN BOYD, Number 7: Alexander Hamilton's Secret Attempts to Control American Foreign Policy (1964)
IRVING BRANT, James Madison (1941–61)
RICHARD BUEL, Securing the Revolution (1972)
WILLIAM N. CHAMBERS, Political Parties in a New Nation: The American Experience, 1776–1809 (1963)
JOSEPH CHARLES, The Origins of the American Party System (1956)
J. A. COMBS, The Jay Treaty (1970)
NOBLE CUNNINGHAM, The Jeffersonian Republicans: The Formation of Party Organization, 1789–1801 (1957)
MANNING DAUER, The Adams Federalists (1953)
ALEXANDER DECONDE, Entangling Alliance: Politics and Diplomacy Under George Washington (1958)
————, The Quasi-War (1966)
RICHARD HOFSTADTER, The Idea of a Party System (1969)
REGINALD HORSMAN, The Frontier in the Formative Years (1970)
STEPHEN KURTZ, The Presidency of John Adams (1957)
DUMAS MALONE, Jefferson and His Time (1948–74)
————, The Public Life of Thomas Cooper (1961)
JOHN C. MILLER, Alexander Hamilton, Portrait in Paradox (1959)
————, Crisis in Freedom (1951)
————, The Federalist Era, 1789–1801 (1960)
BROADUS MITCHELL, Alexander Hamilton (1957–62)
BRADFORD PERKINS, The First Rapprochement: England and the United States (1955)
JAMES M. SMITH, Freedom's Fetters: The Alien and Sedition Laws and American Civil Liberties (1956)
PAGE SMITH, John Adams (1962)
DONALD STEWART, The Opposition Press of the Federal Period, 1789–1800 (1969)
HARRY M. TINKCOM, Republicans and Federalists in Pennsylvania, 1790–1801 (1950)
PAUL VARG, Foreign Policies of the Founding Fathers (1963)
LEONARD D. WHITE, The Federalists (1948)
ALFRED YOUNG, The Democratic Republicans of New York, 1763–1797 (1967)

5

The Age of Jefferson, 1800–1815

The Revolution of 1800

Toward the end of his life Thomas Jefferson wrote that his election in 1800, though effected by suffrage rather than the sword, was "as real a revolution in the principles of our government as that of 1776 was in its form." The words are easily misconstrued. By principles he really meant measures, and by revolution he meant a turning back to the original intent of the founding fathers. Jefferson felt the Federalists had twisted and perverted the spirit of the American Revolution and the Constitution. They had enacted laws that bordered on the tyrannical. Freedom of speech and the press had been compromised. People were fined and sentenced to prison merely for voicing their criticisms. Military expenditures were too large. A standing army of professional soldiers was an unnecessary danger in a democracy. Moreover, according to Jefferson, Hamilton's financial program had benefited the rich and privileged in society. The people were saddled with heavy taxes and debts. Speculation in securities had corrupted congressmen. Their actions in the 1790s certainly seemed more responsive to moneyed interests than to the public. Finally, there was the problem of how America could pursue an independent foreign policy when the Federalist fiscal system made the United States utterly dependent upon the goodwill of Britain. As president Jefferson did not propose a program of remedial legislation—in fact, he had none. Rather he simply suggested removing a number of their laws and practices and then letting nature take its course. The results are what might be called the revolution of 1800.

Jefferson believed the national debt should be retired as quickly as possible. He saw no intrinsic economic value or political benefits in maintaining it. The chief goal of his administration, he told a friend, was "to reform the waste of public money, and thus drive away the vultures who prey upon it." He instructed his Secretary of the Treasury, Albert Gallatin, to devise a plan for the gradual extinction of the public debt. In eight years, despite fifteen million dollars spent to acquire the Louisiana territory, the debt was reduced from eighty million to fifty-seven million, and there was a treasury surplus of fourteen million—a formidable accomplishment.

Jefferson also thought that internal taxes should be

Thomas Jefferson continues to be judged one of America's ablest yet most controversial and enigmatic figures. Frances Trollope called his writings "a mighty mass of mischief." Henry Adams claimed that the weakness of "the Jeffersonian system lay in its rigidity of rule." Franklin Roosevelt praised him for leading "the steps of America into the paths of the permanent integrity of the Republic."
(Culver Pictures)

repealed. They were onerous and unnecessary. The cost of their collection was high. Evasions were frequent. They fomented discontents, such as the whiskey rebellion. And they added only a small percentage (9 percent) to the national coffers. By 1802, at Jefferson's instigation, most of the hated excise, carriage, and direct property taxes had been repealed. Economy in government was another of his major concerns. As Dumas Malone remarks, Jefferson "wielded his shears in the spirit of a gardener, pruning shrubs of their excess foliage." Ministerial posts in Holland, Portugal, and Prussia were withdrawn; the foreign missions to Great Britain, France, and Spain were reduced. Most navy frigates were decommissioned and no new ones were built. The army was cut to a single regiment of three thousand men. Finally Jefferson believed the style of government should be plain. He had never approved of the elegant levees of George Washington and John Adams, and he made a point of holding simple receptions. Even his presidential inauguration—he walked from his boarding house to the Capitol—was an exercise in republican simplicity. He was a most accessible president, but his casual disregard for protocol occasionally was resented. The British minister to the United States, Anthony Merry, complained that Jefferson once received him in slippers and that on another occasion no distinction in rank was observed at a presidential dinner party.

Jefferson did not tinker with the Bank of the United States, which was permitted to continue under its twenty-year charter. Most of the Alien and Sedition Acts lapsed in 1800, and the Naturalization Act was repealed with little debate. As for state-federal relations, Jefferson promised in his inaugural address to "support the State governments in all their rights, as the most competent administrators for our domestic concerns and the surest bulwarks against anti-republican tendencies." His foreign policy, Jefferson stated, was to be based upon "peace, commerce, and honest friendship with all nations—entangling alliances with none." Thus, moderately, pragmatically, more by example than by law, Jefferson hoped to set the ship of state back on a republican course. He held out the olive branch to his political opponents. "We have called by different names brethren of the same principle," said Jefferson. "We are all republicans—we are all federalists." His words were a plea to end partisan bickering, to replace past bitterness with a spirit of trust and harmony, above all to think in terms of American interests, not European conflicts.

If the election of 1800 was a revolution, it was a mild one, and Federalist leaders did not know how to cope with it. Although they greeted each successive Republican move with laments and threats, the public remained unconvinced. The churches remained standing. No bloodbaths took place. The country continued to prosper. Far from the metaphysician the Federalists had pictured, Jefferson proved an enormously capable politician.

Having lost control of both the executive and legislative branches, the Federalists took refuge in the judiciary. When Jefferson ordered an attack upon the courts, the Federalists resisted tenaciously. Their funereal dirge turned into shrieks of frightened rage. Actually the Republican attack was restrained, justified, and based entirely on political—not theoretical—grounds. Federalist judges, not judicial power, were the target.

Jefferson and the Judiciary

In 1802 the Republicans attempted to repeal a judiciary law, enacted the previous year, that had created sixteen new circuit courts, to which Adams had appointed only members of his own party as judges. Federalists argued that the act could not be repealed without violating the clear mandate of the Constitution. The basic law of the land guaranteed the tenure of federal judges. So long as the judges exercised "good behavior," their salaries could not be diminished, and they could not be removed except by the process of impeachment. Federalists accused Jefferson and his followers of seeking to upset the highly sensitive federal balance of power, of destroying the independence of the judiciary, and of thereby harming the Constitution. Jefferson responded that the Federalists had retreated "into the judiciary as a stronghold. . . By a fraudulent use of the Constitution, which has made judges irremovable, they have multiplied useless judges merely to strengthen their phalanx." Taking their cue from him, Republicans reasoned that the legislature had authority, by constitutional provision, over inferior federal courts. The Constitution had given Congress the power to establish—and thus, logically, to abolish—all except the Supreme Court. Were this not so, they argued, a defeated party could establish thousands of judicial sinecures to be filled by its members. The repealing act passed. Its only effect was to reduce the number of courts.

Federalist congressmen called upon Chief Justice John Marshall, asking him to outmaneuver the Republicans by persuading the Supreme Court to declare the repealing act unconstitutional. Marshall wisely refused to do so, much to their disappointment. In 1803, however, he won the esteem of his party for his masterful opinion in the case of *Marbury v. Madison*. William Marbury, a Federalist appointed to a minor judicial post by John Adams, had not received his commission. Signed and sealed, it had not been delivered in the rush and confusion of changing administrations. Now Marbury asked the Court for a writ of mandamus ordering the Republican secretary of state, James Madison, to deliver it. Marshall knew that a writ, if he issued it, would have been ignored. Instead, speaking for the Court, he declared that the writ could not be issued because section 13 of the Judiciary Act of 1789, which gave the Court authority to do so, was unconstitutional. Marbury lost his job, but the precedent of judicial review of federal legislation was established.

Jefferson's response was typical. Privately he was incensed by the decision, for he never considered the Supreme Court the ultimate arbiter of constitutional issues. But he did not wish to arouse ebbing partisan emotions over the question of judicial review, and so he did nothing.

Understandable, but ill considered, were the Republican impeachments of two Federalist judges in 1803–05. District Court Justice John Pickering was insane and should not have been tried. Several Republican congressmen were squeamish about convicting a deranged man. By a strict party vote, however, Pickering was found guilty. Associate Justice Samuel Chase was not insane, but he had conducted cases in an outrageously biased manner and had expressed from the bench the most prejudiced opinions concerning Republicans. To convict Chase the Senate would require construing his actions as legal crimes or misdemeanors, which clearly they were not. Several Republicans broke party ranks to vote with the Federalists, and Chase was acquitted. "Impeachment," stated Jefferson, "is a farce which will not be tried again."

The Louisiana Purchase

The Federalists could not awaken any serious public discontent over the judiciary, but for a time they believed another national problem might carry them back into power. Since 1800 it had been rumored that Spain had ceded the Louisiana territory to France. By 1802, when the port of New Orleans was closed to American traffic, the rumors had been confirmed. Naturally Jefferson was alarmed. A lethargic, feeble Spain on the western frontier was not to be feared; an energetic, imperialistic France was a menace. "The day that France takes possession of New Orleans," Jefferson predicted, "we must marry ourselves to the British fleet and nation." The Federalists could see only two distasteful alternatives for Jefferson. Either he must declare war on France to satisfy the war fever spreading through the American West, or, by continuing a pacific policy, he must risk unpopularity and a consequent Federalist renaissance.

Jefferson's political genius was equal to the problem. His public addresses took on a military tone, but secretly he requested and received from Congress an appropriation of two million dollars to purchase New Orleans and West Florida from France. James Monroe was appointed as minister extraordinary to join Robert R. Livingston in Paris for the negotiations. If they failed, the American diplomats were instructed to cross the channel and sign a treaty of alliance with Great Britain. Napoleon, meanwhile, had decided to sell the entire territory. His dream of building a Caribbean empire had collapsed because of catastrophic losses in Santo Domingo against the black revolutionaries. In 1802 alone approximately fifty thousand French soldiers died either in battle or from yellow fever. Moreover, war between France and Britain was imminent, and Napoleon could not spare troops to defend Louisiana. And he needed money. "I renounce Louisiana," Napoleon told his ministers. "It is not only New Orleans that I mean to cede; it is the whole colony, reserving none of it." Monroe and Livingston were totally unpre-

Expansion of the United States

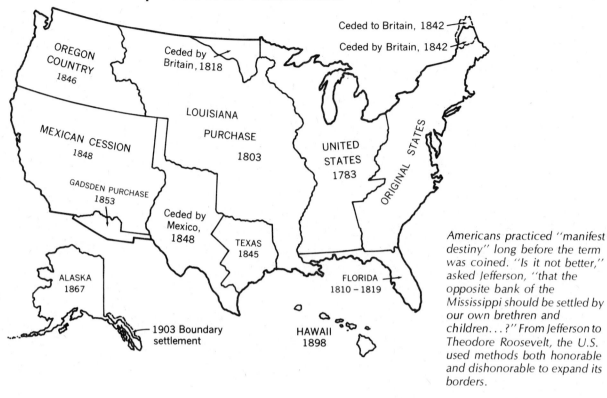

Americans practiced "manifest destiny" long before the term was coined. "Is it not better," asked Jefferson, "that the opposite bank of the Mississippi should be settled by our own brethren and children...?" From Jefferson to Theodore Roosevelt, the U.S. used methods both honorable and dishonorable to expand its borders.

pared and somewhat mystified by his offer, but they did not hesitate. Louisiana was purchased for fifteen million dollars, subject to ratification by the American government. "We have lived long," Livingston told Monroe, "but this is the noblest work of our lives."

Jefferson was enthusiastic, for the purchase would eradicate the perennial concern of trade on the Mississippi. It would quiet western discontent, eliminate Indian raids instigated by foreign powers, ruin Federalist hopes of regaining office, and free the United States from the necessity of an alliance with Britain. Most important, it would double the size of the country and open a boundless land to settlement. Jefferson was troubled by doubts concerning the constitutionality of the treaty, since there were no provisions in the Constitution for acquiring territory. Jefferson was a strict constructionist; he believed that the federal government could not do what was not specifically authorized by the fundamental law. He had so argued a decade earlier when Hamilton proposed the incorporation of the Bank. But the nation would benefit by possessing Louisiana, Jefferson concluded, and thus justified the violation of his principles. He submitted the treaty, asking the Senate to ratify it "with as little debate as possible, particularly so far as respects the constitutional difficulty."

"Is it not better," Jefferson once asked, "that the opposite bank of the Mississippi should be settled by our own brethren and children?" He had long wanted details about the land between the Mississippi River and the Pacific Ocean, which no white man had yet seen. Was there a feasible overland route? Could the fur trade be developed there? What riches did it hold? What unique plants and animals? As early as 1786 Jefferson had encouraged John Ledyard to undertake a fantastic voyage across Russia, Siberia, and the Bering Sea, and to return through the interior of North America. Ledyard actually got as far as Irkutsk before Russian police stopped his journey. He was then escorted to the Polish frontier and warned not to enter Russia again "or he would certainly be hanged." In 1792 the American Philosophical Society, prodded by Jefferson, financed a proposed trip across the continent by a French scientist, André Michaux. The venture collapsed because of Michaux's involvement in political intrigues. In 1803, months before Louisiana was ceded to the United States, Jefferson obtained a secret appropriation from Congress to finance an expedition "to the Western Ocean." To head the expedition Jefferson selected his secretary, Meriwether Lewis, who was skilled in wilderness survival; and Lewis chose as his associate William Clark, a younger brother of George Rogers Clark, familiarly known to the Indians as "Red Head." By the time they gathered and trained a crew of frontiersmen and broke winter quarters near St. Louis, secrecy was no longer necessary, since Louisiana was American territory. Their journey from 1804 to 1806, beginning with the hard push up the Missouri river; their encampment at Fort Mandan (in North Dakota); the help they received from the remarkable Indian woman, Sacajawea; their discovery of the narrow passes through the Rockies; their descent to the Pacific by way of the Columbia River; and their slow, arduous return to St. Louis, constitutes one of the greatest adventure tales in western history. They brought back an enormous body of knowledge about western North America for scientists and information of value to fur traders. Moreover, they established the basis for the American claim to Oregon. It was with understandable pride that Lewis reported to Jefferson: "In obedience to your orders we have penetrated the Continent of North America to the Pacific Ocean and sufficiently explored the interior of the country to affirm that we have discovered the most practicable communication which does exist across the continent."

There were other less successful expeditions Jefferson fathered during his presidency. William Dunbar and John Hunter, both scientists, received a congressional grant in 1804 to explore the Red River to its source. The fear of Spanish resentment caused them to turn northward along the Ouachita River instead. In 1806 Thomas Freeman, a surveyor and astronomer, led a party some six hundred miles in two flat-bottomed barges on the Red River, but Spanish troops from Texas forced their retreat. Concurrently, in 1805 and 1806, Jefferson sent Lieutenant Zebulon M. Pike to seek out the source of the Mississippi River. He never reached it, though—understandably—both Pike and Jefferson believed he did. Pike's next voyage, in 1806 and 1807, along the upper reaches of the Arkansas River to the Rocky mountains, became more renowned. He failed to climb the mountain that bears his name (Pike's Peak), and he explored in vain for the source of the Red River. A Spanish force intercepted his expedition and escorted him to Albuquerque, then to Chihuahua (in northern Mexico), and finally back to American soil. Pike's account of his travels did much to form the popular impression that the land between the Missouri and the Rockies was a vast desert best left to the Indians.

Jefferson received "with unspeakable joy" news of the safe return of Lewis and Clark. At the same time, with good reason, he had gloomy suspicions about the western plans of Aaron Burr. Jefferson did not trust him, especially after the tied electoral vote between the two in 1800, when Federalists supported Burr for the presidency against the obvious understanding of the electorate. It seemed to Jefferson that Burr was an unprincipled schemer whose actions were grounded in expediency and whose interests were solely personal. Thus, he repudiated the vice-president, withholding patronage from Burr and Burrites. In 1804 Burr entered the New York gubernatorial race, receiving the informal endorsement of many Federalists. But there another enemy, Alexander Hamilton, did all in his power to have Burr defeated. "He threw himself against Burr's ambition," Broadus Mitchell, a biographer of Hamilton states, "and died to satisfy his rival's revenge." Some of Hamilton's derogatory comments, personal in nature, appeared in print, and Burr—who lost the election—demanded a retraction, which Hamilton refused to make. The duel that followed (across the Hudson River at Weehawken, New Jersey, on July 11, 1804) resulted in Hamilton's death and the destruction of Burr's political career. With his avenues to power blocked both in Washington and in New York, Burr sought personal glory in a western scheme that ended in his arrest and trial for treason.

The Burr Conspiracy

Precisely what he planned will probably never be known. Some historians believe he wished to promote the separation of the Southwest from the Union. Others feel he planned to establish a colony in Louisiana that would be used as a base to conquer Spanish territory. Most likely Burr envisioned an empire stretching from the Ohio to Mexico over which he would preside, and he intended to take whatever steps were necessary to achieve it. A party to the conspiracy was the governor of Louisiana, General James Wilkinson, whose recognized abilities were matched by his unparalleled corruptions. Wilkinson had long acted as a spy for Spain while in the service of the American government. "The gods invite us to glory and fortune," Burr wrote to Wilkinson. "It remains to be seen whether we deserve the boon."

The staging area for the venture began on an island in the Ohio River, near Marietta, owned by a rich Irish exile, Herman Blennerhasset. Burr joined it later on, at the mouth of the Cumberland, and a few more recruits were picked up as the expedition floated down the Ohio and Mississippi rivers. Meanwhile, Jefferson, though aware of this illegal gathering of armed force, was strangely quiescent. Why he did not act remains a subject of considerable speculation. However, when Wilkinson doublecrossed Burr and informed Jefferson of the conspiracy, the president was forced to issue a proclamation (November 27, 1806) that led to the collapse of the plot and Burr's arrest. Wilkinson had written that "a numerous and powerful association . . . was formed to levy and rendezvous eight or ten thousand men in New Orleans" for an invasion of Mexico. At that moment Burr commanded sixty men. His conspiracy must be judged as one of the strangest and wildest enterprises of western history.

The subsequent trial held at Richmond, Virginia, presided over by Chief Justice John Marshall, was replete with ironic twists and significant precedents. Jefferson, his better judgment marred by his deep hatred for Burr, acted in a most partisan and vindictive manner. Pardons were offered to Burr's associates who agreed to testify for the government. One of Burr's friends, a Frenchman, was offered an army commission. Jefferson, a scholar notes, "made himself a party to the prosecution" by dispatching evidence to the United States attorney handling the case. However, when Marshall issued a subpoena requiring Jefferson to submit certain documents bearing on the case, the president—on the ground of executive privilege—refused. Marshall's conduct of the case was prejudiced by his enmity toward Jefferson. He construed the law of treason quite narrowly. Organizing "a military assemblage," he stated, was not equivalent to "levying of war." Recruiting followers for an expedition with treasonable intent was not in itself treason. Unless there were two witnesses testifying to an overt act, the accused must be found innocent. Guided by this definition and despite the array of evidence, the jury took a mere twenty-five minutes to acquit Burr. His career was over, however. Marked by the public as a traitor, still wanted for murder in some states, threatened by angry mobs in Baltimore, Burr gathered some money from friends and fled to Europe.

The Barbary Pirates

"History will hardly furnish an example of such oppressive tyranny," a Federalist newspaper declared during the Burr trial, "as has been practiced under the administration of Mr. Jefferson." Nevertheless, Jefferson's popularity was at its peak in the middle years of his tenure as president. In the election of 1804 he captured every state except Connecticut and Delaware. He was applauded for abolishing internal taxes, for reducing the national debt, for acquiring Louisiana, and even the merchant class was pleased with his decisive action in dealing with the Barbary pirates. When a Virginia lawyer, William Wirt, composed a list of Jefferson's practical accomplishments, he thanked the president for "the lesson taught the inhabitants of the coast of Barbary, that we have the means of chastising their piratical encroachments, and awing them into justice."

For years it had been the custom of European nations to pay tribute to the states on the Barbary coast—Algeria, Tripoli, Tunis, and Morocco—to ensure the safety of their merchant vessels. The United States did the same. During the administrations of Washington and Adams two million dollars was spent in this way, and still American ships occasionally were seized and American sailors captured and held for ransom. In May 1801, two months after Jefferson took office, the pasha of Tripoli, demanding still larger payments of tribute, declared war on the United States. Jefferson decided to meet this extortion by an appropriate use of force. Without asking the permission of Congress, he dispatched a naval squadron to the Mediterranean. Several members of his cabinet, especially Levi Lincoln and Albert Gallatin, thought the action unconstitutional. But Jefferson could not abide bribery, and no constitutional scruples could delay his determination to crush the Barbary pirates. (Later Congress did declare war.) It took four years—including some daring military feats—before the pasha conceded. One of the spectacular moments was Lieutenant Stephen Decatur's destruction of the American frigate, *Philadelphia*, which had grounded on a reef, been captured by the Tripolitans, and was to be refitted by them. Decatur's force entered the harbor at night, set the *Philadelphia* afire, and then escaped to safety. (Lord Nelson described Decatur's raid as "the most bold and daring act of the age.") Instead of three million dollars ransom initially demanded by the pasha for the release of American prisoners, the final treaty of 1805 provided for a payment of sixty thousand dollars. Moreover, the amount of tribute was substantially reduced. Ten years later it was entirely eliminated. The Dey of Algeria, attempting to take advantage of the United States' involvement in the War of 1812, once again began to seize American

"Money and fear," the Count of Vergennes once advised Jefferson (in 1786), "are the only two agents" to be used with the Barbary Coast pirates. Jefferson advised a retaliatory war. He hoped Naples and Portugal would join the United States in such a venture—but nothing came of it. As president, Jefferson used a combination of force and diplomacy against the Barbary states which, writes Dumas Malone, accomplished more "than any previous administration or any European power had done." (The Bettmann Archive)

merchant vessels. Decatur returned to the Mediterranean with a squadron, defeated the Dey, and forced a treaty whereby *he* had to pay. The same tactics, yielding the same results, were imposed upon Tunis and Tripoli.

The Problem of Neutrality

During his second administration Jefferson's image became somewhat tarnished. War between Britain and France again bedeviled the United States. Jefferson's task was to steer a course that would convince both powers to respect American rights on the high seas, that would not commit the United States to an open conflict, and that would be acceptable to the majority of Americans. A policy meeting all these conditions was never found. Jefferson did keep the peace, as one of his eulogists stated in 1809, "through a season of uncommon difficulty and trial." Yet his policies really failed, and James Madison, his successor, inherited issues that had been postponed rather than resolved.

Britain was the master of the seas, particularly after Lord Nelson's naval victory at Trafalgar in 1805 ruined Napoleon's plans for invading England. France was master of the continent, its armies marching from the victory at Ulm to the celebrated conquests at Austerlitz, Jena, and Friedland. Within their respective spheres the two contenders were impregnable. Not being able to hurt one another with arms, they turned to economic weapons. It was the spectator—the United States, the world's leading neutral producer and carrier—that suffered. By the *Essex* decision in 1805 a British court declared that French cargoes on American vessels might be seized. Thereafter, British ships were stationed near key American ports, boarding and inspecting merchantmen, confiscating cargoes, and, worst of all, impressing American seamen. The British insisted that citizenship was inalienable—once an Englishman, always an Englishman. American naturalization papers, real or fraudulent, were worthless when a British ship decided that it needed more hands. To be sure, many sailors were British deserters; but many were not, and impressed sailors could anticipate only low pay, filthy quarters, brutal treatment, and possible death in naval battles.

Napoleon's Berlin (1806) and Milan (1807) decrees established—at least on paper—a blockade of the British Isles. They declared that any neutral vessel that permitted itself to be boarded by the British or touched at a British port was subject to capture. Britain reciprocated by Orders in Council, which proclaimed that neutral vessels bound for a port controlled by France must first land in Britain, pay full duties, and receive permission to continue. The problem for the United States was clear: to obey the decrees of one country was to violate those of the other. Despite these regulations, American merchants prospered because of the war. The value of reexports of West Indian products mounted from fourteen million dollars in 1803 to sixty million in 1806. Nearly four thousand new seamen were employed on American vessels, and shipping increased at the rate of seventy thousand tons annually. Although they prospered, the merchants were irritated by Britain's blockades, seizures, and impressment, and they demanded that the administration take appropriate steps to defend the rights of neutrals.

The first step in attempting to retaliate against Britain came in 1806 when Congress—after much debate and bickering—passed the Nonimportation Act. Although its weaknesses were apparent, Jefferson signed the measure. John Randolph called the act "a milk and water bill, a dose of chicken broth to be taken nine months hence." According to the Nonimportation Act certain British goods would be prohibited from being imported into the United States after November 15, 1806, unless, before that date, the two nations could resolve their differences. Jefferson extended the deadline to afford his ministers, William Pinkney and James Monroe, every opportunity to conclude an acceptable treaty. They were instructed to secure from Britain an abandonment of the practice of impressment and resumption of the right of "broken voyages." Instead of adhering to their instructions, Monroe and Pinkney signed a draft that dismayed the Republican administration. By its terms the British made some minor concessions regarding the West Indian trade; and they agreed to sign a diplomatic note assuring the United States that they would try to avoid impressing bona-fide Americans. However, there was no mention of impressment in the treaty itself. More important, at the last moment the British insisted upon an important condition: for ten years the United States must promise not to employ a policy of economic coercion against Britain. Finally, in a separate note attached to the treaty, the British reserved the privilege of nonratification if the United States did not take positive measures against Napoleon's recently enacted Berlin Decree—which, of course, might well mean war.

Jefferson had no intention of surrendering the tactic of economic pressure for a decade, so he never bothered to submit the Monroe-Pinkney treaty to the Senate. Some scholars believe Jefferson should have accepted it as a realistic settlement of Anglo-American differences. According to one critic, A. L. Burt, Jefferson "threw away an irreplaceable instrument for stifling the growing strife between the two countries, and he also contributed to the increase of this strife." Many Federalists and a few antiadministration Republicans also felt this way. But most Americans sided with Jefferson. Even the British minister to the United States, David Erskine, reported to his government: "I think public opinion will support the President in his objections to the Treaty."

The fundamental causes for a declaration of war were present, and on June 22, 1807, an immediate provocation occurred. The British frigate, HMS *Leopard,* fired three broadsides at close range into the side of an American naval ship, the *Chesapeake.* A number of Americans were killed or wounded, and the British removed four alleged deserters. Two were black, two white, and only one was clearly an Englishman. War fever swept the country as news of the attack radiated from Norfolk, Virginia. "Never since the battle of Lexington," Jefferson wrote to his old friend Lafayette, "have I seen this country in such a state of exasperation. . . . And even that did not produce such unanimity." Jefferson could have seized the moment of aroused nationalism, sent a war message to Congress, and enjoyed the enthusiastic support of virtually all Americans. Personally and politically he would have

Negotiating with Britain

profited by such a move. But he knew that the United States was not prepared for war. And war would be an admission of diplomatic bankruptcy, which he was not yet ready to concede. There was a penultimate policy Jefferson first wished to try: not partial, temporary, and ineffective laws restricting commerce but a total embargo that would truly coerce Britain and France. "Let us see whether having taught so many other useful lessons to Europe," wrote Jefferson, "we may not add that of showing them that there are peaceful means of repressing injustice, by making it to the interest of the aggressor to do what is just."

Jefferson's Embargo

Precisely six months after the *Leopard*'s attack, on December 22, 1807, Jefferson signed the Embargo Act. Supplemented four times by additional legislation to enforce its provisions, the act prohibited virtually all exports from the United States by land or sea and forbade the importation of specified British manufactured goods. Only vessels engaged in the coastal trade were permitted to operate.

Theoretically the embargo seemed a sound alternative to war; in practice it proved a costly failure for several reasons. First, Jefferson overestimated the dependence of France and Britain upon American products. The West Indies did run short of food, the Lancashire mills of cotton, and the Irish linen industry of flax. But in general the British economy was not seriously disrupted. In fact, British shipowners were delighted by the act, which removed their American competitors from the high seas. France appeared completely indifferent to the embargo. "We have somewhat overrated our means of coercing the two great belligerents to a course of justice," the United States minister to France reported in August 1808. "Here [in France] it is not felt, and in England it is forgotten." Second, it required a considerable sacrifice on the part of the American people, which they were not prepared to make. The effect upon the economy was catastrophic: idle

Alexander Anderson's cartoon illustrates an attempt to smuggle tobacco, thwarted by the snapping turtle, a symbol of governmental oppression, during the period of the Embargo Act. "Ograbme," embargo spelled backward, was just one of the ways citizens, angered by the law that forbade the export of goods, transposed the word. *(New York Public Library)*

ships, falling prices, mounting unemployment, and bankruptcies. The embargo was most detested by the very classes—shipowners and merchants—it was designed to protect. Exports plummeted from a value of one hundred eight million dollars in 1807 to twenty-two million in 1808. "Would to God," thundered one Federalist, "that the Embargo had done as little evil to ourselves as it has done to foreign nations."

Despite the rigorous enforcement provisions, the law was widely evaded. Smuggling, mainly through Canada, became a major enterprise in New England. On Lake Champlain large rafts joined together, fortified and carrying enormous quantities of contraband, openly defied the American customs. Informed of these efforts, Jefferson responded that it was "important to crush every example of forcible opposition to the law." But the evaders prevailed. A mob at Gloucester, Massachusetts, destroyed a United States revenue cutter. Coastal vessels frequently cleared port without papers and transferred their cargoes to British vessels at sea. The lawbreakers suffered no qualms of disloyalty. "Let every man who holds the name of America dear to him," declared a typical Massachusetts circular, "stretch forth his hands and put this accursed thing, this Embargo, from him."

Jefferson suffered much personal abuse because of the embargo. A precocious youth of thirteen, William Cullen Bryant, penned a satirical poem suggesting that Jefferson "resign the presidential chair" and return to the "charms" and "sable arms" of his alleged mulatto mistress. Such gossip had long been rampant in the Federalist press. Jefferson usually ignored it. In 1808 he was certainly more concerned with the political effects of the embargo. The Federalists were regaining strength. Their representation in Congress had doubled. They controlled every gubernatorial office in New England. Many, while pursuing legitimate political goals, openly voiced secessionist sentiments. Years later Jefferson commented: "I felt the foundations of the government shaken under my feet by the New England townships." In New York the Republicans were split; in Virginia John Randolph pushed the candidacy of James Monroe for president in opposition to the administration's choice, James Madison. Nevertheless, the fundamental popularity of Jeffersonian Republicanism could be read in the results of the presidential election. Outside New England, Madison swept most of the country, receiving 122 electoral votes; the Federalist candidate, Charles C. Pinckney, gained 47; George Clinton had 6, all of which were from New York. In Virginia Madison triumphed over Monroe by more than a four-to-one margin. Republican power in the House decreased, but they still enjoyed an impressive majority of forty-six over the Federalists.

Jefferson's joy at the prospect of retiring to Monticello was boundless. He was bone weary. Yet he had preserved his party. Burr's bizarre expedition and the hopeless secessionist plots of Federalist extremists had been aborted. Republican party schisms remained a minor irritant, which Jefferson, through wise leadership, never permitted to spread. But the embargo was a disaster. After fifteen months he was forced to concede its failure. Shortly before leaving the presidency he signed the act for its repeal.

"Poor Jemmy! He is but a withered little apple-John," was writer *Madison as President* Washington Irving's caustic opinion of James Madison. Though Madison's electoral victory in 1808 was decisive, he lacked Jefferson's administrative talent and political ability. New figures in Washington, including the aggressive Henry Clay and the incisive John C. Calhoun, overshadowed the drab chief executive. Madison's anxiety to preserve Republican harmony resulted in numerous party defections, and his attempts to preserve the peace resulted in a series of crucial diplomatic blunders that led finally to war.

Madison made his first mistake only a few months after he assumed office. The embargo had been replaced by the Nonintercourse Act forbidding trade with England and France. However, the law provided that commercial relations with either country could be resumed, at presidential discretion, if their decrees against neutrals were removed. The British minister to the United States, David Erskine, eager to improve Anglo-American relations, signed an agreement that bound Britain to lift its Orders in Council. "Great and Glorious News," proclaimed one newspaper, "Our Differences with Great Britain Amicably Settled." Americans were jubilant, and for weeks the event was celebrated throughout the nation. Madison immediately opened trade with Britain, and hundreds of American ships loaded with raw materials raced across the Atlantic. Then came news of Britain's repudiation of the Erskine agreement. But the damage had been done. The cumulative effects of the embargo and the nonintercourse measures, which had begun to pinch the British, were relieved by the American cargoes.

By 1810 coercion had been abandoned, and in its stead Congress passed and Madison reluctantly signed Macon's Bill No. 2, a measure that amounted to economic bribery. According to the new legislation, trade with Britain and France was reopened without restriction. However, the bill also stipulated that if either belligerent repealed its decrees against neutrals, the United States would enforce commercial restrictions upon the other. Napoleon was quick to take advantage of the opening. He instructed his foreign minister, the duke of Cadore, to inform the Americans that France's decrees would be removed after November 1, 1810, if in the interim Britain did the same or if in the interim the United States imposed restrictions against Britain. Cadore's letter, carefully edited by Napoleon, was purposely equivocal. But again Madison acted precipitously. He announced that the edicts of France had been revoked and gave Britain three months to suspend its orders or suffer the resumption of commercial restrictions.

It soon became obvious that Napoleon had no intention of respecting America's neutral rights. Indeed, French hostility seemed to increase after the Cadore letter. Some American ships and cargoes were burned at sea; others were auctioned off, and the proceeds were placed in the French treasury. Britain naturally refused to lift its orders as long as the French decrees were being enforced. "The Devil himself," declared the Republican Nathaniel Macon, "could not tell which government, England or France, is the most wicked." Madison was not deceived by Napoleon's bad faith.

Nevertheless, he insisted on maintaining commercial restrictions against Britain. Twenty months later, seeing that those restrictions had had no apparent effect on Britain and prodded by the martial spirit of some congressmen, Madison asked for a declaration of war.

The martial spirit had been heightened by two events of 1811—one off the coast of New York, the other on the frontier in Indiana. In May 1811 an American frigate of forty-four guns, the *President,* defeated a British corvette of twenty guns, the *Little Belt* (mistaking it, in the dusk, for a more powerful warship that had been stopping United States merchant vessels and impressing American seamen). Nine British sailors were killed and twenty-three wounded. There were no American casualties. Though the fight was uneven, the nation applauded the victory for squaring accounts with the British: had they not done the same to the *Chesapeake* four years earlier? It reminded one writer of 1776 when patriots had attacked the British lion, "knocked down his teeth and scowered his blackhell throat." The British were also blamed for provoking Indian attacks on frontier settlements. Actually the conflicts with Indians were precipitated by the constant territorial encroachments of Americans. Two Shawnee chiefs, Tecumseh and his twin brother, the Prophet, realized that the Indian tribes would be wiped out unless they united and resisted. On November 7, 1811, General William Henry Harrison destroyed their main village at the battle of Tippecanoe. Fighting continued, but thereafter the alliance of Indian tribes steadily deteriorated. Few Americans doubted, as a Kentucky newspaper reported, that "the War on the Wabash is purely British. The British scalping knife has filled many habitations both in this state as well as in the Indiana Territory with widows and orphans."

An analysis of congressional balloting reveals that the strongest sentiment for war originated with westerners and southerners; a majority of New Englanders opposed it. "When a man rises in this House," a northern congressman chided his colleagues, "you may almost tell how ardent he will be [for war] by knowing how far distant he lives from the sea." A Boston newspaper complained: "We, whose soil was the hotbed and whose ships were the nursery of Sailors, are insulted with the hypocrisy of a devotedness to Sailors' rights, and the arrogance of a pretended skill in maritime jurisprudence, by those whose country furnishes no navigation beyond the size of a ferryboat or an Indian canoe." The complaint was not without merit. Those whom their opponents labeled war hawks were usually younger men, proud and nationalistic, and tired of diplomatic procrastination. They regarded British violations of American rights on the high seas virtually as a personal insult. They demanded a war of conquest. "We could fight France too, if necessary, in a good cause," Speaker of the House Henry Clay boasted, "the cause of honor and independence." (In fact a proposal to include France in the declaration of war was narrowly defeated in the Senate, eighteen to fourteen). Most war hawks were expansionists. They never doubted that someday the American flag would fly over Canada. Henry Clay promised Congress "that the militia of Kentucky are alone competent to place Montreal and Upper Canada at your feet." John Randolph, who joined New Englanders in opposition to a declaration of war, charged that "we have heard but one word, like the whippoorwill, but one monotonous tone—Canada! Canada! Canada!" Southerners also itched to expand American boundaries to the southwest. In 1810 American settlers occupied the Spanish fort at Baton Rouge and promptly requested its annexation by the United States—which President Madison proclaimed. In 1811 the governor of Georgia, George Mathews, with Madison's knowledge, attempted to stir up a revolution in East Florida, which was owned by Spain. Spain was Britain's ally, and a war with the latter would afford Americans the opportunity to seize not only Canada but Florida.

In June 1812 Congress responded affirmatively to President Madison's war message. By a vote of seventy-nine to forty-nine in the House and nineteen to thirteen in the Senate, the United States declared war against Great Britain. If Madison had delayed a few months, no conflict would have been necessary. The news that Britain had suspended its Orders in Council arrived after hostilities had begun.

It soon became obvious, contrary to the boasting jingoistic predictions of war hawks, that the United States could not conquer Canada or Florida, that a military offensive could not be sustained, and that a desperate struggle would be necessary merely to avoid total disaster. The United States was a seriously divided nation and poorly prepared for war. The regular army consisted of fewer than seven thousand men, and these were spread over an area so large that communications among outposts took months. Madison authorized the enlistment of fifty thousand volunteers. After half a year scarcely five thousand had signed up. Military leadership ranged from poor to mediocre. Madison's secretary of war, William Eustis, resigned and was replaced with a number of equally forgettable successors. The ranking major general, Henry Dearborn, was old and incompetent. "The old officers," stated a younger one, Winfield Scott, "had very generally slunk into either sloth, ignorance, or habits of intemperate drinking." The most significant and undeniable mistake of the Jeffersonian Republicans was their failure to prepare the United States for war. Financially, too, the federal government was hard pressed. In 1811 the Republicans permitted the twenty-year charter of the Bank of the United States to expire without renewal. Had the Bank been operating the administration could have borrowed without difficulty. As matters stood, when Secretary of the Treasury Albert Gallatin asked for public support to finance the war, the loans were undersubscribed. Boston businessmen refused to participate. When Madison approved a call for a hundred thousand state militia, the Federalist governors of New England were openly defiant, refusing to permit their militia to fight outside state boundaries.* Federalist newspapers were filled with disloyal and inflamma-

Divided and Unprepared

---

*There were in fact 695,000 militia on state rolls in 1811–1812, but the quality varied considerably. The best equipped were in Massachusetts and Connecticut. In some other states, including Delaware and Maryland, the militia possessed one firearm for every ten men.

tory appeals. "Anything, everything," advised one Bostonian, should be done "not to be involved in the war." Another writer suggested the formation of a league of commercial states to "defy the enmity and machinations of the slaveholders and backwoods men." Madison was reelected in 1812, but in New England he won only in Vermont (a frontier state). In that region the conflict was commonly called "Mr. Madison's war," and the possibility of secession advanced with each year of the war. Many observers predicted it as a certainty. Little wonder, then, that a visitor reported Madison looking "miserably shattered and woebegone. His mind is full of the New England sedition."

Scarcely a month after Congress declared war General William Hull led a force of twenty-two hundred men out of Detroit into Canada, promising the residents that they would "be emancipated from Tyranny and oppression and restored to the dignified station of freemen." A good many Canadians responded, coming over to the American side, but not enough, and Hull soon retreated to Detroit. British regulars and Canadian militia, with their Indian allies, captured Chicago. Another British force, led by General Isaac Brock, took Detroit without firing a shot! Hull was later court-martialed, tried for treason, cowardice, neglect of duty, and bad conduct. Cleared of the first two charges, he was sentenced to death for the last two, but Madison remitted the sentence. Even more disgraceful was the account of the American invasion of Canada across the Niagara River in October 1812. Though shot through both thighs and with a force of only 240 men, Captain John Wool had gained command of a strategic height and waited in confidence for reenforcements from the New York militia. But many militiamen refused to go, knowing they could not be made to fight outside their state; and they warned their officers that any attempts to punish them would be remembered at the next election. Wool's troops had to surrender. General Henry Dearborn led a third expedition from Plattsburgh, New York, with Montreal as the objective. At the border he authorized a unit of six hundred regulars under the command of Colonel Zebulon M. Pike (the explorer) to invade; and a separate column of four hundred militia decided to cross, taking a different path. They met at dawn and in error fired on each other, at a cost of fifty casualties. Other militia refused to leave New York. Dearborn was not really anxious to fight and marched the remaining troops back to Plattsburgh. "It would appear," he concluded, "that something like fatality has pervaded our military operations through the course of this campaign."

On the seas a different story unfolded in 1812. Much of the Royal Navy was stationed elsewhere, and though they still possessed a numerical superiority in American waters, their ships were slower and less maneuverable. In a series of individual engagements the United States scored some impressive victories. The *Constitution*, under the command of Captain Isaac Hull (a nephew of the general), took the measure of HMS *Guerriere* in half an hour. So humiliated was the British government that it permitted no word of this debacle to be reported in England. Moreover, they ordered British naval officers to try to avoid single-ship combat with American warships.

Defeats and Victories

In August 1812, the Constitution, with a crew of 456, defeated the British frigate Guerriere, carrying 272 men. Seven Americans and thirteen British sailors were killed; seven Americans and sixty-two British were wounded. So devastating was the effect of American firepower that when the British surrendered, Hull ordered the Guerriere scuttled as a useless wreck. (The Bettmann Archive)

Captain David Porter of the *Essex*, the smallest American frigate, captured seven British ships in two months. The *United States*, commanded by Captain Stephen Decatur, sailing near the Azores, engaged the British *Macedonian* in October 1812, killed and wounded 108 of the enemy to 12 American casualties, and brought the defeated warship back to New York as a prize. There were other victories (and a few losses) for the United States— and Britain, so absolutely confident of its prior invincibility upon the oceans, did not relish the taste of defeat. The British began to concentrate more warships off the American coast in 1813, tightening a blockade that bottled up most of the American navy for the remainder of the war.

By that time the fortunes of war on the continent had improved for the United States. Captain Oliver Perry captured a British squadron on Lake Erie. "We have met the enemy," he reported in words that were to become famous, "and they are ours: two ships, two brigs, one schooner, and one sloop." The British, abandoning Detroit, were pursued and defeated by General William Henry Harrison at the battle of the Thames (near Ontario) in October 1813. Tecumseh was killed in this engagement. An American raid on Toronto got out of hand. Though the British troops surrendered, the Americans proceeded to burn the parliamentary buildings and the governor's residence. The British retaliated by capturing Fort Niagara and burning the town of Buffalo.

In 1814, after Napoleon's defeat and abdication, the British decided to put an end to the military stalemate in America. Thousands of British veterans were brought over as part of a three-pronged offensive—in the north, to march from Montreal to Lake Champlain and down the Hudson valley; in the south, to take New Orleans and secure control of the Mississippi; and a third amphibious force to raid and harass the Chesapeake region. The last was most successful. The British troops of General Robert Ross marched virtually unopposed to the outskirts of Washington, D.C. They easily defeated an American force, which broke and fled after token opposition (the battle of Bladensburg), and then proceeded to burn much of the capital. The British enjoyed the spectacle, joked about it, and dined at the White House (at a table already set for the president's dinner) before setting it afire. But they could not take Baltimore. They pounded Fort McHenry for twenty-five hours, and when an observer, Francis Scott Key, saw the flag still flying at daybreak, he composed what was to become the national anthem. The destruction of Washington was psychologically shocking—thousands of angry Americans hastened to enlist—but of no particular military significance. In the North, however, an American victory in the naval battle at

Admiral George Cockburn and General Robert Ross took pride and delight in burning Washington in 1814. Cockburn went so far as to personally supervise the destruction of the offices of the National Intelligencer, *ordering his soldiers to "destroy all C's so they can't abuse my name." Americans protested that even Napoleon, who had entered many an enemy capital in triumph, had never burned them. Some British citizens agreed. "If there is such a thing as humanized war," commented the* Annual Register, *a British journal, "it's principle must consist in inflicting no other evils upon the enemy than are necessary to promote the success of warlike operations." (Courtesy of the Boston Public Library, Print Department)*

Plattsburgh (September 11, 1814) was decisive in stopping the main British invading force. British troops under General George Prevost far outnumbered the Americans (eleven thousand to thirty-three hundred). Prevost, however, would not proceed unless he had control of Lake Champlain. It was Captain Thomas MacDonough's superior tactical skill in naval warfare and hard fighting, gunwale to gunwale, that vanquished the British and prompted Prevost to retreat to Canada.

Scarcely four months later, on January 8, 1815, at New Orleans, a large army of seasoned British troops, men who had fought against the French in Spain, led by Sir Edward Pakenham, met a motley army of Tennessee and Kentucky militia and local volunteers consisting of blacks, Indians, Creoles, pirates, and sailors led by Andrew Jackson. Neither side realized that a peace treaty had been concluded a few weeks earlier. Neither side could have predicted how spectacularly one-sided would be the outcome. In fact, all the assumptions were that the British would win. Thus, when the results were reported—192 British (including Pakenham) to 13 Americans killed; 1,265 British to 13 Americans wounded, for that one day alone—the spirit of the nation swelled in nationalistic pride, a spirit that had been dormant through the war. "INCREDIBLE VICTORY!! GLORIOUS!" read the newspaper headlines, "RISING GLORY OF THE AMERICAN REPUBLIC!"

The numerous ironies of the war were all but forgotten. The War of 1812 had been declared after Britain had repealed its Orders in Council. Its greatest battle took place after a peace treaty had been signed. And that treaty was silent on the main issues, neutral rights and impressment.

The Treaty of Ghent

News of Russia's offer to act as mediator between the United States and England first reached America in March 1813. The way in which Federalists and Republicans responded to the offer tells us much of their respective attitudes. Federalists, unbelieving and distrustful, attacked the news as either spurious or worthless. Some considered it to be false information designed to spur lagging subscriptions to government war loans. Gouverneur Morris accepted it as the truth but said it accorded perfectly with Madison's desire to continue the war, "for if he did not he would have declined a Mediation which tends to delay." Actually Madison was so anxious to have the war negotiated that he appointed a bipartisan mission without knowing whether Great Britain would agree. Albert Gallatin and James A. Bayard sailed for St. Petersburg where they joined the American minister, John Quincy Adams; there they learned that Britain had spurned Russia's offer. Then Britain agreed to direct negotiations. Madison appointed Henry Clay and Jonathan Russell as additional ministers, and the five Americans finally met with British diplomats at Ghent in Belgium in 1814.

Peace was made possible only after both sides relaxed their demands. The American team had been instructed that Britain's abandonment of impressment was an indispensable condition of peace. But by the summer of 1814, with Napoleon's defeat and serious internecine divisions in New England, Madison was prepared to abandon that position. He sent instructions granting the American mission the right to sign a treaty, as a last resort, without mention of impressment. Besides, since the European war had terminated, impressment became a theoretical question rather than a practiced abuse. The Americans were told to negotiate a treaty based upon status quo ante bellum (the same conditions as before the war). The British, however, came to Ghent with extravagant demands. They wanted cessions of territory in New York, in Maine, and along the Great Lakes; and the creation of a separate, independent Indian nation in the Northwest to act as a buffer between the United States and Canada. The American ministers flatly rejected such terms. John Adams, in retirement, advised Madison that he "would continue this war forever rather than surrender an acre." Not until November 1814 did Britain retreat from its position. The duke of Wellington advised the British cabinet that to prolong the war would be prohibitively expensive and strategically unwise. "The state of military operations" in America, he said, did not warrant their territorial demands. Besides, the possibility of renewed conflict in Europe made it expedient for Britain to settle the war in America.

The Treaty of Ghent, signed on Christmas Eve, simply restored prewar boundaries. The United States did not gain a foot of Canadian territory, nor did it extract any concession of neutral maritime rights from the British. Yet Americans regarded the treaty as a triumph. Coming soon after news of Jackson's victory at New Orleans, the two events were celebrated throughout the nation. Almost overnight, Madison became a popular president, congratulated for his perseverance "in a season of darkness and difficulty." Schisms within the Republican party were miraculously (if temporarily) cured. The peace, Albert Gallatin noted, "has renewed and reinstated the national feelings which the Revolution had given and which were daily lessened. The people have now more general objects of attachment with which their pride and political opinions are connected. They are more American. They feel and act more like a nation; and I hope that the permanency of the Union is thereby better secured."

Andrew Jackson's victory at New Orleans came after the peace treaty was signed, but its symbolic and psychological impact upon the American people was enormous. "I cannot, sir, perhaps language cannot, do justice to the merits of General Jackson and the troops under his command," George Troup of Georgia told the House of Representatives. "It is a fit subject for the genius of Homer." The war has ended "in a blaze of glory," wrote one editor. Poems and speeches and stories soon raised the victory at New Orleans to legendary proportions—and Jackson to the White House. (American Antiquarian Society)

The War of 1812, according to Samuel E. Morison, was "the most unpopular war this country has ever waged, not even excepting the Vietnam conflict." Opposition to it, though naturally concentrated in New England, was widespread. Federalist politicians stimulated popular discontents, and the more extreme openly discussed the merits of secession. John Lowell proposed that a new federal constitution be drawn up, safeguarding New England's commercial interests, and presented to other states as an ultimatum. In November 1814 the *Boston Gazette* predicted that "if James Madison is not out of office [by next July], a new form of government will be in operation in the eastern section of the Union." The *Columbian Centinel,* another Boston newspaper, stated: "The bond of union is already broken by you, Mr. Madison." Timothy Pickering was again at the center of disunionist activities, zealous as ever. Finally the Massachusetts legislature issued a call for a convention "to lay the foundation for a radical reform in the National compact." Rhode Island and Connecticut officially accepted the call. Representatives of local groups from Vermont and New Hampshire also indicated their willingness to attend. Were this convention, which met at Hartford for three weeks, beginning in December, 1814, to advocate secession, the people of New England undoubtedly were ready to accept the decision.

From the outset, however, the Hartford Convention was controlled by moderates. "The worst of all evils," said George Cabot, head of the Massachusetts delegation, "would be a dissolution of the Union." Most other delegates, including Harrison G. Otis and Joseph Lyman, shared this sentiment. Extremists railed at the timidity of its members, but in vain. After indicting Madison's administration for poor and partisan leadership—representing only agrarian interests, neglecting the defense of the coast, attempting unconstitutional control of state militia, discriminating against commerce—the Hartford Convention passed a series of suggested constitutional amendments to strengthen the bonds of union:

1. Abrogation of the three-fifths clause.
2. A two-thirds vote of Congress to admit new states.
3. A two-thirds vote of Congress for legislation restricting commerce.
4. A two-thirds vote of Congress for any declaration of war.
5. No enforcement of an embargo for more than sixty days.
6. Only native-born citizens, not naturalized ones, as officeholders in the federal government.
7. A one-term limit for the president; nor could that person be chosen from the same geographical area as his predecessor.

Twenty-six delegates signed the resolutions. Three members—Harrison Otis, William Sullivan, and Thomas Perkins—were assigned the responsibility of presenting them to the national government. By the time they arrived in Washington, news of Jackson's victory at New Orleans and of the Treaty of Ghent made their task futile. "Their position," commented the French minister, Louis Serurier, "was awkward, embarrassing, and lent itself cruelly to ridicule." They paid their respects to Madison but left without performing their mission.

COMMENTARY

Only a quarter of a century had passed since the ratification of the Constitution had launched a new nation, which had survived authoritarian impulses, secessionist plots, political alarms, and British arms. The "withered little apple-John," by a combination of fortune and fortitude, had steered the American people from near disaster to a new era of national self-respect. With a free and open land stretching to the Rockies, with a commercial potential destined to rule the oceans, with a solid peace and flourishing economy, with a vigorous and harmonious people in the full possession of liberty, no one in 1815 could doubt the American future. The party Madison had formed and then codirected with Jefferson was now the obvious party of that future. "A glorious opportunity" presented itself, wrote Joseph Story, "for the Republican party to place themselves permanently in power."

SUGGESTED READING

THOMAS P. ABERNETHY, *The Burr Conspiracy* (1954)

HENRY ADAMS, *History of the United States of America During the Administrations of Jefferson and Madison* (1891)

JAMES M. BANNER, *To the Hartford Convention* (1969)

WINFRED BERNHARD, *Fisher Ames* (1965)

ALBERT BEVERIDGE, *John Marshall* (1916)

ROBERT H. BROWN, *The Republic in Peril* (1964)

HARRY COLES, *The War of 1812* (1965)

NOBLE CUNNINGHAM, *The Jeffersonian Republicans in Power: Party Operations, 1801–1809* (1963)

BERNARD DE VOTO, *The Journals of Lewis and Clark* (1953)

RICHARD ELLIS, *The Jeffersonian Crisis* (1971)

DAVID FISCHER, *The Revolution of American Conservatism* (1965)

LINDA KERBER, *Federalists in Dissent* (1970)

RALPH KETCHAM, *From Colony to Country: The Revolution in American Thought, 1750–1820* (1974)

ADRIENNE KOCH, *Jefferson and Madison: The Great Collaboration* (1950)

LEONARD LEVY, *Jefferson and Civil Liberties: The Darker Side* (1963)

JOHN K. MAHON, *The War of 1812* (1972)

FORREST MCDONALD, *The Presidency of Thomas Jefferson* (1976)

SAMUEL E. MORISON, *Life and Letters of Harrison G. Otis* (1913)

————, FREDERICK MERK, and FRANK FREIDEL, *Dissent in Three American Wars* (1970)

BRADFORD PERKINS, *Prologue to War* (1961)

MERRILL D. PETERSON, *The Jefferson Image in the American Mind* (1960)

NORMAN K. RISJORD, *Forging the American Republic* (1973)

LOUIS SEARS, *Jefferson and the Embargo* (1927)

MARSHALL SMELSER, *The Democratic Republic, 1801–1815* (1968)

RAYMOND WALTERS, *Albert Gallatin* (1957)

LEONARD WHITE, *The Jeffersonians* (1951)

6

Jacksonian Democracy, 1815–1840

An Era of Good Feelings

The year 1815 is a natural dividing point in American history. Until that date the political fortunes of the United States had been intimately connected with those of Europe. After it Americans turned inward to face the task of exploring and conquering the West. Lands had to be settled, Indians removed, lines of transportation constructed, states formed, and boundaries defined. While nineteenth-century Americans pursued what they called their Manifest Destiny, Europeans were occupied with crushing post-Napoleonic rebellions. The spirit of industrial enterprise flowered on both continents, but in Europe (though not in Britain) it was a spindly growth, retarded by old concepts and autocratic governments. By the middle of the century a triangular conflict had developed in Europe between reactionary monarchists, liberal capitalists, and socialist workers. In the United States, on the other hand, enterprise was encouraged by democracy and social mobility. The future was enticing, promising a rich reward open to anyone with initiative. Success, measured in material accomplishment, became part of the American faith.

When President James Monroe visited Boston in 1817 a Federalist newspaper announced the event as marking an "Era of Good Feelings." The phrase is apt, if limited to a relatively brief period following the War of 1812. Jackson's smashing victory at New Orleans was precisely the adrenalin the American people needed. Divided in war, they rejoiced in triumph and united in peace. Although political bickering was vile and scurrilous, it was generally local and personal. The Federalist party continued to function but only in token opposition. Candidates seeking high national office had to operate within the Republican structure if they wanted to be successful. Economically the nation, still principally agrarian, appeared prosperous. Cotton production, stimulated by Eli Whitney's cotton gin, increased as prices in Britain soared in 1816 and 1817. Land values rose accordingly, catalyzed by easy credit and the vast quantities of paper money issued by state banks.

Economic Nationalism

Victory, prosperity, opportunity, and one-party rule fostered the growth of nationalistic sentiment. A Republican Congress in 1816 swallowed its scruples and

Eli Whitney completed the first working model of his cotton gin in 1793. Crude but effective, it consisted of rollers with wire teeth, which tore the cotton from the seed. Operated by hand, it equaled the labor of ten workers; operated by horse power, it equaled that of fifty. The machine was easily duplicated by any plantation blacksmith, and improvements were made by other inventors. (Whitney unsuccessfully sued for patent infringements.) After the War of 1812 Whitney's gin helped stimulate the spectacular growth of cotton. In a decade cotton production quadrupled, with far-reaching social and political consequences. (Library of Congress)

enacted the first tariff in American history designed more for protection than for revenue. In a sense it was an emergency measure; the British were shipping huge quantities of manufactured goods of superior quality and at cheaper prices than the infant American industries could supply. New England cotton manufacturers, mill owners in Carolina, entrepreneurs of iron foundries in Pennsylvania, and hemp producers in Kentucky called for relief. The idea of a protective tariff was definitely Federalist, but James Madison recommended it to provide a competitive edge and to spur the further growth of American industry. The vote in the House of Representatives showed Federalists favored the tariff by a bare majority (twenty-five to twenty-three), while Republicans supported it by more than two to one (sixty-three to thirty-one). How does one explain such a vote? First, many northern Federalists, such as Daniel Webster, reflecting the views of New England's import merchants, believed a high tariff would damage their commercial interests. Shipping and a flourishing foreign trade—not domestic manufacturing—were their primary concerns. Second, many southern Republicans favored the law out of patriotic and nationalistic considerations. Although the chief beneficiaries were northern businessmen, the southerners believed even they deserved protection from the late enemy. "Southern leaders believed that they controlled the triumphant Republican party, and with it the machinery of the central government," George Dangerfield notes. "Their nationalism rose and fell with this sense of control, so one could say, without risking a paradox, that in the last two years of James Madison's Presidency the congressional South was most nationalistic when it was most sectional."

A second important piece of legislation enacted by the Republicans in 1816 established the second Bank of the United States. Its economic value seemed indisputable, but Republican supporters had to answer as best they could the charges of inconsistency and espousal of Federalist measures. James Madison contrasted the "unassuming spirit" of Republicanism to Federalist arrogance. Henry Clay had opposed the rechartering of the first Bank in 1811 on constitutional grounds. Now, as Speaker of the House, he explained his change of heart as resulting from "the force of circumstance and the lights of experience." The vote shows northern and middle state congressmen opposed the Bank (fifty-three to forty-four); southern and western congressmen approved it (fifty-eight to thirty). Obviously, a good many Republicans realized that their old doctrines were impotent and that adjustment was vital. Although their rhetoric remained Jeffersonian, many of their actions were plainly Hamiltonian. The major congressional spokesmen for economic nationalism were Henry Clay of Kentucky and John C. Calhoun of South Carolina. Clay championed the Bank, the protective tariff, and a federal transportation network, later termed the "American system," as vital elements designed to harmonize sectional interests and to free the United States from overdependence on foreign markets. Calhoun agreed. "We are great, and rapidly . . . growing," he warned Congress. "This is our pride and danger, our weakness and our strength. . . . Let us bind the republic together with a perfect system of roads and canals. Let us conquer space."

Still, economic nationalism had limits. In 1817 Calhoun sponsored and Congress passed the "Bonus Bill," which called for using a million and a half dollars plus annual dividends received from the Bank for internal improvements. Madison vetoed it as an improper and "inadmissible latitude" of constitutional construction. "The permanent success of the Constitution," he reasoned, "depends on a definite partition of powers between the General and State Governments." Moreover, the nationalism expressed by Republican leaders was temporary—an immediate postwar phenomenon—and evaporated when it no longer served the interests of their particular section.

Profound and disturbing social changes took place throughout the nation in the decade following the War of 1812. Few quite understood the nature of these changes. Many feared the consequences. Virginia was undergoing an economic and cultural decline. New England was building factories. The West attracted hordes of eastern migrants and, later, foreign immigrants. The lower South dreamed of diversification, but cotton became king. This economic expansion was sparking an egalitarian impulse. Socially the scale was tipping away from old aristocrats to new entrepreneurs. The "good feeling" was merely window dressing. In 1822 Thomas Jefferson complained of "many calling themselves Republicans and preaching the rankest doctrines of the old Federalists." As the window dressing was removed it revealed the beginnings of sectional conflict and the struggle between economic classes for control of the nation.

Chief Justice John Marshall had little use for Republicans, even those who had come to appreciate and preach neo-Hamiltonian doctrines. Their commitment to nationalism was temporary and expedient; his was basic, princi-

Legal Nationalism

pled, compelling, and enduring. For thirty-five years Marshall dominated the Supreme Court. While fashions varied and opinions shifted, he remained an unswerving and persuasive advocate of nationalism. During his tenure, the complexion of the Court changed as Federalists died out and Republican presidents made new appointments, but Marshall's opinions prevailed. Rarely was he in the minority. He spoke for the Court in case after case, defining the federal system to enhance national and limit state authority. When Maryland attempted to tax a branch of the Bank of the United States, the Court struck down the state law. Following Hamilton's logic and even paraphrasing his prose, Marshall declared that Congress had the right to use any appropriate means—including the Bank—to exercise its legitimate powers. Those powers were supreme. A state could not be permitted to tax and perhaps thereby destroy an instrument of the federal government (*McCulloch* v. *Maryland*, 1819). Two years later Marshall delivered a second masterful exposition of the authority of Congress and the federal courts. Two brothers had been arrested, convicted, and fined by a Virginia court for selling lottery tickets in that state, contrary to law. They maintained that the lottery was authorized by Congress and appealed directly to the Supreme Court for relief. Lawyers for Virginia denied that the Supreme Court had any authority to review the finding of the state court. Marshall rejected that argument categorically. If the appellate jurisdiction of the Supreme Court were taken away, declared Marshall, "every other branch of federal authority might as well be surrendered. To part with this, leaves the Union a mere league or confederacy" (*Cohens* v. *Virginia*, 1821). Another opportunity to reaffirm the supremacy of the national government presented itself in 1824. When New York granted a steamship company a monopoly to operate on the Hudson River, a competitor carrying goods between New York and New Jersey objected. Marshall declared the state law unconstitutional. The Constitution had granted Congress the exclusive power over interstate commerce, Marshall reasoned. Therefore, "the subject is as completely taken from the state legislatures as if they had been expressly forbidden to act on it" (*Gibbons* v. *Ogden*, 1824).

On thirteen occasions the Marshall court reversed state laws it held to be contrary to the Constitution. Some of these cases involved interpretations of the law of contracts, which alarmed states' rights advocates. For example, the Georgia legislature, bribed by land speculators, sold some thirty-five million acres for five hundred thousand dollars; an aroused public voted in a new legislature, which promptly declared the act of cession to be fraudulent and void. But in *Fletcher* v. *Peck* (1810), Marshall cited the provision of the Constitution that declares that no state shall pass a "law impairing the obligation of contracts." Once a contract is executed it cannot be invalidated. Thus despite the corruption involved, the state law repealing the sale was found to be unconstitutional. The more famous case of *Dartmouth College* v. *Woodward* (1819) originated in a quarrel between the New Hampshire legislature (controlled by Republicans) and Dartmouth College trustees (supported by Federalists). The college operated under a royal charter granted in 1769. The legislature wished to reverse that charter, appoint new trustees, and thereby convert a private institution into a public one. The counsel for Dartmouth College, Daniel Webster, argued that the royal charter was a grant, that a grant is a contract, and that a state could not impair "the obligation of contracts." "A grant of corporate powers and privileges," Webster stated, "is as much a contract as a grant of land." Marshall, speaking for the Court, agreed. The New Hampshire laws affecting Dartmouth College were struck down, providing a precedent protecting all private educational institutions from state interference. But the impact of the decision was much broader. Business corporations, which received their charters from state legislatures, came under the same ruling: once the grant was made it could not be rescinded or altered.

Marshall's decisions thus served the purpose of fostering nationalism and capitalism. The two, linked in his mind, were vital components for the survival of the United States. "Marshall and his colleagues on the bench expected great things from the unchained forces of capitalism," R. Kent Newmyer concludes. "National commerce would forge lasting bonds of national union. The conservative class of businessmen and lawyers who rose to guide the forces of capitalism would replace the vanishing gentleman ruler of the old republic and counterbalance the untrustworthy professional, democratic politician." But by the mid-1820s economic nationalism was being replaced by sectional selfishness; elitism in politics by the common man; and a new democratic breed of entrepreneurs rallying round the figure of Andrew Jackson began to challenge the power of the privileged few.

Diplomatic Nationalism

Few statesmen have served America more faithfully or conscientiously than John Quincy Adams. The wisdom of President Monroe's decision to appoint him secretary of state in 1817 was confirmed by Adams's accomplishments. Expert in diplomatic affairs, aloof from politics, and dedicated to the national interest, he made several important contributions to the foundations of American foreign policy. Adams believed that the "natural dominion" of the United States extended to the Pacific Ocean, and his purpose was to stretch the country's boundary across the entire continent. Two nations, Britain and Spain, contested American territorial rights in the West. Adams's diplomacy with each was masterful. Using persuasion or intimidation, as the case warranted, ready to compromise but unwilling to yield on essentials, he accomplished his goal in two years.

In 1818 a treaty was concluded with Britain establishing the American-Canadian boundary from the Great Lakes to the Rocky Mountains. The land beyond was left open to colonization by citizens of both countries for a ten-year period. This arrangement was continued until 1846 when a permanent boundary was set for the Northwest. Adams's negotiations with Spain were more difficult but equally successful. By the Adams-Onís Treaty of 1819 the United States acquired Florida. To western expansionists the treaty was most significant for its definition of the Spanish-American boundary. A jagged line was drawn from Louisiana to the forty-second latitude and then

Taken shortly before his death in 1848, this picture of John Quincy Adams conveys his iron-willed character. A confirmed nationalist and expansionist, he wanted the United States boundary extended to the Pacific Ocean. He also urged America to support the cause of republicanism in other lands. "Wherever the standard of freedom and independence has been or shall be unfurled," he stated in 1821, "there will her heart, her benedictions and her prayers be." But, he warned, the United States should not go "abroad in search of monsters to destroy." The danger is that America "might become the dictatress of the world. She would no longer be the ruler of her own spirit." (Brown Brothers)

west to the Pacific. Although Adams sacrificed American claims to parts of present-day Texas, he opened a gateway to the Pacific. "The acknowledgement of a definite line of boundary to the South Sea forms a great epoch of our history," recorded Adams with pride. "The first proposal of it . . . was my own."

Monroe's outstanding achievement during his second term was the announcement of the Monroe Doctrine, although credit for it properly should be shared with John Quincy Adams. In 1823 the British suggested to the United States that the two governments guarantee the independence of South American countries against any invasion by European powers. The agreement was designed to prohibit both countries from ever acquiring any of these territories. Jefferson and Madison advised acceptance, and Monroe was prepared—if the British foreign secretary, George Canning, had not changed his mind—to conclude the arrangement. The threat of an invasion of Latin America by armies of the Holy Alliance convinced several cabinet members of the necessity of the agreement. French and Austrian troops had suppressed revolutions in Naples, Piedmont, and Spain. A Russian note stated that the intention of the Holy Alliance was the restoration of "tranquility" everywhere. Secretary of War John C. Calhoun, certain that an army of ten thousand would sail from Cadiz, argued for cooperation with Britain.

"It would be more candid, as well as more dignified," stated Adams, "to avow our principles explicitly to Russia and France, than to come in as a cockboat in the wake of the British-man-of-war." He correctly guessed that there was little chance of an invasion of Latin America by European powers. Even if one were attempted, he knew that Britain's navy was powerful enough alone to stop it. Nor did Adams want to restrict the possibility of American growth, as he suspected Britain intended to do by the alliance. Perhaps some day, Adams hoped, Texas and Cuba might be peacefully annexed to the United States. It is "a settled geographical element," he had informed an earlier cabinet, "that the United States and North America are identical." Adams's logic persuaded Monroe. Largely from his concepts, then, was born the doctrine of 1823, which was included in a presidential address to Congress. It contained three major points:

1. The United States would not tolerate any future colonization by European powers in the Western Hemisphere.
2. The United States would regard any foreign interference with or attempted control over any independent nation in the Western Hemisphere as an unfriendly act, "dangerous to our peace and safety."
3. The United States would stay out of European wars with which it was not concerned. "It is only when our rights are invaded, or seriously menaced, that we resent injuries, or make preparations for our defense."

The Panic of 1819

The exuberance of the era of good feelings received its first rude shock from a financial crisis that began in 1818, became a panic in 1819, and lingered for years. It was the first major depression to strike America. Like those that followed throughout the nineteenth and twentieth centuries, the cause of the panic was partly international: a shortage of specie brought about by South American revolutions, a shift in European demands for American staples, rapidly increasing world competition, and declining commodity prices. And part of the cause was domestic: an enormous postwar speculation in land.

Before the War of 1812 one in seven Americans lived west of the Appalachian mountains; ten years later one in four was a westerner. New states were added to the Union in rapid succession: Indiana in 1816, Mississippi in 1817, Illinois in 1818, and Alabama in 1819. By 1820, it should be remembered, Ohio had a larger population than Massachusetts. Under the United States Land Act of 1804 a citizen could purchase one hundred sixty acres at two dollars per acre with only a 25 percent down payment (eighty dollars); the remainder fell due within four years. But even the down payment could be paid with paper currency borrowed from state or private banks, and the value of this money was often questionable. In 1817, just before the economic collapse, those banks issued over a hundred million dollars in paper money, much of which was not negotiable in other communities. There seemed no limit to land values: credit was easy, cotton was selling at more than thirty cents a pound because of the apparently insatiable demand of British textile manufacturers, and Europe was calling for more tobacco and more grains, causing prices to soar. In 1815 land sales amounted to one million acres; by 1819 the figure was five million acres. Town and city lots were selling at record levels. In the Southwest, the so-called Black Belt of Alabama and Mississippi, land was being auctioned off at more than a hundred dollars per acre.

The first signs of economic collapse came when cotton prices on the British market tumbled, and land prices in the South and West plunged disastrously. At the same time the Bank of the United States, which had initially abetted the speculative frenzy by easy credit, under new management in 1818, began to tighten its loan regulations. Its branches were ordered to redeem their holdings of state and private bank paper in specie. These banks in turn were forced to call in their loans to farmers and speculators. The inflationary bubble was pricked and the deflation was immediate. The entire American economy shuddered. Tens of thousands lost their savings. Bankruptcies multiplied. Commerce faltered. Unemployment mounted. In New York City and Philadelphia alone, there were forty thousand laborers out of work. Every class was affected: bankers, merchants, planters, farmers, industrialists, workers. Imprisonment was common for nonpayment of debt, an anachronism in a capitalist society whose very foundations rested on the concept of credit.

The depression was most acute in the urban West. In Pittsburgh, Cincinnati, Lexington, and Nashville, property values plummeted, and scores of businesses failed. Some westerners, seeking a scapegoat, attacked the second Bank of the United States. "All the flourishing cities of the West," Thomas Hart Benton of Missouri later remarked, "are mortgaged to this money power. They may be devoured by it at any moment. They are in the jaws of the monster! A lump of butter in the mouth of a dog! One gulp, one swallow, and all is gone!" The Bank may have precipitated but it hardly caused the depression. Nevertheless, a western legacy of hatred for the Bank lingered for many years. Not until the end of the 1820s did the Bank regain the esteem of many westerners as an important source of capital for agricultural loans.

A second event that tarnished the nationalism of the era of good feelings was the unanticipated reemergence of sectional controversy over the territory of Missouri, which petitioned for statehood in 1819. An obscure New York congressman, James Tallmadge, Jr., introduced an amendment to the enabling bill that prohibited the further introduction of slavery into Missouri and provided that the children of slaves born there were to be freed at the age of twenty-five. Scholars have puzzled over Tallmadge's motives. Was he a sincere abolitionist? Or was his amendment inspired by political considerations? Northerners had long sought a way to curb the extension of southern political power. Yet Tallmadge's words seem to show a conscience sincerely outraged by slavery. "It is the cause of the freedom of man!" he argued. "If a dissolution of the Union must take place, let it be so! If civil war . . . must come, I can only say, let it come!" Enough northerners in the lower house agreed with him to pass the amendment. In the Senate, where southerners were equal in strength, the amendment failed.

Americans at this time generally avoided the issue of slavery. Nevertheless, almost a year after Tallmadge's amendment was defeated, the subject of Missouri was again on the floor of Congress. The debates were short but bitter. Southerners were offended by what they regarded as northern hypocrisy and pointed out that prejudice against the black man was quite common above the Mason-Dixon line. Some congressmen (from the lower South) delivered impassioned orations in defense of slavery. Others (from the upper South) preferred to stand on constitutional grounds, denying the right of Congress to impose conditions on the admission of a state. Largely through the benevolent offices of Senator Jesse B. Thomas of Illinois, a compromise was arranged. Slavery was prohibited in the Louisiana territory north of latitude 36°30'. Missouri was permitted to enter the Union as a slave state and Maine as a free state, thus maintaining sectional balance in the upper

Missouri Compromise, 1820

Missouri Compromise, 1820

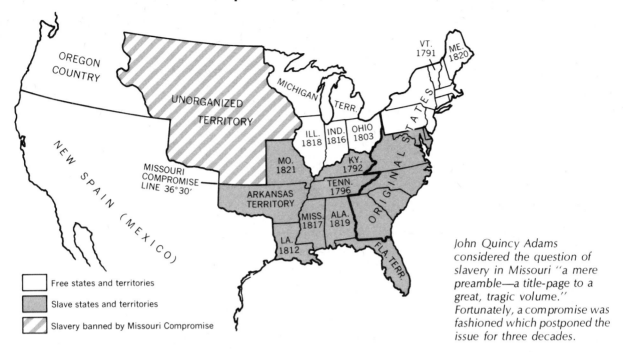

John Quincy Adams considered the question of slavery in Missouri "a mere preamble—a title-page to a great, tragic volume." Fortunately, a compromise was fashioned which postponed the issue for three decades.

house. Although sectional emotions receded, the misunderstanding and distrust remained. "You have kindled a fire," a congressman from Georgia hurled at the North, "which all the waters of the ocean cannot put out, which seas of blood can only extinguish."

Republican Divisions

Still another characteristic of the era of good feelings, Republican unity, was undermined by inept party direction and divisive factions. At the zenith of its power after the War of 1812, the party began to decay because of Monroe's careless political leadership. Monroe was honest and dedicated; he was also simple and unimaginative. His reelection in 1820—in which he received all but one of the electoral college ballots—signified not Republican agreement but popular indifference. Like Washington, Monroe wished to govern by consensus. He chose not to meddle in local affairs, manipulate patronage, or cultivate congressmen. In effect, he refused to captain the Republican vessel. His subordinates schemed and quarreled over his successor.

The political cement crumbled in 1824 when at least five favorite sons sought the presidency. There were "coalitions of every description without the least regard to principle," complained Albert Gallatin. "I see nothing but . . . the fulfillment of personal views and passions." In Tennessee three men—William B. Lewis, John H. Eaton, and John Overton—plotted strategy in behalf of Andrew Jackson. In New York a shrewd politician, Martin Van Buren, decided to continue an old alliance and joined in supporting the choice of the Virginia dynasty, William H. Crawford of Georgia. In Mas-

On January 8, 1824, before the election of that year, Secretary of State John Quincy Adams hosted a reception for his political rival Andrew Jackson. Mrs. Adams prepared decorations made of tissue paper and evergreens. On the floor were chalked eagles, flags, and the words "Welcome to the Hero of New Orleans." A thousand guests were invited. "The ladies climbed on chairs and benches to see General Jackson," Phoebe Morris wrote to Dolly Madison. "Mrs. Adams very gracefully took his arm and walked through the apartments." From left to right, as an artist pictured the scene, the men are John C. Calhoun, Daniel Webster, Jackson, Henry Clay, and Adams.   (Library of Congress)

sachusetts the Republicans opted for their distinguished statesman, John Quincy Adams. In Kentucky the supreme politician, Henry Clay, campaigned for his "American system." John C. Calhoun from South Carolina also sought the main prize. However, he discerned that public opinion was in Jackson's favor. Reluctantly, but wisely, he postponed his own candidacy and joined the Jackson bandwagon.

Old Hickory—an affectionate nickname that Jackson's soldiers invented and his admirers adopted—received a plurality of both the popular and the electoral votes. Adams ran a close second. Crawford and Clay lagged far behind. Since no candidate obtained a majority, the choice—by constitutional provision—fell to the members of the House of Representatives voting by states. A selection was to be made from the three front-runners. Rumors of intrigues and bargains, similar to those that had arisen during the election of 1800, were whispered throughout the capital. They centered on Henry Clay. The Kentuckian had lost the election but controlled enough western congressional votes to make his influence decisive. He ruled out Crawford on several grounds, including the Georgian's ill health and hostility to the tariff. He dismissed Jackson for other reasons, ranging from personal animosity to intellectual unfitness. "I cannot believe that killing 2,500 Englishmen at New Orleans," wrote Clay, "qualifies for the various, difficult, and complicated duties of the Chief Magistrate." Adams was the only logical choice. The two men met together several times. An understanding was reached between them, although Jackson and his followers considered it as a corrupt bargain.

Clay's supporters in the lower house voted for Adams, who won the presidency with thirteen states to Jackson's seven and Crawford's four. A few days later, Adams announced that Clay would become his secretary of state. One scholar has termed this arrangement the result of an entente cordiale. Jackson used a biblical analogy: "The Judas of the West has closed the contract and will receive the thirty pieces of silver. His end will be the same. Was there ever witnessed such barefaced corruption?" The Jacksonians relentlessly and successfully rode the issue of corruption for the next four years. Their man had been cheated. It would not happen again.

Adams could never convey his love of country to the people, nor could he project an exciting image. He was not a great orator. Physically he was short and plump, with a massive bald head. Jackson, by comparison, was long and lean, shaggy-haired, exuding firmness and inspiring confidence. The two would have made an unbeatable political combination. One newspaper in 1824 came out for a ticket of

Adams's Administration

> John Quincy Adams
> Who can write,
> And Andrew Jackson,
> Who can fight.

When Adams was secretary of state he had defended Jackson's high-handed actions in Florida. In 1818, while pursuing the Seminoles, Jackson's forces had captured and summarily executed two British citizens who were suspected of inciting the Indians. Calhoun, Crawford, and other members of the cabinet wanted to punish Old Hickory by court-martial. Adams resisted them, supported Jackson's right to invade Florida, and won Monroe over to his position. Jackson, however, did not know the details of the debate. He assumed that Calhoun had been his defender. After 1825 the Republican party was largely in the hands of the Jacksonians, who began to style themselves "Democrats." Their representatives in Congress sought to stymie, badger, and embarrass Adams.

Historians do not measure presidential greatness by criteria of courage or intelligence. If they did, John Quincy Adams would rank near the top. Success has always been the test, and Adams's administration, it is agreed, was a failure. Adams remained constant while the nation changed. He was too much the elitist, the idealist, the nationalist, in an age that apotheosized the common man. His proposals to encourage science, education, and internal improvements were largely rejected. Even his decision to have the United States participate in a Panama congress ended pathetically. "The American Union, as a moral person in the family of nations," said Adams after he left the presidency, "is to live from hand to mouth, and to cast away instead of using for the improvement of its own condition, the bounties of Providence."

The tariff was not a significant issue in American politics until the 1820s. Gradually, however, and especially after the Tariff of Abominations was passed in 1828, southern leaders came to feel that the tariff penalized their section to the benefit of the North. They viewed it as a tax imposed upon southern agriculture solely to protect commercial and manufacturing interests. In the above cartoon the North grows fat and the South remains skinny because of the tariff. (U.S. Weekly Telegraph, 1832)

The Tariff of Abominations

The failure of the Adams administration was reflected in the Tariff of Abominations passed in 1828. The measure was fashioned chiefly by Jacksonians and was reluctantly signed by Adams. He and Clay had long favored a high tariff to protect infant industry from foreign competition. To the Jacksonians the tariff was a political payoff. Every politician wanted something. Thomas Hart Benton of Missouri wanted duties placed on fur and lead. Mahlon Dickerson of New Jersey asked for one on vermicelli. The bill at first provided for high duties on coarse wool and other raw materials to satisfy the growers. A significant amendment, however, raised the tariff on finished woolen products to please manufacturers. The Jacksonian leaders in Congress had calculated that southern support for Jackson was secure; that northern protectionists could be won over by duties on specified products; and that objectionable provisions in the act could be blamed on the Adams administration. It did not work out that way. The tariff that emerged was impractical and jumbled. Many southerners expressed their outrage at its provisions. The Jacksonians, who had expected to wound Adams, found that they had opened a fissure in their own ranks.

Textile manufacturing had advanced considerably in New England in a decade and now competed with commerce for economic precedence. When commerce was dominant, New England had consistently favored low tariffs; as a center of manufacturing, however, the area wanted no competition from British goods. Daniel Webster of Massachusetts, who had advocated free trade in the past, dramatically declared himself in favor of protection. Four other New England senators agreed with him. Their votes, completely unexpected, were instrumental in passing the Tariff of Abominations. Many southerners had also reversed their stands. In 1816, in the first flush of postwar nationalism, southern leaders had supported protection. Since then they had come to regard the North as an economic foe and the tariff as an unjust tax imposed upon their section. "We of the South," wrote Thomas Cooper of South Carolina, "hold our plantations as the serfs and operatives of the North." The southerners opposed the tariff almost to a man. John C. Calhoun, the ultranationalist of 1816, secretly became a spokesman of states' rights. Expecting to follow Jackson into the presidency, he felt it would not be wise to express his hostility to the tariff openly. Moreover, he and other southerners thought that Jackson would correct the tariff inequities after the election.

The tariff had no appreciable effect on the election of 1828. Jackson's charismatic personality transcended all issues. Unlike the hydraheaded race of 1824, there were only two factions. Adams represented the aristocratic past, Jackson the democratic future. Jackson swept the election of 1828 by approximately forty thousand votes. He captured every western and southern state except Maryland, which divided its electoral vote. Pennsylvania was overwhelmingly behind him; New York gave him twenty of its thirty-six votes. Only in New England did Adams secure a majority. During the inauguration ceremonies on March 4, 1829, an enormous crowd poured into the capital to celebrate the election of Old Hickory. Jackson inspired their confidence and adulation, but many older Federalists and Republicans despaired. There was a quality about Jackson that the elite distrusted. John Quincy Adams called him a "barbarian." Chief Justice Marshall's reaction was typical. "Should Jackson be elected," he prophesied, "I shall look upon the government as virtually dissolved."

Jackson's Victory

Three particular qualities of Andrew Jackson initially attracted the admiration of the American people. First, he was the war hero who had conquered the haughty British at New Orleans. But he was not regarded as a professional soldier. Rather, he was idealized as the citizen-soldier, beloved by all, who had traditionally left the farm to defend their country from invasion. Second, he was the recognized head of the emerging Democratic party. But he was not regarded as a compromiser, like Henry Clay, or a self-seeking professional politician. Rather, he was seen as a selfless private citizen who reluctantly had accepted a political post to restore government to the people. Third, although Jackson was actually a rich man, a slaveholder, and a plantation aristocrat, the people chose to envision him as a champion of the masses. "If elected, which I trust in God you will be," his friend John Branch had predicted, "you will owe your election to the people, Yes Sir, to the unbiased, unbought suffrages of the independent, grateful yeomanry of this country. You will come into the Executive chair untrammeled, free to pursue the dictates of your own judgment." What those judgments were remained an enigma.

The significance of Jacksonian democracy is to be found partly in the figure and personality of Andrew Jackson, partly in the way people perceived him. He represented the different, even contradictory aspirations of groups with different, even contradictory, interests in American society. Jackson was not politically astute or sophisticated enough to project these various images. His judgments and decisions were mainly instinctive. Sometimes people imputed meanings to Jackson, and interpretations of the democracy he symbolized, that he would scarcely have recognized. For whom did he speak? The western farmer? The urban worker? The party stalwart? The rich planter? The new entrepreneur? The so-called common man? Jackson spoke for all. He was their demigod, created by them to serve their purposes. The fierce loyalties he evoked were understandable but irrational, for in 1829 no one knew Jackson's attitude toward any major issue or his philosophy of government. In the campaign he displayed a positive mastery of political double-talk. He swore to uphold states' rights, but he also insisted that the states must acknowledge their membership in an indestructible union. He assured voters of his Jeffersonian beliefs, and he also claimed no hostility to "domestic manufactures or internal works." Was he entitled to wear the Jeffersonian mantle? In 1824 Jefferson told Thomas Gilmer that "one might as well make a sailor of a cock, or a soldier of a goose, as a President of Andrew Jackson."

Calhoun Versus Van Buren

The vice-president, John C. Calhoun of South Carolina, and his supporters in Congress and the Cabinet expected to steer Jackson toward the South. Calhoun had every hope of succeeding Jackson to the presidency. If Jackson were "King Andrew," as the opposition labeled him, Calhoun wanted very much to be the heir apparent. Within two years of the election, however, a complete change took place. Jackson repudiated Calhoun and dismissed his followers. Virtually all the national influence Calhoun possessed, the result of the meticulous political labors of a decade, disintegrated. The national destiny, represented and guided by Jackson, took on a northern and western complexion.

The story of Calhoun's downfall involved a saucy and reputedly promiscuous woman, Margaret (Peggy) O'Neale, whose family owned one of Washington's most renowned boardinghouses. O'Neale eventually married, and Jackson in 1824 became acquainted with her as Mrs. Timberlake. He saw nothing exceptional in her behavior: evenings she entertained at the piano; Sundays she and the O'Neales accompanied Jackson to church. To capital gossips, however, Peggy had long been a subject of speculation. She was alleged to have been the cause of a young man's suicide and of an old general's daft behavior. Timberlake often was at sea as a ship's purser, and Peggy was squired by Jackson's close friend, Senator John Henry Eaton. Eaton was young, wealthy, and a widower. He helped finance Peggy's father, and she was naturally grateful. The capital in 1828 buzzed with scandalous stories of their relationship. When Timberlake died at sea, Eaton—at Jackson's insistence—married Peggy. Eaton became Jackson's secretary of war. His wife, who looked forward to a round of pleasant parties, dinner engagements, society balls, and carriage rides with other ladies, was cruelly disappointed. The Eatons were snubbed, notably by the wives of Calhoun's supporters in the cabinet. Apparently their wives had more influence upon them than the president. "John C. Calhoun and his followers remained conspicuously uncooperative with Old Hickory's effort to induce society to accept the marriage he had pushed his friend into," according to Marquis James. One cabinet member who did accept an Eaton invitation, however, was Calhoun's competitor, the widower Martin Van Buren. The public humiliation of the Eatons became a major internal issue in Jackson's administration. All over Washington the question of Peggy Eaton's previous virtue, or lack thereof, was debated. Evidence was collected, depositions taken. A rather unique meeting of the cabinet was held to consider the question, at which Jackson exploded. "She is as chaste as a virgin!" he shouted at a doubter, who probably remained unconvinced.

An astute student of human character who understood Jackson's fierce loyalties, Van Buren used the Eaton affair as one of several means to ruin Calhoun and to elevate himself in the president's eyes. Van Buren was not called the "Little Magician" without reason. His goal was the presidency, and to obtain it required dexterity. He had earned Jackson's gratitude by accepting the Eatons when Calhoun and his followers had not. Now he had to convince Jackson of Calhoun's duplicity and of his own trustworthiness without leaving the slightest evidence of his own personal political interest. Some of his friends gave Jackson indisputable evidence of Calhoun's recommendation that Jackson be court-martialed for the Florida campaign of 1818. Calhoun had twice before vigorously denied insinuations to this effect. Now Jackson requested an explanation of the documents he had received. Calhoun, completely distraught, took two weeks to compose a fifty-two-page apologia. Jackson answered curtly: "Understanding you now. . . . No further communication is necessary."

At the correct psychological moment, when Calhoun's position had badly deteriorated and the Eaton episode was deadlocked, Van Buren offered to resign from the cabinet. Convinced of Van Buren's loyalty and of the wisdom of his proposal, Jackson acquiesced. From that point each move followed Van Buren's calculations. As expected, Eaton also withdrew. Jackson then felt free to request the resignations of Calhoun's friends, which they reluctantly tendered. At last the Eaton issue was terminated. The naive president could never understand Peggy's subsequent coldness to him. In essence, Eaton had been sacrificed on the altar of Van Buren's presidential plans. With his enemies removed from high office, and his standing with Jackson never higher, Van Buren became the favorite to win the Democratic nomination and the presidency in 1836.

Even without Van Buren's machinations, Jackson and Calhoun seemed destined to split. The Tariff of Abominations had convinced Calhoun that high tariffs were responsible for South Carolina's ailing economy. In 1828 he secretly wrote the *South Carolina Exposition and Protest,* which concluded that a state could nullify an act of the federal government it considered

The Tariff and Nullification

unconstitutional. The theory stemmed from Jefferson's Kentucky Resolution of 1798. Jefferson had advanced the doctrine as a means of defending freedom of speech and the press. Calhoun elaborated upon it as a means of preserving the national power of the southern planters.

Jackson—and Van Buren—counseled a "judicious" tariff. They also advocated restrictions on the power of the national government. But Jackson could never accept the implication of the *Exposition and Protest* that the federal government was merely the agent of the sovereign states. At a Jefferson Day dinner in 1830 that Calhoun and his friends had arranged, Jackson pointedly warned against nullification in a toast: "Our *Federal Union—It must be preserved.*" Calhoun, although shaken, responded with an opposing toast: "The Union—next to our liberty, most dear."

In 1832 Congress passed a tariff that the administration regarded as a reasonable corrective to the inequities of the Tariff of Abominations. Protection was maintained in certain vital areas, but the overall level of duties was actually lowered. Jackson believed that the law would pacify the lower South. Instead, aroused South Carolinians decided not to obey the law. "He that dallies is a dastard," swore one nullificationist. "He that doubts is damned." A convention was held in Columbia at which the "nullifiers" outnumbered the moderate "unionists." The members swiftly approved an Ordinance of Nullification, which was to go into effect on February 1, 1833. The ordinance stated that after that date, South Carolina would not allow the federal tariff to be collected within its boundaries, and no appeals from state to federal courts would be permitted that involved the tariff. The next move was Jackson's. Privately he was incensed; he referred to Calhoun as demented and threatened to hang the nullifiers for treason. Publicly his position was remarkably tempered. A "Proclamation to the People of South Carolina" was issued, actually drafted by Secretary of State Edward Livingston, which declared that nullification was "incompatible with the existence of the Union, contradicted by the letter of the Constitution, unauthorized by its spirit . . . and destructive of the great object for which it was formed." Each side moved cautiously. Jackson admitted that the tariff might be reduced further. South Carolina postponed putting the nullification ordinance into operation.

Meanwhile Henry Clay seized upon the issue as a perfect vehicle to advance his political standing in the South. Despite his previous advocacy of high protection, Clay now suggested a compromise measure. The tariff would be lowered over a nine-year period to a general level of 20 percent ad valorem. On March 1, 1833, the Compromise Tariff was completed. With it was passed the Force Act, which permitted the president to employ military force, if necessary, to collect the tariff. South Carolina accepted the tariff by repealing the Ordinance of Nullification but, wanting the last word, defiantly nullified the Force Act. It is difficult to say who had the final victory. South Carolina, a single state, had succeeded in coercing the federal government into revising the law of the land. On the other hand, it had learned that it stood alone: no other state had openly agreed with the doctrine of nullification.

The struggle over nullification was not the only melodrama of the Jacksonian administration. Concurrent with it, on another stage, with a slightly different cast of Jacksonian heroes and aristocratic villains, was portrayed the Monster Bank performance.

In 1816 Congress had chartered the second Bank of the United States for a twenty-year period. The Bank's directors were undistinguished, even incompetent; its policies were injudicious. By 1818 it verged on insolvency. Jealous states—including Tennessee, North Carolina, Georgia, Ohio, Maryland, and Kentucky—attempted to tax its branches. The Bank refused to pay, and the question of sovereignty was brought to the Supreme Court in the case of *McCulloch* v. *Maryland* (1819). The greatest orators in the nation

The bill establishing the Second Bank of the United States, signed by President Madison on May 10, 1816, also authorized the creation of branch banks—and almost immediately the Second Bank began to establish branches. In many areas they were regarded as unwelcome and unnecessary competitors of local banking institutions. President Jackson accused some of the branch managers of aiding local politicians hostile to his party.

The Bank of the United States and Its Branches, 1830

addressed the Court: Luther Martin for Maryland and Daniel Webster for the Bank. Marshall's opinion, which struck down the state tax, saved the Bank from possible ruin.

The appointments of Langdon Cheves and Nicholas Biddle as successive presidents of the Bank resulted in a distinct improvement in its financial condition. They dismissed corrupt employees and applied conservative fiscal policies. By 1830 the Bank was a prosperous institution that held one-third of all the deposits and specie in American banks. Biddle was the opposite of Jackson. Educated and urbane, he was equally at home in the worlds of poetry and business. Jackson was a simple man by comparison; he hated all banks because he did not understand their function. Biddle did what he could to appease Jackson. He investigated charges that some branch managers had contributed funds to anti-Jackson politicians, cultivated members of Jackson's cabinet, appointed some of Jackson's closest friends to Bank posts, and called upon Jackson personally to assure him of the Bank's goodwill, its value to the country, its future goals. But nothing could really alter Jackson's distrust of the Bank. At times he masked it, would drop a friendly word, counter that with a threat, and seemed to delight in Biddle's discomfiture. The more erratic Jackson appeared, the more edgy Biddle became. Nervous about the future of the Bank, Biddle permitted himself to be persuaded by Henry Clay and Daniel Webster to seek a congressional recharter in 1832, four years earlier than necessary. They felt that they could persuade enough Democrats to join them to pass the bill through Congress. Jackson would have to sign it or, by a veto, lose the key state of Pennsylvania and the presidential election. The plan seemed to work well. The recharter bill was enacted by a vote of 28 to 20 in the Senate and 107 to 85 in the House of Representatives. Jackson regarded the recharter as a challenge and a provocation. Four of his advisors—Roger Taney, Amos Kendall, Andrew Donelson, and Levi Woodbury—helped the president compose a veto message, which amounted to a campaign manifesto. Jackson's action, to Clay and Webster, spelled his political demise. But Senator Willie Mangum of North Carolina thought otherwise. "The whole [issue] may ultimately take the appearance of a trial between General Jackson and the Bank—In that case the Bank will go down."

Jackson's ringing threat, "The Bank is trying to kill me" (as he told Van Buren), "but I shall kill it," is evidence of the president's determination to completely scuttle the Bank. He appealed over Congress to the people to support his veto. In 1832 Clay was the nominee of the National Republicans (the nucleus around which the Whig party later would develop). An anti-Masonic party, which had originated a few years earlier in upstate New York as a protest against secret orders and exclusive privileges, entered the national political scene, nominating William Wirt. South Carolina went its separate way, isolated from the mainstream of national politics, supporting John Floyd of Virginia.

The issue was never in doubt. Wirt took Vermont, South Carolina voted for Floyd, Clay carried six other states (but not Pennsylvania), and Jackson

Andrew Jackson's veto of the bill to recharter the Bank of the United States was considered by his opponents to be economically disastrous and nationally divisive. His message, Daniel Webster said, "manifestly seeks to inflame the poor against the rich; it wantonly attacks whole classes of the people, for the purpose of turning against them the prejudices and the resentments of other classes. It is a state paper which finds no topic too exciting for its use, no passion too inflammable for its address and its solicitation." This anti-Jackson cartoon portrays him as a man who always sought personal glory and popularity, equating his military victories with his destruction of the Bank. (Courtesy of the Boston Public Library, Print Department)

had all the rest. He swept to victory in seventeen states and rolled up an electoral majority of 219 to Clay's 49. In fact his triumph was so commanding, and his control of the large Democratic majority in Congress so firm, that all hopes for the Bank were dead. Clay and Webster had badly miscalculated. Jackson had slain the Monster. But for whom? And to what purpose?

Disparate elements had united behind Jackson's war on the Bank. First, *Democratic Unity*
eastern workingmen agreed with him in opposing all banks. Like Jackson,
they were advocates of hard money. They conceived it to be immoral for a
bank with only three or four million dollars in assets to issue thirty or forty
million dollars in paper currency. Since workingmen were, at times, cheated
because they were paid in depreciated or worthless currency, their animosity is understandable. The workingmen of New York City endorsed a resolution to the effect "that more than one hundred broken banks, within a few
years past, admonish the community to destroy banks altogether." Although
they did not approve of Van Buren, by 1832 Jackson's attack on the Bank
had won their enthusiastic support.

Second, many state bankers were jealous of the Bank's powers and profits.
As a depository for government funds, the Bank enjoyed a privileged
economic position. It was also identified with the old aristocracy of inherited
wealth and established social position. The new entrepreneurs were self-
made men, the rugged individualists of nineteenth-century fact and fable,
who—with Jackson—shared an antiaristocratic bias. They resented the
Bank's fetters on credit and paper money. They sought to destroy the
monopolistic controls of the Chestnut Street grandees. They were energetic,
crass, determined, and resourceful, and they would brook no limitations—
legal, moral, political, or otherwise—in their pursuit of wealth.

Third, although many westerners, such as Thomas Hart Benton, were
opposed to the Bank, their attitude did not represent that of the vast majority.
Bank policies had changed the minds of many in the West. The St. Louis
Beacon, established in 1829 with Benton's support, came out flatly against
the Bank veto in 1832. A pro-administration paper, the Cincinnati *Republican,* warned that "a national Bank is important to the prosperity of the
West." The scholar Jean Wilburn has written: "These people were very short
of capital and lacked a currency. For the most part they bought and sold
through New Orleans and needed a ready and stable market for their bills of
exchange. Only the Second United States Bank with its system of branches
. . . could fulfill this need." Surely many westerners supported Jackson's
war upon the Bank. But the main thrust originated from the East. The editor
of the Boston *Post* exulted that the Bank was "BIDDLED, DIDDLED, AND
UNDONE." Theodore Sedgwick, Jr., of Massachusetts boasted, "We have as
yet scarcely begun to see the advantageous results . . . which are yet to
ensue."

As long as Jackson fought the Bank, he could keep the Democratic party *Inflation and Panic*
united; thus he did not let the issue rest during the concluding four years of
its charter. He was determined to remove government deposits and relocate
them in state banks. The secretary of the treasury, Louis McLane, refused to
carry out the order and was shifted to the state department. The next
secretary of the treasury, William J. Duane, also refused and was dismissed.
The next, Roger Taney, later to be rewarded with the post of chief justice of
the Supreme Court, accomplished Jackson's purpose. Taney made all the

government's deposits in state banks, known as "pets," and for expenditures he drew upon the reserves in the Bank of the United States. By 1833 Biddle was forced by the dwindling reserves to curtail the Bank's operations. However, the credit contraction that he ordered—a drastic reduction of loans to businessmen, and pressures upon state banks to redeem their notes and checks in specie—was probably exaggerated. Biddle frankly hoped that the economic distress would force Jackson to restore government deposits to the Bank. Hundreds of businessmen sent petitions to the president requesting some form of relief. Others called on him. "Go to the monster, go to Nicholas Biddle," Jackson stormed. "I never will restore the deposits." By 1834 Biddle relented, reversed his policy, and ended the artificial shortage of credit. The value of Bank stock continued to fall, and in 1836 it ceased to function as a nationally chartered institution.

Meanwhile credit expanded rapidly—too rapidly—once the Bank was stripped of its power and could no longer act as a restraining influence. Hundreds of new banks were formed. The amount of bank notes in circulation, without adequate reserves of specie, jumped from eighty-two million dollars in 1835 to one hundred twenty million in 1836. People borrowed recklessly to speculate in real estate. The value of town lots increased astronomically. Federal income from the sale of public lands, which amounted to $2.6 million in 1832, climbed to $14.8 million in 1835, and then to $24.9 million in 1836. Alarmed at the speculative frenzy, "Old Bullion" Benton of Missouri angrily declared to the Senate, "I did not join in putting down the Bank of the United States, to put up a wilderness of local banks. I did not join in putting down the paper currency of a national bank, to put up a national paper currency of a thousand local banks. I did not strike Caesar to make Anthony master of Rome." Urged on by Benton, Jackson in the summer of 1836 issued the Specie Circular. The order directed government land agents to accept only hard money in payment for public lands. Unfortunately the circular came too late and too abruptly, bringing about a rapid deflation. Politically it destroyed Democratic party unity. The radical wing, itself a conglomeration of older Jeffersonian agrarians and urban workers who were dubbed "locofocos," supported Jackson. The conservative wing of bankers and entrepreneurs pressed for its repeal. Moreover, the circular also unsettled the international money market. British financiers feared overinvestment in the American economy. If the United States government did not trust Yankee money, why should they? British firms with heavy American commitments collapsed. Secondary explosions rocked the cotton trade as well. In 1837 merchants in both countries were squeezed into bankruptcy.

The panic of 1837 was not over until 1843. A large number of banks, including some "pets," temporarily suspended specie payments. Many others defaulted and never reopened. Since there was no national bank to blame for the depression, guilt centered on banks in general. Van Buren, who was elected president in 1836, faced an excruciating problem. Radical

Van Buren's Solution

Democrats demanded that the government withdraw its funds from all banks. Jackson vigorously endorsed their position. Conservative Democrats, with whom Van Buren was closely allied, wanted the deposits maintained. The radicals had the votes, the conservatives the organization. Only a political magician like Van Buren would attempt to bridge the dilemma. His solution was masterful. In 1837 he summoned a special session of Congress and there publicly flayed the malefactors of wealth. Locofocos cheered. Jackson's faith in Van Buren was confirmed. The proposal Van Buren placed before Congress called for an independent treasury system to divorce the national government from banking entirely. Only gold and silver would be accepted and disbursed by the treasury. Public funds would be housed in government vaults in Washington and in subtreasuries in other cities.

The plan failed to unite the Democrats. The business world could see only the short-term losses, not the long-term gains. In fact, Van Buren's system offered them the culmination of laissez-faire. "The less government interferes with private pursuits," he stated, "the better." Without government regulation, legal interference, or public supervision, enterprise would be completely free. But businessmen did not grasp the opportunity. To them the fact that government deposits would be removed from state banks was sufficient evidence of Van Buren's betrayal. They left in droves to join the Whig opposition.

The independent treasury was twice defeated in Congress, passed in 1840, repealed in 1841, and reenacted in 1846. The robber barons of a later age reaped the benefits of the system. The free enterprise Van Buren espoused was to become an eleventh commandment for the American businessman. And the common man suffered from the absence of a central banking system until the twentieth century.

The crowning paradox of the Jacksonian period was revealed in the election of 1840. For years an assemblage of oddly assorted interests, bound only by their mutual antipathy toward Jackson and Van Buren, had been coalescing into the Whig structure: adherents of Clay and his "American system," ex-Democrats disillusioned with the administration's financial policies, states' righters who followed Calhoun, educated classes disturbed by the anti-intellectual tone of Jacksonianism. They all joined to overthrow the Democratic machine. In 1836 the Whigs had nominated no single candidate but ran favorite sons, making Van Buren's victory all the easier. In 1840 they changed their strategy. Knowing that their party was considered by the public to be high-toned and aristocratic, the Whigs purposely selected a candidate, William Henry Harrison, whom they could dress in the image of Jackson. Harrison was already known as the hero of Tippecanoe. The Whigs pictured him as a simple and honest Ohio farmer, born in a log cabin, a man of unswerving principle. To complete the irony, the Whigs identified Van Buren as a spendthrift politician who perfumed his whiskers, drank champagne, ate off golden plates, and reclined on a "Turkish divan." Neither Harrison's upbringing nor Van Buren's living habits remotely resembled the

Election of 1840

campaign propaganda. But the symbols, along with free liquor, torchlight parades, and incendiary speeches, excited popular emotions and elicited a record response of the electorate. Harrison won by a small popular majority. More significantly, the election of 1840 represented a crest of the democratic tide that had commenced decades before. An immense number of people voted, nearly 25 percent more than in any previous presidential election.

Harrison died a month after taking office and was succeeded by John Tyler of Virginia, a southern Whig whose antagonism to the Bank matched Jackson's. Thus, when Congress in 1841 passed a bill creating a third national Bank, Tyler vetoed it. When it was rewritten to satisfy Tyler's constitutional objections, he again vetoed it. Fifty Whig congressmen caucused and read Tyler out of the party. But the existence of a national Bank was not really crucial to economic expansion: the antebellum economy was not truly national in character and local sources and foreign investments were generally sufficient to meet the capital needs of industry.

America was on the move; in the first half of the nineteenth century its economic landscape was changing as rapidly as its political practices. "The American flies at everything," a nineteenth-century Scottish traveler observed." 'Go ahead anyhow,' that is his motto. . . . The American people diffuses itself, its energy, and its capital over a whole continent." Unlike the Europeans, steeped in history and bound by the traditions of class and craft, Americans at this time were enormously mobile, wonderfully adaptive, and relatively classless. "Machines, not men, became specialized" in America, Daniel J. Boorstin has commented. Eli Whitney produced muskets for the United States government, manufacturing each part separately but uniformly. This "uniformity system" or "Whitney system" provided the foundation of the concept of interchangeable parts, upon which the twentieth-century American miracle of mass production would be built. Another foundation was the "factory system." Samuel Slater, an Englishman, had built the machinery for the first American textile factory at Pawtucket, Rhode Island, in 1790. Cotton textile factories thereafter expanded in number—particularly at Lowell, Massachusetts, and later at Utica, New York—and in size and sophistication, uniting all aspects of production under one roof. In 1800 only two thousand spindles were in operation; by 1840 there were two and a quarter million. Other industries did not develop quite so spectacularly, nor did household production disappear, but scores of factories were constructed near waterfalls in New England and New York, manufacturing a variety of goods—woolens, furniture, nails, cutlery, clocks, firearms, machine tools. In Massachusetts the "Suffolk system," a model of sound banking, supplied industry in that state with credit at low interest rates and provided the public at large with paper money of reliable, predictable value.

In little more than a generation following the War of 1812, sleepy New England communities were transformed into thriving production centers. The territory of the United States nearly doubled, expanding from the Missis-

WESTERN EMIGRATION.

JOURNAL

OF

DOCTOR JEREMIAH SIMPLETON's

TOUR TO OHIO.

CONTAINING

An account of the numerous difficulties, Hair-breadth Escapes, Mortifications and Privations, which the Doctor and his family experienced on their Journey from Maine, to the 'Land of Promise,' and during a residence of three years in that highly extolled country.

BY H. TRUMBULL.

Nulli Fides Frontis.

BOSTON--PRINTED BY S. SEWALL.

ments---that provisions abound in such profusion, that geese, turkeys, oppossums, bears, raccoons and rabbits may be seen running in the woods in droves, ready cooked, with knives and forks stuck in their flanks, crying out to the newly arrived emigrant, come eat me.'---The reverse of this, friend Scruple, is the case, as you may perceive by my account of the mishaps and disasters that I met with. You will, on your arrival there, be obliged to sleep in a hollow tree, or build yourself a log hut, for here are no carpenters---kill and dress your own game, for here are no butchers---clothe yourself in skins, when your stock of apparel is worn out, for here are no factories, shoemakers, tailors, hatters or tanners---and pound your own corn, for you may travel in this wild wilderness fifty miles, without discovering the sign of a mill---in short, nothing an be obtained here without costing more for the transportation than the original price of any article you may want. As to *society*, if you wish to converse in any human language out of your family, you must go twenty or thirty miles to your next door neighbor, with your axe instead of staff---for you must cut your way thither, for want of roads---and perhaps, after all, find him almost as hoggish as the 'swines in your pens' or the more numerous class of the inhabitants of Ohio, the wild-cat, panther, &c. who frequently associate with our tame animals to their sorrow, and sometimes with young children to *our* mourning ;---And fags I'd rather be a hog-reeve in good New-England, than hold any office in this back woods country, where the inhabitants walk on all fours, with the exception of a few double headed fools. Take my advice, therefore, Scruple, and put off your journey, till you think a little further on the subject.

F I N I S.

sippi to the Pacific; population trebled; national wealth multiplied fivefold. Eastern cities, swelled by immigrants, began to bulge in size and in problems. But the most spectacular growth was in the West. Hundreds of thousands of land-hungry Americans poured into Alabama and Arkansas, Mississippi, Michigan and Missouri, Ohio, Indiana and Illinois. Whitney's cotton gin—a device that could remove the seed from short-staple cotton mechanically—accelerated the western expansion of southern planters. The steamboat also hastened the opening of the Mississippi Valley by drastically reducing freight charges. In 1812, when Nicholas Roosevelt sailed his thirty thousand dollar steamer into Louisville, the inhabitants were startled. Most had never seen and some had scarcely heard of such a phenomenon. By 1820 there were sixty steamboats operating on the Mississippi; by 1830 there were over two hundred.

New Orleans, tapping the commerce of the Mississippi Valley, became one of the world's leading ports and might have eclipsed New York City were it not for an engineering marvel of the age: the 350-mile Erie Canal. Completed in 1825, at a cost of seven million dollars, the Erie Canal provided a cheap and efficient means of transportation between the Hudson River and the Great Lakes. New York City, as De Witt Clinton predicted

While tens of thousands of easterners sought to begin life anew in the fertile lands of the Ohio Valley, others who remained poked fun at the migrants, as this 1819 pamphlet illustrates. In Ohio, the author claimed, "the inhabitants walk on all fours, with the exception of a few double-headed fools." By 1820 Ohio ranked fifth in population in the Union. (American Antiquarian Society)

when he sponsored the canal, became the principal gateway to the North-west. The undertaking proved so successful that merchants of other cities pressed their state legislatures to finance similar ventures. By 1840 Pennsylvania had almost a thousand miles of canals; its major system extended from Philadelphia to Pittsburgh. Ohio joined the Great Lakes and the Ohio River by two routes: Cleveland to Portsmouth and Toledo to Cincinnati. In Indiana the Wabash and Erie Canal ran from Terre Haute to Fort Wayne and then connected with the Ohio system. Seventy-five percent of all canal investments were made or sponsored by state governments. Illinois piled up a debt of eleven million dollars and Ohio twenty-seven million. Michigan's debt for internal improvements, prorated by population, amounted to fifty-three dollars for every man, woman, and child. In 1840 the burden of the states reached the staggering sum of two hundred million dollars. Most of the bonded indebtedness was purchased by British citizens looking for low-risk, high-return investments. They recognized the profits that America's capital scarcity yielded, and they regarded state securities as extremely safe investments.

Eventually the canal-building boom declined, particularly after the superiority of railroads became evident. Neither the absence of a central Bank nor the lessons of the panic of 1837 had any sobering effect on raising capital for railroads. In the decades before the Civil War over one billion dollars was invested once it became apparent that railroads were profitable ventures. Cities, counties, states, and later the federal government, either by monetary gifts, stock purchases, bond guarantees, or land grants, financed about 25 percent of the cost. The other sources were private—and abundant. In transportation, as well as in manufacturing and in politics, a revolution had occurred. The face of America had been altered.

In the age of Jackson politics became popular, enterprise became free, and both became passions that the American people assiduously pursued. Pursuit meant progress, to which most Americans (outside the South) were committed. But consummation bore some bitter fruit, to which other Americans objected.

Consequences of an Age

Administratively, a distinct lessening in the quality of public officials was apparent. Jackson and his aides, in the name of reform, had created the spoils system. Wholesale removals of civil servants did not take place. In fact, Jackson in eight years dismissed only one-tenth of all federal officeholders, a proportion comparable to Jefferson's record. However, the replacements were judged on party fidelity and personal loyalty to Jackson. Jefferson conceived of office as a service. Under Jackson it became a reward. "Office-seeking and office-getting," one Democrat commented in 1838, "was becoming a regular business, where impudence triumphed over worth."

Politically, more people than ever before participated as voters. Candidates had to affect simplicity. As America moved away from its agrarian roots, Americans insisted that their leaders possess rural or frontier origins. A log-cabin birth became imperative, for it symbolized virtue and independence. Daniel Webster had to admit that he was not so fortunate. "But," he added, "my elder brothers and sisters were born in a log cabin." Jeffersonians had tried to cultivate and educate the public. Jacksonians and Whigs tried to manipulate opinion. Duplicity and cynicism became part of the political system. Yet the system functioned, the people approved, and the democratic volcano Jacksonianism had activated occasionally spewed up political leaders of remarkable ability.

Economically, the United States was afflicted with all the evils of rapid and unplanned industrial growth. In comparison with other nations, the American standard of living was high. Nevertheless, 65 percent of those employed in cotton mills were women and children who worked twelve hours a day for bare subsistence wages. Their lives were regimented. Malcontents were blacklisted. Strikes were forbidden by the judiciary. Some mills set aside "whipping rooms." Outside of New England education was for the rich. In 1833, it is estimated, a million children between ages of five and fifteen attended no school whatsoever. In large cities the poverty stricken were crowded into slums. Periodic unemployment bred crime and prostitution. It was commonly remarked that a slave in Kentucky or Virginia was better compensated in terms of food, housing, and even personal treatment than a northern worker.

COMMENTARY

The American was impatient with the present, never doubted the future, yet looked longingly to the past. The more his character was stained in the pursuit of wealth, the more he sought purity at home. The more his civilization seemed mechanical, the more he displayed affection for the natural. Slums, bread riots, and multiplying urban problems evoked romantic memories of his rural past. Rapid economic growth and social movement made him acutely conscious of the need for social order. Politics, a national game in which all whites could participate, continued to fascinate him, but the quality of his leaders caused him to yearn for the incorruptibility of George Washington. Acquisitive, he sought lost innocence. Materialistic, he wallowed in sentimentality. Beset by conflicting localisms, he became increasingly chauvinistic. He built bridges and railroads, sent clipper ships to the far reaches of the world, transformed prairie towns into thriving commercial centers —or promised to do so. Truth was measured by success, and success was measured by economic growth. If that growth proved an illusion —as it did in hundreds of small towns that failed —the American moved on to where it would become a reality. For all his business confidence, there persisted an uncertainty, a confusion, and a vague dissatisfaction about the meaning and the purpose of the nation. Had men died in revolution and war so that America might become nothing more than a vast countinghouse? Did economic progress mean that humanitarian values must be sacrificed? An army of reformers rose to correct abuses, to combat evils, to rectify inequalities, to amend America's institutions, and redirect its historic mission to something more than capital accumulations. "We are to revise the whole of our social structure," Ralph Waldo Emerson advised in 1841, "the state, the school, religion, marriage, trade, science, and explore their foundations in our own nature."

THOMAS P. ABERNETHY, *From Frontier to Plantation in Tennessee* (1967)

HARRY AMMON, *James Monroe* (1971)

SAMUEL F. BEMIS, *John Quincy Adams and the Foundations of American Foreign Policy* (1949)

———, *John Quincy Adams and the Union* (1956)

LEE BENSON, *The Concept of Jacksonian Democracy: New York as a Test Case* (1961)

VAN WYCK BROOKS, *The World of Washington Irving* (1944)

WILLIAM N. CHAMBERS, *Old Bullion Benton: Senator from the New West* (1956)

GEORGE DANGERFIELD, *The Era of Good Feelings* (1953)

CLEMENT EATON, *Henry Clay and the Art of American Politics* (1957)

JOHN HOPE FRANKLIN, *The Militant South* (1956)

W. W. FREEHLING, *Prelude to the Civil War: The Nullification Controversy in South Carolina, 1816–1836* (1966)

PAUL GATES, *The Farmer's Age* (1960)

BRAY HAMMOND, *Banks and Politics in America from the Revolution to the Civil War* (1957)

WALTER HUGINS, *Jacksonian Democracy and the Working Class: A Study of the New York Workingmen's Movement* (1960)

MARQUIS JAMES, *Andrew Jackson* (1937)

SHAW LIVERMORE, *The Twilight of Federalism* (1962)

RICHARD McCORMICK, *The Second American Party System* (1966)

JOHN McFAUL, *The Politics of Jacksonian Finance* (1972)

MARVIN MEYERS, *The Jacksonian Persuasion: Politics and Belief* (1957)

NATHAN MILLER, *The Enterprise of a Free People* (1962)

R. KENT NEWMYER, *The Supreme Court under Marshall and Taney* (1968)

RUSSELL NYE, *The Cultural Life of the New Nation, 1776–1830* (1960)

DEXTER PERKINS, *History of the Monroe Doctrine* (Rev. ed. 1955)

EDWARD PESSEN, *New Perspectives on Jacksonian Parties and Politics* (1969)

ROBERT REMINI, *The Election of Andrew Jackson* (1963)

———, *Martin Van Buren and the Making of the Democratic Party* (1959)

ARTHUR SCHLESINGER, JR., *The Age of Jackson* (1946)

GEORGE R. TAYLOR, *The Transportation Revolution, 1815–1860* (1951)

PETER TEMIN, *The Jacksonian Economy* (1969)

FREDERICK J. TURNER, *Rise of the New West, 1819–1829* (1906)

GLYNDON VAN DEUSEN, *The Jacksonian Era* (1959)

JOHN W. WARD, *Andrew Jackson: Symbol for an Age* (1955)

LEONARD WHITE, *The Jacksonians* (1954)

CHILTON WILLIAMSON, *American Suffrage* (1960)

CHARLES WILTSE, *John C. Calhoun* (1944–51)

7

Reform and Expansion, 1840–1850

Freedom's Ferment

A ferment for reform, a crusade to eradicate evils, touched thousands of literate people throughout the North. Its particular focus was in New England, but its vision was national. Its leadership was largely clerical, but its goals transcended the narrow interests of denominationalism. It was essentially, but not exclusively, nonpolitical. It was zealous, but not violent; radical, but not revolutionary. It was optimistic, naive, and urgent. It believed no challenge was insuperable, and all triumphs were close at hand. And it was comprehensive. Every institution and every practice was questioned, investigated, and debated—liquor, slavery, dietary habits, penal institutions, marriage, money, state power, war, women's rights. One reformer called for a Convention to Emancipate the Human Race from Ignorance, Poverty, Division, and Misery. All good causes were related, and reformers, many of whom served several movements simultaneously, made up an interlocking directorate.

Unfortunately, and perhaps inevitably, cranks and crackpots were attracted to it, as well as obnoxious extremists whom Emerson called "narrow, self-pleasing, conceited men." A number of transcendentalists were food faddists; social revisionists and physiological reformers often went hand in hand; and, while some hooted, other intellectual progressives were intrigued by the "science" of phrenology. William Alcott, widely known for his household manuals, moral guides, and physiology handbooks, cautioned against tea drinking as a dangerous sexual stimulant. "The female who restores her strength by tea, the laborer who regains strength by spiritous liquors, and the Turk who recruits his energies by his pill of opium," warned Alcott, "are in precisely the same condition." Horace Mann, who singlehandedly launched an educational renaissance in New England, advised young men to undergo a phrenological examination before deciding upon a career. Lewis Hough thought everyone should eat fruit and whole grain wheat, take no fluid, sun themselves in the nude, and engage in sexual intercourse just once a year. Sylvester Graham's program for mental and physical health included frequent baths, hard mattresses, the whole wheat cracker he made famous, and chastity.

By 1850 the pioneering work of Thomas H. Gallaudet led to the creation of special schools for the education of the deaf in fourteen states. Shown is a classroom in one such institution, from Leslie's Illustrated Weekly.

Practical Reformers

Numerous men and women devoted themselves to practical social reforms, with substantial results. "Every creature in human shape should command our respect," wrote Samuel Gridley Howe. "The strong should help the weak, so that the whole should advance as a band of brethren." Howe practiced what he preached. He fought for Greek independence in the 1820s and returned to America to work for the blind. For forty-four years he directed the Perkins Institute in Boston, training teachers of the blind in new techniques he had developed. Charles Dickens, who saw little to admire in America during his tour, thought Howe's system a model other countries should emulate. Dorothea Dix, a Boston schoolmistress, investigated the appalling treatment accorded the insane in Massachusetts and submitted her findings to the state legislature in 1843. "Insane persons confined within this commonwealth," she reported, "are in cages, closets, cellars, stalls, pens! Chained, naked, beaten with rods, and lashed into obedience!" Before the Civil War more than a dozen states passed corrective legislation because of her efforts. She even went to Europe, where conditions for the insane were equally heinous, and enlisted the support of Queen Victoria and Pope Pius IX. Thomas H. Gallaudet had gone to Europe years earlier to study techniques of teaching deaf mutes. While in Britain he found that one family had for generations monopolized the field, and they preferred to keep their methods a profitable secret. Gallaudet received a better reception in France, where he studied with Abbé Sicard; he then returned to establish the first free school for the deaf in Hartford, Connecticut. Like Howe's it became a model for the nation.

Other groups of reformers alerted the public conscience to social abuses in orphanages, poorhouses, and correctional homes for juveniles. John Sargent attempted to eradicate prostitution. Josiah Quincy, a pioneer in municipal reform, also fought prostitution and made a remarkable address to the Suffolk grand jury in Massachusetts on the effects of jailing young offenders with hardened criminals. James Russell Lowell spoke out against capital punishment. Louis Dwight headed a society dedicated to the improvement of prison conditions. Robert Rantoul successfully argued for the legitimacy of unions and labor's right to strike. His logic helped persuade Chief Justice Lemuel Shaw of Massachusetts to overturn previous court decisions by recognizing that unions were not criminal conspiracies (*Commonwealth* v. *Hunt,* 1842).

Utopian Reformers

The first voices raised in criticism of capitalism were European. The dichotomy between the rich and poor was more striking than in the United States, and the conditions of the working class more appalling. Long before Karl Marx and Friedrich Engels wrote the *Communist Manifesto,* dozens of socialistic proposals were formulated. The theories of two men in particular, a Welshman named Robert Owen and a Frenchman, Charles Fourier, were given a limited trial in the United States.

Owen was a successful industrialist whose cotton mills and company town at New Lanark, Scotland, attracted worldwide attention for their advanced educational facilities, humane treatment of employees—and profits. Despite his own example, Owen became convinced that wealth was not created by entrepreneurial wizardry, but by science and society. Before 1820 he shifted from social reformer to socialist. Fourier's career and personality were radically different. An economic casualty of the French Revolution, he became an impoverished eccentric. For thirty years he patiently awaited the arrival of a rich patron to finance his socialist dreams. Both men envisioned a series of village utopias where people, isolated from the debilitating effects of competitive struggle, could develop intellectual independence and true social equality. Cooperation was to be the motivating force, harmony the result. Both men hoped that if the communities functioned as planned, the idea would spread until, gradually, capitalism would be replaced entirely by socialism. The United States was an ideal place to attempt the experiment. Land was cheap. Americans already possessed the requisite political freedom. Religious communitarianism had long been practiced by fundamentalist sects, mainly German pietists.

Owen's chance came first. He purchased the land and buildings of a religious group, the Rappites, in Indiana, and invited settlers. The response was heartening. More arrived than could be accommodated, including several eminent scientists and educators imbued with the teachings of the European pedagogist Johann Pestalozzi. Owen's son described the colonists as "a heterogeneous collection of radicals, enthusiastic devotees to principle, honest latitudinarians, and lazy theorists, with a sprinkling of unprincipled sharpers thrown in." But dedication and faith were not enough to make a success of a backwoods utopia. Largely because skilled workers were in short supply, the collapse of New Harmony was quick. On July 4, 1826, Owen issued a "Declaration of Mental Independence." It proclaimed his hostility to a trinity of "monstrous evils": private property, organized religion, and marriage. A year before he had been invited to address a joint session of Congress: now he was pilloried in press and pulpit as a whoremonger, and his colony was described as "one great brothel." Bitter fights and ugly recriminations rocked New Harmony. By 1827 Owen withdrew; he had lost two hundred thousand dollars, and his community was practically extinct. For the next dozen years, with one minor exception, no new secular communitarian experiments were attempted.

Fourier's philanthropic millionaire never appeared, but he had several disciples, one of whom—Albert Brisbane—carried his gospel to the United States. Brisbane converted Horace Greeley, publisher of the New York *Tribune,* and the two propagandized for Fourierism with considerable success. Marx's later "scientific" socialism rested on what he saw as the natural enmity between labor and capital, the growing class consciousness of the former, and the ultimate overthrow of the latter. Fourier's utopian socialism, on the other hand, rejected class struggle as well as revolution. He aimed instead "to content all classes, all parties." Dozens of Fourierist communities, called "phalanxes," were opened after 1840. They all existed briefly and died quietly. Contrary to Brisbane's advice, the phalanxes were founded with inadequate capital. The most prestigious was Brook Farm in Massachusetts, an established community of New England transcendentalists, which adopted Fourierism in 1844. Transcendentalism was different from Fourierism in its roots, its spirit, and its method, but both shared similar goals. The transcendentalists believed that mankind was corrupted by mass society and materialism. Their utopian objective, wrote George Ripley, was "to combine the thinker and the worker, as far as possible in the same individual." Nathaniel Hawthorne labored at Brook Farm with a pitchfork and manure pile. Afterward he mocked the transcendentalists in his book, *The Blithedale Romance* (1852). But even Hawthorne testified to Brook Farm's "scheme of a noble and unselfish life. . . . I feel we struck upon what ought to be a truth. Posterity may dig it up and profit by it."

The heady optimism of Brook Farm members had already started to wane when they decided to convert to Fourierism. If successful, they felt, Brook Farm could continue to operate and could become a center of the Fourierist crusade to proselytize America. Debts, fire, and smallpox, however, drained the resources and spirit of the members. In 1847 Brook Farm closed down.

The quest for social justice was not the exclusive prerogative of utopian socialists. Other reformers sought to cure the cancers of enterprise by rapid

Some Pet Panaceas

surgery. New York City workingmen, for example, organized politically to gain better hours and wages, to destroy banks, to abolish the practice of imprisonment for debts, to end compulsory militia service, and to obtain a workers' lien law for the protection of wages. Their demands were largely practical; some of their leaders were not.

Thomas Skidmore considered it a grave mistake on the part of Thomas Jefferson to have based his theory of democratic government on only the rights of man. For democracy to be meaningful, said Skidmore, there must be economic equality. Property must be redistributed and inheritance laws altered. Skidmore's crude communism was outlined in his book, *The Rights of Man to Property! Being a Proposition to Make It Equal among the Adults of the Present Generation: and to Provide for Its Equal Transmission to Every Individual of Each Succeeding Generation, on Arriving at the Age of Maturity* (1829). Workingmen at first followed Skidmore, then rapidly disowned him when public opinion became hostile. "We have no desire or intention," their journal announced, "of disturbing the rights of property."

Frances Wright and Robert Dale Owen (son of the utopian socialist) exerted a considerable influence on the New York workingmen after Skidmore's decline. Their ideas were equally exotic and, to the general public, just as outrageous. Wright's public expressions of atheism and her intemperate attacks on organized religion shocked society. One newspaper called her "the Red Harlot of Infidelity." Owen audaciously suggested birth-control measures to alleviate the miseries of the indigent. The major panacea of both Wright and Owen, however, was education. "I believe," wrote Owen, "in a National System of Equal, Republican, Protective, Practical Education, the sole regenerator of a profligate Age, and the only redeemer of our suffering country from the equal curses of chilling poverty and corrupting riches, of gnawing want and destroying debauchery, of blind ignorance and unprincipled intrigue." According to their plan each state would establish and maintain a school system in which all class distinction would be obliterated. All children would receive identical food, clothes, board, and instruction. Then they could enter the competitive world on an equal basis as "useful, intelligent, virtuous citizens." The scheme was rejected by some as too radical and idealistic, by others as unnecessary and inappropriate. Working-class distress, the New York Typographical Society commented, "is caused not by anything Owen could reform, but by the introduction of labor-saving machinery during the last thirty years. Has Owen any remedy to propose? Far from it."

George Henry Evans believed he had the remedy for mechanization. As early as 1833, and for the rest of his life, Evans championed free western land grants to bona-fide settlers. Man had as natural a right to land, said Evans, as he had to air or sun or water. A farm boy himself, he toiled for years in a drab New York printing shop, nearly destitute, composing eloquent arguments to convince eastern workers that happiness and independence could be found only in agriculture. The first homestead bill, providing for free western land grants, was introduced in Congress by Andrew Johnson of

Tennessee in 1846. Every year thereafter the legislation was reintroduced and defeated. Evans' theories were united with abolitionism in the slogan of the Free Soil party: "Free Soil, Free Land, Free Labor, Free Men." Not until 1862, after Evans's death, was the Homestead Act passed. Then the fallacy of his panacea became obvious. Agrarianism was no cure for the evils of industrialism. Workers did not have the capital, the knowledge, or even the desire to go West and become farmers. Whatever the merits of the Homestead Act, it failed to act as an avenue of escape for discontented eastern workers.

Other attempted reforms, such as peace and temperance, generated much verbal debate but few satisfying results. Both causes had dedicated leaders, national organizations, and significant clerical support, though liquor was considered a more serious evil than war. Temperance was the largest and strongest, and peace the smallest and weakest of the reform movements.

Peace and Temperance

PEACE If all agreed on the desirability of peace, still there were bitter arguments among pacifists about methods of achieving it. Some sought to devise legal techniques to settle disputes between nations. "It is high time," wrote William Ladd, founder of the American Peace Society, "for the Christian world to seek a more rational, cheap, and equitable mode of settling international difficulties." An ex-sea captain and farmer, Ladd led the pacifist crusade for two decades. His suggested program for a congress of nations to formulate international law and a court of justice to enforce it was admired in the abstract but disregarded in practice. In the twentieth century it would be resurrected as Wilsonianism.

Equally ineffective was another wing of the pacifist movement, which was uninterested in international conferences and unwilling to honor laws or agreements contrary to their rigid ideas. Precursors of Gandhi rather than Wilson, these pacifists championed nonresistance. They held that neither nations nor individuals should use physical force under any circumstances. In 1838 the abolitionist William Lloyd Garrison formed the New England Non-Resistance Society and wrote its Declaration of Sentiments. In it he included the following radical statement:

> We register our testimony, not only against all wars, whether offensive or defensive, but all preparations for war; against every naval ship, every arsenal, every fortification; against the militia system and a standing army; against all military chieftains and soldiers; against all monuments commemorative of victory over a fallen foe, all trophies won in battle, all celebrations in honor of military or naval exploits; against all appropriations for the defence of a nation by force and arms, on the part of any legislative body; against every edict of government requiring of its subjects military service. Hence, we deem it unlawful to bear arms, or to hold a military office.

Henry David Thoreau sympathized with but did not participate in the reform movement. Though influenced by the passive resistance philosophy, he carefully disassociated himself from its anarchist conclusions. "Unlike those who call themselves no-government men," wrote Thoreau, "I ask for, not at once no government, but *at once* a better government." Thoreau was individualistic to the point of selfishness. He objected to the Mexican War and refused to pay taxes as a protest, but he would not cooperate with other pacifists. Elihu Burritt, on the other hand, was completely selfless and cooperative, motivated by no ambition except a desire to aid humanity. After Ladd's death the crusade for peace came to depend upon his exertions. Between 1848 and 1852 he organized four international conferences: each was well attended but produced no visible effects. Pacifism as a movement collapsed rapidly as nations went to war on both sides of the Atlantic—the Crimean War, revolution in Poland, unification struggles in Italy and Germany, and civil war in America. Torn between their hatred of war and hatred of slavery, most reformers adjusted their antiwar philosophy to support the North. "I think we should agree about war," wrote the New England minister, Theodore Parker. "I hate it, deplore it, but yet see its necessity. All the great charters of humanity have been writ in blood, and must continue to be for some centuries." Burritt also supported the Union, though he returned to pacifism as soon as the war ended, this time advocating massive resistance, a worldwide strike of workingmen for peace. "We hope the day will come," Burritt declared, "when the working men of Christendom will form one vast Trades Union, and make a universal and simultaneous *strike* against the whole war system."

TEMPERANCE Physicians, evangelical ministers, students and scholars, renowned theologians, reformed drunkards, and even children all marched together for temperance. Thousands of organizations were devoted to the task, including the American Temperance Union, the Independent Order of Rechabites, the Washingtonians, the Congressional Temperance Society, the Carson League, "Father Mathew" societies, and the Cold Water Army. Over a million people took the pledge of sobriety, including children:

> We, Cold Water girls and boys,
> Freely renounce the treacherous joys
> Of brandy, whiskey, rum and gin;
> The serpent's lure to death and sin.
> Wine, beer and cider we detest,
> And thus we'll make our parents blest;
> So here we pledge perpetual hate
> To all that can intoxicate.

Temperance was the one reform to permeate the South. Senator Robert B. Rhett of South Carolina and Governor Henry H. Wise of Virginia were prominent in the movement, and General John Cocke of Virginia became president of the American Temperance Union. A number of states tried to control the worst effects of excessive alcoholic consumption by various licensing and tax laws. Massachusetts in 1838 passed the "Fifteen-Gallon Law," which forbade the sale of less than that amount at one time. The governor who signed the law, Edward Everett, was defeated for reelection, and it was repealed in 1840. Gradually more-radical reformers came to the conclusion that mere temperance was not enough, and they sought total abstinence to be enforced by legal prohibition. Wherever prohibition was tried—first in Maine and then in a dozen other states—there was fierce resistance. A crowd in Salem, Massachusetts, pelted a prohibitionist clergyman with eggs. Another in St. Paul, Minnesota, attacked the local sheriff. In some states the laws were declared unconstitutional; in others they failed to perform as expected. Observers pointed out that though all the grogshops in Maine were closed, people there were drinking more liquor than ever before. But prohibitionists were notoriously persistent, urged on by a sense of religious fervor and moral certainty, and the issue continued to divide Americans well into the twentieth century.

North and South, women were not easily admitted to participation in reform activities. In fact, most did not respond to the call from leaders of their own sex to fight for equality in education, in marriage, in law, and in politics.

Women's Rights

There were temperance parades, temperance songs, temperance plays, and temperance conventions. "Dear Father, Drink No more" and "Mother, Dry That Flowing Tear" were sentimental favorites sung at their meetings, as was "Father, Dear Father, Come Home With Me Now." Lucius Sargent's Temperance Tales *were widely read; and Timothy Shay Arthur's play,* Ten Nights in a Bar Room, *was a commercial success. Famous reformers, such as William Lloyd Garrison, Elihu Burritt, Lyman Beecher, and Frederick Douglass journeyed to London in 1846 to participate in a World Temperance Convention. Women were active in the movement, though barred from membership in some societies. As the cartoon indicates, children also were expected to take the pledge to renounce all liquor. (Courtesy of the New York Historical Society)*

Pioneer women shared the full burden and responsibilities of homesteading. Working-class women labored in mills and factories. And a woman of the middle and upper classes was expected to stay at home, to be pure, pious, submissive, and totally domestic. Virginity, not intelligence, was her proudest possession, the marriage night the greatest event in her life, and bearing and raising children her sole contribution. Any girl foolish enough to part with her virginity before marriage, Thomas Branagan warned in *The Excellency of the Female Character*, "will be left in silent sadness to bewail your credulity, imbecility, duplicity, and premature prostitution." The home, the stabilizing core of a fluctuating society, was maintained and safeguarded by women. In return for that sovereignty she was expected to renounce all others. "Noble, sublime, is the task of the American mother," one author proclaimed. Those who left the hearth for the lectern "are only semi-women, mental hermaphrodites." Virtuous women possessed the most sublime and divine "rights" at home:

> The right to love whom others scorn,
> The right to comfort and to mourn,
> The right to shed new joy on earth,
> The right to feel the soul's high worth . . .
> Such women's rights, and God will bless
> And crown their champions with success.

Women who dared rebel against the prevailing social code required extraordinary fortitude. At every step their actions were greeted with public derision, taunts, and insults. "Mind," Hannah Crocker observed, "has no sex," but males feared making this dangerous concession. Emma Willard submitted a plan for improving female education to the New York legislature and opened a female seminary in 1821. One paper commented that "the most acceptable degree" for young ladies was "the degree of M.R.S." Elizabeth Blackwell's applications to enter medical school were repeatedly denied. "You cannot expect us," a male dean told her, "to furnish you with a stick to break our heads with." She was finally admitted to a small medical college in Geneva, New York. The townspeople, she reported, theorized that she was either "a bad woman, whose designs would gradually become evident, or that, being insane, an outbreak of insanity would soon be apparent." Elizabeth Cady Stanton, Lucretia Mott, and scores of other women were enthusiastic abolitionists. Yet women who journeyed to London in 1840 to attend the World Antislavery Convention were not permitted to participate. The men who excluded them "would have been horrified at the idea of burning the distinguished women present with red-hot irons," wrote Elizabeth Stanton, "but the crucifixion of their pride and self-respect, the humiliation of their spirit, seemed to them a most trifling matter." Women had stalwartly supported temperance reform since its inception. Yet when Susan B. Anthony attempted to address a temperance society convention in Albany, she was informed that "ladies" could listen but take no part in the proceedings.

Susan B. Anthony (above) and Elizabeth Cady Stanton (below) were central figures in the women's rights movement. Alice F. Tyler notes that "the friendship between the two women was remarkable. Neither was subordinate to the other; both were vital to the cause. Mrs. Stanton wrote and talked easily and well, and for many years she wrote the speeches for which Miss Anthony collected the material. Henry Stanton once said, 'You stir up Susan and she stirs the world,' and Mrs. Stanton herself admitted that she 'forged the thunder bolts' and Susan fired them." (American Antiquarian Society)

A sense of solidarity united feminists who had suffered male rebuffs and male condescension. At Seneca Falls, New York, in 1848, a women's rights convention adopted its own declaration of independence, a paraphrase of the original, which demanded that women "have immediate admission to all the rights and privileges which belong to them as citizens of the United States." Similar conventions followed in Massachusetts, Ohio, Pennsylvania, and Indiana, though men scorned and ridiculed their efforts. At a women's meeting in Akron, Ohio, unsympathetic clergymen invaded and dominated the discussion until Sojourner Truth—an old but fiery black female abolitionist—rose to speak, dramatically reminding her audience that women's rights were not meant for whites only:

> Dad man ober dar say dat womin needs to be helped into carriages and lifted ober ditches, and to hab de best place everywhar. Nobody eber helps me into carriages, or ober mud-puddles, or gibs me any best place! And a'n't I a woman? Look at my arm! I have ploughed, and planted and gathered into barns, and no man could head me! And a'n't I a woman? I could work as much and eat as much as a man—when I could get it—and bear de lash as well! And a'n't I a woman? I have borne thirteen chilern, and seen 'em mos' all sold off to slavery, and when I cried out with my mother's grief, none but Jesus heard me! And a'n't I a woman? Den dat little little man in black dar, he say women can't have as much rights as men, 'cause Christ wan't a woman! Whar did your Christ come from? Whar did your Christ come from? From God and a woman! Man had nothin' to do with Him!

The gains achieved by these activist women were modest. More schools were opened to women. Elementary teaching positions became almost a female monopoly (though women were paid considerably less than men). Massachusetts and Indiana liberalized their divorce laws. New York in 1860 gave women the right to sue as well as control their own wages and property. Most important, a slight breach had been made in the wall of male chauvinism, and examples of female courage sustained later feminists in their struggle for equality.

The humanitarian impulse and Christian love of reformers had distinct limits. It scoffed at the pretensions of women who thought themselves equal to men. And it balked altogether at the idea of equating Catholicism with other faiths. Reverend Lyman Beecher thought that "if it had been the design of Heaven to establish a powerful nation in the full enjoyment of civil and religious liberty . . . where should such an experiment have been made but in this country!" Beecher helped heaven's design by espousing the causes of abolition, temperance, and educational reform. He also wrote *Plea for the West* (1835), a nativist attack upon Catholicism whose policies would "inflame the nation, break the bond of our union, and throw down our free institutions." On one occasion Beecher's anti-Catholic sermons inflamed a Boston mob to attack and burn an Ursuline convent.

Anti-Catholicism was an old and familiar prejudice of Protestants in America, but never before had it flared into full-scale bigotry. In 1830 there

Anti-Catholicism

were 318,000 Catholics in the United States, making up only 3 percent of the population; shortly before the Civil War there were 3 million, some 10 percent of the population. The huge Irish immigration had made Catholicism the largest religion in America. Catholics were "crowding our cities, lining our railroads and canals," a worried critic observed, "and electing our rulers." Samuel F. B. Morse, promoter of the telegraph, spread the alarm in his book, *Foreign Conspiracy Against the Liberties of the United States* (1835). Maria Monk's lurid fiction, *Awful Disclosures of the Hotel Dieu Nunnery of Montreal* (1836), was taken as truth, and it spawned dozens of imitations. There were, of course, numerous rebuttals. If many Protestant intellectuals included anti-Catholicism in their roster of reforms, others such as Parke Godwin in New York and Henry Wise in Virginia denounced the lies and humbug directed against Catholics. Benedict Webb, a Kentucky Catholic, wrote: "The man who impugns my patriotism on account of my religious opinions, is either an insane bigot who claims my pity, or a foul-mouthed slanderer who has my contempt." The defense was less effective than the slander. Because they were frightened by irrational fears of "papal influence" and believing they were fighting to save their country, nativists rioted in cities such as Baltimore, St. Louis, Louisville, and New Orleans.

The Order of the Star Spangled Banner, organized in 1849, combined with other nativist groups and entered politics as the American or Know-Nothing party. The party scored impressive victories in 1854–55, carrying at least seven states (mainly northern) and gaining substantial support in seven others (mainly southern). Then, as quickly as it had blossomed, the Know-Nothing party faded. It had accomplished nothing of substance where it held power. (In Massachusetts, for example, committees spent inordinate sums investigating nunneries and convent schools.) Moreover, it lacked effective leadership. Most important, the Know-Nothing party anticipated that it might achieve victory by uniting a majority of Americans on the basis of anti-Catholic and antiforeign prejudice, only to find its ranks divided over the issue of slavery. Thousands of members deserted the nativist cause to join the major parties. In 1856, Millard Fillmore, the Know-Nothing presidential candidate, could garner no more than eight electoral votes.

Varieties of Religious Experience

A resurgence of religious spirit, a second Great Awakening, crossed over the land in the early nineteenth century. The fastest-growing faiths were evangelical ones that rejected elaborate theological structures understood by the few for emotional appeals appreciated by the many. This movement was in keeping with the temper of the times. The age of deference had passed, replaced by an age of mass participation, of egalitarian values, which sought simpler, more democratic paths, including the path to heaven. There could be no exclusivity in politics, economics, or religion. Old-fashioned Calvinism, with its emphasis on predestination, finally lost its hold upon the New England mind. Unitarianism took its place, at least among the intellectual elite. For the masses, however, Unitarianism was too cold, too cerebral, and too lacking in essential piety. They preferred fiery, declamatory sermons that stirred the soul. "Young men," Lyman Beecher advised prospective ministers, "pump yourselves brim full of your subject till you can't hold another drop, and then knock out the bung and let nature caper." Revivalism became the central element of the Protestant structure. All churches were affected, though the Methodists and Baptists reaped the richest rewards in numbers of converts.

Revivalism seemed to fulfill the psychological needs of society. Men and women under the spell of itinerant preachers twitched their bodies, rolled on the ground, shrieked in agitation (or religious ecstasy), barked like dogs, suffered hallucinations, and often fell unconscious. "Jerking" was a common symptom of their camp meetings. "The hands of the jerking patients flew with wondrous quickness, from side to side in various directions," a witness to a Kentucky revival noted, "and their necks doubled back like a flail in the hands of the thresher. Their faces were distorted and black, and their eyes seemed to flash horror and distraction." All kinds of religions proliferated in America, particularly in rural and frontier areas, including some rather strange and short-lived cultists who followed self-proclaimed seers. Vermont and upstate New York, along the main route of New Englanders journeying westward, was especially "burnt-over" by the fires of religious excitement. Here there originated the Millennial movement of William Miller, who predicted that the second coming of Christ would occur in 1843, then revised the date to 1844. Millennialism spread phenomenally into the urban East and as far west as Iowa. A million converts were claimed, mainly poor and uneducated farmers, workers, and shopkeepers, who accepted Miller's prediction and prepared accordingly. Some disposed of all their material possessions. Some went berserk when the appointed day passed without Christ's appearance. Miller continued to believe, supported by a handful of Adventists; but the rest, terribly disillusioned, abandoned their faith in Millennialism.

The "burnt-over" district also spawned a variety of spiritualists. Many educated people were attracted by clairvoyants, perhaps because they were not zealous holy rollers and claimed to offer direct communion with divine forces. The Fox sisters of Rochester became nationally famous for their alleged ability to contact the spiritual world. "We are convinced beyond a doubt," testified Horace Greeley, publisher of the New York Tribune, "of their perfect integrity and good faith." Though some mediums were exposed as charlatans (including the Fox sisters), prominent figures such as James Fenimore Cooper, Edgar Allan Poe, Harriet Beecher Stowe, the historian George Bancroft, the Workingmen's party advocate Robert Dale Owen, the scientist Robert Hare, and the transcendentalist preacher Theodore Parker, either endorsed the authenticity of or experimented with seances and other spiritualistic phenomena. Every town seemed to have a renowned local medium. Spiritualism as a part of religious faith was widespread. It was an integral component of Shaker religious life and of Swedenborgianism, which several Brook Farm residents took seriously. Andrew Jackson Davis, known

The evangelistic impulse was at the core of American religion in the first half of the nineteenth century, and its geographic center was in New York. There were always critics who disapproved of the emotional excesses displayed at camp meetings and doubted the validity of the religious conversions claimed. Usually the most unrestrained excitement was exhibited at frontier revivals. Others, such as that pictured here at Sing Sing, New York, in 1859, were generally restrained, the sermons and singing complimented by many visitors. (Library of Congress)

as the "Poughkeepsie Seer," swore that he talked with Swedenborg's ghost, as well as with Benjamin Franklin and St. Paul. Adin Ballou, a respected reformer and leader of the Hopedale Community in Massachusetts, was a spiritualist. So was Warren Chase, founder of a Fourierist commune in Wisconsin.

The most astonishing success story in American religion originated in the "burnt-over" district. In 1830 Joseph Smith had dug up golden plates and deciphered them with the aid of magic stones: his work was published as the *Book of Mormon* in Palmyra, New York. Within two decades, despite Protestant hostility, which drove Smith's supporters from New York to Ohio

The Mormons

to Missouri to Illinois and, finally, to Utah, Mormonism became the ninth largest religion in the United States. The governor of Missouri declared Mormon residents to be "public enemies," who must be "exterminated or driven from the State, if necessary, for the public good." At Carthage, Illinois, a wild mob of two hundred, unrestrained by militia, killed Joseph Smith and his brother. Under the leadership of Brigham Young the Mormons moved on to the valley of the Great Salt Lake in Utah. Here they hoped to build, as had the Puritans two centuries earlier, a Zion in the wilderness. Here was virgin land and the promise of salvation. "In this place," wrote a Mormon convert from England, "there is a prospect of receiving every good thing both of this world and that which is to come."

Even in that isolated region hostility pursued the Mormons. Emigrant groups on their way to California complained of the outrageous prices Mormons charged for goods. Brigham Young's autocratic rule conflicted with the authority of territorial judges appointed by the federal government. But most criticism was directed at the Mormon practice of polygamy, which many reformers classed with slavery as a barbaric evil not to be tolerated in America. An agent of the American Bible Society described the Mormon

"I do not believe," a traveler once noted, referring to the Mormons, "that there is another people in existence who could have made such improvements in the same length of time, under the same circumstances." The sturdy character of the Mormons was admired, but their practice of polygamy outraged public opinion. Shown here is an etching from an early photograph of a Mormon pioneer family. (New York Public Library)

colony as a "bedlam, brothel, sink of iniquity, Hades, and vortex of moral ruin." Anti-Mormon feeling reached a pitch when a wagon train of one hundred twenty emigrants was murdered by a combined force of Indians and Mormons. One eastern newspaper demanded that the "beastly heresy" of Mormonism be crushed. "This is the first rebellion which has existed in our territories," President Buchanan declared, "and humanity itself requires that we should put it down in such a manner that it shall be the last." His order dispatching federal troops to Utah territory might have led to war were it not for the good sense of peace negotiators on both sides. Thereafter the Mormons nominally accepted the authority of "gentile" governors from Washington, continued to obey Brigham Young, and set an example of thrift, industry, and piety, which attracted many converts and did much to earn the respect of all Americans.

All told, the cause of religion prospered in the nineteenth century, if one judges by its free expression, its amazing assortment of creeds, its vitality, and its growth. However, theology went bankrupt. In this respect it bore a striking parallel to political developments. No group of political leaders emerged to match the stellar array of intellectual talent that had guided America during the Revolutionary and Federalist eras. And no Protestant theology or theologians of the first order were produced during the century of its greatest expansion.

An energetic and bustling America emphasized practicality rather than theology and applauded material achievements rather than philosophical systems. People interested in either building or reforming had no time for metaphysical hairsplitting or recondite reasoning. One might expect, therefore, that America had little to contribute culturally, that the leveling effects of a democratic society would drive out intellectual creativity. Some authors and artists, disillusioned and disengaged from the American scene, fled to Europe. Some spoke rather bitterly, and with much truth, about the crudity and vulgarity of their own land, with its lack of opportunities for the serious writer. "The utmost any American author can look for in his native country," Charles Brockden Brown told his brother, "is to be reimbursed his unavoidable expenses." James Fenimore Cooper spent much time abroad and complained of the poverty of the imagination in America. "There are no annals for the historian; no follies . . . for the satirist; no manners for the dramatist; no obscure fictions for the writer of romance . . . nor any of the rich artificial auxiliaries of poetry," Cooper wrote contemptuously in *Notions of the Americans* (1828). His indictment was repeated by many other American authors at a later date. Yet Brown and Cooper were distinctively American. Their works marked a shift from the classical tradition of the eighteenth century to the romantic movement of the nineteenth century. Cooper published more than fifty books and pamphlets in thirty years, frequently using the American wilderness as a setting to spin out his themes of conflict between the civilized and the primitive.

As early as 1778 Noah Webster called for a declaration of cultural

Cultural Independence

freedom. "America," he wrote, "must be as independent in *literature* as she is in *politics,* as famous for *arts* as for *arms*." This nationalistic appeal was echoed many times over, but without too much success. In Boston the Anthology Club and in New York City the Friendly Club were formed to encourage American authors to cast off fashionable British styles and to create a national literature. Few agreed with Cooper that the United States was a land of dull uniformity. Rather, it was endlessly diverse, and it required authors of sagacity and skill to exploit the rich materials it afforded. Ralph Waldo Emerson in his Phi Beta Kappa address, "The American Scholar," delivered at Harvard University in 1837, exulted that "our day of dependence, our long apprenticeship to the learning of other lands, draws to a close. The millions that around us are rushing into life cannot always be fed on the sere remains of foreign harvests. Events, actions arise, that must be sung, that will sing themselves." Walt Whitman responded wholeheartedly, setting himself the task of consciously joining democracy to literature, of becoming the poet Emerson envisioned singing of America. "The drama of this country," he once wrote, "can be the mouthpiece of freedom." If Cooper saw mainly contradictions and ambiguities in America, which soured him, Whitman loved the expansive multiplicity of democratic forces at work in the land. As a young reporter on the Brooklyn *Daily Eagle* he asked for "American plays, fitted to American opinions and institutions." "The United States themselves," he once noted, "are essentially the greatest poem." Whitman set the type for *Leaves of Grass* (1855) with his own hand. The twelve poems in free verse were coarse, uneven, sensuous, and mystical; they were also emphatically and authentically American.

The essays of Emerson and Thoreau and the poetry of Whitman mark a turning away from Europe. The trend was equally apparent in the novels of Nathaniel Hawthorne and Herman Melville. Between 1850 and 1855 there appeared *The Scarlet Letter* and *The House of Seven Gables* by Hawthorne, *Moby Dick* by Melville, *Walden* by Thoreau, and *Leaves of Grass* by Whitman. "You may search all the rest of American literature," according to one critic, "without being able to collect a group of books equal to these in imaginative vitality."

In the end the American public reviled Cooper for his criticisms. Thoreau was little appreciated in the United States though hailed as a genius elsewhere. Hawthorne enjoyed some success, as did Whitman, but Melville was too profound to be popular, and he died in obscurity. The masses, then as now, preferred reading sentimental novels that stirred the emotions and did not tax the intellect. Their tastes ran to what was practical or patriotic or moral or pornographic posing as moral. The leading male writer in America was George Lippard, a religious charlatan, pseudoradical, and superpatriot. His novel, *The Quaker City; or The Monks of Monk Hall* (1844), was filled with sinister Jews, hulking blacks, corrupt clergymen, and grasping bankers who raped virgins and killed old women. The combination of sex and social protest was irresistible. The book sold sixty thousand copies the first year of

Mass Culture

publication, and half that number annually for the next decade. Lippard's patriotic writings were equally spurious. His *Washington and His Generals; or Legends of the American Revolution* (1847), another best-seller, began the myth of the "Liberty Bell's" being rung to announce the signing of the Declaration of Independence.

Heartrending stories of poor orphans, ravished innocence, and blighted love—forerunners of the modern soap opera—were favorites of American readers. The fiction of Sir Walter Scott and Charles Dickens was much in demand, and American female authors joined in, virtually monopolizing the "domestic" novel. Mary Jane Holmes's lachrymose books became classics, selling over a million copies. Maria Cummins's *The Lamplighter* (1854) was an instant success. Probably the best-known book was *The Wide Wide World* (1854) by Susan Warner. Her characters, one reviewer commented, "are distinguished for the union of purity, sweetness, and admirable sense. . . . They display a naturalness and beauty of conduct which never fails to touch the moral sensibilities." Little wonder that Hawthorne remarked in anger: "America is now wholly given over to a damned mob of scribbling women, and I should have no chance of success while the public taste is occupied with their trash."

Above all, Americans loved oratory, especially if it was inspiring and educational. The lyceum movement—an association providing public lectures—spread so rapidly that by 1835 there were three thousand in existence in fifteen states. In 1859 *Harper's Magazine* observed that "the lyceum has now become a fixed American institution." For a modest fee anyone could attend and hear talks on various subjects: "The Life of Mohammed," "The Honey Bee," "The Education of Children," "The Memoirs of Count Rumford," "The Progress of Democracy." Emerson was a great favorite on the lyceum circuit, as were Daniel Webster and Horace Mann. The lyceum was undoubtedly a more significant cultural force than formal academic institutions. Besides spreading knowledge to all age groups, they encouraged the establishment of public schools and libraries as well as scientific collections. A Swedish visitor to America, P. A. Siljeström, was so impressed that he advised Europeans to copy the lyceum if they wished to avoid either despotism or revolution.

With the development of more efficient printing techniques, such as the Hoe rotary press, newspapers became inexpensive educational instruments for the masses. To be sure, the "penny press" thrived on sensationalism, emphasizing the three r's of rape, riot, and robbery. And many remained political sheets of no particular distinction. But by the 1840s reputable metropolitan dailies, such as Horace Greeley's New York *Tribune*, helped form American cultural tastes. Political news came first, of course, as well as commercial items, yet the paper also contained book notices, synopses of lyceum lectures, editorials espousing reforms, travel accounts by distinguished journalists, and extended analytical essays by foreign correspondents. Karl Marx, in fact, was the London correspondent for the *Tribune* before the Civil War.

One aspect of the American character dominated all others. An aggressive people, Americans were also incurably sentimental; inclined to materialistic goals, they made a fetish of piety; culturally chauvinistic, still they harbored the idea that Europeans could do it better; if most were boosters and boasters, others were dissatisfied reformers. In this complex of opposites, Americans sought unity in patriotism. Local jealousies and sectional tensions might prevail, but all could unite in veneration of the past—if only the past could be sterilized and sanctified. The figure of George Washington was an obvious and inevitable choice to be mythologized by a public who yearned for an incorruptible father image to glorify.

The Deification of Washington

The process of glorification whereby Washington was converted from a fallible human to a faultless saint began early and was exceedingly rapid and thorough. Even while Americans still mourned his death in 1799, an itinerant book peddler and evangelist, Mason Locke Weems, decided to enrich himself (financially) and the nation (morally) by penning a series of mainly spurious anecdotes revealing the "Great Virtues" of Washington. The work of this clever fraud, which first appeared in 1800, had an enormous impact, probably greater than that of any other single volume in American history. It satisfied the public need to hear homilies of Washington's life and accounts of his piety, wisdom, and dedication. Other heroes might possess blemishes, but Washington as Father of His Country needed to appear spotless. So he was presented by Weems and by dozens of imitators, and so he was envisioned by Americans.

A few resisted the unqualified acclaim. Emerson remarked that people bored with such unstinting praise were apt to remark in private, "Damn George Washington." Artemus Ward poked at the image: "G. Washington was abowt the best man this world ever sot eyes on. . . . He never slopt over." Hawthorne wrote derisively: "Did any body ever see Washington nude? It is inconceivable. He had no nakedness, but I imagine he was born with his clothes on, and his hair powdered, and made a stately bow on his first appearance before the world." Yet those who refused to join in the deification of Washington, who insisted that men, while good enough, are far more complex and fascinating than mere divinities, were in a distinct minority. More typical were the words of Abraham Lincoln, who owned the tenth edition of Weems, and learned its lessons well. "To add brightness to the sun or glory to the name of Washington is alike impossible," he proclaimed on February 22, 1842. "Let none attempt it. In solemn awe pronounce the name and in its naked deathless splendor leave it shining on."

All the patriotic reverence of Washington, together with all the Fourth of July speeches, could not make the issue of slavery disappear. Until the second quarter of the nineteenth century slavery was not a major issue to white Americans. Advertisements for runaway slaves appeared regularly in the northern press. Occasionally a Quaker petition recommending the abolition of slavery raised a flurry in Congress. Americans, North and South, were well aware of the dichotomy between preaching liberty and practicing slavery.

The Abolitionist Attack

But the North was preoccupied with economic development. The southern position was both firm and apologetic. If they would not tolerate interference with slavery, neither would they build any elaborate arguments to defend it. These attitudes began to change in the 1830s and 1840s. The reforming energies directed against the money power were also turned to combat the slave power. "Everybody is opposed to slavery," wrote William Lloyd Garrison sarcastically, "O, yes! There is an abundance of philanthropy among us." The question of what to do about it divided the northerners into bitterly antagonistic camps. At one extreme were abolitionists who followed the lead of Garrison. They preached that slavery was a sin to be atoned only by instantaneous repentance—the immediate and uncompensated emancipation of all slaves. Like other zealots, Garrison had little patience with those who questioned his methods. His newspaper, the *Liberator,* established in Boston in 1831, never attained a circulation greater than three thousand. Nevertheless, to most contemporaries and to many later scholars, Garrison symbolized the antislavery crusade.

A second center of abolitionism existed in upstate New York, western Pennsylvania, and Ohio. This movement stemmed from and borrowed the techniques of religious revivalism. It was at once more practical, more moderate, more influential, and more politically oriented than the Garrisonians. A volume by one of the better-known leaders, Theodore Weld's *Slavery As It Is* (1839), sold over a hundred thousand copies the first year. Weld advocated the doctrine of gradual immediatism: to begin the process of emancipation of slaves immediately and to achieve complete freedom gradually.

Abolitionists alternately cooperated and quarreled among themselves, yet many shared a common martyrdom. Most northerners, although they might admit that slavery was evil, professed that it was not their affair. Abolitionist speeches pricked northerners' consciences and aroused furious reactions. In 1835 Garrison was tied with a rope and pulled through the streets of Boston by an enraged mob, which threatened to lynch him. Elijah Lovejoy was less fortunate. He was killed in 1837 in Alton, Illinois, defending his printing press against a rampaging mob. Nor were these isolated examples: hundreds of incidents occurred in which abolitionists' homes were sacked, or their meetings disrupted, or their offices destroyed, or bodily harm inflicted. Then, in less than a decade, northern opinion shifted. Abolitionism was still hardly popular, but abolitionists came to be tolerated by the masses and toasted by the intellectuals.

The Southern Defense

Partly as a reaction to northern abolitionism, the South began to devote its collective intellectual abilities to proving that slavery was a wise and beneficial practice. Southern ministers cited the gospel as a theological defense. Southern economists asserted that slaves were better treated than many northern workers. Southern politicians reproached northerners for criticizing an institution recognized by the Constitution. Southern scientists concluded that blacks were intellectually inferior to whites and therefore suited to be

Distribution of Slaves, 1820

PERCENT OF SLAVES IN TOTAL POPULATION

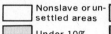

Nonslave or un-settled areas

Under 10%

10% to 30%

Over 30%

Distribution of Slaves, 1860

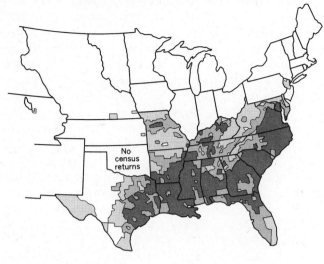

No census returns

Cotton Production, 1820

Cotton Production, 1860

As these four maps indicate, the concentration of slave population followed the areas of highest cotton production. The kingdom of cotton did not remain confined to the East, but shifted westward, first into Georgia, then Alabama, and then into the rich lands of the Mississippi delta. Where cotton was king, there the ratio of slave to free population was greatest.

slaves. Southern historians pointed to the existence of slavery in ancient and contemporary cultures. Southerners may once have questioned the profitability of slavery and speculated about its deleterious effects on whites, but such reservations were swept away by the 1840s. Contrary views were not permitted. Discussion was not tolerated. Slavery was deemed essential to the economic system and the social stability of the South. Indeed, southerners boasted that through slavery they had created a unique civilization, superior to all others. So zealous was the South's attempt at justification that for decades it produced few enduring works in art, literature, philosophy, or science.

Lurking behind this self-assurance was the gnawing fear of slave insurrection. "We regard our Negroes," one southerner commented, "as the *Jacobins* of the country, against whom we should always be on our guard." The black slave was not the docile, contented, loyal servant romantics like to imagine. Nor was he the rebellious firebrand some authors have portrayed. Statistically many more conspiracies were plotted than the small number of open rebellions that were actually attempted. Nevertheless, at times the fear of a "Black Terror" led southern whites to the point of hysteria. Repression and white supremacy became the distinguishing hallmarks of the antebellum South and were passed on to future generations.

The obtuseness and intransigence of southern congressmen helped the abolitionist cause. For some time abolitionist societies had been flooding Congress with petitions to emancipate slaves or to forbid the slave trade in the District of Columbia. These petitions had no practical effect and served

The "Gag" Resolution

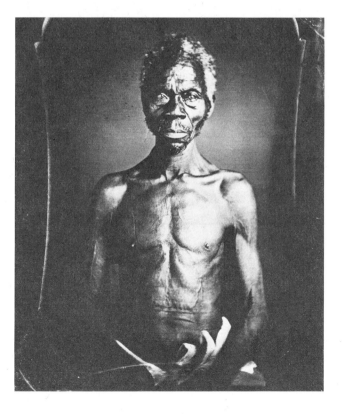

Recently discovered, this daguerreotype of a slave was made in 1850 in Columbia, South Carolina, to aid the research of Louis Agassiz, a renowned scientist. Agassiz theorized that human races did not stem from a common ancestor—a position many Southern intellectuals adopted—and he studied slaves for anatomical evidence to support his belief. (Peabody Museum, Harvard University. Photograph by Hillel Burger)

only to impede the consideration of other business. But they occasionally provoked discussions of slavery, which the southerners wanted to block. Some northern members agreed that the subject was dangerous and should be silenced. Thus, in 1836, the lower house passed a "gag" resolution to receive and automatically table all such petitions. Technically the "gag" rule was not an abridgement of the right of petition, but in effect it constituted a denial of that right.

Massachusetts' most famous congressman, old John Quincy Adams—ex-minister, ex-secretary of state, and ex-president—singlehandedly took up the cudgels for free discussion. Adams was friendly to the antislavery movement, though he was no abolitionist. Indeed, he had voted to maintain slavery in the capital. But the right of petition transcended immediate issues. At stake, Adams told his constituents, was "your freedom of thought and of action, and the freedom of speech in Congress of your representative." For eight years Adams scored southerners in debate, enduring their taunts, their intimidations, and even their attempts to pass resolutions of censure, until the rule was finally repealed in 1844. By that time a solid core of northern congressmen, mainly from the Whig party, had joined Adams. And by that time events in Texas had pushed northern congressmen further toward the antislavery position.

Early American migrants to the Mexican territory of Texas did not journey there with a view to rebellion and the hope of eventual annexation to the United States, though Mexicans, with good reason, came to believe such was the case. Like the movement across the boundary into Canada, migration into Texas was impelled by land hunger. Many were prepared to live under a different flag. A few were outlaws who defied all flags. When a group of Texas settlers revolted in 1826 and established the Fredonian Republic, Americans led by Stephen Austin cooperated with Mexican troops to suppress the uprising. In the next decade, however, Americans in Texas became increasingly dissatisfied. The Mexican government was unstable, inept, corrupt, and despotic. Slave property was not secure. Political and economic grievances over the tariff, immigration, and representation were in turn aggravated by cultural clashes between the proud Texans and the aristocratic Mexicans. Ultimately a short but decisive revolution resulted. On March 2, 1836, Texan independence was declared; on March 6, the Alamo fell; on April 21, at the battle of San Jacinto, the Mexican army of General Santa Anna was routed. Thereafter the Texans quickly ratified a constitution, legalized slavery, made Sam Houston their president, and voted by the overwhelming ratio of sixty to one to abandon their recently acquired sovereignty if the United States would agree to annex Texas.

Abolitionists interpreted American expansion into Texas as part of a southern conspiracy to extend the boundaries of slavery. John Quincy Adams echoed the charge and added some vivid reminders of what annexation of Texas would entail: a costly and bloody war with Mexico. Northern politicians were alarmed at the political weight that would be added to the South if Texas, carved into perhaps five states, were admitted. Eight northern

The Texas Question

states passed resolutions of opposition. Even if Andrew Jackson wanted annexation, he could not act without jeopardizing the election of his successor, Martin Van Buren. Just before retiring from the presidency, Jackson received the minister from the Lone Star Republic, and the United States officially recognized the independence of Texas.

During the administrations of Martin Van Buren, William Henry Harrison, and John Tyler, the annexation question agitated American politics. Andrew Jackson urged Tyler to take some determinative action. Britain was making serious overtures to the Texas Republic. "To prevent Great Britain from getting it, or an influence over it," warned Jackson, "we must have it, *peaceably if we can, but forcibly if we must.*" Some northerners who had purchased Texas bonds and thus had an economic interest in the area's future strongly advised annexation. Tyler needed little encouragement. One of his main purposes in appointing John C. Calhoun as secretary of state in March 1844 had been to fashion a treaty that would bring Texas into the Union. The attempt failed. In addition to the indefatigable Adams, but for different reasons, a bipartisan group, which included Thomas Hart Benton and Henry Clay, voted to defeat the treaty Calhoun submitted. Following nine years of fruitless effort in Congress, expansionists turned to the people. The election of 1844, it was hoped, would finally decide the issue of Texas.

Rejecting Martin Van Buren, the Democratic party nominated a dark horse candidate, the first in American history, James K. Polk of Tennessee. Their platform promised the "reannexation" of Texas and, to satisfy northern Democrats, the "reoccupation" of Oregon to the latitude of 54°40'. Carrying out either plank could well mean war with Mexico or Great Britain. Were the majority of American voters willing to risk it? Democratic orators whipped up sentiment for expansion. The United States was pursuing a divine destiny to attain its natural geographic limits, Democrats proclaimed, a movement at once glorious, inevitable, irresistible—and manifest. The "peace" candidate of the Whig party, the venerable Henry Clay, was also confident of victory. Clay had declared plainly enough that he would annex Texas if it could be accomplished "without dishonor, without war, with the common consent of the Union, and upon just and fair terms." Would a majority respect Clay's experience and trust his cautious judgment? The result was close—and cruelly ironical. Clay lost the election by losing New York State; he lost New York because the abolitionist Liberty party candidate, James Birney, attracted enough antislavery Whig votes to give Polk the edge. Out of a total of 2,636,000 votes cast for the two major candidates, Polk won by only 38,000.

Despite the narrow margin, President Tyler considered the results a popular mandate for the annexation of Texas. Before his office passed to Polk, Tyler suggested that Congress pass a joint resolution to annex Texas. The strategy was constitutionally questionable but undoubtedly shrewd, for a resolution needed only a simple majority while a treaty required a vote of two-thirds. The final ballot was nevertheless close: 120 to 98 in the House of Representatives and 27 to 25 in the Senate.

The Election of 1844

Had Polk been content with the incorporation of Texas, war with Mexico *War with Mexico* might have been avoided, but annexation led to ruptured relations between the two countries. The offended nationalism of the Mexicans clashed with the expansive nationalism of the Americans and stirred martial feelings on both sides. Still, to say that the war was inevitable excuses responsibility for it. War was inevitable because Polk made it so. He wanted California as the basis of an American empire fronting on the Pacific, and one way or another he was determined to wrest the land from Mexico.

Polk was no swashbuckling militarist. He preferred peaceful solutions and was willing to compromise. He had done so with Great Britain over the northwestern boundary between the United States and Canada. In 1846 a settlement had been arranged at the forty-ninth latitude, a compromise that was heartily approved by the people of both countries, despite the opinions of some extremists and disgruntled politicians. To Mexico Polk had dispatched a minister, John Slidell, to offer money for California. The mission failed. "Be assured," Slidell reported, "that nothing is to be done with these people until they shall have been chastised." Polk then ordered American troops commanded by General Zachary Taylor to enter disputed territory between the Nueces and Rio Grande rivers. The results of this deliberately provocative act were all that Polk could ask. Shots were fired; Taylor reported sixteen Americans killed or wounded; and Polk coolly asked Congress to declare war on the grounds that Mexico had commenced hostilities.

An American military victory was never in doubt, though the Mexicans fought courageously against what a later generation would call invading imperialistic forces. Polk's main problem, in fact, was to keep the war small while continuing it until its chief purpose—the acquisition of California—was attained. He was embarrassed, one scholar has written, by "an ephemeral enemy that continued to lose all the battles but refused to ask for terms of peace." At home a substantial number of Americans disapproved of "Mr. Polk's war." Abraham Lincoln, a young Whig congressman from Illinois, received national attention when he demanded to know the precise spot upon which American blood was first spilled. As the war progressed some leading Democrats joined the Whigs in requesting that it be speedily terminated. By accident as much as by design, the war ended as Polk had wished. Nicholas Trist, the chief clerk of the state department, had been sent to Mexico to negotiate. Although recalled by Polk, he ignored the order and stayed to sign the peace treaty of Guadalupe Hidalgo. According to the terms Mexico ceded virtually all its northern half, including New Mexico and California; in return the United States agreed to pay fifteen million dollars and to assume American claims that totaled three and a quarter million dollars. Polk asked the Senate to ignore the circumstances surrounding the transactions and to vote on the merits of the treaty. Thus, one observer commented, the peace "negotiated by an unauthorized agent, with an unacknowledged government, submitted by an accidental president to a dissatisfied Senate, has, notwithstanding these objections in form, been confirmed."

172 [7] REFORM AND EXPANSION, 1840–1850

Polk was no less triumphant in his other presidential objectives. Besides settling the Oregon boundary with Great Britain and seizing California from Mexico, he achieved a reduction of the tariff and engineered the reestablishment of the independent treasury system. An eminent nineteenth-century historian called Polk "one of the very foremost of our public men and one of the very best and most honest and most successful Presidents the country ever had." Yet two problems resulted from the Mexican War, which Polk had clearly foreseen but which he had been powerless to avoid.

One was political. The generals in charge of the Mexican War, Zachary Taylor and Winfield Scott, were both Whigs. Scott was a bit pompous. But Taylor, affecting simplicity, became a popular hero known as "Old Rough and Ready." He fully appreciated the value of the press and conducted each military campaign with an eye to the next presidential election. Polk could not have removed him from command without arousing a storm of public protest. As a result Taylor went on to obtain both the Whig nomination in 1848 and then the presidency, defeating the Democrats' choice, Lewis Cass of Michigan.

The other problem was more significant. During the war Congressman David Wilmot, a Pennsylvania Democrat, attached a rider to an appropriation bill that specified that "neither slavery nor involuntary servitude shall ever exist" in any lands acquired from Mexico. Wilmot's proviso passed the lower house repeatedly but each time met defeat in the Senate. There the South Carolinian John C. Calhoun introduced resolutions—despite ample precedents to the contrary—denying the congressional right to prohibit slavery in any territory of the United States. These were also defeated. In and out of Congress suspicions and jealousies between northerners and southerners created an atmosphere of misunderstanding. The two sections had long coexisted by means of cooperation and compromise, but as the 1840s closed each was regarding the other with increasing distrust and animosity.

COMMENTARY

Few issues in American history have been more persistently divisive than that of slavery, particularly slavery in the West. Many observers claimed that the problem was essentially theoretical. A special set of geographic and climatic conditions were necessary, they insisted, to raise the kinds of crops upon which slave labor could profitably be employed. Since those conditions were not present in the Great Plains, the Rocky Mountains, or the southwestern deserts, slavery could not possibly spread there. Others agreed but maintained that a principle was involved, one that was worth fighting for. And still others regarded the question as neither specious nor academic. They felt that the lush valleys of California could conceivably support a thriving slave economy. California was growing swiftly because of the discovery of gold in 1849 and had in fact already applied for admission to the union as a free state. Theoretical or not, the problem of slavery was ominous for the American future.

Three major Protestant churches— Presbyterians, Methodists, and Baptists— were divided over slavery (and would remain divided until the twentieth century). The issue also crossed party lines. In the North,

"Conscience Whigs" and "Barnburner Democrats" abandoned their traditional political allegiances and joined with ex-Liberty party members to form the Free Soil party. In the lower South a southern rights movement was initiated that ignored the old partisan loyalties. Gradually the institutional links of nationalism were snapping beneath the weight of aroused sectionalism. Most northerners were not abolitionists, but they considered slavery a moral wrong; they wanted it kept out of the territories by congressional law; and they wished to admit California as a free state.

Most southerners were not secessionists, but they believed the western territories belonged to all Americans and that each citizen had a constitutional right to bring slave property there. They reasoned that, since California had been won, in the main, by southern soldiers, it should come in as a slave state or not at all, and they were incensed at northerners who made a mockery of the Constitution by blocking the return of fugitive slaves. Clearly the question of slavery had to be resolved or the consequence would be disunion.

SUGGESTED READING

IRVING H. BARTLETT, The American Mind in the Mid-Nineteenth Century (1967)
ARTHUR BESTOR, Backwoods Utopias (1950)
RAY BILLINGTON, The Far Western Frontier (1956)
———, The Protestant Crusade (1938)
CARL BODE, The American Lyceum: Town Meeting of the Mind (1956)
———, The Anatomy of American Popular Culture, 1840–1861 (1959)
DANIEL BOORSTIN, The Americans: The National Experience (1965)
E. DOUGLAS BRANCH, The Sentimental Years (1934)
FAWN BRODIE, No Man Knows My History: The Life of Joseph Smith (2nd Rev. 1971)
VAN WYCK BROOKS, The Flowering of New England (1936)
HENRY S. COMMAGER, The Era of Reform (1960)
———, Theodore Parker (1936)
WHITNEY CROSS, The Burned-Over District (1950)
MERLE CURTI, The American Peace Crusade (1929)
ARTHUR A. EKIRCH, The Idea of Progress in America (1944)
LESLIE FIEDLER, Love and Death in the American Novel (Rev. ed. 1966)
LOUIS FILLER, The Crusade Against Slavery (1960)
ELEANOR FLEXNER, Century of Struggle: The Women's Rights Movement in the United States (1968)
OCTAVIUS B. FROTHINGHAM, Transcendentalism in New England (1959)
EUGENE GENOVESE, Roll, Jordan, Roll (1974)
NORMAN GRAEBNER, Empire on the Pacific (1955)
JOSEPH R. GUSFIELD, Symbolic Crusade: Status Politics and the American Temperance Movement (1963)
JOHN A. KROUT, The Origins of Prohibition (1925)
GERDA LERNER, The Black Woman in White America (1972)
F. O. MATTHIESSEN, American Renaissance (1941)
FREDERICK MERK, Manifest Destiny and Mission in American History (1963)
———, The Monroe Doctrine and American Expansionism, 1843–1849 (1966)
DAVID ROTHMAN, The Discovery of the Asylum (1971)
CLARA SEARS, Days of Delusion (1924)

CHARLES SELLERS, *James K. Polk* (1957-66)

JOEL SILBEY, *The Shrine of Party: Congressional Voting Behavior, 1841–1852* (1967)

ANDREW SINCLAIR, *The Better Half: The Emancipation of the American Woman* (1965)

HENRY N. SMITH, *Virgin Land* (1950)

KENNETH STAMPP, *The Peculiar Institution* (1956)

ALICE F. TYLER, *Freedom's Ferment* (1944)

BERNARD WEISBERGER, *They Gathered at the River* (1958)

8

Slavery and Civil War, 1850–1865

Compromise of 1850

The spirit of concession, which had so often and so effectively operated in past crises, was invoked once again by Henry Clay. A master politician in the best sense of that term, Clay had long espoused the concept of sectional balance. Now, in the winter of 1850, and in the twilight of his life, he rose in the Senate to plead once again the cause of moderation. "I hold in my hand," he said, "a series of resolutions which I desire to submit. . . . Taken together, in combination, they propose an amicable arrangement of all questions in controversy between the free and slave states, growing out of the subject of Slavery." Clay's proposals encompassed several points.

1. California would enter the Union as a free state.
2. The southwestern regions would be organized into territories by legislation that neither permitted nor excluded slavery.
3. The Texas boundary with New Mexico would be drawn in the latter's favor, and Texas would be compensated by federal assumption of its preannexation debts.
4. The slave trade, though not slavery itself, would be prohibited in the District of Columbia.
5. A new and more powerful fugitive slave law would be enacted, guaranteeing southerners the return of slaves who fled north.

Compromise, by its very nature, is abhorrent to idealists who reason in terms of ethical absolutes. "I think all legislative compromises radically wrong and essentially vicious," Senator William H. Seward of New York declared in speaking against Clay's plan. There could be no compromise on a subject as morally reprehensible and outrageous as human slavery. Some southern extremists were equally vehement in their denunciation of a settlement they regarded as unjust. "The South asks for justice, simple justice," charged Calhoun, "and less she ought not to take." Physically emaciated and near death, Calhoun sat in gloomy silence as his opposition speech was read by a fellow southerner. One particular voice, however, no longer resonant but nevertheless spellbinding, rose in defense of compromise. Daniel Webster, on the seventh of March, addressed the Senate "not as a Massachusetts man, nor as a Northern man, but as an American. . . . I speak for the preservation of the Union. Hear me for my cause."

The magnificent oratory had little effect upon the deep-seated prejudices of the legislators. Clay's proposals were supported mainly by Democrats and southerners, but they had no real possibility of enactment so long as Zachary Taylor was president. Virginia-born and Louisiana-bred, a slaveholder with southern interests, southern friends, and southern ties—his son-in-law was Jefferson Davis—Taylor could have accepted the compromise and received a rousing endorsement from his own section. But he thought California should enter the Union as a free state without that issue being tied to any other. A convention had met at Monterey in September 1849 and drafted a proposed state constitution prohibiting slavery; it had been ratified by the people of California by approximately twelve thousand to eight hundred votes; a temporary state capitol had been selected, and a governor chosen. To delay California's admission or—even worse—to associate it with slave-related issues, Taylor felt, was ill considered and dangerous. Thomas Hart Benton said as much on the Senate floor: "I am opposed to this mixing of subjects which have no affinities. California has washed her hands of slavery at home, and should not be mixed up with it abroad." Taylor's unexpected death, however, removed executive obstruction to the compromise. His successor, Millard Fillmore, one of Senator Seward's bitterest enemies, fully agreed with and facilitated the adoption of each bill. Calhoun's death also

Compromise of 1850

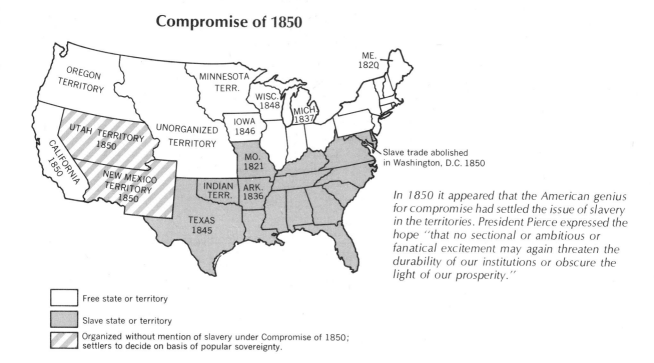

Slave trade abolished in Washington, D.C. 1850

In 1850 it appeared that the American genius for compromise had settled the issue of slavery in the territories. President Pierce expressed the hope "that no sectional or ambitious or fanatical excitement may again threaten the durability of our institutions or obscure the light of our prosperity."

☐ Free state or territory

▨ Slave state or territory

▨ Organized without mention of slavery under Compromise of 1850; settlers to decide on basis of popular sovereignty.

significantly weakened the southern extremists. Piece by piece the acts making up the Compromise of 1850 were skillfully maneuvered through Congress by Senator Stephen A. Douglas of Illinois and signed into law by Fillmore. In Georgia, Alabama, and Louisiana, even in Mississippi and South Carolina (though by narrower majorities), unionist candidates who endorsed the compromise triumphed over secessionists in statewide elections. One could almost sense the national relief: war had been averted.

Relations between northerners and southerners did not improve because of the Compromise of 1850. Americans were torn between an awareness that the compromise had averted a national tragedy and a sheer inability to live up to its terms. Agitators in both sections, momentarily subdued when the compromise was first announced and applauded, returned to foster distrust among receptive audiences.

The Fugitive Slave Act

Northerners found the Fugitive Slave Act impossible to swallow. The act allowed the fugitives no jury trial or even a hearing before a judge. A federal commissioner was authorized to certify the immediate return of an accused slave. Any deputy who refused to carry out the law could be fined a thousand dollars. Any citizen who hid a fugitive could be fined the same amount, imprisoned for six months, and compelled to pay civil damages. Hundreds of panic-stricken free blacks, alarmed at the potential abuses, left their northern homes for Canada. The severity of the law invited popular resistance. A mob in Syracuse broke into a building to free a captured slave. Another in Boston rescued a slave from deportation. In Pennsylvania a slave hunter was murdered. All the New England states, plus Pennsylvania, Ohio, Indiana, Wisconsin, and Michigan, enacted "personal liberty laws" that forbade state officials from assisting in the recapture and return of runaways.

"This filthy enactment," wrote Ralph Waldo Emerson about the Fugitive Slave Act, "was made in the nineteenth century, by people who could read and write. I will not obey it, by God!" Many other northerners felt the same way, as this 1851 poster indicates. (Library of Congress)

CAUTION!!

COLORED PEOPLE
OF BOSTON, ONE & ALL,

You are hereby respectfully CAUTIONED and advised, to avoid conversing with the

Watchmen and Police Officers of Boston,

For since the recent ORDER OF THE MAYOR & ALDERMEN, they are empowered to act as

KIDNAPPERS
AND
Slave Catchers,

And they have already been actually employed in KIDNAPPING, CATCHING, AND KEEPING SLAVES. Therefore, if you value your LIBERTY, and the *Welfare of the Fugitives* among you, *Shun* them in every possible manner, as so many *HOUNDS* on the track of the most unfortunate of your race.

Keep a Sharp Look Out for KIDNAPPERS, and have TOP EYE open.
APRIL 24, 1851.

The supreme court of Wisconsin absolved a newspaperman who had violated the Fugitive Slave Act by declaring it unconstitutional, a decision that was not reversed by the United States Supreme Court until 1859 (*Ableman v. Booth*). Statistically the number of such incidents was small, but each one further strained sectional tensions.

Northern opposition to the Fugitive Slave Act was quickened by the impact of Harriet Beecher Stowe's novel, *Uncle Tom's Cabin* (1852). It sold three hundred thousand copies in its first year and became one of the most remarkable best-sellers in American History. Stowe was a member of a distinguished New England Calvinist family—her father and seven brothers were ministers—and she absorbed their abolitionist sentiments. Her residence in Cincinnati, a favorite crossing place on the Ohio River for fugitive slaves, and her trips into Kentucky to view plantation operations, provided her with some knowledge of the institution. Stowe was not antisouthern. The chief villain of her novel, Simon Legree, was a transplanted Yankee who became a brutal plantation owner. Nevertheless, as one southerner wrote after reading the book, it "greatly tended to influence one-half of the nation against the other, to produce disunion and to stir up a civil war."

Harriet Tubman, in old age, pictured on the left with slaves she helped to escape, was a woman of immense courage. Born into slavery in Dorchester County, Maryland, she escaped to freedom in 1849. Nineteen times she made hazardous journeys into the South to help lead others to freedom. She tolerated no cowardice, telling the faint-hearted she would use her revolver: "Dead niggers tell no tales, you go on or die." (The Bettmann Archive)

The national problem was epitomized in the election of 1852. No important *The Whig Demise* difference separated Whig and Democratic party platforms. Both endorsed the Compromise of 1850. Both labored at the task of maintaining party unity. The Democrats in convention balloted forty-nine times before selecting a nonentity, Franklin Pierce of New Hampshire, as their candidate. The Whigs hoped to win with another hero of the Mexican War, General Winfield Scott. Pierce carried all but four states, and while his popular majority was not extraordinary, he received 254 of 296 electoral votes. The Whigs never recovered. Like their Federalist predecessors they soon vanished as a national party.

But why? How could one defeat spell political oblivion for the Whigs? First, the Whig party had received its direction from political leaders of ability and stature. Those spokesmen of an older generation were gone— Clay and Webster died in 1852—and the party fell to men of small talents and limited imaginations. Second, southern Whigs, alienated by the anti-slavery proclivities of northern members who helped fugitive slaves, deserted the party by the thousands. "There may be no political future for us," Thurlow Weed of New York predicted in 1852, and he was right. The lessons of the Whig demise should have been clear to Democrats, but they were not. Pierce was followed by Buchanan. Both men were incapable of providing the nation with direction. More vitally, instead of seeking ways to moderate sectional grievances, the Democrats blundered by reopening the question of slavery in the territories.

Senator Stephen A. Douglas of Illinois, known as the "Little Giant" because *Bleeding Kansas* of his small size and commanding appearance, bore responsibility for the blunder. Douglas had far more initiative and intelligence than Pierce, Buchanan, or other Democratic chieftains. A fine orator, a clever politician, a rabid expansionist, and a dedicated nationalist, Douglas was immensely popular with northern voters. He had every reason to anticipate becoming president. His chance was considerably lessened, if not destroyed; the Democratic party was ultimately splintered; and the nation was pushed along the road to war all because Douglas—believing it was most democratic to allow the settlers themselves to decide on slavery—introduced legislation that specifically repealed the Missouri Compromise of 1820.

Because Douglas would benefit economically and (he thought) politically, he wanted the federal government to support the construction of a transcontinental railroad from St. Louis to San Francisco. Because the route would pass through Nebraska, it was essential to organize that area into a territory. Southerners, for obvious reasons, favored making New Orleans or Memphis the eastern terminus. In addition, southern congressmen had previously defeated territorial legislation for Nebraska since that region was north of 36°30′ and would be formed into free states. A new Kansas-Nebraska bill, sponsored by Douglas, divided the territory in two, explicitly declared the Missouri Compromise void, and left the settlers to decide whether slavery would be permitted. Southerners, recognizing an opportunity to expand the boundaries of slavery, supported it. For the same reason northerners besieged their legislators with pleas to oppose it. Douglas, however, exerted considerable political pressure. Enough northern congressmen succumbed to pass the Kansas-Nebraska bill in May 1854. A substantial portion of northern opinion was so enraged that effigies of Douglas were burned all across the plains of Indiana and Illinois. So irate was a Chicago audience that Douglas could not speak above the uproar. "Abolitionists of Chicago!" Douglas is alleged to have shouted, "It is Sunday morning. I'll go to church, and you may all go to hell." Chicagoans called him the "Benedict Arnold of 1854." In Boston thousands of United States soldiers and marines, as well as the state militia, were needed to enforce the deportation of one fugitive slave. Douglas had opened a Pandora's box. The railroad was all but forgotten.

Douglas had argued that letting the settlers decide on slavery—a system called popular or "squatter" sovereignty—was the most democratic of all methods. In theory, he may have been right; in practice, he was not. The act turned Kansas into a bloody battlefield. Most settlers were neutral, but from New England came a number of emigrants carrying rifles and ammunition, sworn to keep Kansas free. Funds were collected at church services and public meetings and funneled through various emigrant aid societies to assist the freedom fighters. From the South also came settlers, though not as many, determined to legalize slavery in Kansas. "Border ruffians," as Horace Greeley termed them, crossed over from Missouri. Although they had no real intention of remaining, they spread terror and jammed the ballot boxes with their votes for slavery. Atrocities were committed on both sides; the most celebrated was John Brown's wanton massacre and mutilation of five men at Pottawatomie. Brown considered slavery a form of murder, and he felt no remorse. Emerson, Thoreau, and other northern literati idolized Brown as a man of action. European philosophers regarded him as an authentic American national hero. Brown's role in Kansas was insignificant, but he became a symbol—the just and wrathful prophet—to his admirers and to posterity.

The conflict in Kansas was mirrored in Congress where the dispute also turned from harsh words to physical violence. Senator Charles Sumner of Massachusetts, a devoted but sharp-tongued abolitionist, surpassed his previous vituperative efforts in a two-day speech entitled "The Crime Against Kansas." Some of his most pointed insults were aimed at Senator Andrew P. Butler of South Carolina, who was not present to defend himself. Three days later, while Sumner was seated at his desk in the Senate chamber, he was assaulted by Butler's nephew, Congressman Preston Brooks. Brooks beat Sumner unconscious with his cane and then bragged that he made the northerner bellow "like a calf." Brooks became a southern hero, praised in the press, banqueted, and rewarded for striking back at northern insults.

"I live with my constituents, drink with them, lodge with them, pray with them, laugh, hunt, dance, and work with them," Senator Stephen A. Douglas once boasted. "I eat their corn dodgers and fried bacon and sleep two in a bed with them." Able, aggressive, shrewd, and nationally recognized, he made a serious political miscalculation by introducing the Kansas-Nebraska bill.

The Republican Party

The issue of Kansas gave birth to the Republican party. In 1854, in the old Northwest (various localities claim to be the birthplace) antislavery Whigs combined with old Liberty and Free Soil partisans, dissident Democrats, land reformers, and temperance men to raise the banner against slavery's

extension. The new organization incorporated several groups with antithetical interests. For example, many German political refugees from the unsuccessful European revolutions of 1848, generally idealistic, liberal men to
whom slavery was an abomination, joined the new party. Yet most northern
members of the Know-Nothing movement—a secret, superpatriotic, anti-
Catholic, and antiforeign group that flourished briefly—also joined the Republicans.

The party was completely sectional, representing the mainstream of
northern opinion. It took no stand against slavery in the South, and
abolitionists faced the choice of either going their own ineffective way or
staying with the party to exercise what influence they could. Nor did the
Republicans pretend to be any special friend of the black people. Republican newspapers repeatedly called themselves the "White Man's Party."
None of the states in the old Northwest, for example, permitted blacks to
vote. Illinois even prohibited their entering the state. The Republican party
platform in 1856 was concerned primarily with the West. It denounced
proslavery voting frauds in Kansas and called for congressional action to
forbid "those twin relics of barbarism, [Mormon] polygamy and slavery"
in the territories.

The Republicans became an immediate threat to the Democrats. In 1856
they nominated, in the Whig tradition, a romantic military figure, John C.
Frémont. The son-in-law of Thomas Hart Benton, Frémont was nationally
known for his exploits in California. Their alliterative songs and slogans
asked voters to support "Freedom, Freemen, and Frémont." The Democrats
rejected Pierce and Douglas and nominated James Buchanan, an experienced but inoffensive politician who, though from Pennsylvania, had markedly southern inclinations. Their platform reaffirmed the concept of popular sovereignty contained in the Kansas-Nebraska Act. Buchanan won by
taking all the slave states except Maryland (which voted for Fillmore, who
ran on the remnants of the Know-Nothing movement), plus Pennsylvania,
New Jersey, Indiana, Illinois, and California. The campaign was exciting
and, in retrospect, alarming. Southerners, including those who had supported the Union in 1850, made it plain that if Frémont had won, they
would not have submitted. In the next election Republicans would concentrate on the four northern states they had lost in 1856. By winning these, they
could win the national election. Did the southerners mean what they had
said? Would they in fact secede in the event of a Republican triumph?

Two days after Buchanan took his oath of office the United States Supreme
Court announced its decision in the case of *Dred Scott* v. *Sanford* and
radically altered national perspectives on the question of slavery in the
territories. As a slave owned by a military doctor, Dred Scott had been taken
from Missouri to Illinois in 1834, then to Wisconsin Territory, and back to
Missouri some years later. Scott was suing on the ground that his residence
in a free state, and in a territory where slavery was prohibited by the Missouri
Compromise of 1820, made him a free man. The Supreme Court justices

*The Dred Scott
Decision*

might have disposed of the case in any number of ways. They might have thrown it out as a notorious collusive action; Scott's present owners were abolitionists and would free him regardless of the final decision. Or the Court might have dismissed the case on the grounds that, as a slave, Scott was not a citizen and therefore not entitled to sue. Instead, eight of the nine justices wrote long and separate opinions, some of which were blatantly racist. Chief Justice Taney stated that no blacks, even those who were free, could be regarded as citizens under the Constitution. Two other judges agreed with Taney—not enough for a majority. But six others did concur with Taney that Scott's status had reverted to slavery once he was brought back to Missouri, and slaves could not sue in federal courts.

They might have stopped here, but a majority of the Court went even further. They ruled that slaves were property, that property rights were protected by the Fifth Amendment of the Constitution, and therefore the Missouri Compromise of 1820, which forbade citizens from taking their property into specified American territories, was unconstitutional. Three years before the Compromise of 1820 had been repealed by the Kansas-Nebraska Act. Now the Supreme Court ruled that the compromise had never been constitutional, that Congress had no authority to keep slavery out of any territory. Then, and ever since, scholars have criticized the Dred Scott decision as one of the most poorly reasoned and subjective judgments in Supreme Court history. Northerners were chagrined, angry, openly defiant. The decision confirmed their belief that the five southern justices, headed by Chief Justice Roger Taney of Maryland, were hopelessly biased. The Court, wrote one New York journalist, has "draggled and polluted its garments in the filth of pro-slavery politics." Abraham Lincoln expressed the feelings of Republicans:

> If this important decision had been made by the unanimous concurrence of the judges, and without any partisan bias, and had been based in no part on assumed historical facts which are not really true; or, if it had been before the court more than once, and had there been affirmed and reaffirmed through a course of years, it then might be factious, nay even revolutionary, not to acquiesce in it as a precedent. But when, as it is true, we find it wanting in all these claims to the public confidence, it is not resistance, it is not factious, it is not even disrespectful, to treat it as not having yet established a settled doctrine for the country.

Republicans proposed a variety of constitutional amendments to upset the Dred Scott decision. Southerners were delighted by it, for the Court's ruling confirmed their belief that slaves could be transported to any territory. To Stephen Douglas and the Democratic party, however, the Dred Scott ruling spelled disaster.

The decision drove a wedge between northern and southern Democrats. Party unity had largely depended upon the agreement to uphold popular sovereignty. Many southerners saw no reason to do so when the Supreme Court had ruled otherwise. Moreover, President Buchanan urged the Ameri-

Douglas and Buchanan

can people to accept the Court's ruling as a final settlement; Douglas, on the other hand, was not yet ready to abandon his doctrine.

This opening rift in the Democratic ranks was widened by developments in Kansas. There a rump body of proslavery delegates meeting in the town of Lecompton had drawn up a state constitution legalizing slavery. The Lecompton constitution was submitted to the people in a manner so unfair that it made a mockery of popular sovereignty. Even the territorial governor of Kansas, Robert J. Walker of Mississippi, who had been appointed by Buchanan, denounced the maneuver and advised that the Lecompton constitution be rejected. Nevertheless, Buchanan decided to recommend it to Congress as the basis for Kansas's admission to the union. Douglas objected, and the two men exchanged heated words. "No Democrat ever yet differed from an Administration of his choice without being crushed," Buchanan warned Douglas. "Mr. President, I wish you to remember that General Jackson is dead!" Douglas snapped back. Buchanan did try to crush Douglas by depriving him of patronage, but Douglas's strength among northern Democrats in Congress was enough to prevent acceptance of the Lecompton constitution. Kansas did not enter the union until 1861, and then it did so as a free state.

Republicans began to court Douglas. Horace Greeley's New York *Tribune,* a newspaper of considerable influence throughout the country, admired his stand against the forces of slavery. Any chance of an alliance, however, was killed by the pronounced hostility of Illinois Republicans toward Douglas. They aimed at gaining his senatorial seat in 1858. To do so they were promoting the reputation of a lawyer from Springfield, a tall, angular, awkward politician whom the people intuitively trusted, named Abraham Lincoln.

Douglas and Lincoln

The Illinois senatorial contest between Douglas and Lincoln attracted huge crowds. They met seven times in debate, covering the state from north to south. Never in American history has a public debate surpassed that of these two masterful and articulate speakers.

Douglas was the more consistent debater. When, in the town of Freeport, Lincoln challenged him to defend popular sovereignty, which seemed a farce in the light of the Dred Scott case, Douglas did so. "Slavery cannot exist a day or an hour anywhere," explained Douglas, "unless it is supported by local police regulations." In other words, the people of a territory could ban slavery by the simple expedient of not enacting legislation protecting it. The Freeport doctrine was repudiated by southern Democrats as heretical but remained a viable principle to northern members. Lincoln shaded his speeches depending upon the area in which he spoke. In Chicago, where antislavery sentiment was strongest, he cited the Declaration of Independence: "Let us discard all this quibbling about . . . this race and that race and the other race being inferior. . . . All men are created equal." Two months later in the town of Charleston, where many southerners had settled, Lincoln changed his tune: "I will say, then, that I am not, nor ever have been, in favor of bringing about in any way the social and political equality of the white and black races. . . . I am not nor ever have been in favor of making voters or jurors of Negroes, nor of qualifying them to hold office, nor to intermarry with white people. . . . I as much as any other man am in favor of having the superior position assigned to the white race."

If Douglas was more consistent, he was blind to the moral implications of slavery—and Lincoln was not. The difference was crucial. Lincoln felt that slavery must eventually be extinguished. "I do not expect the Union to be dissolved—I do not expect the House to fall—but I do expect it to cease to be divided," he said in his most famous speech of the 1858 debates. "It will become all one thing or all the other." Lincoln planned no assault on slavery in the states. He made it quite plain that abolitionism had no place in the Republican party. But by confining slavery to the old South Lincoln hoped to promote its gradual attrition and disappearance. Douglas drew no moral distinction between slavery and freedom. "Every sentiment he utters," said Lincoln, "discards the idea that there is any wrong in slavery." While Douglas emphasized that Lincoln's stand could mean only war, Lincoln countered by portraying Douglas as a proslavery conspirator. Let Dred Scott stand, warned Lincoln, and there would soon follow "another Supreme Court decision, declaring that the Constitution of the United States does not permit a *State* to exclude slavery." Douglas won the election, but Lincoln established a reputation that two years later made it possible for him to gain the Republican nomination for the presidency.

The sore festered, and the poison ran through the body politic. At what point the disease became incurable, no one can say. Surely a crisis of some kind seemed imminent. A United States senator from California was killed in a duel with a southerner. Many northerners, having read the immensely popular *Uncle Tom's Cabin*, believed everyone south of the Mason-Dixon line was a Simon Legree. Many southerners believed everyone north of it was an irresponsible abolitionist agitator or sympathizer. Even a northern accent aroused suspicion in the South. Republican attempts to disassociate the party from the extremists failed to persuade southerners. If some were not yet fully convinced, in 1859 an act of northern fanaticism took place that removed any lingering doubts.

John Brown's Raid

John Brown had no trouble raising money in the North. Men of the highest social distinction contributed tens of thousands of dollars to finance his guerrilla warfare. Six men in particular—the so-called Secret Six—who represented the best of northern society, knew that Brown planned an audacious raid into the South itself to arm slaves and to incite them to rebel against their white masters. Brown planned to establish a revolutionary government in the South, with himself as military dictator, and he carefully composed a "Provisional Constitution and Ordinances for the People of the United States." The Secret Six—a philanthropist, a financier, a surgeon, a professor, a minister, and a philosopher—had diverted funds collected for use in Kansas to support Brown's invasion. Lest they become too deeply implicated, however, they asked Brown not to tell them the precise time and place of the attack. Brown struck on a Sunday evening, October 16, 1859. His expedition numbered eighteen men, including five blacks, enough to capture the unguarded federal arsenal at Harpers Ferry, Virginia. But none of Brown's plans worked. The slaves did not rise. "It was so absurd," Abraham Lincoln later commented, "that the slaves, with all their ignorance, saw plainly enough it could not succeed." Ironically the first to die was a free black who failed to heed a command to halt given by one of Brown's men. Four Harpers Ferry residents and a United States marine were killed by the insurrectionists, and others were taken prisoner. A telegraphed alarm brought government troops, headed by Colonel Robert E. Lee and Lieutenant J. E. B. Stuart. Surrounded and trapped in a locomotive roundhouse, Brown displayed the courage of a truly dedicated man. According to an eyewitness: "Brown was the coolest and firmest man I ever saw in defying danger and death. With one son dead by his side, and another shot through, he felt the pulse of his dying son with one hand and held his rifle with the other and commanded his men with the utmost composure, encouraging them to be firm and to sell their lives as dearly as they could." Ten died and a few escaped before Brown and five others were taken prisoner. The revolution had lasted a little more than twenty-four hours. Brown was tried and convicted of murder, criminal conspiracy, and treason against the state of Virginia. He died on the scaffold as bravely as he had fought.

Republican and Democratic political leaders immediately denounced Brown's raid. "No man, North or South," said Lincoln, "can approve of violence or crime." Anti-Brown meetings in Boston and New York were exceptionally well attended. Southerners, however, heard other voices that canonized Brown. He was "not only a martyr," wrote Theodore Parker, "but a SAINT." Thoreau composed an eloquent "Plea for Captain Brown." Wendell Phillips told an audience, "John Brown is the impersonation of God's order and God's law." Emerson believed that Brown's death "will make the gallows as glorious as the cross." Little wonder that when war came northern soldiers went South singing:

> John Brown's body lies a-mouldering in the grave,
> But his soul goes marching on.

In the South, Brown's raid touched off a hunt for subversives and fellow-travelers. Few were found, but hundreds of innocents suffered: a minister in Texas was lashed seventy times; a schoolteacher was ordered to leave Arkansas in thirty-six hours; three sailors off a Maine ship were flogged in Georgia; a Connecticut bookseller was beaten in Charleston; the northern president of an Alabama college was dismissed; an Irish stonecutter in Columbia, South Carolina, was tarred and feathered. A great fear settled over the South. Rumors of northern invasion, of slaves rioting, raping, burning, and killing, and of abolitionist conspiracies to poison all whites multiplied and spread panic. Such was the paranoia in the nation when citizens were asked to vote in the election of 1860.

Many scholars conclude that John Brown was crazy, his scheme for invading the South crackbrained. Yet many northerners, such as Lincoln's law partner, William Herndon, predicted that Brown's name would "live amidst the world's gods and heroes through all the infinite ages." The photograph of John Brown was taken in 1855. (Kansas State Historical Society)

The Democratic party held its convention in Charleston, South Carolina, a rich, quiet city of mansions and tree-lined streets. But the mood of the delegates clashed with their surroundings. Hostile and inflexible, southern delegates brought in a plank declaring protection of slavery in the territories to be a federal duty. "Gentlemen of the South," an Ohioan responded, "you mistake us—you mistake us—we will not do it." Douglas's men were in a majority. When their resolution for popular sovereignty passed, the southerners walked out. Since no presidential candidate could be nominated without a two-thirds majority, the convention adjourned. The Democrats never reunited. Several months later the convention reassembled in Baltimore and chose Douglas; the dissenting southerners held their own meeting and selected John C. Breckenridge of Kentucky.

The Republican party met in Chicago in a noisy carnival atmosphere stimulated in part by quantities of free liquor. John Brown's attack was repudiated, as was abolitionism, and the Dred Scott decision was declared "a dangerous political heresy." The Republicans affirmed that freedom must be national and slavery sectional. But they were no longer a single-issue party: for the Germans there was a plank opposing any changes in the naturalization laws; for midwestern farmers and their sons, a plank recommending passage of a homestead act; for eastern industrialists, endorsement of a high tariff. The platform was carefully drawn to appeal to a variety of northern interests. Selection of a presidential nominee was spirited and caused some dissension. The front-runner was Seward, no longer the radical of 1850, but that image persisted and ruined his chances. Most Republicans wanted a middle-of-the-road figure and, after some backroom manipulations and secret political commitments, particularly of cabinet appointments, Abraham Lincoln was nominated.

The antebellum South has been described as a nation within a nation, and in 1860 southern balloting was an election within an election. No Lincoln ticket was presented in the cotton states, and Douglas was virtually ignored except by a minority of loyal adherents. The choice was between Breckenridge for the southern Democrats and John Bell as the candidate of the Constitutional Union party. The Constitutional Unionists advocated peace and union but offered no fresh formulas. Though Bell polled a respectable 588,000 popular votes, he captured the electoral votes of only Virginia, Kentucky, and Tennessee. Breckenridge polled 849,000 votes and took every other southern state. In the North the contest was entirely between Lincoln and Douglas. Douglas received 1.38 million votes, but they were so spread across the country that he carried only Missouri and part of New Jersey. Lincoln took every free state. His popular total was 1.87 million votes (a minority), but in the electoral college he obtained 180 ballots (a substantial majority).

Secession

With Lincoln's election the lower South seceded. For decades the South had exercised an influence in the national government far out of proportion to its population or productivity. That influence should have reached its peak and declined a generation before, but the southern cause possessed a charm that enlisted northern political advocates, and they helped sustain southern power beyond its time. In the past the South had dominated the presidency, the cabinet, and the Supreme Court, and it had maintained strength equal with that of the free states in the Senate.

Politically southern leaders realized that Lincoln's election signaled the beginning of northern domination. Minnesota's entrance to the Union in 1858 gave the North a predominance in the Senate. Now, they felt, a Republican president elected entirely by northern votes was being imposed upon them. Calhoun had long foreseen this moment and had attempted to alter the federal structure to ensure southern equality in the national councils, or a southern veto over national laws. He had even suggested a dual executive. He had warned that secession would follow unless the South were protected from the tyranny of a northern majority. That moment had come.

Economically, while some southern leaders favored economic diversification, others insisted that the South could prosper only by expanding their slave system into new territory. They saw the economic gap between North and South widen steadily with each passing year. Railroads built in the 1850s connected the trans-Mississippi West to eastern metropolitan centers, tying these sections to one another by mutual interest. True, the tariff had been low. But Republicans, southerners had no doubt, would eventually raise it. They felt isolated, encircled, squeezed. They feared that exploitation would follow.

Culturally, the South was unique. Northern society was mixed and mobile; southern society was a throwback to the feudal past. The South was proud and aristocratic, vaunting superiority to cover a basic insecurity; the North was optimistic, democratic, and self-critical. Southerners were quick to duel over personal insults, real or fancied. Primogeniture was still the custom, if not the law. White women were publicly venerated. Kinship and family meant much to southerners, who were very conscious of history; it meant less to northerners, who looked to the future. The southerner of means revered the traditional, the classical, the agrarian, and the graceful and leisurely way of life. He had no wish to join in the advance of Western civilization. He wanted to preserve his social structure, including its central tenet, white supremacy. The North would not permit it. Northerners had declared slavery wrong, and the South had to resist or see its culture destroyed. "We are a people, a *nation,* with arms in our hands," wrote one southerner, ". . . and we shall never submit the case to the judgment of *another people,* until they show themselves of superior virtue and intellect."

South Carolina was the first to secede. Six more states of the lower South soon followed. By February 1861 the Confederate States of America had been established, and Jefferson Davis was chosen as provisional president. Federal forts and arsenals were seized and declared to be Confederate property. Diplomats selected by the new government prepared to sail. Buchanan in his final month in office did nothing. A pathetic figure, he

Secession

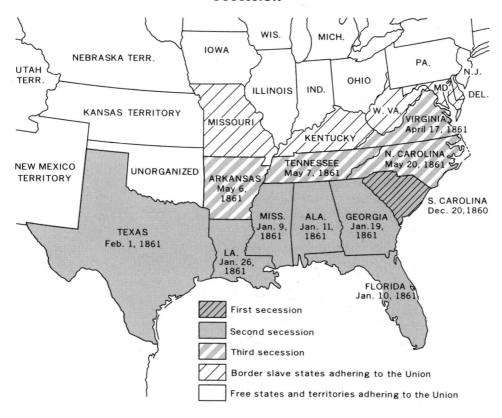

Time table for secession: dates given are for the adoption of ordinances of secession in each state, except in the case of Tennessee, where the date indicates when the legislature ratified the Military League with the Confederacy.

watched each secessionist move with acute discomfort and total irresolution. Eight other slave states, meanwhile, decided to wait for the next president to take his oath. Indeed, the entire nation was eager to know what Lincoln would do.

Lincoln's position was uncompromising. Several desperate bids to preserve the Union were made, one by Senator John J. Crittenden of Kentucky and another by a Peace Convention of 133 delegates, which met in Washington shortly before Lincoln's inauguration. They failed because Lincoln would accept no bargain on the question of the extension of slavery in the territories, nor would the leaders of the Confederacy compromise. In his inaugural address, however, Lincoln renewed the Republican pledge to respect slavery in the states. His words had no effect on southern extremists, who were obsessed with the idea that the president was an abolitionist. But

The War Begins

while some Republicans, like Horace Greeley, advised letting the South secede in peace, Lincoln thought otherwise. "In your hands, my dissatisfied fellow countrymen," said Lincoln, "and not in mine, is the momentous issue of civil war. The government will not assail you. You can have no conflict without yourselves being the aggressors."

Whether North or South was the aggressor in the Civil War is still a subject of historical dispute. Lincoln's first decision as commander in chief concerned two island fortresses, Pickens at Pensacola and Sumter at Charleston. Both were held by federal troops who were running short of supplies. The Confederacy demanded their evacuation and surrender. At Charleston rebel batteries were placed in strategic positions ready to fire upon the fort. The Confederates made it clear that any attempt to send relief vessels to Sumter or Pickens would be regarded as a hostile act. Lincoln pondered, hesitated, sought the counsel of his cabinet, and weighed the consequences of his alternatives. Sending vessels could precipitate war and turn the upper South to the Confederacy. Not sending vessels could be interpreted as a sign of weakness. Seward, who had been appointed secretary of state and had a rather exalted opinion of his own ability, suggested that the United States pick a quarrel with some European power in order to rally all Americans to the flag and thus relieve sectional tensions. Seward and four other cabinet officers adamantly opposed sending reinforcements to Sumter or Pickens, but Lincoln overruled them and ordered the vessels to sail.

Confederate officers at Charleston called upon the commander at Fort Sumter and requested his surrender. Fort Sumter, he responded, still had a two-day supply of food and, as a point of honor, would not surrender until those provisions were exhausted. The Confederates could not wait. Even before the supply ship arrived, at 4:30 A.M. April 12, 1861, Confederate batteries fired the first shots of the Civil War. A burst of indignation swept through the North upon news of Sumter's capitulation. "I utterly abhor peace," the Reverend Henry Ward Beecher announced from his pulpit. "Give me war redder than blood and fiercer than fire." Lincoln rejoiced at the emotional response. "The plan succeeded," he wrote. "They attacked Sumter—it fell, and thus, did more service than it otherwise could." Lincoln issued a call for seventy-five thousand volunteers and proclaimed a naval blockade of the South. Virginia, North Carolina, Arkansas, and Tennessee seceded and joined the Confederacy. However, western Virginia seceded from Virginia and remained loyal to the Union. Delaware, Kentucky, Missouri, and Maryland also remained loyal, though Maryland did so only because it was occupied by federal troops.

Opposing Sides

Certainly the North possessed enormous advantages in resources over the South. Northern population totaled 23 million to the South's 8.7 million (of whom 3.5 million were slaves). Northern real and personal property was valued at $11 billion to the South's $5.37 billion. Northern banking capital amounted to $330 million, more than seven times that of the South. In factories, mines, ships, and railroads, the North enjoyed a marked superiority, which would appear to make their eventual victory inevitable. In 1860 the North produced firearms worth $2.25 million, the South, $73,000.

Southerners were conscious of these discrepancies, yet they calculated according to a different scale. First, they believed cotton was a crucial crop that more than balanced northern advantages. "You do not dare to make war on cotton," a southern senator remarked to Congress in 1858. "No power on earth dares to make war upon it. Cotton is king." Few southerners thought the North had the fortitude for a protracted war. As unemployment in northern cities mounted, as their merchants and manufacturers felt the economic pinch, and early battlefield casualties shocked the Union, causing some sober reflections on the purpose of the war, the South expected Lincoln's administration would be forced to recognize the independency of the Confederacy. Second, in terms of military preparedness, leadership, and morale, southerners were convinced of the superiority their section held over the North. Some three hundred West Point officers remained loyal to the United States; one hundred fifty sided with the Confederacy, but these included some of the leading officers of the regular army: Robert E. Lee, Stonewall Jackson, J. E. B. Stuart, A. P. Hill, Albert S. Johnston, and P. G. T. Beauregard. The military tradition was strongest in the South, and this distinction was evident in the early years of the war. The South had an able commander and a competent military staff while Lincoln still searched for officers of equal talent. In 1861 Ulysses S. Grant, George B. McClellan, and William T. Sherman were in private life. The South soon developed the strategy of conducting a defensive war against northern armies, which, they reasoned, would be less costly, with fewer logistical problems, and with considerable psychological impact. A people protecting their homeland always fought tenaciously against invading forces. Southerners cited the experience of British and Hessian troops in the colonies and of Napoleon's armies in Spain and Russia. After Fort Sumter's capitulation, the southern call to arms resulted in a popular response more impressive than that in the North. Some two hundred thousand volunteers had to return home since there was not enough military equipment available for their use.

In time the high hopes and morale of large numbers of southerners eroded. By April 1862 the Confederate government found it necessary to enact a conscription law—the first in American history—requiring all white men between the ages of eighteen to thirty-five to serve in the army. Later the age limit was extended to fifty. Those who remained committed to the southern cause sneered at "conscripts," and many volunteered rather than suffer that term of opprobrium. Still, thousands who could afford to bought their way out of military service by hiring substitutes, which the law permitted. "A rich man's war and a poor man's fight" was a frequent complaint of those who could not afford the price. The desertion rate in southern armies swelled to more than a hundred thousand as the war dragged on. Casualties rose to a staggering number. At Shiloh the South lost more than ten thousand soldiers; in the Seven Days Campaign, twenty thousand; at Antietam, perhaps eleven

The Confederate States of America

The photograph on the left of Private John Werth of the Richmond Howitzer Battalion, Confederate States of America, is typical of pictures taken of thousands of Confederate and Union soldiers for sending home to their families. For many it was the final and sole momento. The Civil War was dirty and grim, with an unprecedented loss of human lives. Shown at the right is a dead Confederate youth at Petersburg, Virginia, one of more than 600,000 soldiers who died in the war. (The Museum of the Confederacy, Richmond; Library of Congress)

thousand. Northern armies suffered the same high number of casualties—their confidence was also shaken—and their desertion rate was also large—but the North had three times the southern population and thus a proportionately larger reservoir of troops. Before the Civil War ended in 1865 the deaths totaled 618,000 (360,000 northern, 258,000 southern), considerably higher than in any other war in American history.

The wartime problems of the Confederate government were compounded by fundamental political divisions among southerners. Independence from the United States was their common goal, but many southern governors seemed to consider states' rights more important than sectional unity. Governor Zebulon M. Vance of North Carolina, for example, felt the Confederacy had no authority to enact a conscription law and tried to hinder its enforcement. Governor Joseph Brown of Georgia agreed. When the Confederate president, Jefferson Davis, suspended the writ of habeas corpus, a storm of controversy ensued. The states' rightists generally supported the Confederate vice-president, Alexander H. Stephens, who thought Davis was an inept strategist and a potential dictator. Obviously the Confederate administration was wracked with dissension. In four years Davis appointed five secretaries of war. None of the cabinet officials was particularly distinguished, with the possible exception of Judah P. Benjamin, who served consecutively as attorney general, secretary of war, and secretary of state.

His realistic appraisals and sound advice were to no avail as the southern cause grew desperate. The South needed a scapegoat and Benjamin, because of his religion, was an easy mark. He became "the hated Jew." Davis's relations with the Confederate congress were so poor that he vetoed thirty-eight bills, and thirty-seven of these were passed over his veto. (Lincoln vetoed a total of three bills.) In 1864, with supplies dangerously short, General Robert E. Lee journeyed to the Confederate capitol to seek aid from the government. "I visited Congress today," he wrote to his son, "and they did not seem to be able to do anything except eat peanuts and chew tobacco while my army is starving."

Yet the South never lost a battle because of a lack of arms or ammunition. Soldiers ran short of boots, clothes, blankets, food, and medical supplies, but a brilliant chief of ordinance, Josiah Gorgas, was largely responsible for developing policies that kept southern armies supplied with weapons. In four years some six hundred thousand small arms were brought in from Europe by blockade runners. Captured northern equipment was utilized. The Tredegar Iron Works at Richmond, Virginia, was converted into a munitions plant, and foundries were built in South Carolina, Georgia, and Alabama. For all the weaknesses of the Confederate government, by 1863 they had nevertheless raised and maintained a first-class fighting force of 260,000 men.

Jefferson Davis, President of the Confederate States of America, suffered from neuralgia and other nervous disorders. Carl Schurz once described him as "slender, tall, and erect," possessing a "dignity which does not invite familiar approach, but will not render one uneasy by lofty assumption." Others found him imperious and defiant of public opinion. His leadership frequently was ridiculed. After Lee surrendered, and with all hopes shattered, Davis urged southerners to continue the fight. "Three thousand brave men," he told a group of cavalry officers, "are enough for a nucleus around which the whole people will rally." When they disagreed, Davis finally admitted that "all is indeed lost." (Library of Congress)

The South counted on King Cotton to force Britain and France to intervene on its side. Intervention would mean an official acknowledgment of Confederate independence, monetary aid and military assistance, and the possibility of a declared war against the United States. "Why, sir, we have only to shut off your supply of cotton for a few weeks," a southerner told a correspondent of the London *Times,* "and we can create a revolution in Great Britain." Surely, with their textile mills closed and economic collapse imminent, Britain would have to break the northern blockade to obtain southern cotton. That would mean war. In 1860, however, the South had produced a bumper crop, the British mills were oversupplied with fiber, and cotton cloth glutted the market. Southerners tried to speed up the economic pressure upon Britain in a number of ways. In 1861 they imposed an embargo; in 1862 they resorted to limiting the production of cotton; in 1863 they destroyed millions of bales. The coercion was effective. Britain developed new sources of supply from India and Egypt, but the cotton it brought in was hardly sufficient. Some four hundred thousand British workers were left unemployed or partly employed. Yet cotton, contrary to the southern obsession, proved not to be king. First of all, during the Civil War years the British experienced serious grain shortages. They found it expedient to sell munitions to the North in exchange for the needed grains. Second, except for the cotton industry, the British economy was booming. Ship-builders, steel manufacturers, shippers, even the owners of woolen mills (which had been languishing) were profiting enormously. "We are as busy, as rich, and as fortunate in our trade as if the American war had never broken out," reported the London *Times* in January 1864. "Cotton was no King, notwithstanding the prerogatives which had been loudly claimed for him."

On several occasions, though not because of cotton, war between the United States and Britain seemed perilously close. The initial crisis occurred late in 1861, when Captain Charles Wilkes of the U. S. S. *San Jacinto* forcibly removed two Confederate diplomatic agents who were traveling to England aboard the *Trent,* a British mail steamer. The two agents, Senators James M. Mason and John Slidell, and their secretaries, were confined to a federal fortress. Wilkes was instantaneously acclaimed throughout the North as a military hero. But in Britain his action aroused an uproar of protest. "Some may stand for this," Lord Palmerston, the British prime minister, told his cabinet in a rage, "but damned if I will." The British demanded the release of Mason and Slidell and a suitable apology—or war. Lincoln hesitated, since he certainly did not want war, yet he feared the political consequences of releasing the diplomats. After prolonged debate within the cabinet Lincoln—wisely—decided to yield. Mason and Slidell, Secretary of State Seward announced, "will be cheerfully liberated." Northern anger at Britain's martial attitude was widespread. "I now here publicly avow and record my inextinguishable hatred of that Government," an Illinois congressman declared. James Russell Lowell expressed his feelings in a poem:

> It don't seem hardly right, John,
> When both my hands was full,

To stump me to a fight, John—
Your cousin, too, John Bull!

The second crisis came two years later, but this time the war threats were made by the United States. The British had decided to follow a policy of neutrality. Nevertheless, on a legal subterfuge, they permitted Confederate cruisers to be built in British shipyards. Since these vessels were outfitted with armament elsewhere, Britain could maintain that the letter of the law was not being violated. This flimsy argument angered the American government. It was common knowledge that the vessels were designed for and used as warships against the North. Three of the most famous British-built cruisers, the *Shenandoah,* the *Florida,* and the *Alabama,* took a heavy toll of northern commerce before the Civil War ended. (In 1872 an arbitration commission awarded the United States damages amounting to fifteen and a half million dollars, which Britain had to pay for not exercising "due diligence.") However, it was the construction of ironclads at the Laird shipyards, built with pointed prows for ramming and sinking Northern blockade vessels, which posed an immediate danger.* Gradually the northern naval blockade was strangling the South, creating food shortages and driving up the price of merchandise. In 1861, it is estimated, no more than one of every ten southern blockade runners was caught; by 1865 one of every two was caught. If the "Laird rams" had been permitted to leave Britain in September 1863, one historian states, "the South would probably have won its independence." The American minister to Great Britain, Charles Francis Adams, put the matter bluntly in a note to the foreign secretary, Earl Russell: "It would be superfluous in me to point out to your Lordship that this is war." But the British government had decided to detain the Laird rams even before the receipt of Adams's note. The value of Confederate bonds immediately plummeted fourteen points. James Mason was recalled, and British consuls in the South were expelled.

Anyone who served as president during the Civil War would have been memorable. Lincoln, however, did more than preside. He was the one dominant and decisive figure of the war years. Americans have turned Lincoln into a legend, enshrining him with Washington in their pantheon of demigods. However, many of his actions have been harshly criticized. Setting the myths aside and weighing the criticisms, he still emerges an extraordinary individual.

Lincoln was a clever, adroit, and hard-working politician. He had to be. He was attacked by "peace" Democrats who campaigned for a negotiated settlement. Their strength in the southern parts of Ohio, Indiana, and Illinois was formidable. They considered Lincoln a warmonger, and the war itself unjust, inhumane, and unnecessary. Most were loyal to the Union, but a good

Lincoln's Political Problems

---

*In 1862 the Confederate *Virginia* (renamed from the *Merrimac*), specially plated with iron, had some success against wooden blockade ships until it was checked by the U.S.S. *Monitor* in the first naval battle between ironclads. The Laird rams were considerably more powerful than the *Merrimac,* in fact more powerful than any other in the United States Navy.

many were southern sympathizers, known as "copperheads," and a few engaged in subversive acts. Lincoln suspended the writ of habeas corpus in critical regions and permitted the military to suppress hostile newspapers and to arbitrarily arrest and try civilians—actions that the Supreme Court later declared to be unconstitutional. Some fifteen thousand Americans were jailed, and many of them remained in prison without a trial until the close of the war. These arbitrary arrests, according to David Donald, "cannot be passed over lightly: to do so would allow too small a value to civil guarantees. On the other hand a search of the full record will show that anything like a drastic military regime was far from Lincoln's thoughts." Lincoln was no dictator. If he violated the law, he did so cautiously, reluctantly, and with good reason, because without these violations the war—and with it the Union—might have been lost.

Lincoln had as much trouble with his own party as he did with copperheads. A radical wing of the Republicans was bent on revenging themselves on the South and were annoyed by Lincoln's moderate attitude. The Radical Republicans formed and dominated a joint congressional committee on the conduct of the war, and they badgered Lincoln to abolish slavery. To do so, Lincoln felt would (1) violate the Republican platform, which had promised that the federal government would not interfere with slavery in the states and (2) outrage public opinion in some of the border states that had remained loyal, pushing them to the Confederate side. "My paramount object in this struggle," wrote Lincoln, "*is* to save the union, and is *not* to save or destroy slavery." Nevertheless, under constant pressure from the Radical Republicans, Lincoln in 1863 used his wartime presidential powers to issue the Emancipation Proclamation. Ironically, the proclamation ordered freedom for the slaves only in those areas in which Lincoln had no real authority. Some radicals thought Lincoln should have made a more courageous and forthright statement. Democrats, on the other hand, thought Lincoln had acted hypocritically by yielding to the demands of the Radical Republicans:

> Honest old Abe, when the
> war first began,
> Denied abolition was part of his plan;
> Honest old Abe has since made a decree,
> The war must go on till the slaves are all free.
> As both can't be honest, will someone tell how,
> If honest Abe then, he is honest Abe now?

The Emancipation Proclamation was put into effect by northern armies as they gradually conquered southern territory. The Thirteenth Amendment to the Constitution, which abolished slavery everywhere, was not finally adopted until after Lincoln's death, although he was instrumental in forcing it through Congress.

Despite party bickering in the cabinet, in Congress, and among state leaders, Lincoln kept the Republicans fairly well united during his first administration. For a while, however, he thought he might lose the election of 1864. Radical Republicans were less than pleased with his veto of the Wade-Davis bill, a plan for postwar reconstruction of the South that Lincoln considered too harsh. Horace Greeley, on the other hand, accused Lincoln of extending the war for selfish reasons when he could have terminated it by negotiation. This temporary alliance between Radical Republicans and Greeley was strange but nevertheless disturbing to Lincoln. In 1864 he was running on a coalition ticket of Republicans and War Democrats, the National Union party, with Andrew Johnson of Tennessee as the vice-presidential nominee. The regular Democratic organization nominated General George McClellan, whom Lincoln had removed from command for incompetence. When the war swung in favor of the North during the presidential campaign, however, political alignments abruptly altered. Greeley came out for Lincoln, as did the Radical Republicans. The National Union party swept to victory by 212 to 21 electoral votes and a popular majority of nearly

On November 7, 1864, Jefferson Davis said that the Confederate States of America must continue to fight and to fulfill "the task which has been so happily begun—that of Christianizing and improving the condition of the Africans who have by the will of Providence been placed in our charge." Shown here is a black family on the plantation of J. J. Smith at Beaufort, South Carolina, in 1862, typical of those whom Confederates believed were better off in slavery than in freedom. (Library of Congress)

half a million. "The election," said Lincoln, "has demonstrated that a people's government can sustain a national election in the midst of a great civil war."

Lincoln never attempted to evade the military responsibilities of his office. His policy of blockading Confederate ports at the very outset of the war was of fundamental importance in the defeat of the South. He also adopted the idea of fighting the war on several fronts. "We have the *greater* numbers, and the enemy has the *greater* facility of concentrating forces upon points of collision," said Lincoln. "We must fail unless we can find some way of making *our* advantage an overmatch for *his*; and this can only be done by menacing him with superior forces at *different* points, at the *same* time." Lincoln's policy was sound, but he had to find a general equal to Lee to carry it out.

Lincoln's Military Leadership

His first choice, General George McClellan, was a failure. A master at military organization and preparation, he was slow in executing plans, and his best strategies were defensive. One historian states that though McClellan "talked like Napoleon," he "did not like to fight." Another calls McClellan "the General who would not dare." Had McClellan been more aggressive immediately after Antietam, Lee's army might have been crushed; instead, he let the southern forces slip back across the Potomac to regroup at Richmond. Lincoln's next choice, General Ambrose Burnside, was amiable and personable—and mediocre. If McClellan was too cautious, Burnside was too rash. At Fredericksburg in December 1862, his army outnumbered Lee's by 114,000 to 72,000, but the Confederate troops occupied a far superior position. Burnside ordered a futile attack, watched thousands of his men die in vain, cried at the losses, and then resigned. Next came General "Fighting Joe" Hooker, whom Lincoln advised to "beware of rashness, but with energy and sleepless vigilance, go forward, and give us victories." The victories were not forthcoming. Hooker was outmaneuvered by Lee at Chancellorsville, though both armies took heavy casualties. Hooker was replaced by General George G. Meade, whose task it was to stop Lee's bold invasion of the North. On July 1, 1863, at the town of Gettysburg, Pennsylvania, the battle commenced. Its high point came two days later when Lee ordered fifteen thousand Confederates, under General George Pickett, to storm the center of Union strength on Cemetery Ridge. That charge, perhaps the most important military engagement of the Civil War, failed. Months later still-unburied bodies littered the battleground. For the first time Lee clearly had been defeated. "Call no council of war," Lincoln telegraphed Meade. "Do not let the enemy escape." But that is precisely what Meade did. He refused to counterattack, and Lee retreated to safety in Virginia.

Lincoln finally found an effective general in Ulysses S. Grant, who once defined his theory of warfare as follows: "The art of war is simple enough. Find out where the enemy is. Get him as soon as you can. Strike at him as hard as you can and keep moving on." His victories in the western theater of operations, especially the spectacular triumph at Vicksburg, split the Confederacy, giving the Union control of the Mississippi River. In March 1864

Lincoln promoted Grant to the position of lieutenant general in charge of all Union armies. His grand strategy was to squeeze the South in a pincer movement and force its surrender. General William T. Sherman would march from Chattanooga across Georgia to the sea and then turn northward. Grant would move his Army of the Potomac into Virginia and take the measure of Lee. In less than a month, at the battles of the Wilderness (May 6), Spotsylvania (May 19), and Cold Harbor (June 3), the North suffered over fifty-five thousand casualties. Critics labeled Grant a "butcher," and indeed some of the attacks he ordered were foolish. Grant himself recognized the problems. "At Cold Harbor," he later wrote, "no advantage whatever was gained to compensate for the heavy losses we sustained." But Lincoln stood by Grant. They both knew the South lacked reserves, that a point of exhaustion was approaching. The failure of their diplomacy, their defeats at Gettysburg and Vicksburg, the tightened naval blockade of their ports, the bleeding away of Lee's troops, all took a heavy toll of southern morale. Sherman's capture of Atlanta and his devastating march across Georgia to Savannah broke the backbone of the Confederacy. By February 1865 Sherman's troops were in Columbia, South Carolina, pressing north. Lee's army, meanwhile, under a long siege at Petersburg, Virginia, was outnumbered by Grant's 115,000 to less than 50,000. Pressured by the impending collapse, in a move of desperation, Lee attempted to link up with Confederate General Joe Johnston in North Carolina. Cut off and surrounded by Grant, however, Lee surrendered at Appomattox Court House on April 9, 1865. "Give them the most liberal terms," Lincoln instructed Grant. "Let them have their horses to plow with, and, if you like, their guns to shoot crows with. I want no one punished." Five days later, while watching a play at Ford's Theater in Washington, Lincoln was shot. He died the next morning.

Effects of the War

The Civil War resulted in enormous physical devastation to the South. Eyewitness accounts describe a land of ruins and desolation. Between Richmond and Washington it was "like a desert." Charleston was a city "of vacant houses, of widowed women, of rotting wharves." The path of General Sherman's march "looked for many miles like a broad, black streak of ruin." It took nearly two decades before the cotton crop was restored to the level of 1860. Southern industries were crippled. The banks were bankrupt. Overnight a southern investment in slaves valued at two and a half billion dollars was erased. The value of southern lands decreased by half between 1860 and 1870.

What about the North? It is sometimes fashionable to speak of the war as inaugurating or spurring an industrial revolution. It is true that many engaged in wartime business activities made fortunes. Agricultural production expanded and mechanized at a fast rate. Moreover, the Republican party enacted laws consistent with its economic philosophy. It reversed the antebellum drift toward free trade by the Morrill tariff of 1861 and by another tariff act (1864), which imposed duties that were almost half the total value of all dutiable imports. Congress in 1862 voted funds to finance the construction of a transcontinental railroad; and in 1863 and 1864 passed the

In 1864 Abraham Lincoln was assailed by the New York Herald as a ridiculous figure and a disgrace as president. "President Lincoln is a joke incarnated . . . The idea that such a man as he should be the President of such a country as this is a joke . . . His conversation is full of jokes . . . His title of 'Honest' is a satirical joke." Beginning with his death Lincoln's stature began to grow until in time it reached legendary proportions. Today he is rated above George Washington as America's greatest president.   (The National Archives)

National Banking Acts that required member banks to invest one-third of their capital in government bonds—on which they made both substantial interest and profits. Little wonder that Senator John Sherman wrote to his brother, the general: "The truth is the close of the war with our resources unimpaired gives an elevation, a scope to the ideas of leading capitalists, far higher than anything ever undertaken in this country before. They talk of millions as confidently as formerly of thousands." Nevertheless, a good many businesses, such as textiles and ship-building, did not share in the prosperity. Neither did many urban workers, whose real wages failed to rise as fast as inflation. The loss of the large southern market for its manufactured products and the depletion of its labor supply by military demands actually caused northern labor productivity to decline. All significant economic indicators were lower for the Civil War decade than for any other in the nineteenth century.

COMMENTARY

The problems after 1865, however, were not merely economic, but emotional and psychological—and racial. "With malice toward none; with charity for all; with firmness in the right, as God gives us to see the right," Lincoln said in his second inaugural address, "let us strive on to finish the work we are in; to bind up the nation's wounds . . . to do all which may achieve a just and lasting peace among ourselves, and with all nations." But there were too many empty chairs, too many vacant bedrooms, too many maimed, too many bitter memories. While Lincoln pleaded for forgiveness, Edmund Ruffin of South Carolina recorded his "unmitigated hatred to Yankee rule—to all political, social and business connections with the Yankees and to the Yankee race. Would that I could impress these sentiments, in their full force, on every living Southerner and bequeath them to every one yet to be born!" Soon after writing that legacy Ruffin committed suicide. Had Lincoln lived, could he have mastered postwar problems as effectively as he had directed the nation in war? Or would his image have been sullied in the muddy waters of Reconstruction? While deifying Lincoln the people really forgot him. The years after his death, instead of being marked by charity and justice, were filled with vengeance, corruption, and exploitation.

GERALD CAPERS, *Stephen A. Douglas* (1959)
BRUCE CATTON, *The Centennial History of the Civil War* (1961–65)
ARTHUR C. COLE, *The Irrepressible Conflict* (1934)
HENRY S. COMMAGER, *The Blue and the Gray* (1950)
AVERY O. CRAVEN, *The Coming of the Civil.War* (1957)
RICHARD CURRENT, *Lincoln and the First Shot* (1963)
———, *The Lincoln Nobody Knows* (1958)
DAVID DONALD, *Charles Sumner and the Coming of the Civil War* (1960)
———, *Lincoln Reconsidered* (1956)
MARTIN DUBERMAN, *Charles Francis Adams* (1960)
DWIGHT DUMOND, *Antislavery: The Crusade for Freedom in America* (1961)
CLEMENT EATON, *A History of the Southern Confederacy* (1954)
———, *The Mind of the Old South* (1967)
STANLEY ELKINS, *Slavery* (1968)
DON FEHRENBACHER, *Prelude to Greatness: Lincoln in the 1850's* (1962)
ERIC FONER, *Free Soil, Free Labor, Free Men* (1970)
DOUGLAS S. FREEMAN, *Robert E. Lee* (1934)
C. S. GRIFFIN, *The Ferment of Reform* (1967)
HOLMAN HAMILTON, *Prologue to Conflict: The Crisis and Compromise of 1850* (1964)
ALLAN NEVINS, *The Ordeal of the Union* (1947)
———, *The Emergence of Lincoln* (1950)
ROY F. NICHOLS, *The Disruption of American Democracy* (1948)
RUSSELL NYE, *William Lloyd Garrison and the Humanitarian Reformers* (1955)
DAVID POTTER, *Lincoln and His Party in the Secession Crisis* (1942)
———, *The South and the Sectional Conflict* (1968)
THOMAS PRESSLEY, *Americans Interpret Their Civil War* (1962)
J. G. RANDALL, *Lincoln, the President* (1944)
——— and DAVID DONALD, *The Civil War and Reconstruction* (1961)
KENNETH STAMPP, *And the War Came* (1950)
EDWARD STONE, *Incident at Harper's Ferry* (1956)
CARL SWISHER, *Roger B. Taney* (1935)
BENJAMIN THOMAS, *Abraham Lincoln* (1952)
HANS TREFOUSSE, *The Radical Republicans* (1968)

9

White, Black, and Red: The Era of Reconstruction, 1865–1876

It has been said that the Civil War was fought to resolve three issues: secession, the role of the South within the Union, and the role of Negroes within white society. If this is so, the war solved only one of these. Secession, the war proved, was not permissible. At Appomattox, the South bowed entirely to this verdict. The other two issues remained unresolved in 1865. The political role of an agrarian South within an industrializing nation had generated repeated conflicts over national land, transportation, and commercial policies. Victory over the Confederacy did not provide any solution to this recurring problem. Nor did it fully resolve the matter of the relation between the races. Slavery was ended, but this vital advance was only a halfway step. What roles would blacks assume now that they were not owned by other men? This question rose up ominously as the guns were stilled. Reconstruction was a time of confronting those two remaining dilemmas.

Lincoln's 10 Percent Plan

Abraham Lincoln had given some thought to the intertwined issues of race and sectional politics after Gettysburg. In 1863 he had proposed a tentative plan whereby the southern states would be readmitted into the Union upon compliance with a few simple procedures. Excepting high-ranking Confederate officials, all southerners under Lincoln's plan could regain citizenship by taking a loyalty oath. When 10 percent of the electorate of 1860 in any state had taken such an oath, they could set up a state government, draft a constitution, and send representatives to Washington to participate in national policy making. Lincoln's plan required the southern states to recognize the end of slavery, but it did not specify that blacks be given full political rights. This was left to the states. As historian Kenneth Stampp wrote: "For him [Lincoln], reconstruction was to be essentially a work of restoration, not innovation; it was the old Union—the Union as it was—that he hoped to rebuild."

The plan had two objectionable features in the eyes of some Congressmen: leniency toward southern whites and the relegation of Congress to a passive role while the president managed reconstruction. The Radicals in Congress wanted harsher terms, and they wanted Congress to participate fully in the process of reconstituting the Union. They passed the Wade-Davis bill in July 1864, raising Lincoln's 10 percent to a majority of the voters and requiring the new state constitutions to repudiate the Confederate debt and prohibit slavery. Lincoln disposed of the bill with a pocket veto, keeping the initiative in his own hands. Yet the lines were drawn, and it was evident that reconstruction would involve conflicts both between sections and between branches of the federal government.

Lincoln's assassination on April 14, 1865, brought the dour Tennessean Andrew Johnson to the presidency. He had been a vocal critic of the southern ruling classes who had taken the disastrous route to secession, and some Radicals hoped that Johnson would share their determination to force the South not only to repent but also to make far-reaching social and political changes before readmission to the Union. But Johnson shared Lincoln's view that reconciliation with southern whites was the overriding goal. Over the summer and fall of 1865, with Congress adjourned, Johnson offered the South lenient terms not unlike those Lincoln had suggested. By December, when Congress reconvened, every southern state had organized new governments in accord with the president's instruction and had sent representatives to Washington ready to participate in federal politics once again.

This was *presidential* reconstruction, presenting solutions to the problems of race relations and the role of the South in the Union, which a majority of Congressmen and Senators found unacceptable and even infuriating. It seemed that Johnson was abandoning the black man, leaving him not a slave but far from free. All the new southern governments were entirely white, and they had been busy during the summer passing black codes to regulate the position of blacks within the white-dominated society. The codes varied from state to state, but they typically prohibited blacks from bearing arms, taking up occupations outside of agriculture, and moving about freely from job to job and place to place. Unemployed persons were easily classified as "vagrants" and were liable to fines and imprisonment. The black code of Louisiana even went so far as to state that "every negro is required to be in the regular service of some white person . . . or former owner, who shall be held responsible for the conduct of said negro." In the view of all Radical Republicans and many moderates, the war had not been fought for such limited gains for blacks.

The codes were not the worst of the new situation confronting southern blacks. Vicious race riots, invariably initiated by whites, swept several southern cities. Memphis whites, offended by the presence of black troops, looted and burned the black section. A similar incident erupted in New Orleans, and several blacks were killed. "The hands of rebels are again red with loyal blood," announced the *New York Tribune*. Moderates pulled away from Johnson, who seemed largely responsible for the behavior of southern whites.

Northern and western representatives were also quick to note that the newly elected southern senators and congressmen who were waiting in Washington hotels for the opening of Congress were the same class of

Confederate leaders who had recently led the South in grey uniforms. Indeed, the former vice-president of the Confederacy, Alexander Stephens, was the new Senator from Georgia. These men were Democrats by party, agrarian and "unreconstructed" in outlook, sure to oppose Republican policies. Their admission to Congress would jeopardize the program of internal improvements—land grants to western railroads, the Homestead Act, a national banking system, a higher tariff to protect industry—that had been passed by Republican majorities while the South was in secession.

Congress quickly set up the Joint Committee on Reconstruction, barred the *Congress Intervenes* southern representatives, and the struggle over reconstruction entered a new phase. President Johnson held stubbornly to his view that reconstruction should proceed promptly with a minimum of changes forced upon the white South, but he was not an adroit leader of moderate opinion in the country at large or on Capitol Hill. The Radical Republicans, led by men like Senator Charles Sumner of Massachusetts and Congressman Thaddeus Stevens of Pennsylvania, took the upper hand. Their aim was to rebuild the southern political system so that blacks could participate fully, and the Republican party could remain strong in that section. "If all whites vote," Sumner had said, "then must all Blacks . . . Without them the old enemy will reappear, and . . . in alliance with the Northern Democracy, put us all in peril again." Stevens, in the words of historian James G. Randall "that strange mixture of disinterested philanthropy and partisan vindictiveness," quite frankly stated that his policies aimed at "the ascendancy of the Union [Republican] party. . . . If impartial suffrage is excluded in the rebel States, then . . . They [Democrats] with their kindred Cooperheads of the North, would always elect the President and control Congress. . . . For these, among other reasons, I am for negro suffrage in every rebel State."
   Some Radicals wished also to reform the southern social system, giving the blacks an economic base from which full social, as well as political, equality could be developed. This was the intent of Thaddeus Stevens's idea to provide each ex-slave with "forty acres and a mule." Stevens wanted to confiscate the land of the richest "70,000 proud, bloated and defiant rebels," which he estimated at three hundred ninety-four million acres of plantation land, and distribute it to the blacks. Few Americans, however, were committed to full racial equality or willing to go so far in reforming southern life. The operating strategy of the congressional majority was to secure political rights for blacks, trusting to the vote to upgrade race relations and entrench the Republican party in the still suspect South.

With Johnson in defiant opposition, the Radicals passed the Civil Rights Act *The Radical Program* over presidential veto in April 1866 and mustered sufficient votes to override Johnson's earlier veto of a bill extending the life of the Freedmen's Bureau. The bureau, headed by General Oliver Otis Howard, projected the northern helping hand deep into the South with a program of education and relief for uprooted populations. The important civil-rights law forbade the states from discriminating on the basis of race, thus invalidating all of the black codes.

To protect it from constitutional challenge, Congress submitted to the states the Fourteenth Amendment. It declared that "all persons born or naturalized in the United States, and subjected to the jurisdiction thereof, are citizens of the United States and of the State wherein they reside." Another part of the amendment read: "No State shall make or enforce any law which shall abridge the privileges or immunities of citizens of the United States; nor shall any State deprive any person of life, liberty, or property, without due process of law; nor deny to any person within its jurisdiction the equal protection of the laws." Although the amendment did not explicitly give Negroes the right to vote (that would come with the Fifteenth Amendment ratified in March 1870), it provided a reduction in representation for states that denied the suffrage on the basis of color.

The Civil Rights Act and the Fourteenth Amendment were the heart of congressional Reconstruction. An active federal agency operating in the South, the Freedmen's Bureau, was expected to do what it could to promote black independence through education and relief, but the right to vote was central to Republican strategy. Andrew Johnson advised the ten southern states remaining out of the Union (Tennessee had been readmitted in 1866) to refuse to ratify the Fourteenth Amendment. All took his advice. Johnson took the issue to the voters in the autumn of 1866 in a series of impassioned stump speeches. But the public apparently favored a firm line toward the recalcitrant white South and gave the Republicans a two-thirds majority in both houses of Congress. With this mandate and the evidence of continued abuse of blacks by southern whites, Congress moved into the military phase of Reconstruction.

The First Reconstruction Act came in March 1867; it divided the former Confederacy into five military districts controlled by Union generals. Troops would be withdrawn only when the states ratified the Fourteenth Amendment (enough of them had done so by July 1868 for official ratification) and adopted new constitutions satisfactory to Congress. Two other Reconstruction Acts followed over presidential vetoes, clarifying and extending the first. So began the relatively brief but intense period of military Reconstruction, an unprecedented era in which white-black coalition governments conducted southern political life. It was unquestionably the greatest period of social experimentation in the nation's history, "in a certain sense all a failure," wrote historian W. E. B. Du Bois, "but a splendid failure."

Reconstruction was a varied experience for the southern states, lasting as briefly as two years in some states and ending in all cases in 1876. Yet during that time southern life was sharply changed, and powerful feelings were generated that have colored the memory of Reconstruction to this day. To the white South it was a tragic era, a vengeful invasion of the section by outside power. Reconstruction was seen as producing corrupt regimes dominated by a large black electorate unready for self-government. This view was carried to millions by the movie *The Birth of a Nation* (1915) and by the best-selling novel (and Clark Gable-Vivien Leigh movie) *Gone with the Wind* (1935). Historians sympathized with this perspective on Recon-

The Experience of Reconstruction

struction until the mid-twentieth century when new research efforts and altered perspectives brought a different view.

It must be remembered that Reconstruction was brief, lasting between two and eight years in the ten states where it took place. During that time there was no black domination of the South. No Negro was elected governor, only two reached the United States Senate, and fourteen were elected to the House. Blacks held many lesser offices across the South, such as county supervisor or mayor, but in no state—with the exception of South Carolina during a brief period—did black legislators outnumber whites in state government. Black voters just barely outnumbered the whites by a margin of about seven hundred thousand to six hundred sixty thousand. Reconstruction governments were racial coalitions, but whites were in the majority.

Some whites were the northern carpetbaggers who went South out of idealism or restlessness or opportunism and southern "scalawags" who decided to cooperate with the new regime for any number of motives. These whites with their Negro allies compiled a mixed record but one not without its constructive aspects. There was graft and inefficiency, but this was true of all governments in the aftermath of war. Taxes were raised, and the southern bonded debt went up by a hundred million dollars by 1874. The increase was inevitable for the South was rebuilding after a destructive conflict. Reconstruction governments wrote enlightened new state constitutions, broadened the suffrage, and increased spending for public education for both races. These efforts, combined with northern philanthropy and the work of the Freedmen's Bureau, put six hundred thousand black southerners into public schools in the South by 1876; a negligible number had received such education ten years earlier. During Reconstruction the great Negro colleges of Fisk, Howard, Atlanta, and Hampton Institute were founded. While making these gains, blacks in office for the most part exercised great restraint and moderation, displaying none of the vindictiveness that might have been expected of former slaves. For a brief season, the southern Negro made rapid strides toward the distant goal of political equality with whites.

This social experiment lasted only so long as the Republican white-black coalitions could hold power against the resurgent all-white Democrats. By 1870 the Democrats had control of Virginia, North Carolina, and Georgia. Texas Democrats overthrew Reconstruction regimes in 1873, Alabama and Arkansas were "redeemed" (the phrase used by Democrats to describe the termination of Republican rule) in 1874, Mississippi in 1875. Only three states were left in Republican hands on the eve of the 1876 election—Florida, South Carolina, and Louisiana.

   The process of redemption was complex and virtually irresistible. Black voters could be persuaded not to vote Republican in a number of ways. The ex-slaves, often illiterate and naturally inexperienced in political life, could often be tricked or defrauded. Informal intimidation could be brought to bear when trickery failed. After all, whites occupied superior economic positions, hired and fired black workers. In areas where overwhelming black majorities made informal pressure inadequate, more organized intimidation appeared. Secret societies of whites sprang up to utilize selective terrorism. The Ku Klux Klan became the most famous, but it shared the scene with the Knights of the White Camelia, the Red Shirts, and others. With the use of night rides, burning crosses, and occasional lynchings, the secret orders counterattacked against the newly enfranchised black electorate.

   Against these tactics and the superior economic and social position of southern whites, the new Republican coalitions were everywhere over-matched. There was some grumbling in Congress as news came North of Democratic resurgence, and two Force Acts (1870, 1871) and the Ku Klux Klan Act (1871) authorized the President to use military power to keep order in the South. Yet both President Ulysses Grant, elected in 1868, and the

Redemption

A contemporary cartoon depicts hooded Ku Klux Klansmen in an armed attack on a black family. The cartoon presumably meant to express criticism of the Klan for its cowardly attack on defenseless people, but the racial stereotypes in its depiction of blacks seriously limited its helpfulness in discouraging inter-racial conflict. Woodcut after a drawing by Frank Bellew. (The Bettmann Archive)

Congress were steadily losing their interest in Negro rights. Said Grant's attorney general upon hearing news of more counterattacks against Reconstruction governments: "The whole public are tired of these annual autumnal outbreaks in the South." Radical congressmen who did not become weary of the struggle were often not reelected. Democrats in the North gained seats in the congressional elections of 1870 and, especially, 1874, and their presence weakened the thrust for social reconstruction in the South.

The Democrats came back strongly in 1876, nominating Samuel J. Tilden of New York. Tilden probably won the 1876 election, for he carried all redeemed southern states and added four northern ones for a 203 to 165 lead in the electoral vote. Yet in the three troubled Reconstruction states still under military rule—Florida, Louisiana, and South Carolina—disputed totals were reported. Historians believe that Tilden carried at least two of these, and he only needed one of their combined nineteen electoral votes. But in the case of disputed votes the Constitution provides that the Senate (which was dominated by Republicans) and the House (controlled by Democrats) must open and count the ballots. The constitutional language is unclear as to procedure, and a deadlock ensued, Republicans insisting that all nineteen disputed votes be counted for their candidate, Rutherford B. Hayes. A special electoral commission finally decided by a partisan vote to count all votes for Hayes, and the Democrats accepted the verdict only when Hayes agreed to give southern Democrats control of patronage in their section, to offer generous internal improvements, and to withdraw troops from the last three states. Bargaining over these arrangements took from November until the spring of 1877 and was justly seen as a major crisis bringing back memories of the schism of 1860. In the end, political compromise seemed better than intransigent resistance. The Compromise of 1877 formally ended the Reconstruction era. Hayes toured the South after his inauguration, allowed former Confederate General Wade Hampton to join his train, and appointed a Tennessean, David M. Key, as attorney general. "Received everywhere heartily," he wrote about his journey: "The Country is again one and united." The price of this unity was the abandonment of the Negro to whatever fate the Southern economic and social system arranged for him. As Hayes told a meeting in Atlanta: the "rights and interests" of Negroes "would be safer if this great mass of intelligent [Southern] white men were let alone by the general government." The southern Negro would now have to work out his destiny within the region; he could expect no more help from the national government, which had marched south in 1861 to strike off the chains of slavery.

End of Reconstruction

One lasting effect of Reconstruction was that the American Constitution was altered by the addition of three amendments: the Thirteenth prohibiting slavery, the Fourteenth requiring that states extend equal protection of the laws to all citizens, and the Fifteenth extending the vote to all males. These

Lasting Effects of Reconstruction

amendments were obviously intended to help black Americans by granting emancipation and full political rights. Only the Thirteenth was immediately effective. The other two were honored only for the short period of federal intervention and then became largely ignored. This nullification of constitutional rights did not happen overnight, for southern whites discovered that the right to vote did not necessarily have to be withdrawn for other political and social rights to be severely circumscribed. Without economic power, education, or experience in political activity, blacks could not use their vote effectively as a ladder to full participation in southern society. Redeemer governments found that Negro suffrage was not a serious impediment to white domination of southern affairs, and for more than a decade after Reconstruction, blacks continued to vote in substantial numbers. It was not until the 1890s that agrarian unrest threatened conservative Democrats and convinced them that the vote of poor black farmers was potentially dangerous and must be withdrawn. From 1890 through the early years of the twentieth century southern governments systematically disfranchised blacks, easily evading the Fifteenth Amendment by avoiding explicit reference to color in their voting provisions. Two principal devices were the poll tax or other form of property qualification and the literacy test. Some whites were pushed from the voting rolls by these measures, but southerners considered this an acceptable price to pay for the almost total exclusion of blacks. Some states also used the so-called grandfather clause, which allowed whites who could not meet property qualifications to vote if their grandfathers had voted before the war. The federal government was in no mood, by the 1890s, to return to the South and enforce the Fifteenth Amendment. Eventually the grandfather laws would be overruled by the Supreme Court, but other patently discriminatory measures remained to close southern political life to blacks.

The Fourteenth Amendment was evaded with equal ease. It required equal protection of the laws, but the Supreme Court held in the civil-rights cases of 1883 that this language did not bar segregation in private facilities. This ruling was broadened in the *Plessy* v. *Ferguson* judgment of 1896, when the Court declared that segregation in public transportation (in this case, a railroad) was permissible so long as "separate but equal" facilities were provided for blacks. Thus the Court removed any possibility of constitutional challenge to the network of Jim Crow laws passed in southern states to segregate the races in separate schools, gathering places, restaurants, toilets, even drinking facilities.

Thus the Fourteenth and Fifteenth amendments appeared for many years to have been Reconstruction-era achievements that made no difference at all—to the Negro. (Corporations were pleasantly surprised in the period from the 1880s to the late 1930s to find the courts including them as "persons" under the equal-protection and due process language of the Fourteenth Amendment, sheltering them from much state economic regulation.) But time would reveal that the dead constitutional letters of one era might be dynamically revived in another. The Fifteenth Amendment began to come to life in the 1940s in the case of *Smith* v. *Allwright* (1944) when the Supreme Court prohibited the Texas Democratic party from excluding blacks from voting in the party primaries. Other judicial decisions, combined with the Voting Rights Acts of the late 1950s and 1960s, eventually gave the Fifteenth Amendment full application some one hundred years after its passage.

The Fourteenth Amendment was to have an even greater impact as interpreted by the Supreme Court in the latter years of the Roosevelt administrations and thereafter. In 1948 the justices ruled that racially restrictive real estate covenants could not be enforced by state courts. In 1950 separate dining car facilities on railroads were rejected, and in the celebrated *Brown* v. *Topeka Board of Education* decision in 1954 segregation in education was ruled a violation of the equal protection clause. The Fourteenth Amendment was utilized for other challenges to ancient political habits in the states; examples are the reapportionment cases—*Baker* v. *Carr* (1962), and *Wesberry* v. *Sanders* (1964), and *Reynolds* v. *Sims* (1964)—in which gerrymandered congressional and state legislative districts were outlawed. The Fourteenth Amendment, ruled the Court, required that "as nearly as practicable one man's vote . . . is to be worth as much as another's." Today the Supreme Court interprets the Fourteenth Amendment as obliging the states to observe almost the entire Bill of Rights, even though the first ten amendments were originally written to apply only to the power of the national government. No group in America has benefited more than black Americans from these amendments, even though they had to wait almost a century before the nation was ready to live up to the spirit of laws passed in the aftermath of Civil War.

The Reconstruction-era constitutional amendments had a beneficial effect—at least in the long run—but this cannot be said of another constitutional impact of the passions of Reconstruction: the impeachment and trial of President Johnson. Johnson's collisions with Congress had become exceptionally bitter and frequent. In 1867 the Congress passed over presidential veto the Tenure of Office Act, making it impossible for the chief executive to remove high-level appointees without Senate consent; it also passed the Army Appropriation Act, which severely limited the powers of the president as commander in chief by requiring all army orders to be issued by the general of the army. Johnson thought the laws unconstitutional, with good reason, and arranged to violate the Tenure of Office Act by firing Secretary of War Edwin Stanton in February 1868. Two days later the House voted 124 to 47 to impeach him. The charges were violating the Tenure of Office Act, acting reprehensibly and attempting to bring Congress into public "disgrace, ridicule, hatred, contempt, and reproach," and being guilty of "a high misdemeanor in office."

The president, through his attorneys, went to trial before the Senate, with Chief Justice of the Supreme Court Salmon P. Chase presiding. For once Andrew Johnson held his tongue. He remained silently, even humble, in the White House as a parade of witnesses heaped scorn upon him. But none

Impeachment of Andrew Johnson

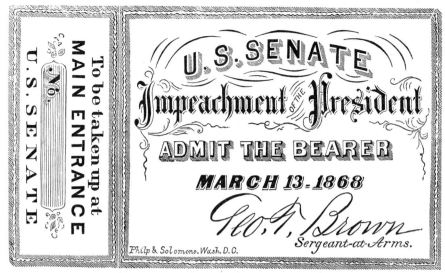

FAC-SIMILE OF TICKET OF ADMISSION TO THE IMPEACHMENT TRIAL.

Was impeachment, as The Nation *magazine said, "an allowable means of getting rid of an executive officer whose administration the majority believe to be injurious to the public welfare"? Seven Republicans decided that it was not, insisting that "high crimes and misdemeanors" meant more than merely obnoxious policies. (Culver Pictures)*

could produce evidence of "high Crimes and Misdemeanors." Finally realizing that they were doing their cause far more harm than good by prolonging the trial, the Radicals called for a vote on May 16. To their mortification the result was thirty-five to nineteen, one short of the two-thirds necessary for conviction. Not willing to accept the verdict, the Radical leadership unmercifully badgered, threatened, and cajoled the seven members of the Republican party who had refused to toe the line. In another vote, taken ten days later, the result was the same, and the impeachment was abandoned.

As one of the stalwart seven, Lyman Trumbull, later explained, if Johnson had been removed for such obviously insufficient cause, then any president would be at the mercy of Congress whenever he was opposed by half the House and two-thirds of the Senate. This would have ended the separation of powers and was a step that seven Republican Senators refused to take.

The impeachment of Johnson, though unsuccessful, nonetheless had the short-run effect of weakening the presidency. Not until Theodore Roosevelt came to the White House in 1901 did the chief executive regain the initiative in guiding national affairs that Lincoln and Jackson had exercised. Yet in the longer run, the Johnson impeachment seems to have contributed something to the imperial presidency of post–World War II America; the Radicals' impeachment of Andrew Johnson was so partisan and shabby that it discredited the constitutional provision for removal of presidents from office. As historian Henry Jones Ford wrote in 1898, impeachment was "a rusted blunderbuss, that will probably never be taken in hand again." It was lost as one of the potential checks upon presidents as the office began to gather overwhelming power and arrogance in the second half of the twentieth century.

The post-Reconstruction denial of political rights was not the worst feature of the freedman's role after withdrawal of federal troops. Nothing in Reconstruction had laid the basis for the economic recovery of the whole South or provided clear avenues for black economic progress. The region's staggering economic problems were burdening both races. Never as prosperous as the North, the South at the end of the war had seen much of its transportation network damaged and its commercial life profoundly disrupted. Apart from the wartime destruction of property, the end of slavery eradicated $2.5 billion worth of capital assets, and the debacle of Confederate money wiped out much more. Not until 1877 would the South raise as much cotton as 1860, and one sign of the region's economic weakness was the tendency to see cotton production as the prime measure of revival. Southern soil remained fertile, but the one-crop system ruled too much of the region. Whether cotton or tobacco, single-crop farming depleted the soil and encouraged a narrow diet.

Within this flawed economy the blacks were generally worse off than the struggling whites. Only in a very few places, such as Sea Island off the coast of Georgia, did war or Reconstruction stimulate land redistribution from owners to ex-slaves. For the most part the blacks were landless; yet with only agricultural skills, most had no alternative but to remain on someone's farm. A new economic system—called tenancy or share cropping—grew out of the ashes of war. Since cash was scarce, blacks (and many whites) without land often worked on large farms in return for a wooden shack, agricultural tools, and a division of the crop—usually on a fifty-fifty basis.

The system was hard on both land and people. Cash crops, cotton, and—to a lesser extent—rice, corn, or tobacco claimed every available acre. The diet of the postwar South continued to reflect an inattention to dairy farming, livestock, vegetables, fruit. The sharecropper was totally dependent upon the landowner for food and supplies through the year, paying exorbitant rates of interest at the local (often the landowner's) store. At the time of settlement there might be no cash payment at all in poor years, and in better years the cropper could never be sure that his share was a fair one. Semiliteracy and black skin discouraged self-assertiveness. The landowner who exploited his own labor was in turn exploited by high interest rates from local and eastern banks, by freight rate differentials favoring the Northeast, by drastic and unpredictable fluctuations characteristic of export-crop agriculture. The land was exploited by everybody. Farming was not a prosperous occupation anywhere in America in the last decades of the nineteenth century, and the person at the bottom of a sickly cotton economy in the South was the black ex-slave.

Some economic progress was slowly made even in the face of these conditions, since southern people were hardworking and the region had impressive resources. Commercially minded people in southern cities spoke of a "New South" and promoted the growth of industrial capacity—steel in Birmingham, cotton textiles in the Carolinas, coal in the southern Appalachians. By 1880 the South could claim 80 percent more manufacturing plants than on the eve of the war. But the region lagged behind the rest of the country. The industrial production of the entire South in 1890 did not match that of New York State. In 1880, the average per capita wealth outside the South was $1,086; inside the South it was $376.

Thus it was not a very "reconstructed" South that emerged when the Compromise of 1877 ended the era of federal intervention. Blacks had moved up from slavery, but the vast majority had reached only up to a form of peonage within a one-crop agricultural economy. Further progress, if it came, would not come from outside. President James A. Garfield confirmed the preoccupation of the federal government with other matters when he said in 1881 of the southern racial problem: "Time is the only cure." So the Negro must produce his own strategy for improvement, just as the white spokesmen of the New South were at work devising plans for the community as they conceived it.

For a time it seemed that political resistance was feasible, especially when poor farmers of both races could join in grievances against landlords, railroads, and banks. The agrarian unrest that reached from greenbackism through the populism of the 1890s included many black farmers, but this sort of insurgency was too easily quashed by a combination of violence and Negro disfranchisement. The depression of the 1890s all but wiped out the struggling black middle class of artisans and shopkeepers and brought Negro life in America to what historian Rayford Logan called the nadir at the turn of the century. In desperation, some black spokesmen turned to colonization: "Africa is our home," said Bishop Henry M. Turner of Georgia. Racial solidarity in self-help communities was urged by others. "Let us stand up like men in our own organizations," said T. Thomas Fortune who founded the Afro-American League in 1887, "[and] if others use violence . . . it is not for us to run away from violence." But these strategies had no large appeal. Then in 1895 a major leader emerged in the person of Booker T. Washington, who charted a difficult path to Negro progress through accommodation to the harsh realities of a world without Lincoln, Thaddeus Stevens, or Charles Sumner.

The Negro Dilemma

Born a slave in 1856, Washington was educated at Hampton Institute in Virginia, and in 1881 was chosen to organize a new black normal school at Tuskegee, Alabama. In 1895 he made a speech at the Cotton States and International Exposition in Atlanta that made him the nation's leading black educator and an internationally known figure. Washington laid out a strategy for the progress of the Negro people, and his themes were accommodation, self-help, the avoidance of politics, the importance of middle-class values of work and thrift. He counseled blacks to stay in the South, learn the manual and agricultural trades, prove their worth to a skeptical white population, and accept segregation: "In all things that are purely social we can be as separate as the fingers, yet one as the hand in all matters essential to mutual progress."

Booker T. Washington

"Let us, in the future," said Booker T. Washington, "spend less time talking about the part of the city that we cannot live in, and more time in making the part of the city that we can live in beautiful and attractive." It was a message of self-help, and most blacks found it to be wise counsel. (Culver Pictures)

His message of gradualism, accommodation, and conciliation pleased a listening white world, which recognized Washington as his race's leading spokesman until his death in 1915. Critics have found Washington in retrospect to have been a harmful influence on his people, remembering him as the apostle of resignation. They forget the occasions when Washington exerted his influence for justice, risking his contacts with the white power structure. Whether his message was realistic or excessively timid depends upon one's assessment of the possibilities open to blacks in turn-of-the-century America, a time of rampant racism, high lynching rates, and the complete absence of sources of organized support for social intervention to moderate Southern race relations. But in advising his people to turn away from politics and look to their own labor—to "let down your bucket where you are" —Booker Washington was dealing with the implications of the end of Reconstruction and the turning of the national mind and conscience toward other problems.

The Other Colored Race—the Indian

When the nation was fighting its only Civil War over a cluster of issues in which black-white relations were central, another colored race within the society was forcing itself upon the national agenda in a new way. The native American had always been "a problem" to white settlers, for he owned and occupied the land and resisted encroachment. Yet the Indian wars of the 1860s represented something different in white-Indian relations. A final phase had arrived in the latter half of the nineteenth century. Although the wars against the Plains Indians were to be the most savage and epic in the long history of conflicting civilizations in North America, they were also to be the last. During these years the Indian, resourceful and indomitable to the end, finally ran out of space, numbers, and time. The post–Civil War generation of whites thus inherited two of the most difficult problems ever to face citizens of the United States: the devising of new roles for freed slaves and the fashioning of a new policy toward the native American as armed resistance entered a spectacular but culminating phase.

At the close of the Civil War the Indian roamed freely over roughly half the continent. The survivors of five eastern tribes occupied reservation lands in Oklahoma, and, along with the shattered tribes of California, they were incapable of further resistance to white encroachment. But a quarter of a million Indians of undiminished vigor occupied their ancestral lands in the West, and the mobile, buffalo-hunting tribes of the Great Plains were especially formidable: the Blackfeet of southwestern Canada, the Sioux of Minnesota and the Dakotas, the Cheyenne of Colorado and Wyoming, the Comanche of northern Texas, the Apache farther to the west in New Mexico. They resisted the white advance with resourcefulness, courage, and savagery.

In 1851 the federal government, in the Treaty of Fort Laramie, had attempted to evolve a policy to put an end to the increasing friction between Indians and the wagon trains bound for California and Oregon. Under the treaty a number of the plains tribes, including the Sioux, Cheyenne, and Arapaho, were induced to accept separate reservations off the main line of white advance. In return, the whites promised food supplies to the hard-pressed tribes, who were beginning to suffer from the decline in the buffalo

A Ute warrior and his bride pose for a photographer in Utah's Wasatch mountains in the 1870s. (Smithsonian Institution National Anthropological Archives)

herds. A familiar cycle of events brought these peacemaking efforts to nothing. On the Indians' side, the younger braves could not be held to the agreements made by the chiefs; they despised confinement to reservations and doubted the good faith of the whites. They were usually correct in their doubts. The government intended to honor its promises of supplies, but the agents chosen to distribute them were unreliable, and the food was too often either stolen by whites or was inferior in quality. Nor did the army prevent the constant encroachment of settlers upon reservation lands. As whites continued to move into Indian-occupied areas, a broad revolt flared. Its timing coincided with the beginning of the Civil War when federal troops were diverted from the frontier. For five years, from 1862 to about 1867, the Indians conducted running warfare throughout the West, raiding isolated cabins and settlements with devastating effect. The whites struck back in kind, and carried the fight to the "civilian" population of the enemy, as Sherman did in the March through Georgia in 1864. In that same year, for example, a unit of the Colorado militia caught some five hundred Cheyenne and Arapaho braves and their families at Sand Creek, Colorado, in November and within a few hours annihilated virtually all of them with gunshots, knives, and clubs. "Kill and scalp all, big and little," the commander, Colonel Chivington, told his men: "Nits make lice." A white observer recorded: "They were scalped, their brains knocked out; the men used their knives, ripped open women, clubbed little children . . . beat their brains out, mutilated their bodies in every sense of the word."

The Chivington massacre had its parallels on both sides. In 1867 the principal chiefs among the plains Indians agreed to a government demand that the Indians accept reservations in the Black Hills and in Oklahoma. Again many tribesmen refused to give up their way of life, and the war went on. As General Philip Sheridan said: "We took away their country and their means of support, broke up their mode of living, their habits of life, introduced disease and decay among them, and . . . they made war. Could anyone expect less?" In the end, the material and human resources of the whites were irresistible. The Sioux under Crazy Horse surrendered in the fall of 1876 and returned to their Black Hills reservation. The Nez Percé of Idaho and Oregon, led by Chief Joseph, resisted until 1878; The Apaches under Geronimo gave up in 1886. American folklore preserves the memory of the Indian wars in the West as a story of courageous white settlers who were eventually victorious in a good cause. But for the original Americans it was a historical moment of unfathomable sadness. "I don't want to settle," wrote a Kiowa chief, who surely spoke for all the plains Indians: "I love to roam the prairie. . . . These soldiers cut down my timber, they kill my buffalo, and when I see that, it feels as if my heart would burst with sorrow." Perhaps the most succinct summary of Indian-white relations in the late nineteenth century was uttered by a chief of the Ogala Sioux: "They made us many promises, more than I can remember, but they never kept but one; they promised to take our land, and they took it."

Chief Joseph of the Oregon Nez Percé tribe. In 1877 the resourceful Joseph led his braves on the warpath against encroaching whites, and tied up 5,000 troops for two years before surrendering to disease, starvation, and superior numbers. (Smithsonian Institution National Anthropological Archives)

Formulating an Indian Policy

The clash of civilizations was fundamental and inevitable. While no one can defend the ethical basis of the white invasion of the land of the red men, there was no historical alternative to the displacement of the Indians. Given this conflict, however, the mutual disengagement afforded by reservations could have been more humanely managed by the whites. Actually, the policy of extermination distressed many Americans, especially in the East. By the late 1870s, many intellectuals and segments of the press had developed sympathy for the red man in his desperate struggle for survival. In 1881 Helen Hunt Jackson published a stirring indictment of United States relations with the Indian in *A Century of Dishonor*, rallying humanitarians to the denunciation of past policy. In 1887 Congress passed the Dawes Allotment Act, authorizing the president to divide up tribal lands, allotting one hundred sixty acres to each head of family and lesser amounts to dependents or unmarried individuals. To prevent unscrupulous whites from cheating Indians out of their land without compensation, a twenty-five-year waiting period was provided before title to the lands could be transferred. The philosophy of the Dawes Act was quite simple and had deeply American roots: at the slight cost of one hundred sixty acres of semiarid land, the Indian was to be transformed from a primitive, stone-age hunter into a small agricultural capitalist on the white model. There is a great irony here. The laissez-faire philosophy was at its zenith in America at this time, and society's best minds agreed with William Graham Sumner that "stateways cannot change folkways"—that law was ineffective in regulating human conduct. Yet in the Dawes Act the government proposed by a statute to brush aside centuries of history and propel a primitive people into "the habits of civilized life" by conferring upon them a potential farm.

Not surprisingly, the history of Indian policy under the Dawes and subsequent acts was a dismal failure. With very few exceptions, the Indian did not become a successful farmer or become assimilated into white culture. He occupied a no-man's-land between old and new cultures, lacking both the strengths of the tribal way of life (now economically untenable) and the ability or desire to enter the competitive white world even at its agricultural fringes. Social disorganization ravaged the Indian populations.

By the 1930s, Indian life expectancy was two-thirds of the national average, infant mortality was twice as high, and the total number of American Indians was just the same as fifty years earlier while the white population during that time had increased five times. Some tribes had disappeared altogether. The one-hundred-sixty-acre freehold had not provided a viable economic basis for Indian survival. In 1934 it was calculated that ninety million of the original one hundred forty million acres allotted under the Dawes Act had passed into white hands, often at ridiculously low prices. In that year the government inaugurated a new policy (a "New Deal" for Indians, it was hoped) accepting the tribal unit and customs and abandoning the effort to force the Indians into individualistic agricultural habits. In the 1970s, the nation still gropes for a just policy toward the original inhabitants of the continent.

Politics of the Grant Era

With the end of Reconstruction in the 1870s and the enactment of Indian reform in the 1880s, the Civil War generation ended its painful grapple with two great racial issues: how to absorb black and red peoples into a predominantly white America. A third racial problem involving nonwhite people in the United States was dealt with in 1882 when Congress passed the Chinese Exclusion Act to prohibit immigration from China, which had spurted from four thousand to nearly forty thousand a year as the railroad era arrived in the West.

Today we know that the solutions devised for each of these racial and social problems were unjust, impermanent, and full of potential for future conflict. Yet given the assumptions of the era a vast majority of citizens found these solutions acceptable and turned their political energies to other problems. New issues were to dominate the 1880s and 1890s at the national level of politics: civil service reform, the money question, railroad regulation, the tariff, the trusts, and a growing class conflict.

General Ulysses S. Grant, elected to the presidency in 1868, was a transitional figure between political epochs. He symbolized the war and Union victory and reminded contemporaries of the great era of sectional division and sacrifice. Yet in two presidential terms he presided over the loss of wartime idealism, and when he left office, the Grand Old Party could no longer dominate national politics through the old sectional appeals. The social and racial idealism generated by the abolitionists and nourished by a national war effort would have dissipated eventually in any case, but Grant's administration of the affairs of state hastened the process. In his first term he appointed many old army cronies and allowed the administration to be tainted by the Crédit Mobilier financial scandal of 1868. He kept company with notorious stock-market manipulators Jay Gould and Jim Fisk. In the second term there were revelations of corruption in the navy, treasury, and Bureau of Indian Affairs. A whiskey ring of treasury officials operating out of St. Louis defrauded the government of millions of dollars, and Grant's personal secretary Orville Babcock was saved from indictment only by the president's intervention.

Grant's personal honesty was never in question during these scandals, and they came too late to imperil his 1872 reelection in any event. In that year he easily defeated the aging editor of the *New York Tribune* Horace Greeley, nominated by a splinter group of Liberal Republicans and the still-demoralized Democrats. The Grant administration had a relatively strong record in foreign affairs, his Secretary of State Hamilton Fish successfully resolving Anglo-American disputes over the *Alabama* claims (The *Alabama* was a Confederate vessel, built in England, which preyed upon Union shipping) and reestablishing strong relations with Great Britain. Yet the taint of corruption darkened the administration's reputation, and a financial panic in the autumn of 1873 was followed by a deep depression for which Grant had no remedies. Holding the standard "hard money" views of most Republicans (and many Democrats), Grant persuaded Congress to enact in 1874 a bill resuming specie payments that would effectively eliminate the nearly four hundred million dollars of greenbacks still in circulation. This deflationary step in the second year of a major depression raised even more enemies against the administration and stimulated the establishment of the Greenback party in 1876.

Thus economic troubles began to press sectional disputes to the background as the 1870s advanced. By 1876 memories of the Civil War had sufficiently faded to allow the Democrats to mount a vigorous presidential campaign behind Samuel J. Tilden. The voters probably elected a Democratic president that autumn, just eleven years after Appomattox, even though Hayes was eventually installed as president. Civil War political alignments were being rearranged, and a new, confused political era was ahead. "We are in a period when old questions are settled," confessed the new President in 1877, "and the new ones are not yet brought forward."

COMMENTARY

"The old questions were settled"—how odd these words sound to our own age! In the twenty years after the Civil War, white civilization had reached fundamental decisions about the place of black and red peoples within the American union, and time was to prove these decisions flawed. The black would not forever remain in the rural peonage that was arranged after the fall of slavery, and the "Indian problem" would continue to vex policymakers from the 1920s onward. Yet in the short run these interracial issues were indeed settled, in that the groups who set the agenda of American politics had accepted a compromise and began to turn to other social problems. Yet if racial questions had finally been somehow resolved after a long national ordeal, there were those who anticipated the future without optimism. Whites, it seemed, would have abundant reasons to struggle against whites as the Reconstruction era ended. The reformer Henry George wrote, on the eve of the 1876 election:

It is the dark background to our national [centennial] rejoicing, the skeleton which has stood by us at the feast. Our Fourth of July orators do not proclaim it; our newspapers do not announce it; we hardly whisper it to one another, but we all know, for we all feel, that beneath all our centennial rejoicing there exists in the public mind today a greater doubt of the success of Republican institutions than has existed before within the memory of our oldest man.

SUGGESTED READING

HOWARD K. BEALE, *The Critical Year: A Study of Andrew Johnson and Reconstruction* (1930)

MICHAEL L. BENEDICT, *The Impeachment and Trial of Andrew Johnson* (1973)

G. F. BENTLEY, *A History of the Freedmen's Bureau* (1955)

RAY A. BILLINGTON, *Westward Expansion: A History of the American Frontier* (1967)

WILLIAM R. BROCK, *An American Crisis: Congress and Reconstruction, 1865–1867*

JOHN H. and LA WANDA COX, *Politics, Principle, and Prejudice, 1865–1866* (1963)

DAVID H. DONALD, *Charles Sumner and the Rights of Man* (1970)

W. E. B. DU BOIS, *Black Reconstruction* (1935)

WILLIAM T. HAGAN, *American Indians* (1961)

LOUIS T. HARLAN, *Booker T. Washington: The Making of a Negro Leader, 1856–1901* (1972)

STANLEY I. KUTLER, *Judicial Power and Reconstruction Politics* (1968)

ERIC L. MCKITRICK, *Andrew Johnson and Reconstruction* (1960)

ROBERT W. MARDOCK, *Reformers and the American Indian* (1970)

LORING B. PRIEST, *Uncle Sam's Stepchildren: The Reformation of United States Indian Policy, 1865–1887* (1942)

WILLIE LEE ROSE, *Rehearsal for Reconstruction* (1964)

KENNETH M. STAMPP, *The Era of Reconstruction, 1865–1877* (1960)

WILCOMB E. WASHBURN, *The Indian in America* (1975)

JOEL WILLIAMSON, *After Slavery* (1965)

C. VANN WOODWARD, *Reunion and Reaction: The Compromise of 1877 and the End of Reconstruction,* (1951)

10

Expansion and Discontent, 1876–1900

The American "Takeoff" into Industrialism

In the United States, we remember our transition from a predominantly rural to an industrialized society as a difficult period. But in the perspective of recent world history, for a nation to achieve the transition at all is a remarkable feat. Most nation-states today fall into the category of "lesser developed" societies still in the early stages of modernization. Economists doubt that many of them will succeed in the race to increase productivity faster than population growth. The desire for modernization may be intense in Third and Fourth World peoples, but formidable barriers impede the takeoff into industrialism. Even the social regimentation of communism or military dictatorships is not always sufficient to catalyze the leap from a subsistence economy to the benefits (and costs, chiefly environmental pollution) of modern industrial life.

The United States accomplished this takeoff from an agricultural to an industrial economy between 1850 and the end of the nineteenth century. Time has obscured for us the fortunate circumstances that made the passage so dramatically successful. We have forgotten the dynamism, the excitement, the enormous effort, and sufferings of the process. The essential prerequisites for the establishment of a strong industrial economy are natural resources, a large and vigorous labor supply, investment capital, an entrepreneurial class, an adequate base in pure and applied science, a transportation network, and reasonable political stability. The United States in the second half of the nineteenth century possessed all of these assets. Within its borders were found not only fertile soils and abundant water but also huge deposits of iron, coal, oil, copper, and other minerals and metals vital to industrial development. A population of thirty-five million at the end of the Civil War grew to seventy-six million by 1900 through natural increase supplemented by waves of primarily European migration. It was a population of great vigor, a high degree of literacy, and a strong dedication to material advancement. The American people also placed a high value upon thrift, the deferral of gratification, and savings, and to their own internal savings were added investment funds from Britain and France. In land, labor, and capital, the classic factors of production, the United States was favorably endowed for material advancement.

Political circumstances were also fortuitous. The impact of the Civil War on the economy seems to have been ambiguous; productive capacity was not significantly enlarged, but wartime profits did provide capital for subsequent expansion. In addition the war's political impact was clearly favorable to industrial growth. National unity was ensured, and the southern Democrats with their agrarian predispositions were pushed to the periphery of governmental influence. The victorious Republican party was sympathetic to the business community and quickly established a political climate friendly to the aspirations of rising industrialists. Legislative encouragement for economic development took form just after secession: the protective tariffs of 1861, 1890, and 1897, the establishment of a national banking system, the maintenance of a gold standard against agrarian inflationist pressures, and the land grants and loans to railroads, which began in 1862.

Favorable Political Conditions

Federal assistance to railroad builders stimulated a tremendous expansion of railroad mileage and traffic. Prior to the war, sectional rivalries had prevented the granting of subsidies to lure private capital into the building of a

Transportation

Expansion of Railroads, 1860-1900

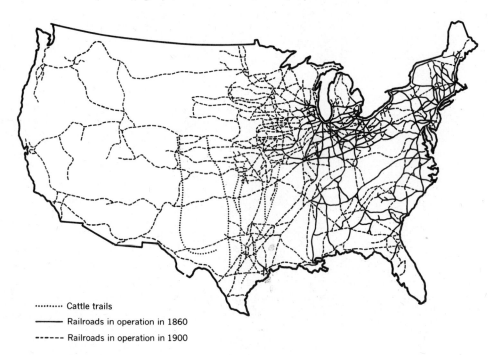

··········· Cattle trails
——— Railroads in operation in 1860
------ Railroads in operation in 1900

"You may stand ankle deep in the short grass of the uninhabited wilderness," wrote one observer, and within a month the railroad would deliver enough men and material to build a town at that site. The railroads opened the West to rapid settlement, but their economic and political power caused agrarian resentment.

transcontinental railroad across the virtually unpopulated West. Government grants of land commenced in 1861, when the southern influence was absent from Washington. On May 10,1869, at Promontory Point, Utah, the Central Pacific (working eastward from Sacramento) and the Union Pacific (moving westward from Council Bluffs, Iowa) were joined by a golden spike. Federal subsidies also made possible the completion of three other transcontinental links: the Atcheson, Topeka, and Santa Fe link to Los Angeles in 1883, the Southern Pacific–Texas Pacific link between Texas and California in 1882, and the Northern Pacific link between Duluth and Portland in 1882. The relentless James J. Hill, working without government aid, pushed the Great Northern to the Washington coast in 1893. But these successes in spanning the continent with track were only the dramatic highlights of a stupendous transportation achievement. There were only thirty-five thousand miles of track in America at the end of the Civil War; in eight years that had been doubled, and by 1900 a fivefold expansion gave the United States two hundred thousand miles of track, approximately the total for all of Europe. Supplemented by roads, barge canals, and navigable rivers, the railroads gave industrializing America an unprecedented access to materials and markets.

Technology

There can be no industrialization without science, and its application, through technology, to practical problems. After the war there came a flood of technological discoveries—new sources of power, new means of applying power to production, and new products for the consumer market. Between 1790 and 1860, Americans patented thirty-six thousand new devices and products; in the thirty years after the Civil War they patented four hundred forty thousand. The list of important technological breakthroughs is impressively long. By 1870 the typewriter and the vacuum cleaner were in production; in the 1870s Thomas A. Edison and Stephen Field perfected the electric dynamo and utilized it to drive electric streetcars in New York City; in 1876 at the Philadelphia exposition, Alexander Graham Bell's telephone dazzled the crowds; at the beginning of the 1880s Edison invented a practical incandescent light bulb. By the end of that decade, Americans in some major cities could ride electric trolleys, enjoy electric lights, facilitate clerical work with typewriters and adding machines, take pictures with a hand camera, write with fountain pens, and make telephone calls. Behind these were less publicized but equally fundamental industrial discoveries, such as the Bessemer steel process (1867), the linotype composing machine (1886), the combined harvester-thresher for wheat (1881), and machines that applied electric and steam power to the tasks that human labor had painstakingly performed. American industrialization rolled forward upon the wheels of such discoveries.

Role of Industrialists

As vital as scientists and inventors are to the accelerating pace of industrialization, a nation must also produce an elite to marshal the energies of its working masses. In America, this elite was the industrial capitalists who imagined profitable ventures where there had been none, borrowed capital, and brought men and material together to found commercial empires. From the beginning America had both attracted and produced such individuals, and in the latter half of the nineteenth century there appeared a group of capitalists so imperious that they came to be called democratic America's "robber barons." There was some admiration in the phrase, but much opprobrium. They were frequently stupendous characters. Collis P. Huntington drove thousands of strong Chinese laborers through forty-foot drifts of snow to build a railroad across the Sierras; James J. Hill, blind in one eye, charted the course of the Great Northern Railroad on a dogsled; Commodore William H. Vanderbilt growled to critics: "What do I care about the law? Haint I got the power?" Even the more conventional of the robber barons, such as the taciturn John D. Rockefeller, were abundantly endowed with energy, self-confidence, large vision, and courage. They usually had the vices that went with their virtues—arrogance, single-minded materialism, narrow social outlook, philistinism, and greed for power and wealth. They have been charged with illegal financial manipulations, with ruthlessness toward labor, with the creation of menacing monopolies; they have been defended as the bringers of affluence, as men who ironed out the irrationalities and inefficiencies in a chaotic economy, and—by historian Allan Nevins—as the men who established the industrial base that won the cold war. They were the authors of both social progress and social dislocation. Their own contribution was only one part of the equation that produced industrialization, but it was a crucial one. For it, they were well rewarded.

Andrew Carnegie was a leader not only in the steel industry, but also in philanthropy. In The Gospel of Wealth he argued that men who had drawn wealth from the growing American economy had the obligation to return most of it in the form of gifts for social improvement. While Carnegie endowed a national system of libraries, and other men gave to schools and universities, many ignored Carnegie's message and kept all their wealth. (Underwood and Underwood)

The rewards, in fact, were functionally related to the process of economic expansion. Nation building in today's world often has primary driving emotions that are collective—nationalism, Marxist ideologies. But in nineteenth-century America the hope for individual gain catalyzed the other factors required for industrialization. The post–Civil War era was an exceptionally materialistic age, even by the standards of this raw new continent that had always excited the hope of wealth. Mark Twain and Charles Dudley Warner surveyed the years of headlong economic and geographical expansion in 1873, and published their novel *The Gilded Age,* describing an America full of "an all-pervading speculativeness," vulgar taste, and "shameful corruption." Historians have usually agreed. In historian Vernon L. Parrington's words: "Exploitation was the business of the times. Freedom had become individualism, and individualism had become the inalienable right to preempt, to exploit, to squander." Any number of contemporaries would have affirmed the right to preempt, if asked. The president of the Louisville and Nashville Railroad, for example, said in the 1870s that "society, as created, was for the purpose of one man's getting what the other fellow has, if he can, and keep out of the penitentiary."

This comment may have been an extreme statement of the aggressive materialism that helped propel the nation toward industrial and geographical expansion. Such self-seeking was modified in practice by the influence of religion, philanthropy, community spirit, and various other sources of social idealism. But thoughtful people in this era seemed to understand that great individual efforts must be sanctioned and encouraged in the interest of social progress. Thus it is not surprising that there grew up a social theory justifying struggle and acquisitiveness. This was later to be called social Darwinism, an adaptation of the biological ideas contained in Charles Darwin's *The Origins of Species* (1859). Darwin saw all forms of life engaged in a continuing struggle for existence, and the "survival of the fittest" allowed the strong to transmit superior qualities to their offspring and improve their kind. Thus, in the natural world, struggle and the defeat of the weak seemed a harsh but necessary path to general progress. The British philosopher Herbert Spencer led in the adaptation of these ideas to nineteenth-century society. He and some American theorists, such as Yale's William Graham Sumner, argued that the unregulated competitive struggle in the business world was Darwin's elemental contest transferred to human society and that the success of men like John D. Rockefeller and his Standard Oil Corporation was evidence of their superiority on the evolutionary scale. Any interference, especially through governmental regulation, would interrupt the march toward progress by handicapping the fit and perpetuating the unfit. "The millionaires," wrote Sumner, "are a product of natural selection. . . . They get high wages and live in luxury, but the bargain is a good one for society. There is the intensest competition for their place and occupation. This assures us that all who are competent for this function will be employed in it." As for those who lost in the competitive struggle, social Darwinism discouraged any idea of assisting them. The Reverend Russell

A Materialistic Age

Conwell wrote: "Let us remember there is not a poor person in the United States who was not made poor by his own shortcomings."

This social philosophy that justified competitive individualism and the pursuit of wealth combined with abundant resources, favorable political conditions, a maturing technology, a vigorous labor force, and aggressive entrepreneurs to produce a surge of economic growth; by 1900 the United States was in the front rank of nations. The economic advance of the country was broad, affecting agriculture as well as manufacturing, but the latter took the lead. American steel production, at a scant twenty thousand tons in 1867, passed the British total of six million tons a year by 1895 and reached ten million by 1900. Oil, discovered in Pennsylvania in 1859, was refined at a rate of ten million barrels a year by 1873, twenty million by 1885, and fifty million ten years later. The electrical equipment industry, nonexistent in 1870, accounted for an output worth twenty-two million dollars in 1890. While the entire country throbbed with new commercial schemes and dreams of jobs and ownership, certain sections were breathtakingly transformed. Iron ore was discovered around Lake Superior, and in some places—most notably the great Mesabi Range—it literally lay upon the surface to be skimmed with steam shovels. The Great Lakes hummed with barge traffic, carrying ore toward a booming Pittsburgh. Shipping tonnage through the Sault Sainte Marie Canal between Lake Superior and Lake Huron jumped from one hundred thousand tons in 1860 to twenty-five million tons by 1900. Cleveland surged with oil and steel production; Birmingham awoke to a regional steel production; Chicago's dynamic growth rested upon many industries, chiefly meat-packing. Small manufacturing cities doubled and tripled in size—Akron, Scranton, Paterson, Troy, Youngstown, and Bridgeport.

This expansion in industrial production was only the most striking sign of a dynamically growing society. Agriculture remained the basic economic activity, the number of farms increasing from 2.6 million to 5.3 million from 1865 to 1900. Farm acreage nearly doubled, and livestock numbers nearly tripled in the same period. The human population reached seventy-six million by the end of the century, and with this growth there was also enormous geographical mobility. Two especially powerful growth patterns characterized late nineteenth-century human settlement in the United States—the westward movement and urbanization.

The first major thrust of population was the westward movement of settlers across the Great Plains to the Rockies and the Pacific Coast. While the growth of cities involved many more people than the settling of the West, the latter seemed to contemporaries the most exciting challenge of the century. The 1870s and 1880s today conjure up images of cattle drives, cavalry and Indian battles and marches, gunfights in rough western towns.

At the end of the Civil War a vast area of more than a billion acres between Kansas City and San Francisco remained essentially unsettled. A

The Scope of Industrialism

Westward Movement

generation later, in 1890, the Bureau of the Census announced that the frontier, as a continuous line between settled and unsettled areas, had ceased to exist. The trapper, miner, lumberman, rancher, and merchant had come to the West in irresistible waves and had begun to exploit its riches. Only pockets of wilderness remained, ringed about by energetic men. New cities and a dozen new states had replaced the scattered bands of Indians. The population shift is readily seen in these dates of statehood: 1889 for North and South Dakota, Montana, and Washington; 1890 for Wyoming and Idaho; 1896 for Utah. In 1890, the superintendent of the U.S. Census announced that "there can hardly be said to be a frontier line" in view of the incursions of white settlement into the formerly "empty" (meaning, empty of whites) West.

The motives for western settlement—excluding those guiding the Mormons of Utah—were chiefly material, although there was also the lure of an adventure with the unknown. In the eyes of whites, at least, those who settled the West were also idealists. The Americans had penetrated the West well before the Civil War, when a few trappers had begun to work the Northern Rockies and Great Plains. Between 1860 and 1875 the white presence greatly expanded as eager prospectors combed the mountains and deserts in search of silver, gold, and copper. In 1859–60 gold was discovered west of Denver, near Pikes Peak, and the Comstock Lode was found in Nevada. Strikes in Idaho, Montana, and the Dakotas followed. The mining towns that quickly grew up were rough and essentially lawless, the depots for a transitory population of prospectors, gamblers, and prostitutes. But the people attracted by precious metals became the first resident white westerners, contributing not only their labors but also their offspring to the populations that brought the West into the national mainstream.

The short stories and novels of the brilliant American writer Samuel Langhorne Clemens (Mark Twain) are perhaps the best source of information about the American frontier—from the towns on the Mississippi River to the Nevada mining camps and California during the gold rush days. (American Antiquarian Society)

THE CATTLE ECONOMY   Behind the trappers and miners came the cattle-men. Cattle raising on a reasonably large scale—herds of one thousand head were common—had been established in Illinois and Ohio during the 1840s and 1850s. When it was discovered that the semiarid Great Plains, from Texas through Kansas and Nebraska, had sufficient water to support cattle, a new pressure was added to the westward drive. Beginning in 1866, great cattle drives of Texas longhorns brought beef from Texas to Missouri where rail connections could be made to dressing centers. Shortly, the towns of Abilene and Dodge City in Kansas and Kearney and North Platte in Ne-braska became rail heads for the eastward shipment of beef, and the short, lusty age of the cattle towns commenced. By 1873 rail service to Texas began to eliminate the great drives up the Chisholm Trail, but by then the western states from Texas north to Montana were well stocked with herds. For a few years cattle ranching attracted men with a desire for quick money, but by the end of the 1880s overexpansion had driven prices down and the blizzard of 1887 had decimated the herds. The boom days were over. Cattlemen began to organize against disease, oversupply, rustling, and en-croaching "dirt farmers." In time, ranching became a well-controlled, reasonably profitable business in the West. Its earlier, reckless days had been short—no more than fifteen years—but had produced an enduring American folklore, which captivates millions to this day in television and film recapitu-lations. While it was still a growing industry, ranching lured to the West additional recruits for the expansion into the breathtaking emptiness of frontier America. As a foremost historian of the West put it:

> In after years the drive of the Texas men became little short of an American saga. To all who saw that long line of Texas cattle come up over a rise in the prairie, nostrils wide for the smell of water, dustcaked and gaunt, so ready to break from the nervous control of the riders strung out along the flanks of the herd, there came a feeling that in this spectacle there was something elemen-tal, something resistless, something perfectly in keeping with the unconquera-ble land about them.

WESTERN AGRICULTURE   Behind the ranchers came thousands of farmers, hoping to combine profitably the free land under the Homestead Act, the availability of rail transportation, and the fertility of prairie soils. The agricul-tural migration began during the war years when nine western states or territories received three hundred thousand people from the East. The movement accelerated after Appomattox. The railroads stimulated westward migration, carrying on promotional campaigns to spread the word of one-hundred-sixty-acre free homesteads throughout the East and even to Europe. At first the semiforested lands of Missouri, Iowa, and Minnesota were settled; then the migrants pushed out into Nebraska, Kansas, and the Dakotas and into the treeless Great Plains. A series of droughts in the early 1870s and again in the mid-1880s ruined many farmers who had ventured too far into the arid prairies, but those who remained developed new techniques for farming where trees would not grow—the barbed wire fence, the sod house, and the windmill to bring water up from wells a hundred to five hundred feet deep. The hardships of agricultural life on the Great Plains tried the human spirit. Weather cycles alternately lured the farmer into new expansions of tilled acreage (with accompanying debt), then brought withering heat, drought, and seasons of almost total loss. Winters were severe, distances immense, and the loneliness of life in the drab single-family homes was a trial to the women and children especially. But hope for a series of good years, love of the vast quiet spaces of the plains, and the desire to move always to the western edge of America to try one's talents kept settlers coming to replace those who failed. By 1900, 1,141,000 new farms had been established in the nineteen western states and territories. Midwestern cities received and processed the mountains of wheat, corn, and beef produced in the new agricultural regions. This great agricultural success gave Americans an abundant food supply during the years of industrialization, keeping food prices low for urban labor and offering a livelihood for millions of the dissatisfied or the restless from Europe, the East, or the South. American culture would preserve memories of cowboys and buffalo herds while largely forgetting the undramatic sacrifices of those who broke the sod of the Great Plains.

Urbanization

While a rapidly growing population spread into the western spaces, it flowed in even greater numbers toward the urban frontier. The cities became a magnet, especially for the young. The urban population grew approximately seven times between the Civil War and World War I, surpassing the rural population by 1920, which had merely doubled in those sixty years. All major cities experienced growth, some of them so fast as to be virtually unrecognizable every decade. Chicago between 1860 and 1910 grew twentyfold, Minneapolis expanded to one hundred twenty times its former size. Less spectacular but steady rates of growth pushed the population of New York to a million and a half by 1890, Philadelphia to over a million, Boston and Baltimore to half a million. And such figures underestimate the total human movement involved; as many people were leaving the cities as were arriving. Careful studies estimate that 25 to 30 percent of the urban population of major cities moved out every decade, presumably for another city or for the West.

In view of the extreme discomforts of city life, one must wonder at the sustained appeal of urban living. Much of the answer lies in the economic opportunities of population centers where the new industrial economy produced and distributed its products. It was widely held that men could grow rich in the cities as they could not in the countryside, and the careers of Rockefeller, Jay Gould, and others offered proof. More routinely, both men and women came to work in the mills, offices, foundries, and stores. The cities seemed to offer advancement to those who were self-employed or had professional status much more surely than had been true in rural or small-town settings, especially at a time when agriculture was caught in a long-term downswing of earnings. Furthermore, the cities offered the excitement of various human contacts, the freedom of anonymity, the stimulation of places full of energy, bustle, light, and sound. William Allen White, arriving in Kansas City in 1891 after a small-town upbringing, reveled in the city's intellectual and artistic delights. He attended concerts and plays and heard James Whitcomb Riley read his poetry. "It got me," said White, "I went raving mad. Life was certainly one round of joy in Kansas City." Such comments call attention to the relative drabness of rural life in the nineteenth century. Life on the farm, one emigrant to the cities recalled, was "hard work and no holidays . . . no books, no papers, no games, no young company." In an age before radio or television, with no telephones or automobiles, no electric lights outside the cities, poor roads, and little machinery to ease the relentless drudgery of agricultural work, even the crowded, dirty, chaotic late nineteenth-century city came to have an irresistible appeal.

IMMIGRATION   Another source of urban growth was European immigration. In the forty years between 1860 and 1900, about fourteen million people came to America, lured by reports of economic opportunity and driven by religious and economic hardship from Europe. Through the 1880s the bulk of these immigrants came from northern Europe—from the United Kingdom (particularly Ireland), Germany, and Scandinavia. But in the 1880s the composition of the influx began to change. Increasingly the arrivals were Austrians and Hungarians from the Danube basin, Serbs from the River Save, Russian Jews from the Volga or the steppes of the Ukraine, olive-skinned Italians from Sicily. By the end of the century, more than half the immigrants to America were coming from southern and eastern Europe. Unlike earlier arrivals, the "new immigration" brought non-Protestant (Catholic, Greek Orthodox, or Jewish) peoples from poor, rural backgrounds. Economically, at least, the immigrants were welcome. Industrialism had by no means eliminated the need for a large reservoir of manual labor. Irish and Chinese immigrants built the Union Pacific and Central Pacific railways; Poles and Ukrainians fired the blast furnaces of Pittsburgh; central European Jews worked in the garment trades of New York; Italians laid track for eastern railroads, dug sewers, and worked in the mines.

Yet before the new century was far advanced the new immigrants that started to arrive in force in the 1880s had come to be seen as a major social problem, despite their physical contributions to economic development. Earlier settlers, with the chief exception of the Irish who had come in large numbers in the 1840s and 1850s, had tended to go West and cultivate land. Except in places like St. Louis and Milwaukee, where Germans clustered, there seemed to be an assimilation of newcomers into the dominant white-Protestant norm, an active "melting pot" in which all ethnic groups were submerged. (Black and red Americans were not assimilated, but no one intended that they should be; indeed, many states passed laws against interracial marriage.) But the new immigrants, who were on the whole poorer and more alien to the dominant culture than earlier arrivals, tended to remain in cities for the multiple reassurances of ethnic group life. The decision was hardly a free one; becoming established in farming took at

least some capital, and the new immigrants were usually too poverty stricken to resume the rural way of life they had just managed to escape. As a result, many of the new immigrants did not disperse but remained in the eastern cities where they were quite visible. New York City soon held the largest Jewish population of any city in the world, along with (at the turn of the century) half a million Italians and Russians, large numbers of every European ethnic group, and some Orientals. Many Afro-Americans arrived from the South, and they, like the other minorities, took up residence in ethnic ghettoes. Many other cities east of the Mississippi soon had a majority of minorities—Fall River, Passaic, Chicago, Cleveland, and Detroit. The rapid urbanization of the late nineteenth century would have produced social tensions in any event, but the urban concentration of the new immigrants added to the strains of modernization. Native whites were uneasy with the newcomers, and, the more alien their dress and habits and the darker their skins, the more uneasiness gave way to hostility. To a lesser extent, the interactions of the minorities themselves were abrasive.

This family of seven cooked, ate, slept, and stored all of its tangible possessions in one room of a tenement. The eldest son is unusually well-dressed, a reminder that parents in such circumstances often clung stubbornly to the hope that their children—particularly the sons—could work their way out of the slums. (Photo by Jessie Tarbox Beals, 1910. Jacob A. Riis Collection, Museum of the City of New York)

URBAN PROBLEMS Ethnic tensions were overshadowed in the bulging cities of the latter nineteenth century by more pressing problems. As the unanticipated, uninvited millions flocked to America's cities, a state of sustained emergency was reached. Housing, transportation, and sanitary facilities lagged far behind the demand, and population density reached such proportions as to suggest that the countryside was fully settled, which was far from the case. In a nation still sparsely settled, one and a half million people jammed onto the southern end of Manhattan Island in 1890, and wards in the center of Chicago counted nine hundred people per acre, exceeding the tally in Bombay, India. Basic municipal services, inadequate at the beginning of the explosive post–Civil War period, could not cope with the influx of people. Two-thirds of Chicago's streets were mud in 1900; cities like Rochester and Pittsburgh were at best half sewer and half privy; Baltimore and New Orleans had virtually no municipal sewage facilities at all. Water, both in quantity and quality, was a problem everywhere. In Washington, D.C., the water pressure was so low in the eastern portion of the city that half the city schools had no operative toilets (not surprisingly, most of these were in the black ghetto). The streets of late nineteenth-century cities, paved and unpaved, were often littered with garbage, for collection services were ill organized. The tenement house coped with the need for living space after a fashion. These were high buildings with narrow, dank air shafts at the center and a few communal toilets. Above the crowding rose the inevitable smells of human habitations without adequate sewage and garbage disposal systems, without effective burning and smoke abatement codes. Baltimore in the 1880s, H. L. Mencken reported, smelled "like a billion polecats." "The stink," said a resident of New York, "is enough to knock you down." "A solid stink" permeated Chicago, affirmed another sufferer.

Under such conditions both disease and crime flourished. Three out of every five babies died in a downtown section of Chicago in 1900, due to disease spread by crowding, bad water, and poor waste disposal. Most cities had a large incidence of tuberculosis, especially Washington, D.C., and New York. In the latter city, one notorious corner, the "lung block," reported one hundred cases in five years. Other illnesses, such as alcoholism, nonfatal diseases, and mental disorders, were inadequately reported but were unusually high in overcrowded areas. If a citizen escaped disease, he might fall victim to some form of violent crime, which was on the increase in urban areas in the decades after the Civil War. The number of prison inmates doubled in the 1880s, and the number of reported homicides tripled. The sketchy statistics of the day suggest a similar increase in robbery, shoplifting, and vandalism. There were tranquil neighborhoods, pleasant days, and wholesome entertainment in American cities during these years, and many residents left memoirs filled with fond nostalgia. But the evidence of social disorder was on the increase everywhere and gave alarm to urbanites who saw in the city the hope of a more liberating, fulfilling future. Out of that alarm would come, at the turn of the century and after, a nationwide urban reform movement designed to modernize city governments and services. Even in the 1870s and 1880s some cities forged ahead of the crisis by appropriating money for street lighting and paving, sewage disposal systems, electric trolley lines to permit population dispersal, building codes, and other reforms. But the struggle against the dirt, the confusion, and the sheer human mass and movement of late nineteenth-century America kept the great cities in a constant state of crisis.

The growing pains of the cities could not discourage an optimistic nation that knew it was on the road to progress. And there was indeed much to applaud as the decades of industrialization went by. Those who attended two celebratory events of the late nineteenth century, the 1876 Philadelphia Centennial Exposition and the Chicago World's Columbian Exposition seventeen years later (1893), could only be struck by the evidence of the nation's advances. The scientific, architectural, and artistic exhibits on display in Chicago, impressive as they were, seemed eclipsed by the miracles of American technology: reapers, typewriters, Pullman railroad cars, the first Ferris wheel, the dynamo, the Westinghouse alternating current generator. Philadelphia's three arc lights in the rambling warehouses thrown up in Fairmount Park contrasted sharply with Chicago's "Great White City" along the lake front.

Industrial Expansion: Benefits and Costs

As modernization went forward the average working person shared in the gains. From 1860 to 1890 the real wages (corrected for inflation) of nonagricultural workers rose by 50 percent and went up by another 37 percent by the eve of World War I. Average hours of work declined slowly but steadily over that half-century. In manufacturing the average work week was down to sixty hours in 1890 and to fifty-five hours by 1914. While social mobility was never so great in America as presented in the era's Horatio Alger novels depicting poor boys making good, industrialization did open up opportunities for many.

Although the historian may see that the long trend of wages and living standards was inexorably upward, contemporaries found the half-century of rapid expansion between civil war and world war a time of painful economic instability. Depressions came every decade (1873–77, 1884–86, 1893–97) as the century closed, and these caused massive suffering. Unemployment averaged 10 percent of the work force every year in the 1870s and again in the 1890s. To the risk of unemployment was added the risk of injury on the job, for America's factories, mines, and transportation systems had little safety equipment, and many workers were wounded, maimed, or killed. Wages may have been rising slowly, but when the average industrial worker in the 1890s earned only thirteen dollars for a seven-day work week and women brought home five or six dollars a week making shirts, Andrew Carnegie pocketed twenty-three million dollars from his steel company in one year and paid no income taxes. The distribution of wealth did not change noticeably between 1860 and 1900, judging by inadequate statistics. It was extremely inequitable. The richest 2 percent owned a third of the wealth, and the richest 50 percent owned virtually all of it. Fabulous homes were being built on Long Island, New York, and Newport, Rhode Island, not far from the festering slums of New York City and Providence.

Industrial unrest, strikes, and violence became main themes of the era of *Protest in Industry* expansion. In the spring of 1877, a year after the nation's centennial, a great railroad strike broke out upon the announcement of a series of wage cuts in the industry. The strike spread from Baltimore to Pittsburgh, then all the way to St. Louis. President Rutherford B. Hayes dispatched federal troops, and virtual open warfare broke out along miles of track and railyards. It was more than a strike, said a St. Louis newspaper, rather like "a labor revolution." In another view, "it seemed as if the whole social and political structure was on the very brink of ruin." Twenty-six men were killed in violence in Pittsburgh, thirteen more in Chicago.

The great strikes of 1877 eventually subsided, but troubled labor relations became a constant feature of late nineteenth-century life. Between 1880 and 1900 there were twenty-three thousand strikes, an average of three a day for twenty years. Employers used Pinkerton detectives and private armies to combat unionism and strikes and could count upon the backing of the courts, state governors and, when necessary, the president to utilize militia to restore order. By one estimate state troops were called out five hundred times between 1875 and 1910. Punctuating the almost continual outbreak of small strikes were large conflicts that arrested national attention and deeply alarmed the public: the railroad wars of 1877, the bombing and police retaliation in the mass demonstrations at Chicago's Haymarket Square during the Knights of Labor strikes in 1886, the bloody Homestead Steel strike led by the American Federation of Labor in 1892, the American Railway Union strike against the Pullman Company in 1894 where Eugene Debs emerged as a national figure. Virtual class warfare seemed to have become a permanent and unwelcome part of American life.

Much of the violence in industrial relations arose from the efforts of workers to unionize and the stubborn resistance of employers who could not imagine coexistence with industrial unions. Workers turned to organization to match the power of corporations, but the road to unionization was strewn with many failures. The National Labor Union born in 1866 foundered in the depression of the 1870s, and the void was filled by Terence V. Powderly's Knights of Labor, which had organized in 1869. The Knights hoped to organize all those who worked for a living—excluding lawyers, doctors, politicians, and bankers, who were thought to exploit the real working classes. They envisaged a mass organization that would engage in the production and distribution of goods on a cooperative basis. The Knights did not favor strikes, but they were drawn into the great walkouts of the 1880s and could not survive the combination of employer resistance and depression. Out of the decade came the labor organization that eventually charted a successful, if arduous, strategy for unionization. Founded in 1886, the American Federation of Labor shunned an image of radicalism and had little interest in political activity. It aimed at "business unionism," organizing the skilled elites of the American working class into craft unions for the pragmatic purpose of wage/hour bargaining with employers. Under Samuel Gompers's leadership the AFL survived the terrible depression of the 1890s when the Knights did not and entered the twentieth century with a modest but growing membership of 625,000.

Protest on the Farm

Most of the American middle class did not share in the insurgent mood of industrial workers and did not sympathize with social reform until after the turn of the century. One exception was the midwestern and southern farmer, that yeoman of the soil who thought of himself as the backbone of American society. Yet he seemed to be rapidly losing ground to industrial and commercial groups as the years passed, and he watched fearfully as a plutocracy of capitalists and a proletariat of workers appeared to be massing for class conflict. The last three decades of the nineteenth century were not happy ones for agriculture as a whole, even though the volume of food production mounted. Staple crops such as wheat and cotton fell in value per unit by nearly 50 percent between the Civil War and the 1890s, as productivity advanced and more Great Plains lands were brought into production. Economic hardship plus an irritating decline in status nourished waves of radicalism in rural America, which chiefly took the form of support for monetary inflation and public control of railroads and grain elevators. The inflationary Greenback party, which grew out of the unrest of the 1870s, elected fourteen congressman from midwestern districts by 1878, only to disintegrate in the 1880s. In the Grange (1867–) the nation's farmers found an organization that solved some of their social needs but would not focus farmer protest upon the national political arena. That development would await the Populist party of the 1890s.

The Grange, initially formed as a fraternal body providing social opportunities for farmers, quickly developed as a politically-oriented anti-railroad organization. This cartoon shows an active Grange member arousing a listless public to the dangers of the fast-approaching railroad monopoly. (Puck)

As huge industrial and financial organizations menaced the middle class from above and a restless labor force fought back with militant organizations of its own, a deep anxiety captured the mood of late nineteenth-century America. Social critics appraised the polarization of the classes and feared a final, bitter struggle between the lords of capital and a desperate, property-less work force. Henry George, in his influential *Progress and Poverty* (1879), criticized the maldistribution of wealth and proposed a confiscatory single tax upon land to recapture for society the social increment in rising land values, which currently went to speculators. Another widely read contemporary critic, Edward Bellamy, sold over a million copies of his utopian novel *Looking Backward* (1888). The book described a happy socialist commonwealth in which all shared in work and its material rewards. Another powerful call for social reform came in Henry Demarest Lloyd's *Wealth Against Commonwealth* (1894), published in the year of the bitter Pullman strike. These and other social theorists argued that current trends in economic and social power would end in either plutocracy or revolution if the public did not awake and demand reform remedies through the political system.

Theorists of Social Reform

Late nineteenth-century national politics remained remarkably little affected by the radical currents and discontents stirring within an industrializing society. Politics was characterized by high emotion and large voter turnout, yet historians have been struck by the confusion of the time and the preoc-cupation of both parties with what now appear to have been frivolous issues. From 1876 to 1896 the two major parties were evenly matched. Republicans took the White House four times (with Rutherford B. Hayes in 1877–81, James A. Garfield in 1881, who was assassinated and whose term was served out through 1885 by Chester A. Arthur, then Benjamin Harrison from 1889 to 1893). Yet not one of these presidents received more than 50.8 percent of the popular vote. Indeed Hayes and Harrison lost the majority popular vote and won only in the electoral tally. The Democrats controlled the House of Repre-sentatives most of the time, and their candidate Grover Cleveland was elected twice (1885–89, 1893–97).

Politics as Usual

It appeared to make little difference which party was in power at the White House or on Capitol Hill, for the political era from Reconstruction to the end of the century produced very little significant policy making of any kind. A series of confused money laws were passed making minor changes in the relation between gold, silver, and paper money. These were preceded by much fervent rhetoric but brought no real change to the nation's mone-tary system, and failed completely to enhance the government's ability to influence the money supply in some routine fashion. An important law of 1887 set up the Interstate Commerce Commission, the basis of the modern regulatory state. Three years later came the seminal Sherman Antitrust Act, which ironically looked in an entirely different direction from the ICC. The thrust of the first was toward regulation on a permanent basis, the second was toward a governmentally protected competitive economy. This contradiction did not trouble the statesmen of the day, perhaps because they knew both laws were full of ambiguities and subject to court review. Beyond these two tentative beginnings, and the Dawes General Allotment Act, the national government of this period produced little in the way of law or programs to influence the country's direction.

Historians have often probed for the reasons behind the "issueless politics" of the era, to use Vernon L. Parrington's phrase. Many groups had deep grievances toward the raw new industrial-urban order, with its gulf between wealth and laboring classes, its crowded cities, its successive economic depressions. Yet the problems were not evident from the issues of national politics. Some economic issues were raised, such as "the money question" and the tariff. Grover Cleveland attempted to make the latter a major debate topic and spoke of the deplorable rule of privilege and wealth, but even he eventually concentrated upon moral uplift rather than upon institutional reforms. Noneconomic issues held central place: civil service reform, temperance, the characters of various public officials, the South's attitude on the verdict of Appomattox. Historian Henry Adams wrote to a friend:

> The amusing thing is that no one talks about real interests. By common consent they agree to let these alone. We are afraid to discuss them. Instead of this, the press is engaged in a most amusing dispute whether Mr. Cleveland had an illegitimate child, and did or not live with more than one mistress; whether Mr. Blaine got paid in railways bonds for services as Speaker; and whether Mrs. Blaine had a baby three months after her marriage. Nothing funnier than some of these subjects has been treated in my time.

Adams's comment fits both parties. Each skirted the serious economic problems of the society and turned passionately to questions of morality, behavior, sectional rivalry, and memories of sectional division. Elections were fought with high public emotion, while politicians in power proposed few changes and enacted almost none. The presidents of the era are difficult to recall; they appear in retrospect as a succession of grey-bearded men whose elevation to power hardly seems to have been worth the torchlight parades and fiery oratory of their campaigns. Certainly it made little difference when the Democrats managed to edge out the Republicans, or vice versa. The two national parties, said a contemporary, "were like two bottles. Each bore a label denoting the kind of liquor it contained, but each was empty."

One source of such vacuous politics was the Whig philosophy that animated every president of the era. They saw the chief executive's role as chiefly symbolic and passive, never imagining their office as a place from which "to move a nation," to use a modern president's phrase. Under the American political system, if presidents do not move the policy machinery, that role falls to other institutions even less suited for or eager to undertake the assignment: a hydraheaded Congress, the Supreme Court, or political parties. Post–Civil War parties enjoyed the intense loyalty of citizens, but they had no permanent party machinery and disbanded after each election.

With elections always so close, the parties crowded toward the center of the political spectrum and shunned that sort of clarity on important issues that might have alienated more voters than were attracted. Third parties with sharp programmatic focus found it impossible to become established.

Recent scholarship has extended our understanding of late nineteenth-century politics, suggesting that the two major parties did indeed mobilize around the big issues of the day—as the public then saw them. These issues, however, were not primarily economic but cultural. Two reasonably distinct cultural images had emerged in America. The Republicans were identified as the party of the Anglo-Saxon Protestants, America's old stock. The Democrats encompassed non-British immigrants, Irish and Polish Catholics, German Lutherans, and others. The Republicans had a tendency to take an evangelical approach to politics, were eager to use local, state, and even federal government to regulate morality—to outlaw drink, boxing, gambling, even parochial schools. The Democrats tended to be pietists who intensely resisted attempts by the Anglo-Saxon Protestants to utilize governmental power to interfere in matters of personal morality. Given this framework of perception, the voters conducted cultural struggle through politics. The Republicans were usually the nativist, anti-immigrant, Americanizing forces, the Democrats usually fighting off these efforts with traditional states' rights doctrine. In this light, the politics of the era were hardly issueless. They were saturated with cultural issues, most of them local questions—whether to retain or prohibit saloons, gambling halls, Sunday recreation, church schools, and the like. The national parties retained the sharp cultural images that had emerged locally, although there was less for national politicians to do in these cultural areas other than symbolize their own beliefs and berate the opposition. Thus, skirting the edge of most of the deep-seated economic and social problems of the day and conducting mostly symbolic struggles over interethnic and interreligious group rivalries, Gilded Age politics produced much sound and fury but seem to have made little difference in the lives of the people.

Ethnocultural Politics

The terrible depression of the 1890s so intensified the economic suffering of farmers and workers that a protest movement eventually formed in the South and Midwest and forced economic issues to the front of national politics. The origins of the Peoples' or Populist party were in the farm organizations formed in the 1880s called Wheels or Alliances. By the 1890s the farmers' alliances counted one million members, and a Colored Farmers Alliance added nearly that many more.

The Populist Movement

At first the alliances tried to remain nonpartisan and nonpolitical, but farmers despaired of help from the two major parties and pressed for political action. Accepting the advice of the Kansas firebrand, Mary Lease, to "raise less corn and more hell," they entered national politics in 1892, organizing the Populist party. The party platform conveyed their sense of urgency:

We meet in the midst of a nation brought to the verge of moral, political, and material ruin. Corruption dominates the ballot box, the Legislatures, the Congress, and touches even the ermine of the Bench. The people are demoralized. . . . The Newspapers are largely subsidized or muzzled, public opinion silenced, business prostrated, our homes covered with mortgages, labor impoverished, and the land concentrating in the hands of the capitalists. . . . The fruits of the toil of millions are boldly stolen to build up colossal fortunes for a few, unprecedented in the history of mankind. . . . From the same prolific womb of governmental injustice we breed the two great classes—tramps and millionaires.

An old radical warhorse, James B. Weaver, was nominated for the presidency, and a platform was designed to appeal not only to farmers but to laborers and other discontented Americans. It urged government ownership of railroads and telegraph systems, the direct election of senators, a postal savings bank, the secret ballot, an increase in the money supply, a graduated income tax, an eight-hour day for labor. The platform blended many themes, among them distrust of a national government supposedly in the control of eastern bankers, but it's main significance was the vastly enlarged role for government intervention that it projected. When a million votes were cast for Weaver in 1892, the Populists looked forward with anticipation to 1896.

By 1896 a depression had greatly enhanced the Populists' appeal. The financial panic of 1893 contracted the money supply and helped produce the severe economic slump. A gold drain in 1894 was stopped only by the intervention of New York banker J. P. Morgan, who underwrote a new bond issue. The spectacle of a private banker saving the nation's treasury appeared to substantiate the charges of the Populists. Hard-pressed farmers turned increasingly to the lure of "free and unlimited coinage" of silver into dollars at a sixteen to one ratio, which meant a dollar cheaper than the golden eagle and hence inflationary. Free silver had many prophets, perhaps foremost among them William H. Harvey, whose pamphlet *Coin's Financial School* (1894) described free silver as a panacea for all the nation's economic ills; it sold three hundred thousand copies in the first year. In fact, the money supply should have been expanded in 1894 to counteract deflation, and substantial coinage of silver dollars at sixteen to one would have been one way to accomplish that goal. In their enthusiasm, the Populists expected too much from this useful reform, and free silver increasingly overshadowed their other ideas. Among their advanced ideas was the conviction, articulated most forcefully by Georgia's Tom Watson, that black and white farmers must become allies: "You are kept apart that you may be separately fleeced of your earnings," he told a racially mixed audience. "You are made to hate each other because upon that hatred is rested the keystone of the arch of financial despotism which enslaves you both."

Before the Populists could nominate their candidate in 1896, the Democrats named theirs—a crusading, charismatic Nebraskan named William Jennings Bryan, a free silverite who had stampeded the convention with his

Battle of the Standards: Gold Versus Silver

"Cross of Gold" speech. With the Democratic party now turning its back upon the conservative pro-gold policies of Grover Cleveland and led by a midwestern reformer for whom silver money was a matter of faith, the Populists had little choice. They, too, nominated Bryan (preserving a vestige of independence by naming Tom Watson for vice-president), hoping for a union of reform forces to defeat the Republicans and take national office. The GOP did its part to make the 1896 election a choice between sharp extremes, nominating the conservative Ohioan William McKinley on a platform that pledged to preserve the gold standard against all tampering.

Bryan campaigned with unprecedented vigor, traveling eighteen thousand miles by rail to deliver over six hundred speeches to massive crowds. Speaking before the era of radio or audio equipment, he roused audiences with his magnificent speaking voice and his appeals for social justice. More Americans voted for Bryan than had ever voted for any presidential candidate—6.5 million of them. Yet McKinley was an easy winner. Rural enthusiasm for Bryan seemed to produce urban fears of this man from the Great Plains who was committed to free silver and backed by the radical Populists. For every vote that Bryan attracted, more than one flowed to the safe GOP candidate who sat upon his porch in Canton, Ohio, radiating moderation. Republican manager Mark Hanna saw to it that Republican orators and literature spread the word that Bryan would cheapen the dollar earned by workers and consumers, and McKinley carried the cities, all but parts of the Midwest and the South, and won the election. The Republicans became the majority party for the first time, and with their new urban base were to dominate national politics until the depression of the 1930s. This defeat plus rising prices in the late 1890s finished the Populists as a party, although many of their ideas were to come to fruition in the urban reform movement called progressivism that lay just ahead. As historian Richard Hofstadter remarked in a study of Populism: "Third parties are like bees: once they have stung, they die." The sting made a difference in the years ahead, but this was surely small consolation to the embattled farmers who had hoped for a yeoman commonwealth.

The "Great Commoner," William Jennings Bryan, strikes a classic campaigning pose. While he never attained the presidency, Bryan was virtually the undisputed leader of the Democratic party from 1896 to 1912. He led the party on a variety of crusades which, though uniformly unsuccessful, dramatized important issues and prepared American thinking for a shift in priorities. (Underwood and Underwood)

With the defeat of Bryan and the Populists, the 1890s lost whatever potential they had for a decisive redirection of the nation's internal affairs. Yet this troubled decade did produce a momentous shift in America's relation to the rest of the world. The United States became a world power and established an empire in the 1890s. In an important sense, the nineteenth century ended with the Spanish-American War in 1898, since that event terminated more than eighty years of isolation and noninvolvement. The roots of that transformation lay deep in American society itself.

A nation preoccupied with an intersectional war, with resolution of the problems arising out of the end of slavery, and with settling its own western frontier was understandably one with little interest in the outside world. This inward orientation came to an abrupt end for many reasons. Expanding industrial and agricultural production led to a rise in American exports and awakened a sense of exciting commercial opportunities abroad. The depression that began in 1893 convinced many that America's productive capacity was greater than the domestic demand for the products of field, factory and mines. This analysis added a new rationale for expanding foreign commerce: not only was foreign trade profitable, it might well be necessary to stave off depression and social unrest at home. Such ideas gained credibility from the surge of labor violence and political radicalism spawned by the depression of 1893–97.

The crisis was more than economic. America's middle class, while somewhat cushioned from the mass unemployment of industry and the agricultural glut that hurt many farmers, discovered other reasons for disquiet at the direction of the national life. Its ranks seemed depleted by the ascent of a few to plutocratic wealth, the descent of many more into the ranks of a propertyless labor force. The small businessman faced an uphill struggle against powerful corporations. And in 1890, a minor news event signaled the apparent closing of a major avenue of upward mobility for Americans: the census director announced that the frontier had been invaded by settlement so extensively that only pockets of unpopulated areas remained.

As the open door to America's western spaces began to close, the harbors of eastern cities continued to receive the crowded boatloads of immigrants. Yet the immigration of 1880–1920 was different from what had gone before in two important ways: size and composition. Immigration jumped from a two million per decade average to reach 5.2 million in the 1880s; 3.6 million more persons came to America in the 1890s, 8.7 million in the first decade of the twentieth century, and 5.7 more by 1920. Even more striking than the increased volume of immigration was the national and social characteristics of newcomers. The "new immigration" was not drawn from the familiar northwest European nations but from central and eastern Europe, as well as southern Italy. Great numbers of eastern European Jews sought to escape the repression and pogroms of czarist Russia, Poland, and Germany. Italians came from poverty-stricken southern Italy. These new immigrants tended to congregate in eastern cities rather than to move to the interior as had the English, Scandinavians, and Germans. Here they were crowded into ghettoes and caused concern that the cities might not be able to assimilate urban masses of such different cultures. Native Americans—the term for white people who had immigrated earlier—became worried that the new immigration was a threat to the homogeneity and vigor of American society.

Nativism

Depression; new immigration; the end of the frontier—these new developments created what one historian called "the psychic crisis of the middle class" in 1890s America. One result was an intensification of nationalistic feeling, or nativism. The Anglo-Saxon Protestant majority became aggressively self-assertive in the face of what it saw as threats to the ethnic and political dominance of a superior northern European stock. Groups such as the Immigration Restriction League and the American Protective Association sprang up, dedicated either to excluding the "inferior races" who were pouring in through America's open ports or to badgering the aliens—especially Catholics—who were already there. When anti-immigrant sentiment runs high, jingoism often is not far behind. Only a pretext was required to focus the self-assertiveness of the dominant culture upon foreign adventure. To many citizens of the 1890s, a foreign escapade of some kind began to emerge as the best solution to a host of internal problems.

Expansionism

Expansionism was not a sentiment plotted in the boardrooms of the large corporations. Some businessmen urged that America join Great Britain, France, and Germany in the search for imperial footholds from which to capture a large share of world trade, but most were cautious about the risks involved. The nation's farmers were even more expansionist than the businessmen; as early as the 1860s they had begun to press for economic and even territorial expansionism as the solution to overproduction at home. "We must go abroad," said a rural congressman in 1890: "we must . . . build up our navy and merchant marine . . . and go upon the high seas." The Populist "Sockless" Jerry Simpson added in 1892: "We have some very serious problems to face. Our country is filled up. There is no west to go to. We are full, and we will have to acquire Canada, British America, and Mexico, or overflow." Agricultural surplus lay behind these sentiments. Many intellectuals came to similar conclusions. In a popular book written in 1886, *Our Country,* the Reverend Josiah Strong wrote: "God is training the anglo-saxon race for its mission. . . . Is there any room for reasonable doubt that this race, unless devitalized by alcohol and tobacco, is destined to dispossess many weaker races . . . until, in a very true and important sense, it has anglo-saxonized mankind?" Other writers, among them Henry and Brooks Adams, Henry Cabot Lodge, and Theodore Roosevelt, feared that urbanization, rather than alcohol or tobacco, might devitalize the race. War, perhaps, would reawaken the primal virtues. "I should welcome almost any war," wrote Roosevelt in 1897, "for I think the country needs one." In this climate, Admiral Alfred Thayer Mahan's *The Influence of Sea Power upon History* (1890) directed attention to the strategic as well as commercial advantages open to the United States if it accepted the role of a great naval power.

Spanish misrule in Cuba served to catalyze the various sources of American restlessness and dissatisfaction and to focus them outward upon Spain's crumbling empire. The Cuban population revolted against Spain in 1895, and the Spanish tactic of relocating large numbers of villagers to isolate them from the revolutionaries led to brutalities, which the American press reported with enthusiasm. A circulation battle between William Randolph Hearst's *New York Journal* and Joseph Pulitzer's *New York World* spurred the newspapers' efforts, but the principal result was an aroused public opinion. In February 1898, a letter from the Spanish minister critical of the American president was published. This was followed within days by a mysterious explosion that sank the U.S. battleship *Maine* at its anchorage in Havana harbor. War fever engulfed much of American society. The McKinley administration, not eager for war, was tempted to accept the April offer of Spain for a truce with the rebels. But key Republicans reported to the president that a decision for war would not only be highly popular but would also focus domestic discontents away from the administration. On April 11 McKinley demanded independence for Cuba. One week later, Congress demanded such independence and announced American willingness to fight for it. Spain had no choice but to break relations, and Congress declared war on April 25. "The president could have worked the business without a war," said Senator John Spooner, "but the current was too strong, the demagogues too numerous, and the fall elections too near."

The war lasted but 113 days. American forces were victorious in the battle of Manila Bay in the Philippines in May (only six days after war was declared, Assistant Secretary of the Navy Theodore Roosevelt had eagerly primed Admiral Dewey's Pacific fleet) and in operations around Santiago in June and July. It was not, as Secretary of State John Hay wrote later, "a

The Spanish-American War

Most depictions of the American charge at San Juan Hill show Lt. Colonel Theodore Roosevelt leading his "Rough Riders," the first volunteer cavalry regiment. This one, however, reveals the important combat role of two black units, the 24th and 25th Infantries. (Chicago Historical Society)

splendid little war, carried on with magnificent intelligence and spirit," for the eager American volunteer forces were wretchedly supplied and poorly directed. But Spanish resistance was uniformly inept, and four remarkable centuries of empire came to an end with surprising ease. The rapid success of American arms was no more startling, however, than the swift acquisition of the beginnings of America's own empire. Hawaii was annexed in July 1898, planting the flag two thousand miles out in the Pacific. The treaty with Spain in 1899 added the Philippines, Guam, and Puerto Rico.

This step was not taken without heated debate. Anti-imperialists, a coalition of Democrats that included Grover Cleveland and William Jennings Bryan, Republicans like Carl Schurz, and the writers Mark Twain and William James, objected that imperialism violated the spirit of the Declaration of Independence, was too expensive, and would bring under the flag races that might prove incapable of assimilation. Cleveland called the first step, Hawaiian annexation, "a perversion of our national mission," which was "to build up and make a great country out of what we have instead of annexing islands." President McKinley, allegedly after prayer, decided to acquire the faraway Philippines on the assumption that some naval power would seize them if the United States did not. The administration was soon embarrassed when the U.S. Army found itself involved in a bloody four-year war to put down a revolt led by Philippine nationalist Emilio Aguinaldo. Three times more Americans were killed in suppressing the revolt than had died fighting Spain, and Americans had a foretaste of the unsavory role of Westerners resisting Asian nationalism that was assumed in Vietnam sixty years later.

The decision for empire was a close one, taken on a narrow Senate vote on the Philippine issue in February 1899. Democratic leader William Jennings Bryan mistakenly advised that the main struggle be shifted from the Senate to the election of 1900. But by that time the anti-imperialists could no longer focus public attention upon imperialism. The nation acquired territory in Asia and the Carribean, which it held in benign submission, joining the European powers whose race for colonies so many Americans had scorned. Time, however, vindicated much of the anti-imperialist argument. Actual colonies were not necessary to an expanded American trade abroad and were more trouble than they were worth. Defined formally as colonies, the American empire began to contract soon after it was acquired. The Platt amendment to the peace treaty guaranteed Cuban independence with the American right to intervene in the event of instability. This arrangement was sufficient to ensure American economic dominance (until 1959, when Fidel Castro came to power), and Cuba remained formally independent. The U.S. Army withdrew from the Philippines in 1902, partial home rule was granted in 1916, and independence in 1946. Puerto Ricans were admitted to citizenship and the advantages of semiterritorial status in 1917, and Hawaii became a state in 1958. The American empire, launched so abruptly in the years 1898–1899, evolved away from the European territorial colonialism toward a more informal economic and strategic hegemony.

United States Possessions, 1898

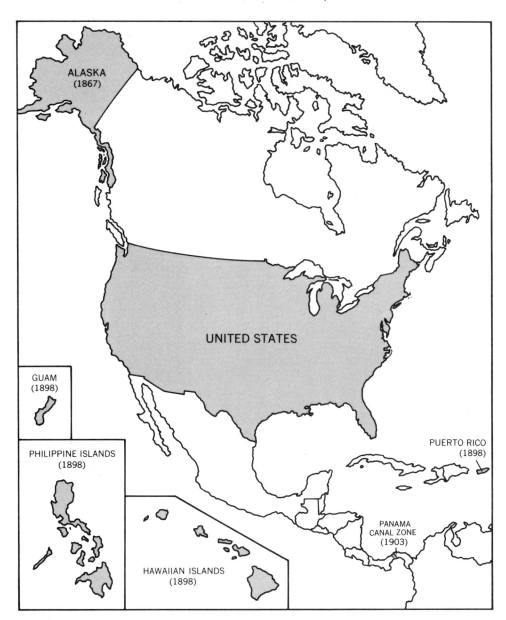

ALASKA
(1867)

UNITED STATES

GUAM
(1898)

PHILIPPINE ISLANDS
(1898)

HAWAIIAN ISLANDS
(1898)

PUERTO RICO
(1898)

PANAMA
CANAL ZONE
(1903)

The U.S. entered the Spanish-American War denying ambitions of conquest, yet acquired Puerto Rico, Guam, and the Philippines. Colonialism and later economic imperialism in Latin America were justified on the basis of racial superiority. Stated Indiana's Senator Beveridge, "We are Anglo-Saxons and must obey our blood and occupy new markets, and if necessary, new lands."

COMMENTARY

| The decade of the 1890s had been one of the most difficult in the nation's history. To both middle and lower class alike, it brought a grinding depression; to the affluent, it brought the frights of political and intellectual radicalism on a scale never before seen in the United States. To ethnic and racial minorities it was the culminating decade in a swell of nativism and intolerance; to the white, Anglo-Saxon Protestant majority, it was a time of the deepest anxiety. The crisis was not resolved by internal upheaval, nor even by significant readjustment of the roles, positions, and expectations of groups. It was resolved first by war, and then by a race for empire. The journalist Henry Watterson wrote in 1899:

From a nation of shopkeepers we become a nation of war-riors. We escape the menace and peril of socialism and agrarianism, as England has escaped them, by a policy of colonization and conquest.

Watterson's language reflects the excessive emotionalism of the last years of the 19th century, typically exaggerating what was at stake and what had been achieved. The joys of empire would not be so sweet as American enthusiasts imagined, and domestic radicalism would flourish again from time to time. But certainly Watterson spoke in a year of relief for men of property. In 1899, the Spaniards, Bryan, Debs, and the depression had all been defeated, and Mark Hanna's words to William McKinley upon his election could take on a new meaning: "God's in His Heaven, all's right with the world!"

SUGGESTED READING

THOMAS COCHRAN and WILLIAM MILLER, *The Age of Enterprise* (1942)

HAROLD U. FAULKNER, *Politics, Reform and Expansion, 1890–1901* (1966)

JOHN A. GARRATY, *The New Commonwealth, 1877–1890* (1968)

RAY GINGER, *The Age of Excess: The U.S. from 1877 to 1914* (1965)

PAUL W. GLAD, *McKinley, Bryan, and the People* (1964)

LAWRENCE GOODWYN, *Democratic Promise: The Populist Movement in America* (1976)

RALPH W. and MURIEL E. HIDY, *Pioneering in Big Business, 1882–1911: History of the Standard Oil Company, New Jersey* (1955)

RICHARD HOFSTADTER, *Social Darwinism in American Thought* (1955)

RICHARD J. JENSEN, *The Winning of the Midwest: Social and Political Conflict, 1888–1896* (1971)

EDWARD C. KIRKLAND, *Industry Comes of Age: Business, Labor, and Public Policy, 1860–1897* (1961)

J. MORGAN KOUSSER, *The Shaping of Southern Politics: Suffrage Restriction and the Establishment of the One Party System, 1880–1910* (1974)

MARGARET LEECH, *In the Days of McKinley* (1959)

WALTER LAFEBER, *New Empire: An Interpretation of American Expansion, 1860–1898* (1963)

ROBERT H. MCCLOSKEY, *American Conservatism in the Age of Enterprise, 1865–1910* (1951)

ERNEST R. MAY, *Imperial Democracy* (1961)

H. WAYNE MORGAN, *From Hayes to McKinley: National Party Politics, 1877–1896* (1969)

WALTER T. K. NUGENT, *The Tolerant Populists: Kansas Populism and Nativism* (1963)

HENRY PELLING, *American Labor* (1960)

JULIUS W. PRATT, *The Expansionists of 1898* (1936)

JOSEPH F. WALL, *Andrew Carnegie* (1970)

C. VANN WOODWARD, *The Strange Career of Jim Crow*, 3d rev. ed. (1974)

———, *The Origins of the New South, 1877–1913* (1951)

11

The Age of Reform, 1900–1916

America in 1900

At the beginning of the twentieth century, there were seventy-six million people in America. This population produced a gross national product (GNP) valued at seventeen billion dollars and a per capita share of $231 if it had been distributed that way; of course it was not. America was now chiefly a manufacturing country; the percentage of the national income that went to agriculture had slipped below that of industry in the early 1890s. Farming occupied 31 percent of the work force in 1900, but 60 percent of the population lived in rural areas. On the farms there was neither electricity nor telephones. Rural postal service was reasonably good, and the Sears and Roebuck catalogs had expanded farmers' access to some of the consumer pleasures of the cities, such as ready-made clothes, kitchenware, and cosmetics. In the larger cities, streetcars ran noisily in the daylight hours, but all urban streets were still jammed with horses and horse-drawn carriages. There were no radios in American homes, no motion pictures (the "nickelodeon" movie theater first appeared in 1905), and only four thousand automobiles. Trains were efficient and fast, and the citizen might learn of coming wonders in entertainment, medicine, and transportation from a visit to the Chicago World's Fair of 1893. Life expectancy for the average American in 1900 was forty-seven years at birth (for whites, forty-eight years; for nonwhites, thirty-three) and was rising. Illiteracy was 10.7 percent, and falling.

With the Spanish-American War successfully concluded and prosperity easing the discontents of the 1890s, the future looked good to many people. "Laws are becoming more just," was the euphoric summary of one contemporary, "rulers humane; music is becoming sweeter and books wiser; homes are happier, and the individual heart becoming at once more just and more gentle."

Others recognized signs of difficulties ahead. The merger movement in industry, which had alarmed the social critics of the late nineteenth century, had not abated, and monopolies appeared to grow without effective resistance from the marketplace or government. Extreme disparities in income and wealth persisted. At the turn of the century, John D. Rockefeller was enjoying an income of a hundred million dollars a year, tax free, while workers in New York's garment district averaged less than ten dollars a week, and most farm families earned less than five hundred dollars annually. Available statistics are somewhat unreliable, but it has been estimated that in 1910 the top 10 percent of the population claimed 34 percent of the national income, the bottom 10 percent receiving 3.4 percent. Robert Hunter, in his book *Poverty* (1904), calculated that ten million urban Americans lived below the subsistence level, and he was not counting the millions in rural areas who eked out a marginal existence as tenant farmers, migratory laborers, or owners of small farms on submarginal land.

Urbanization continued at its reckless pace. Chicago attempted to absorb fifty thousand new residents each year; cities like Seattle, Pasadena, and Flint tripled in size between 1900 and 1910, and Birmingham added one hundred thousand new residents in the same decade. The cities staggered under the resultant problems in housing, sanitation, crime, and congestion. America's factories, mines, and railroads produced a mixed yield; consumer goods were offset by a high rate of industrial accidents, low wages, and long hours. Contemporaries found it difficult to ignore graft and inefficiency in government, the social damage caused by alcoholic beverages, the degradation of prostitution. Some were concerned about the inability of most women to attain positions of influence and about the prohibitions on their voting. A few thought the treatment of American Negroes was deplorable.

These were imposing problems. Yet all had existed in the 1890s also, in a setting of economic depression, when only a portion of the agricultural and laboring communities had risen in protest. The distinguishing feature of the era between 1900 and World War I was not the intensity of its problems, for sustained economic growth made these years in important respects more pleasant than the recent past. The big news of these years, nonetheless, was a wave of insurgency that came to be called progressivism, the mounting of a thousand campaigns to bring under control and redirect American development toward more democratic, humane, and orderly forms. This insurgency touched the agricultural and working classes, but its base was in the urban middle class, which had been largely immune to the social discontents of the 1890s.

The Progressive movement began first with the word—with an outpouring of literature designed to expose social problems and shock an apathetic public into action. Although social critics had never been lacking in America's atmosphere of freedom, the turn of the century saw an expansion in inexpensive magazines and newspapers, which provided readier access to the public mind. Journalists in increasing numbers turned to the themes of exposure, and Theodore Roosevelt in an uncharacteristic moment of irritation labeled them "muckrakers." They wore the label proudly. Lincoln Steffens wrote of the graft and corruption in city government, in his *The Shame of the Cities* (1904). *McClure's Magazine,* which published Steffens's articles, also ran important criticisms of the oil industry by Ida Tarbell and Ray Stannard Baker's series on southern race relations. Thomas W. Lawson

Muckraking

exposed high-level theft in New York financial centers in the pages of *Everybody's*, and David Graham Phillips wrote on similar conditions in the U.S. Senate for *Cosmopolitan*.

Novelists, too, made important contributions. Upton Sinclair described the exploitation of workers and unsanitary conditions in the meat-packing industry in *The Jungle* (1906). Frank Norris wrote of railroad domination of California politics in *The Octopus* (1903). Scholars joined in the mood of debunking. Charles A. Beard's *An Economic Interpretation of the Constitution of the United States* (1913) questioned the founders' solicitude for property rights, and Edward A. Ross raised doubts about traditional views of right and wrong in *Sin and Society* (1907). Clergymen joined in the literature of social introspection; Walter Rauschenbusch and Charles Sheldon insisted that Christ would have condemned America's slums, factory working conditions, and inequalities of wealth had he returned to the early twentieth-century cities.

The Cities

Stimulated by muckraking, reform began in the cities where social problems were the most visible. Good government campaigns sprang up in Chicago in 1896, in Toledo in 1897, in Detroit in 1899. By the first decade of the twentieth century they were flourishing throughout the country. A crusading contingent of mayors replaced the city "bosses", and with the help of citizens' coalitions devised a set of institutional changes for improving urban life. The city manager idea caught hold, city charters were reformed, departments of public health and sanitation were mobilized against disease and pollution, and municipal ownership was extended to transportation and other utilities. Although some men—including "Golden Rule" Jones, Hazen Pingree, and Tom Johnson, who reformed Toledo, Detroit, and Cleveland respectively—took part in spectacular campaigns, it was typically women who took the leadership in a nonpolitical reform, the settlement house movement. In renovated houses located in the midst of urban slums, Jane Addams, Lillian Wald, Mary Simkhovitch, and others established places where the poor could find shelter, social activities, night classes, and the beginnings of political cohesion.

The States

Reform campaigns in the major cities did not end poverty, overcrowding, urban pollution, and misgovernment. Considering the dimensions of the urban dilemma, however, reform efforts made some headway against both chaos and suffering. More progress would surely have been made had urban governments possessed sufficient powers to deal with all the problems within their borders, but they did not. Reformers soon learned that the states held the key to broader urban powers, as well as to the regulation of intrastate industry and transportation.

Reformers moved first to democratize the political system upon which state government rested. They forced through such measures as the direct primary, suffrage for women, and a trio of devices that allowed the people to go around obstructionist legislatures—the initiative, referendum, and recall.

The pinched faces of working children like this young boy in a glassworks (1910) aroused reformers to angry protest. The Keating-Owen Child Labor Law of 1916 appeared to cap a generation of efforts to outlaw most child labor and regulate the rest. It was declared unconstitutional in 1918. (The Bettmann Archive)

The leadership in these battles came from a series of energetic governors, among them, Wisconsin's Robert M. La Follette, Hiram Johnson in California, Charles Evans Hughes in New York, Woodrow Wilson in New Jersey. Political reform was invariably followed by efforts to regulate business and protect the disadvantaged. States set up railroad and public safety commissions, shifted tax burdens from agriculture toward corporations, and passed laws to guard against fraud in the sale of securities. While the struggle to impose regulatory controls upon the robust private enterprisers of pre–World War I America took its toll on Progressives' energies, some enthusiasm remained for what later generations would call welfare legislation. States passed child labor laws (thirty-one states), limited working hours (thirty-nine states), put a floor under the wages (fifteen states) of women, and enacted workmen's compensation systems (forty-three states).

The political rhetoric of both reformers and their opponents at the state level suggested something of a social revolution. But astute observers on both sides knew that the many Progressive campaigns and the resultant legislative record had not gone very far toward easing the problems that the muckrakers had identified. Laws were often diluted when business interests participated in drafting or administering them. Legislatures often failed to appropriate sufficient funds for enforcement. And even where state laws were adequate, it became obvious that many problems of industrializing America could be effectively addressed only at the national level. No city or state could hope to regulate interstate commerce, banking, and industry. Only national action could do something about the trusts. State-by-state legislation was slow, but one national law could bring the vote to women, legalize the progressive income tax, prohibit alcoholic beverages. And certainly no governmental level could match the power of the Washington government, especially the White House, in mobilizing public opinion and exerting moral leadership. And so progressivism soon moved from the state house to the north bank of the Potomac.

Reform arrived in Washington in the person of Theodore Roosevelt, the robust ex-governor of New York who had reluctantly accepted the vice-presidency in 1900 on the ticket with William McKinley. McKinley's assassination in 1901 placed in the White House a man with a strong taste for activism, one eager to focus national energies upon unmet social needs and problems. Republican strategist Mark Hanna thought TR a radical and had resisted his vice-presidential candidacy on the ground that "there's only one life between this madman and the White House." But the patrician Roosevelt was both more complex and more cautious than Hanna suspected. Time would prove him a nationalist, a friend of large institutions, efficiency, and order. His chief contribution to reform was to publicize and focus its concerns rather than to offer original ideas.

Theodore Roosevelt

His first task as president was to confront the monopoly problem. To demonstrate his independence from corporate power, he encouraged his attorney general to press a landmark antitrust suit against the Northern Securities Company, a huge holding company formed to merge the railroads of James J. Hill and Edward H. Harriman. A federal court in 1903 ordered the company to dissolve, and Progressives cheered while Roosevelt's administration undertook more prosecutions for restraint of trade in meat, tobacco and oil. But TR, while glad to accept an increasingly popular label as trustbuster, was no enemy of bigness. Although he acknowledged that corporations often abused their power, he believed that this was "an age of combination", and saw no reason to lose the benefits of large-scale production in a futile effort to restore nineteenth-century individualism. The solution to the monopoly problem was not atomization of the economy but a judicious combination of select antitrust actions with regulation. Between the two modes of directing corporate conduct, Roosevelt always had more faith in regulation than in the marketplace.

It was an indication of Roosevelt's political genius, as well as his basic philosophy, that he could convince both sides of the trust controversy of his support. Even while developing a national reputation as a trustbuster, he satisfied the capitalists that he was not their enemy. Big businessmen quickly perceived that Roosevelt was their best protection against more radical alternatives proposed by others. His rhetorical wrath and infrequent antitrust actions would ease public concern about monopoly, but regulation in a friendly spirit would leave the structure of the American economy essentially unchanged. Only to those who accepted the trustbusting myth was it a surprise when the Morgans, Rockefellers, and other captains of industry donated generously to the Republicans in the 1904 presidential campaign.

Square Dealing

During this campaign the phrase "square deal" came to be widely associated with Roosevelt's political program. The president himself first used it in reference to his settlement of one of the most trying crises of his first term. In May 1902 anthracite coal miners, organized as the United Mine Workers, struck for higher wages and shorter hours. The mine owners, who did not recognize the union, were incensed. George F. Baer revealed the owners' attitude by proclaiming that "the rights and interests of the laboring man will be protected and cared for—not by labor agitators, but by the Christian men to whom God in His infinite wisdom has given the control of the property interests of the country." The miners, abstaining from violence and asking only for arbitration, won the sympathy of most Americans. The strike dragged on into the summer and fall with no sign of settlement. Early in October, Roosevelt decided to act. The mine owners were told that unless they took steps to settle the strike through arbitration, the president would consider using the United States Army to work the mines. Frightened at this unprecedented show of executive power, the owners capitulated.

While this settlement seemed to be a great victory for labor, in fact it was a compromise of the kind Roosevelt preferred. The miners received a 10 percent wage increase; the owners were encouraged to raise prices 10 percent. The president had sided with labor, but he steadfastly refused to approve of union shops, arrangements under which only members of a union were permitted to work. Big labor, Roosevelt believed, could be just as dangerous to the common welfare as big business. He felt that the government should guard against the abuse of any private power in an effort to obtain justice for all sides. Public approval of such square dealing contributed to Roosevelt's resounding victory in the election of 1904 against the comparatively lackluster Democrat, Alton B. Parker.

President Theodore Roosevelt is shown here—as usual—in a self-consciously athletic moment. The horse has his eye on the jump, but the president has his eye on the camera. TR was a matchless showman, yet he also left behind much solid accomplishment. (Max Pohly/Black Star)

Having won the presidency in his own right and sensing the mounting *The Hepburn Act*
national enthusiasm for reform, Roosevelt planned to press forward with
square deal progressivism. At the head of his program was the regulation of
business in the public interest, and the business he most desired to regulate
was transportation. Despite previous legislation such as the Interstate Commerce Act and the Elkins Act, the railroads continued to set rates and grant
privileges that many citizens regarded as grossly unfair. Roosevelt's attempts
to obtain an effective law were initially thwarted by strong opposition from
conservatives in Congress. Finally, after months of involved political maneuvering, he achieved passage of the Hepburn Act in 1906. The new
legislation empowered the Interstate Commerce Commission to set and
enforce rates in response to shippers' demands. The railroads might protest
through the courts, but meanwhile the altered rates would be in effect.

Although the Hepburn Act disappointed the more radical Progressives, it
greatly expanded the federal government's role in controlling business. The
year 1906 became a banner one for Roosevelt with the passage of the Pure
Food and Drug Act and the Meat Inspection Act. Widely demanded by
muckrakers, these laws made it clear that not only interstate commerce but
any industry directly affecting public health and safety was also subject to
federal control.

During the Progressive era, for the first time in their history, large numbers of *Conservation*
Americans became concerned about their environment. Formerly the abun-
dance of natural resources had been taken for granted. Waste had had no
meaning when the West was wilderness. But beginning in the 1890s the
public became aware that the nation was pressing against the limits of its
resources and that a program of conservation was essential. Progressives in
particular found the idea highly appealing. In the first place, conserving
resources for the future needs of the nation seemed democratic. "The natural
resources must be developed and preserved for the benefit of the many,"
asserted Gifford Pinchot, "and not merely for the profit of a few." Conservation also appealed to the typical Progressive's passion for expert, efficient
management. He looked forward to planned, scientific development replacing careless, shortsighted exploitation. Finally the Progressives' anxiety concerning rampant American materialism found expression in enthusiasm for
the part of the conservation movement that sought to preserve scenic beauty
and wilderness. This aesthetic conservation and the resulting preservation
movement, to be sure, were often at odds with Pinchot's utilitarian conservation, and the bitterest conservation controversies were frequently family
affairs among the Progressives.

The Newlands Act of 1902, which launched federal reclamation activities
in the arid West, began Roosevelt's conservation crusade. In the next few
years the president worked closely with his chief forester and close friend,
Gifford Pinchot, to add one hundred fifty million acres to the federally
regulated national forests. He also created the Inland Waterways Commission as a multipurpose planning agency and designated the Grand Canyon a

national monument. In May 1908 Roosevelt made "conservation" a household word by hosting a conference on the subject at the White House. One thousand participants, including forty-four governors, were invited to exchange ideas on what Roosevelt termed "the gravest problem of today." Pinchot, who regarded the conference as "a turning point in human history," hoped it would lead to extensive action on both the state and federal levels. The lawmakers, however, were not inclined to respond favorably to a president who had announced that he would not run for reelection. Congress was weary of being led by a strong executive and, in a gesture of independence, refused to appropriate funds for conservation.

Stimulated by Roosevelt, the forces of reform were now well mobilized in both parties. TR underestimated the momentum of progressive change and invited trouble for the Republicans when he confidently handpicked his secretary of war, William Howard Taft, as his successor. This undemocratic arrangement was out of step with the temper of the times, as was the huge, honest, and deeply conservative Taft. Within a year of his victory over Democrat William Jennings Bryan, Taft had allowed his party to fall into a bitter factionalism. In the first weeks the president endorsed "Boss" Joseph Cannon of Illinois as Speaker of the House, angering insurgents in the Congress. In 1909 the president infuriated reformers by siding with protectionist interests in the shaping of the Payne-Aldrich Tariff Act. In 1910 he fired the hero of the conservation movement, Chief Forester Gifford Pinchot, who had publicly criticized the administration's handling of a scandal surrounding a minor Interior Department official, Richard A. Ballinger. In 1911 he supported a central banking bill that Wall Street favored. This was much too conservative for the Progressives, who chose to ignore the occasions when Taft moved in their direction—for example, in supporting reorganization of the executive branch and the army and in initiating twice the number of antitrust suits in four years than TR had produced in seven. In retrospect, Taft was indeed a Progressive, albeit a conservative one, and he possessed both integrity and intelligence. But his 330-pound body matched his temperament, which was cautious, even sluggish, entirely lacking in that vitality with which TR had electrified the public. By 1912 Progressives in his party were irreconcilable to his renomination, and eager for an alternative.

William Howard Taft

Few elections have presented the American electorate with the clear-cut alternatives of 1912. The sitting president had split his party, and his renomination was accomplished only by a rigged convention. He offered conservatives a candidate who would stand firmly against further changes in the status quo. At the other extreme, reformers who concluded that only the replacement of the capitalist system by public ownership of the principal means of production could vote for the dynamic Eugene V. Debs, who had been building the Socialist party since the merger of socialist factions in 1901. Debs's appeal came as much from his attractive humanitarianism as it did from his socialist program. Many were ready to follow a man who could

The Choices of 1912: Stand-Patism, Socialism, New Freedom, New Nationalism

say: "While there is a lower class, I am in it; while there is a criminal element, I am of it; where there is a soul in prison, I am not free."

Most voters in 1912 preferred a Progressive candidate. Back from a safari in Africa and angry at Taft's failure to sustain the momentum of reform, Theodore Roosevelt first attempted to gain the Republican nomination, then agreed to head the ticket of the new Progressive party. The Bull Moose (Roosevelt claimed to feel as fit as one, giving the new party a nickname) platform of 1912 took on a radical tinge; it endorsed women's suffrage, a popular referendum on judicial decisions, a minimum wage and a maximum hours for women in industrial occupations, social insurance against unemployment and old age, and "a strong Federal administrative commission . . . which shall maintain permanent and active supervision over industrial corporations engaged in inter-State commerce." TR had moved somewhat to the left since leaving office in 1908 and was thoroughly at home with his party's platform. Influenced by Herbert Croly's book, *The Promise of American Life* (1909), Roosevelt called for a "new nationalism" in which a strong central government would continuously regulate the nation's economic life in the public interest.

Another version of progressivism was articulated by the Democratic party's candidate, Governor Woodrow Wilson of New Jersey. A gifted orator, historian, and former president of Princeton University, Wilson offered another approach to social reform in his "new freedom." At its core was the assumption that an economy based on freely competing small units could be restored in the United States. Wilson, and particularly his chief advisor in matters of political philosophy, Louis D. Brandeis, believed that bigness in business stifled opportunity. Instead of regulating the trusts and assisting the

Woodrow Wilson campaigned vigorously in the 1912 election. In his inaugural address he appealed for action on tariff, banking, conservation, and other measures to benefit "humanity": "Men's hearts wait upon us; men's lives hang in the balance. . . . I summon all honest men, all patriotic, all forward-looking men to my side. God helping me, I will not fail them, if they will counsel and sustain me." (Library of Congress)

little man, as Roosevelt promised, Wilson would strip power from the wealthy and privileged and then retire to the role of referee, avoiding paternalism of any kind. This was a vision of active government, but an activism strictly confined to the role of preserving competition. TR tended to see the national government as exerting social guidance, while Wilson would rely upon the market once the government had freed it from monopoly power. It is only a small oversimplification to say that Roosevelt was the friend of a large-scale, managed capitalism and Wilson the ally of a small-business, competitive order. Both sounded somewhat radical, but they took different paths toward the preservation of the essentials of an American industrial-capitalist system.

Between the two reform candidates there was a significant doctrinal as well as personal choice, and the campaign of 1912 offered voters an unprecedented range of alternatives. Debs polled fourth, but earned over nine hundred thousand out of fifteen million votes, the highest proportion of votes a Socialist had won (or would ever win) in a presidential election. Taft ran third, carrying only Utah and Vermont. Roosevelt's third party drew more votes than the dominant Republicans, earning more than four million. But the Democrats received six million three hundred thousand votes, and Woodrow Wilson moved to the White House in early 1913.

With his party in control of both houses of Congress, President Wilson quickly put his new freedom into practice. His first major achievement, the Underwood Tariff of 1913, lowered rates substantially, levied a small tax on personal incomes, and shifted other federal taxes to bear most heavily on the rich. The Federal Reserve Act of the same year sought to reform America's anachronistic banking system by freeing its credit supply from the control of a few private financiers. Actually the act was a compromise between the Progressives and the banking community. The panics of 1873, 1893, and 1907 had demonstrated the inelasticity of the money supply, as well as the need for central control of monetary policy. Bankers wanted to establish a giant, privately directed bank, while the more radical Progressives were set on government regulation in the name of the public welfare. After much haggling the Federal Reserve Board, its members appointed by the president, was established in Washington. Its twelve regional branches were designed to achieve the new freedom goal of decentralizing control over the money supply, but this feature of the law was to disappoint its sponsors. The Federal Reserve Act shifted the center of monetary power from New York to Washington, not to the grass roots, and was thus more in the spirit of the new nationalism than the new freedom.

The ideological purity of Wilson's program was further diluted when he turned to the monopoly problem. The new freedom idea suggested antitrust action, and Wilson skillfully led the Democratic congressional majority to the enactment of the Clayton Act in 1914. The law attempted to specify unfair trade practices, and outlaw them. Yet as the president worked with the problem he realized that no law could cope with all situations in a changing

The Democrats as Progressives

industrial order. Thus he backed legislation that became the Federal Trade Commission Act of 1914, a capitulation to TR's idea of continuous administrative regulation of the economy. In the face of modern complexity, reform was pragmatic, borrowing from all schools of thought.

Surveying his administration's reforms in tariff, antitrust, and banking, Wilson announced that the new freedom was fulfilled. The path to economic opportunity was again open. His conclusion was premature. He may have been satisfied with what had been done, but other Progressives thought more was required. As the 1916 election approached, Wilson realized that he must become the acknowledged leader of progressivism, since the Republicans were likely to be united as they had not been in 1912. Thus in 1915–16 he supported farm credit legislation and the Adamson Act, which brought the eight-hour day to railway labor, and appointed Progressive lawyer Louis D. Brandeis to the Supreme Court. (Brandeis was also a Jew, which made the appointment a bold and—to some—unpopular one.) Wilson's reelection over New Yorker Charles Evans Hughes was a narrow one and could not have been achieved had the president not fashioned an energetic and multifaceted reform program that erased many doubts that the southern-dominated Democratic party could govern in the twentieth century.

Black Frustration

For black Americans the Progressive movement offered promise without fulfillment. While writers and politicians filled the air with cries for social justice, the black man's lot continued to be one of broken dreams. The hopes that flared in 1901 when Theodore Roosevelt invited Booker T. Washington to luncheon in the White House quickly died. Neither of the three Progressive administrations passed significant legislation concerning the rights of blacks. If anything, disenfranchisement and other forms of discrimination increased in these years. Racial violence, moreover, broke out in the North and South. Over a hundred blacks were lynched in 1900 alone—over a thousand by 1914—and most of the deaths testified to the bigotry of whites rather than the transgressions of blacks. Ugly riots in Atlanta, Georgia, Brownsville, Texas, and Springfield, Illinois, resulted in white mobs' running roughshod over black communities.

In the face of continuing prejudice and political apathy, some blacks began to organize in an effort to secure equal rights. W. E. B. Du Bois, who held a Ph.D. from Harvard, took the lead in the early protest movement. His *The Souls of Black Folk* (1903) challenged Booker T. Washington's doctrine of accommodation and conciliation. According to Du Bois, second-class citizenship was intolerable. Taking issue with Washington, he contended that blacks should not surrender, even strategically, their insistence on full equality. Exceptional blacks, the "talented tenth" as Du Bois termed them, must obtain higher education, enter the professions, and win respect for their people.

For these ends Du Bois spearheaded the militant Niagara movement in 1905 and five years later participated in the organization of the biracial

An eloquent spokesman for black intellectuals, Dr. W. E. B. Du Bois edited the journal of the NAACP, The Crisis, from 1910 to 1934 and pressed to gain complete constitutional rights for all blacks. With the passing years, Du Bois became a confirmed Marxist, viewing the struggle for black rights in the context of international class conflict. (Culver Pictures)

National Association for the Advancement of Colored People. The NAACP launched a vigorous crusade. By 1918 its magazine, The Crisis, was alerting a hundred thousand Americans a month to the problems and desires of black America. Its Legal Redress Committee attacked all forms of segregation and discrimination. After 1911 the NAACP was joined by the National Urban League, an organization concerned with the plight of the increasing numbers of black migrants to metropolitan areas. But without the cooperation of the political establishment and the majority of white Americans, the effect of these organizational efforts was quite limited. Since blacks were substantially disfranchised, no politician had any incentive to address their problems. When TR invited Booker T. Washington to a meal at the White House in 1903, a storm of abuse broke over both men, and Roosevelt felt obliged to apologize to whites for offending their sense of propriety. Progressives in general were unconcerned with the race question. President Wilson brought traditional southern attitudes to Washington; the segregation of federal facilities in Washington actually increased during his administrations, and the percentage of black federal employees declined. "I say it with shame and humiliation," the president told a leader of the NAACP, "but I have thought about this [racial] thing for twenty years and I see no way out. It will take a very big man to solve this thing." Some progressives, however, began the struggle to change racial attitudes and habits. A few muckrakers courageously addressed the issue, some settlement workers showed a special concern for the black poor, and white Progressives Mary White Ovington, Charles Edward Russell, and Oswald Garrison Villard were among those who founded the NAACP in 1909.

The crusade for women's rights was more productive. Its roots ran back to an 1848 convention of reform-minded women at Senaca Falls, New York. The presence of Frederick Douglass at the meeting linked the causes of the nation's foremost minorities: blacks and women. But the movements split in the Civil War era, and only the blacks were to secure any federal assistance during the ensuing years. Indeed on the federal level white American males extended suffrage to black men fifty years before they granted it to women.

A complex set of attitudes and institutions served to keep women in their male-defined places in the nineteenth and early twentieth centuries. The belief that a woman's place was in the kitchen, bedroom, and nursery was supported by laws denying her the opportunity to vote, hold office, testify at trials, and even own property. Legally women were shadows of their fathers and husbands. Socially they found themselves officially revered in their assigned roles as mother and homemaker but excluded from full access to male conversation, social gatherings, intellectual opportunities, recreation. Many lower- and middle-class women entered the work force, but they usually shared the prevailing notion that femininity was demeaned in the world of work, and they were compensated at wages far below those paid to males.

The movement for women's rights drew inspiration from the Enlightenment conception of the dignity and capability of every human being. The related ideal of human freedom also figured prominently. To advance it in

Women's Struggle for Equality

Persuading the states to grant suffrage to women was a slow, torturous battle—even when, as in Ohio, Theodore Roosevelt's "Square Deal" slogan was borrowed. The suffragists decided upon a national constitutional amendment in 1913, and by 1919 had secured the long sought goal. (The Bettmann Archive)

the United States, feminist leaders Elizabeth Cady Stanton and Susan B. Anthony organized the National Woman's Suffrage Association in 1868. A group only for women, it demanded immediate suffrage and called for radical modifications in the institution of marriage. In the eyes of some critics this amounted to advocacy of free love, and the association of extreme feminists like Victoria Woodhull and Tennessee Claflin with the NWSA did not help in this respect. As a more respectable alternative Lucy Stone and Julia Ward Howe founded the American Woman Suffrage Association, but the groups merged in 1890 under the leadership of Elizabeth Stanton. The new coalition increasingly concentrated upon voting rights for women, a conservative tactical decision that increased the chances of tangible success but narrowed the movement's potentialities for altering women's roles.

The climate of progressivism both stimulated the drive for female equality and drew strength from it. The new women's colleges, such as Vassar (1865), Smith (1875), Bryn Mawr (1885), and Radcliffe (1893), produced a rising generation of leaders eager for useful careers. The General Federation of Women's Clubs (GFWC), founded in 1890, mobilized female energies in the direction of social activism. The federation's president in 1904, Sarah P. Decker, told the membership (then nearing the one million mark): "I have an important piece of news for you. Dante is dead. He has been dead for several centuries, and I think it is time that we dropped the study of his inferno and turned attention to our own." Women took her advice and provided vital recruits for Progressive reforms at many points. They took a special interest in the prohibition of alcoholic beverages, prostitution, and child labor. The social settlements were predominantly female in leadership and staff, and it was two remarkable women, Florence Kelley and Josephine Shaw Lowell, who founded the National Consumers League in 1891. While the GFWC attracted the upper-class clubwoman, more radical feminists found a fulcrum for their efforts to aid the working girl in the Women's Trade Union League.

It is difficult to generalize about the results such organizations were able to secure. Perhaps, as historian William O'Neill has observed, the various reform activities of women in the pre–World War era were more important in providing useful social roles for the female reformers themselves than in actually changing society. But one should not underestimate the social benefits flowing from their efforts.

One cause united virtually all female reformers, whatever their other interests: the vote. Although all suffragists were not feminists, as Winnifred Cooley noted in 1913, all feminists were suffragists. (A few men were too in this age of surging idealism.) The struggle for the vote was at first conducted at the state level, and it produced victories in several western states in the 1890s. But the state-by-state strategy was costly in time and effort, and several eastern industrial states rebuffed suffragettes in crucial contests. Liquor interests led the resistance, along with both female and male an-

Suffrage for Women

tifeminists whose reasons for opposition ranged from a fear of black female voting to a reluctance to expose women to the coarseness of the "real" world.

A decade of disappointing results in state contests led suffragettes to focus their efforts at the federal level. President Wilson had announced his opposition, but suffragettes believed in moving obstacles. A British-born radical, Alice Paul, led the new Woman's party in militant "nuisance tactics," marching and picketing at the White House gates in 1916 and 1917. Carrie Chapman Catt held the moderate suffragettes on a course designed to influence Wilson and the Congress rather than to alienate them, massing public opinion behind a constitutional amendment. World War I offered a wavering president the chance to accept women's suffrage without appearing to yield to a pressure group. Women had proven themselves capable workers and citizens through participation in the war effort. Their enfranchisement could easily be justified as part of a war to make the world safe for democracy, and Wilson did so in 1918. Congress ratified this last of the Progressive reforms in 1919 as the Nineteenth Amendment.

Suffragettes who expected the vote to bring immediate improvement in national political behavior, as well as in the lives of American women, were disappointed. Yet many, perhaps most, were not so naive. Many feminists understood that the long battle for the vote was only a small aspect of a larger struggle to remove discrimination on the basis of sex from American life. They had always intended to move on to more fundamental reforms when the vote was won. "Women," said the radical feminist Crystal Eastman as the Nineteenth Amendment was ratified, "are saying, 'now at last we can begin.' Now they can say what they are really after . . . freedom." Historian William O'Neill, writing in the 1970s, put the women's movement of the Progressive era in sharper perspective, when he wrote that "no such obviously desired and modest a reform ever required so much effort":

> Most gains for women in those years were accidental. . . . Victorian women had worn confining, sometimes dangerous clothes. . . . In the 20th century matters improved considerably. . . . By 1915 or so it was clear that women meant to dress more sanely. Skirts got shorter. The slip replaced layers of petticoats. The corset gave way to a simple elastic girdle. Drawers were replaced by panties. This transformation, which began in the progressive era, was in practical terms worth considerably more to women than the vote.

Historians continue to disagree sharply on the impact and significance of the era of reform that churned the years prior to World War I. For many years they tended to take Progressive rhetoric at face value and concluded that the reformers had been what they claimed to have been—crusaders who meant to invigorate political democracy, discipline big business, and succor the weak. In the 1950s a more critical view developed. Richard Hofstadter, in his noted *The Age of Reform* (1956), explored certain neglected themes within the Progressive mentality: anxiety about the new urban lower

The Progressive Balance Sheet

classes, a desire to regain the status that small-town elites had lost to metropolitan entrepreneurs, a debilitating nostalgia for the simpler world of the late nineteenth century. Other scholars soon joined Hofstadter in focusing attention upon the not so liberal side of much Progressive activity. They underlined the extent to which reformers sought to control behavior through prohibition and sumptuary laws, supported immigration restriction, ignored the desperate situation of the black American. The affection of many Progressives for the economic individualism of the nineteenth century was seen as hopelessly dated in the twentieth-century world of large institutions.

In this light the Progressives actually constituted a conservative coalition, striving to prevent radical changes by sponsoring marginal reforms and blunting class conflict. Perhaps many Progressives would have agreed with this analysis. Critics have also concluded that the reformers were ineffective, for they had not busted the trusts or made much improvement in urban life where the poor struggled to survive. At least one influential historian, Gabriel Kolko, has insisted that the Progressives' central achievement was not social welfare measures—which were insignificant—but the establishment of national economic regulation designed to stave off a disruptive competition and a gathering rural radicalism. Another prominent writer, Robert Wiebe, saw the typical Progressive not as a businessman but as a rising young technoprofessional, eagerly building a network of institutions designed to rationalize and bring order to American society as it broke out of the comfortable channels of late nineteenth-century small town life.

Each of these perspectives contains its truth, and the problem for historians remains that of assessing the whole record. The democratic and humanitarian commitment of the Progressives has recently been too obscured, and the best judgment of pre-World War reform appears to be that of John Higham, who recently wrote: "In a long-term perspective, the distinctive feature of the period from 1898 to 1918 is not the preeminence of democratic ideals or of bureaucratic techniques, but rather a fertile amalgam of the two."

COMMENTARY

While the attention of national political leaders and much of the public was focused upon the internal reforms and conflicts which we call the Progressive Era, America between the Spanish-American War and World War I was being transformed by forces more potent than politics or the journalism of exposure. Her population stood at seventy-six million when the twentieth century opened, and had climbed to one hundred two million when Wilson was elected for the second time. This increase reflected a high birth rate, a falling death rate, and a flood of European immigration which brought nearly ten million new residents to America in the first decade of the century. The American economy, drawing upon an expanding scientific and technological capacity and nourished by abundant resources, continued the expansion that had made the United States the world's strongest economy when the century opened. Americans had not much noted the steady increase in their economic interdependence with other nations, as the volume of foreign trade expanded. The share of our national product going to foreign trade was no more than 11–13 percent (compared to 54 percent for France, 44 percent for the United Kingdom), but the volume increased from a value of 2.5 billion dollars in 1900 to 8.8 billion dollars in 1916. This was only one index of America's involvement in the world community of nations, and its consequences were not foreseen in the busy years of internal discussion and reform.

But an assassination in a corner of the Austro-Hungarian Empire on June 28, 1914, set in motion a chain of events that would vastly educate the American people in their new world position and would signal an end to the century of "free security" in between the Napoleonic wars and World War I.

SUGGESTED READING

JOHN M. BLUM, *The Republican Roosevelt* (1956)
————, *Woodrow Wilson and the Politics of Morality* (1956)
ROBERT BREMNER, *From the Depths: The Discovery of Poverty in the United States* (1956)
MELVYN DUBOVSKY, *We Shall Be All: A History of the Industrial Workers of the World* (1969)
SIDNEY FINE, *Laissez Faire and the General Welfare State* (1956)
ELEANOR FLEXNER, *Century of Struggle: The Woman's Rights Movement in the United States* (1959)
OTIS L. GRAHAM, JR., *The Great Campaigns: Reform and War in America, 1900–1928* (1971)
JACK T. KIRBY, *Darkness at the Dawning: Race and Reform in the Progressive South* (1972)
SAMUEL P. HAYS, *Conservation and the Gospel of Efficiency* (1959)
RICHARD HOFSTADTER, *The Age of Reform* (1956)
GABRIEL KOLKO, *The Triumph of Conservatism: A Reinterpretation of American History, 1900–1916* (1963)
ARTHUR LINK, *Woodrow Wilson and the Progressive Era: 1910–1917* (1954)
HENRY F. MAY, *The End of American Innocence* (1959)
GEORGE MOWRY, *The Era of Theodore Roosevelt, 1900–1912* (1946)
WILLIAM L. O'NEILL, *Everyone Was Brave: The Rise and Fall of Feminism in America* (1969)
DAVID THELEN, *The New Citizenship, 1885–1900* (1972)
ROBERT WIEBE, *The Search for Order: 1877–1920* (1967)

12

War and Prosperity, 1917–1929

Those who conclude that the Progressive movement had run out of ideas and energies by the end of Wilson's first term can never prove their case, for a world war began in 1914 that soon intruded into the patterns of American domestic life. On June 28, 1914, the assassination of Archduke Franz Ferdinand, heir to the Austro-Hungarian throne, touched off a spark in the powder keg of European international relations. Sides were immediately chosen. Austria-Hungary and Germany, the Central Powers, opposed France, Russia, and Great Britain. By August a full-scale war was in progress. Americans reacted with surprise, coupled with a sense of satisfaction in being geographically isolated from such conflicts. It quickly became apparent, however, that the New World's immunity to Europe's problems was not as complete as many hoped. Trade, and the ships that carried it, involved the United States in European affairs. So did all considerations of security and many Americans' sense of responsibility for the kind of world in which they lived.

Neutrality

When the European war began President Wilson urged impartiality. Yet almost immediately the conduct of the belligerents made this course difficult. Britain established a naval blockade of the Central Powers, stopping virtually all American trade with Germany and Austria. Commerce with those nations, valued at one hundred seventy million dollars in 1914, fell to a mere million two years later. Americans were perturbed at England's insistence on stopping, searching, and sometimes confiscating cargoes, but their anger was somewhat mitigated by the booming trade with the Allied nations. While America's neutral rights were violated by England, no American lives were lost, and Wilson contented himself with sharp protests.

U-Boats

German violations of America's neutral rights, however, took a different and more provoking form. In an effort to strike back at the British blockade, Germany announced that after February 4, 1915, its submarines, or U-boats, would attempt to sink all enemy ships on sight. Neutral vessels were advised to remain clear of the North Atlan-

The German government ran advertisements in New York newspapers to warn American travelers against sailing on the Cunard liner, Lusitania, which flew a British flag and was reputed (correctly) to carry munitions. More than one hundred Americans sailed in May 1915, despite the warnings.

tic in order to avoid unfortunate mistakes. Yet American trade with Great Britain continued. Inevitably an American ship, the *Gulflight,* was torpedoed, though not sunk. The country had hardly recovered from this affront when the news arrived that a submarine had sunk the British passenger liner *Lusitania* on May 7, 1915, with the loss of 1,198 persons, including 128 Americans. Extremists cried for war with Germany, arguing that the *Lusitania* was a defenseless vessel on a peaceful mission. Recent evidence, however, suggests that the giant liner was actually heavily armed and carried an enormous cargo of munitions bought in the United States by the Allies. Britain's successful efforts to conceal this from the American public stemmed from the hope that the sinking of the *Lusitania* would draw the United States into the war against Germany. But while Wilson, and especially his new secretary of state, Robert Lansing, leaned in this direction, they contented themselves in 1915 with Germany's pledge that henceforth it would not attack passenger ships without providing for the safety of the lives of noncombatants. The necessities of submarine warfare weakened the promise: surprise attacks were the U-boats' forte and their small size did not permit taking on survivors. Thus it was not really unexpected when on March 24, 1916, a submarine crippled the French liner *Sussex* with a heavy loss of life. Wilson responded with so strong an ultimatum that the German government agreed not to torpedo merchant ships without first searching them for neutral passengers. The *Sussex* pledge succeeded in restricting submarine warfare for nine months.

Woodrow Wilson's hatred of war, his fear of American involvement, and his sense of world responsibility led him to make several efforts to settle the differences between the European belligerents. On two occasions he sent his closest advisor, Colonel Edward M. House, to Europe in unsuccessful attempts to arrange peace negotiations. The British stalled, gambling that eventual American intervention would enable them to achieve all their war objectives. The Germans, with some justification, regarded Wilson as basically pro-British and rebuffed his efforts to volunteer as an impartial mediator. The president knew that his achievement in forcing an end to unrestricted submarine warfare carried with it a great risk. As he put it, one German submarine commander could break the *Sussex* pledge and undermine U.S. neutrality. Wilson wanted peace. He campaigned against his Republican opponent in 1916 on the slogan "He Kept Us Out of War" and was narrowly reelected. A second term assured, he asked England and Germany in December to state their war objectives as a prelude to compromise, and in January urged "peace without victory" in a speech before the Senate. It was already too late. At a meeting in January, the German high command, judging that Wilson could not be trusted to mediate an acceptable settlement and that their submarine force could bring the Allies to their knees before American intervention could become effective, decided to resume unrestricted submarine warfare. The United States was informed on January 31 that U-boats would attack all ships, including neutral ones, in the war zone beginning on February 1.

Wilson had no choice but to break relations, yet he shrank from the decision for war. Over congressional protests the American merchant fleet was provided with weapons, and armed neutrality was tried as a step short of belligerency. Three developments in the months of February and March changed the public mood and Wilson's mind. First, Americans learned from British interceptors of the secret instructions that the German foreign minister, Alfred Zimmermann, had sent to the German minister in Mexico. In the event of war between the United States and the Central Powers, Zimmermann's note read, Mexico should be invited to join the latter and to conquer Texas, Arizona, and New Mexico. Publication of the note exposed American isolation as a delusion and generated a wave of anti-German feeling that Wilson could not ignore. Second, revolution against the czar placed a democratic government in control of Russia. Thus it now appeared that the Allies were united in carrying the banner of democracy against autocratic systems. For Americans, war on the Allied side became more appealing. Third, between February 3 and April 1, 1917, German U-boats sank eight American ships in the North Atlantic. Each successive sinking made more Americans favor war.

Nevertheless, the actual decision to fight was agonizing, particularly for a Progressive president who believed in the efficacy of reason, the possibility of Christian brotherhood, and the blessings of peace. Given his uncertainty, it was incumbent on Wilson to state America's objectives in highly idealistic terms. "The world must be made safe for democracy," declared his war message of April 2, 1917; "we have no selfish ends to serve." As the president conceived it, the war was to be the greatest crusade of all. The goal was no less than freedom and justice for all mankind. On April 6, by a vast majority, Congress passed the war resolution.

The immediate cause of United States intervention in World War I was Germany's resumption of unrestricted submarine warfare. But the fundamental cause was the American disposition to favor the Allies. This bias in favor of the Allies had several components. Just after the war scholars and public figures raised the charge that American intervention stemmed primarily from economic motives. It is true that America had a considerable economic stake in the Allied war effort. Since 1915 United States bankers had made enormous loans to England and France: $2.3 billion by April 1917, as compared to $27 million to Germany. A diplomatic break with the Allies, or their defeat, would have meant the loss of these funds. Moreover, most of the loans were used to purchase munitions in the United States. American prosperity was thus intertwined with Allied military fortunes. Charges that profit-hungry industrialists and bankers dictated intervention appear entirely unfounded. Wilson and his advisors did not take their cues from munitions manufacturers or the House of Morgan. But the desire to maintain American prosperity did lead to decisions that allowed strong trade links to be formed with the largest available markets, which happened to be in England and France. This fact warmed U.S.-Allied relations and chilled all American contacts with Germany.

The Reasons for Intervention

The fact that United States financial support went to England rather than Germany points up a deeper aspect of the American bias. Culturally and intellectually most Americans sympathized with England. Memories of a shared history, added to ties of language and political ideals, made the bond strong. Some ethnic groups in the United States, notably those of Irish and German extraction, dissented from the general sympathy for Britain, and the central and western portions of the country were less ardent than the East. Yet the basic pro-Allied bias was always strong, and Wilson's entire circle of advisors (with the major exception of Secretary of State Bryan) confirmed the president's leaning in that direction. At first seeing the war as a pointless struggle between equally selfish rival blocs, Wilson and many Americans gradually came to perceive the Allies as defending values to which Americans also subscribed. British "propaganda" (the word was coined at this time), more effective than the German variety, associated the Allied cause with human rights and democracy, while portraying the Germans as barbarous Huns who bayoneted children. Although American indignation may have been greater at times between 1914 and 1917 against England than Germany, the main currents of thought and feeling flowed the other way.

To some writers, this pro-British bias seems to have been an inappropriate basis upon which to build such a fundamental foreign policy position. Leaders and public alike should make such judgements upon the basis of realistic assessments of the national interest, not upon sentimental ethnic or historical ties. Yet there is some evidence that Wilson reached his decisions, at least to an extent, through realistic as well as idealistic thinking. His sympathy with Britain came partially from a far-sighted awareness that Britain and France were, like the United States, members of "the Atlantic community" whose cohesion would be vital to the future security of the American people.

Wilson's war message was delivered on the evening of April 2 before a tense, expectant, and then cheering session of Congress. The United States would fight not for territory or mere victory but for "peace and justice. . . . The world must be made safe for democracy." After four days of sharp debate, an overwhelming vote put America into the war on the Allied side. The United States' contributions to the Allied victory were fourfold.

Declaration of War

MORALE   When America joined the war in April 1917 the Allied will to resist was at a low ebb. The U-boat blockade of food and supplies had proved so successful that England doubted its ability to hold out for more than a few months. Russia had lost a million men in 1916 alone and was preoccupied with internal revolution. On the western front, France seemed to be collapsing before the German onslaught. America's decision to intervene brought vital encouragement even before its forces could be mobilized.

NAVAL AID   Immediately upon entering the war the United States Navy challenged the submarine menace. At the suggestion of American Admiral William S. Sims, convoys were organized to protect Allied merchant vessels. An antisubmarine mine field was planted in the North Sea, also an American idea. United States destroyers and airplanes joined British forces in seeking out and combating U-boats in the Atlantic. The results were impressive. Within six months after American intervention Allied shipping losses due to submarine attack had been reduced sharply, and not a single American troop ship was sunk during the war.

FOOD AND MUNITIONS   Dwindling Allied supplies made it imperative for the United States to gear its economy to the war effort with the utmost speed. President Wilson had created the Council of National Defense which, in turn, organized the War Industries Board, headed by Bernard M. Baruch, to increase manufacturing efficiency. Agricultural mobilization was entrusted to Herbert Hoover's Food Administration. The Emergency Fleet Corporation built, purchased, or confiscated enough ships to transport the products of America's farms and factories to Europe. By increased taxes and the sale of "liberty bonds" the United States not only paid its own wartime expenses but also gave considerable financial assistance to the Allies.

TROOPS   With the Germans planning a final, crushing offensive for the spring of 1918, Americans rushed to place men on the western front. Six months of congressional debate was required to choose a universal draft over a volunteer army as the basic manpower strategy of the mobilization. In

The Western Front, 1918

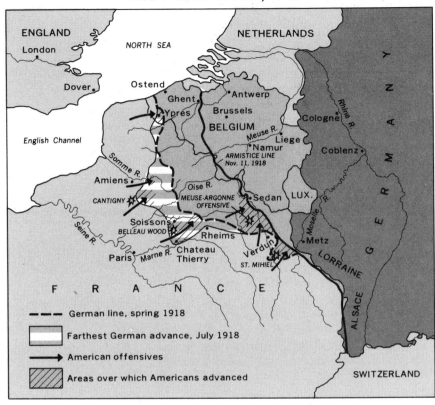

ENGLAND

NORTH SEA

NETHERLANDS

London

Dover

Ostend

Ghent

Ypres

Antwerp

Brussels

BELGIUM

Cologne

Rhine R.

English Channel

Somme R.

Amiens

CANTIGNY

Oise R.

Meuse R.

Namur

Liege

ARMISTICE LINE
Nov. 11, 1918

Coblenz

MEUSE-ARGONNE
OFFENSIVE

Sedan

LUX.

GERMANY

Soissons

BELLEAU WOOD

Rheims

Moselle R.

Metz

Seine R.

Paris

Marne R.

Chateau
Thierry

Verdun

ST. MIHIEL

LORRAINE

F   R   A   N   C   E

ALSACE

- - - - German line, spring 1918

Farthest German advance, July 1918

→ American offensives

Areas over which Americans advanced

SWITZERLAND

An elderly French couple greet Yankees of the 308th Infantry Regiment, 77th Division, on their arrival in France in 1918. The Yanks soon learned that their welcome reflected the near-exhaustion of the Allied war effort. (U. S. Army)

September 1917 the Selective Service Act required all men from the age of twenty-one (eighteen after 1918) to thirty to register for the draft. Those inducted (officials were shocked when 34 percent of the male youth who reported for examination failed the physical tests, and 25 percent were functionally illiterate) received up to six months' basic training and were pressed into service. Five million men, both black and white, were put into uniform, and two million served in Europe, most of them not arriving until March 1918.

Under the command of General John J. Pershing, the American Expeditionary Force cooperated in turning back the German offensive. At Chateau-Thierry (only fifty miles from Paris), between Reims and Soissons, at St. Mihiel, and again in the Meuse-Argonne region, American troops participated in fierce battles. After the turning point at Argonne, they joined in the counteroffensive that led to the armistice of November 11, 1918.

Modern war required an unprecedented degree of governmental mobilization of society's energies and resources. The War Industries Board coordinated a vast cooperative effort by which American industry supplied the implements of war at prices established by Washington bureaucrats. Food administrator Herbert Hoover set prices in basic commodities and channeled a great flow of grain overseas. The War Labor Board mediated labor-management disputes, and another agency established wages and hours. The fledgling Federal Reserve system helped finance the war, which eventually cost some thirty-three billion dollars; one-third of that amount was raised by taxes and two-thirds by loans from banks and war bond sales. Never had the federal government been so deeply engaged in social management, and Wilson presided over this vindication of the new nationalism with some reluctance. *The Home Front*

Among sectors of the population, enthusiasm for the war was unqualified. Enlistments ran high, war bonds were oversubscribed, and most citizens never questioned the president's high justifications or the sacrifices required by belligerency. Many Progressives were especially pleased, for the war offered an occasion for social control, cooperation, and self-sacrifice, which were the elements of the reform vision as it emerged out of the turbulent 1890s. As one Progressive social worker wrote in 1917: "Enthusiasm for social service is epidemic. . . . A luxuriant crop of new agencies is springing up. We scurry back and forth to the national capital; we stock offices with typewriters and new letterheads; we telephone feverishly, regardless of expense. . . . It is all very exhilarating, stimulating, intoxicating."

Yet there was significant dissent. Ethnic groups that were not cordial to the British cause were joined in their opposition to the war by pacifists who rejected all wars and by socialists whose loyalty ran not to nations but to the international working class. Although most American socialists eventually supported the war, many split off into vigorous opposition for the reasons advanced by Eugene Debs, who said: "I have no country to fight for. My *Opposition to the War*

The American socialist leader Eugene V. Debs deliberately tested the right of free speech in an address at Canton, Ohio, in June 1918. He criticized the war effort, as he had for many months, and predicted the ultimate triumph of socialism. He was arrested under the Espionage Act, and sentenced to ten years in prison. (United Press International)

country is the earth, and I am a citizen of the world." The Wilson administration regarded such views as intolerable and set out to mobilize public opinion as effectively as it had commanded the material resources of the nation. The Committee on Public Information, headed by Progressive journalist George Creel, produced pamphlets, films, and lecture tours to intensify public devotion to the Allied cause, as well as a dislike for Germany. It was only a step from propaganda to the suppression of views that might weaken the war effort. Wilson signed the Espionage Act in 1917 and the Sedition Act in 1918. The latter was a particularly sweeping law imposing fines and imprisonment on any person who did "wilfully utter, print, write or publish any disloyal, profane, scurrilous, or abusive language" about the government or the war effort. The administration welcomed these laws and vigorously moved against its critics. The mails were closed to "subversive" literature, which included the socialist newspaper *The Masses* and many minor publications. Some fifteen hundred people were arrested and many were imprisoned, including Eugene Debs, sentenced to a ten-year term in 1918.

It had not been Wilson's intention to set off a public outburst of intolerance when he accepted and administered laws against critics of the war. Yet the war had intensified fear of foreigners and heightened concern about internal division. Given a cue by the federal government's zeal in searching out subversives, vigilante groups and governments at the grass-roots level began to organize to take part in the drive for loyalty. At first the target was anything German. Many schools dropped German language instruction, German music was banned, even the word sauerkraut was deemed offensive and the dish renamed "liberty cabbage." But the intolerance persisted after the armistice of November 1918 and broadened to include radicals, labor

Red Scare

organizers, Catholics, Jews, Negroes—all those who by creed or color seemed to threaten some change to the established white, Anglo-Saxon order. Schoolteachers suspected of deviant opinions lost their jobs, pacifists and militant labor unionists were beaten or jailed. Without question the ugliest expression of the heightened nativism of the 1918–20 years was the series of race riots that swept twenty-two cities in the summer of 1919, from Chicago and Tulsa to Washington, D.C. Hundreds were killed, and the recorded number of lynchings mounted in 1919 to over seventy.

The Wilson administration had not intended that the drive for "100 percent Americanism" should take such vicious forms. Indeed Wilson privately—although not publicly—complained about the intolerance that war invariably fostered. But his government played a leading role in the red scare—much of it under the guidance of the attorney general, A. Mitchell Palmer. His antisubversive fervor increased by hopes of securing the Democratic nomination in 1920, Palmer sensed the public resentment against the great wave of strikes in 1919 that idled some four million workers and moved to smash a mine workers' walkout led by United Mine Workers' John L. Lewis. Events gave Palmer's crusade a further boost in 1919 when civil wars swept eastern Europe, Russia underwent its Bolshevik revolution and established the Third International to spread communism, and a series of bombings by confessed anarchists horrified the public. Palmer authorized mass raids upon radical groups, rounding up six thousand in January 1920 for interrogation and eventually deporting 600 to the Soviet Union. He predicted a huge uprising of communists on May Day 1920 and sounded the alarm: "The blaze of revolution is sweeping every American institution of law and order. . . . licking at the altars of the churches, leaping into the belfry of the school house, crawling into the sacred corners of American homes, seeking to replace marriage vows with libertine laws." Only when May Day came and went without incident did the wave of intolerance, nourished by involvement in the war, begin to ebb.

If the government's mobilization of public opinion went too far and in unnecessary directions, its management of material resources was impressive. Both Allied and U.S. forces were supplied, and the war boom brought prosperity, high employment, rising profits, and only modest inflation. Although Wilson at once demolished all of the wartime machinery of mobilization when the war ended, the 1917–18 experience had created a favorable impression of the possibilities of cooperative planning. The seeds of the military-industrial complex were planted in the world war partnership of military officials and business executives, and the experts from the universities learned their first lessons in the rewards of serving the state in the defense of liberty. The war years gave Americans a foretaste of the future they faced—a society of close business-government-university-military connections, large-scale operations, planning, and the imposed unity of a common danger. In many ways, the twentieth century began for Americans in 1917.

Impact of Mobilization

The armistice of November 1918 soon evolved into surrender; Germany was too exhausted to continue. In early 1918 Woodrow Wilson had set forth fourteen principles on the basis of which he believed a just and lasting peace could be established. Eight of the points called for adjustments of European boundaries according to the ideal of national self-determination. Five concerned guidelines for the conduct of nations in their relations with other nations: avoidance of secret treaties, freedom of the seas, removal of impediments to free trade, reduction of armaments, and impartial adjustments of colonial claims. The final point in Wilson's address urged "a general association of nations . . . for the purpose of affording mutual guarantees of political independence and territorial integrity to great and small states alike." The Allied governments thought this formula for peace too broad and idealistic and too lenient in respect to Germany. Nevertheless, they accepted it, with some reservations, as the basis for peace discussions.

Wilson's fourteen points and his country's timely entry into the war gave him a savior's reputation abroad. At home, however, the president fell into increasing disfavor with politicians and public alike. The first ominous signs of discontent appeared during the election of 1918. Voters ignored Wilson's specific appeal for an endorsement of his policies and returned Republican majorities to both houses of Congress. A reaction against the crusading zeal of the war was under way. At this inopportune moment Wilson decided to lead the American peace delegation to Paris personally. There he stood practically alone against the vindictiveness and greed of the Allies. The fourteen points had promised "open convenants of peace openly arrived

Armistice—and Fourteen Points

President Wilson and British Prime Minister Lloyd George as they appeared at Versailles toward the end of the treaty discussions of 1918–1919. (State Historical Society of Wisconsin)

at," but the treaty was drawn up behind closed doors and incorporated many secret inter-Allied territorial agreements. Many people under the treaty would not have self-determination but would live as permanent minorities in states designed with security against Germany uppermost in mind. After months of haggling, during which Wilson steadily lost ground, the Treaty of Versailles was finally presented to the Germans. While disappointed with the treaty, Wilson took hope from the fact that it provided for the establishment of a League of Nations in accord with his fourteenth point. The creation of this body, Wilson felt, justified all his concessions and, indeed, the war itself.

Even as Wilson labored at Paris, it became apparent that some of his countrymen, particularly some members of the Senate, were not in sympathy with either his ideals or his methods. Part of the president's problem was caused by his political ineptitude in failing to include a prominent Republican, or any senator, in the peace delegation. Wilson created the impression of forcing his personal conception of world organization on the country. While such self-righteous leadership had its merits in a wartime situation, it offended those seeking a return to normal conditions.

The Senate and the League

The Senate, to which Wilson presented the Treaty of Versailles, was split three ways on the question of the peace settlement. Wilsonian Democrats accepted the president's leadership and prepared to ratify the treaty, including the league, as it stood. Their number, however, was far short of the two-thirds needed for approval. Twelve to fifteen "irreconcilables" opposed the treaty absolutely. They especially feared that the league's provisions for collective security would involve the United States in an endless series of overseas wars. According to the irreconcilables, America had erred in entering World War I and should henceforth isolate itself from Europe's problems. The "reservationists," including most Republicans, would have accepted a revised treaty. They insisted upon a reduction of the authority of the league consistent with national sovereignty. Compromise on this point was intolerable to the president. "Never!" he had exclaimed when told that article 10 (U.S. adherence to the League of Nations) might have to be modified to meet senatorial objections. "Never! . . . I'll appeal to the country." In Wilson's view, the reservationists, led by Senator Henry Cabot Lodge of Massachusetts, were partisans who were tampering with fundamentals. The treaty might be flawed, but if every nation wholeheartedly adhered to the league a means of adjustment would be available and the peace secured. He feared the impact in Europe if America attached reservations. Certain of his rightness, his judgment somewhat impaired by fatigue, Wilson did indeed go to the country in September 1919 in an eight-thousand-mile speaking tour. The people, he was sure, would respond to his appeals and force the Senate to accept the League on Wilson's terms. While traveling, Wilson collapsed, the victim of a paralyzing stroke. Still he remained adamantly opposed to compromise. In November 1919 and again in March 1920 the unrevised treaty failed to win the approval of two-thirds of the Senate.

Wilson wanted the election to be "a solemn referendum on the League." And indeed the Democratic nominee, James M. Cox, endorsed U.S. participation in this first world government. If American presidential elections were held when a fundamental issue arose, perhaps Wilson's hopes would have been realized. But by November 1920 the public was tired of idealism, international crusades, and the Democrats. With twenty-six million women enfranchised, the Republicans returned to the White House behind Warren G. Harding of Ohio. He was a tall, handsome man, genial to his friends, without any enemies, and totally devoid of the driving energy and idealism that had characterized TR, Wilson, and the entire Progressive generation. In place of crusades, the public was promised "normalcy," in Harding's new word: "Not heroics, but healing; not nostrums, but normalcy; not revolution, but restoration; not agitation, but adjustment; not surgery, but serenity; not the dramatic, but the dispassionate; not experiment, but equipoise; not submergence in internationality, but sustainment in triumphant nationality." Politically, at least, the American people were now in a mood for stability, for an end to the turbulent change that had begun twenty years earlier when Theodore Roosevelt took the oath of office.

The Election of 1920: From Idealism to Normalcy

Beneath the placid surface of Harding-era politics, America was undergoing a transformation. The population continued to grow and to shift in both its occupational and locational characteristics. Americans had numbered seventy-six million when the century began; they totaled one hundred six million at Harding's election and one hundred twenty-three million at the end of the decade. The 1920 census revealed that the urban (defined as places of twenty-five hundred or more people) population had just surpassed the rural, by fifty-four to fifty-two million, and the urbanizing trend would continue. Farm workers were now outnumbered by the nonrural work force by a wide margin, eleven and a half to thirty million. People of north European stock made up 75 percent of the population, but their dominance was not considered secure. The black population was 10 percent of the total and increasing its proportion, even as black immigration out of the South jumped from the prewar figure of forty-five thousand to seventy-five thousand annually in the 1920s. Mexican-American immigration accelerated in the 1920s, and as the decade opened the flow of "new immigration" from central and eastern Europe had resumed.

Socioeconomic Change in the 1920s

To the average citizen, these changes in demographic patterns were probably less striking than the products of a new consumer era. The automobile industry led the way in the postwar industrial expansion, with 2–5 million cars a year rolling off the assembly lines that Henry Ford had perfected in 1914. An inexpensive radio receiver was in mass production by 1920, and Americans responded enthusiastically to early broadcasts of public events, such as Grantland Rice's play-by-play report of the 1922 World Series. By 1930, 618 stations broadcast daily to an audience of thirteen million families. The movie industry found a base in Hollywood, California, and lavish

Growth Industries

theaters were built in every city and town so that Americans could watch (but not hear; "talkie" movies were not common until the 1930s) Rudolph Valentino, Douglas Fairbanks, Mary Pickford, and Theda Bara. The fledgling airline industry began regular commercial flights in 1920 and was boosted by federal subsidies under the 1925 Kelly Act. In 1927 Charles A. Lindbergh's historic thirty-three-hour solo flight in *The Spirit of St. Louis* from New York to Paris dramatized the global shrinkage being worked by modern transportation modes. Along with autos, the radio, and motion pictures, the airplane shortened both physical and cultural differences between regions and classes of people and attuned the average citizen to a way of life more intensely packed with speed, movement, noise, and sensation.

Growth industries in the fields of communication and transportation were joined by chemicals, electric home appliances, and synthetic textiles. A brief recession in 1921–22 was soon overcome, and a general prosperity tinted the 1920s with optimism. Wage gains were recorded in most occupations, with real per capita income advancing by 20 percent across the decade. Inflation rates held at an astonishing average of 1 percent per year, and unemployment oscillated around 4 percent; both figures represented an economic achievement that later generations would envy. American capitalism seemed a cornucopia of good things, and few worried that the economic structure was shifting steadily toward concentration, as a merger wave absorbed some eight thousand manufacturing and commercial corporations into larger units. It was difficult to question technological and economic change so long as the national product expanded and living standards continued to climb.

Charles A. Lindbergh and his wife, Anne Morrow Lindbergh, are shown here prior to a training flight. In 1927 Lindbergh flew The Spirit of St. Louis *from Long Island to Le Bourget airport near Paris in thirty-three hours. (United Press International)*

Growth of Farm Tenancy: 1910, 1930

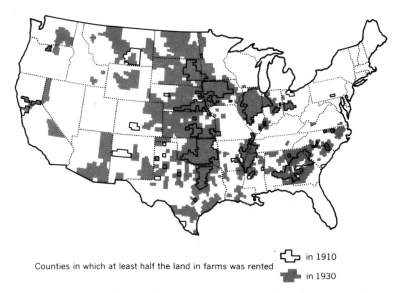

By 1930 over 42 percent of all farms were worked by tenants, and the percentage was much higher for particular crops such as cotton, corn, and wheat. Improved techniques continually expanded the capacity to produce. But the tenants rarely derived any benefits. The sturdy yeomanry of American legend had become an exploited, neglected, and rootless people.

Counties in which at least half the land in farms was rented — in 1910 — in 1930

Poverty amid Prosperity

Yet prosperity had never been completely realized. Many millions still did not earn enough to enjoy the radios, automobiles, and other consumer luxuries of an expanding economy. These were years of grinding poverty for coal miners living in company towns in West Virginia and Pennsylvania. Male and female textile mill workers were underpaid and overworked, sometimes laboring sixty hours a week for less than twenty cents per hour. Child labor was still common throughout the South. Poor whites and poor blacks lived in the festering slums of northern cities, spilling into neighborhoods that were being abandoned by the middle-class exodus to suburbia.

The economic sector that shared least in the boom of the 1920s was agriculture. The American farmer was indeed excited by the idea of prosperity, for he had had a rare sample of its merits during the war and was keenly frustrated by its disappearance with the coming of peace. Now European demands for American produce began to contract. Canada, Australia, and Argentina became more serious rivals for agricultural world markets. Americans, moreover, adopting new dietary fads, were eating less meat and starch. All these factors aggravated the old problem of overproduction. While dairy products, citrus fruits, and truck gardening flourished, traditional staples like wheat and corn did not. The 1920s were consequently a time of unrelieved recession in the large export-crop sectors, although this and other soft spots in the economy were not much noticed by the general public.

An irresistible optimism was in the air, a faith that the American business system was a flawless engine of progress. Commercial values suffused popular culture at every level—literature, art, music, the cinema, even religion. Social commentators concluded that the precepts of capitalism and Christianity were identical. An insurance company pamphlet described

Moses as "the greatest salesman and real-estate promoter that ever lived." A Rotarian boasted that his organization was "a manifestation of the divine." The best-selling nonfiction book of 1925, Bruce Barton's *The Man Nobody Knows,* called Jesus "the founder of modern business." Once a check upon the intense materialism of the New World, Protestantism in the 1920s had substantially thrown off its other-worldly leanings. A president of the era, Calvin Coolidge, gave voice to the new secularization of religion when he said: "The man who builds a factory builds a temple; the man who works there worships there."

Warren Harding had not burned to become president; that position was his wife's dream for him rather than his own. He had no sense of mission about the office, but then neither did his party, which was entirely satisfied with the status quo. He was soon a victim of the materialistic spirit of the era and his own geniality in the face of unscrupulous friends whom he had appointed to high office. His crony Charles Forbes allowed a quarter of a million dollars worth of frauds in the Veterans Bureau and was eventually sent to Leavenworth Penitentiary. The alien property custodian was convicted of taking bribes, and Harding's attorney general, Harry M. Daugherty, was forced from office under charges of receiving payments from bootleggers. The largest scandal involved Secretary of the Interior Albert Fall's lease of naval oil reserves at Teapot Dome, Wyoming, and Elk Hills, California, in return for cash, bonds, and a herd of cattle donated by petroleum company executives. "My damn friends!" Harding said in despair. "They're the ones that keep me walking the floors nights!" He died during a West Coast tour in 1923, just as the scandals were gathering momentum.

Normalcy in Politics

His successor, Calvin Coolidge, shared Harding's satisfaction with the state of economic and social affairs and ably projected the values of small-town America. He extolled thrift, Bible reading, early rising, and hard work—although he took naps each afternoon in the White House because he did not find very much to do. Above all, Coolidge was a fiscal conservative; he believed in a balanced budget and sound dollar and no government interference with business. Nine out of ten problems, he liked to say, would solve themselves if one remained calm. He remained calm, allowed himself to be photographed on his Vermont farm pitching hay, and was easily elected in 1924 with 54 percent of the vote as against the 29 percent cast for the Democrat John W. Davis. Relative prosperity aided Coolidge, as did the divisions within the Democratic party, which led it to ballot 103 times in a futile effort to choose between the "wet" Al Smith and the "dry" William G. McAdoo. The conservatism of the two major parties produced the Progressive candidacy of aging Senator Robert M. La Follette, who pulled 16 percent of the vote on a platform calling for higher taxes on the wealthy and an attack upon monopolies.

The Harding-Coolidge years were hardly a time of laissez-faire policies. They were rather an era of cordiality and cooperation between government and business. Secretary of the Treasury Andrew Mellon was able to reduce

Calvin Coolidge was a very popular president—partly because he was an astute politician and partly because his laconic style and simple tastes reminded the country of its rural childhood. He encouraged photographers to take pictures of him in "down home" poses on his Vermont farm. The final reason for Coolidge's success, of course, was that he knew when to retire. (Brown Brothers)

federal taxes on corporations, tariff protection for industry was raised in the Fordney-McCumber Act of 1922, and the economic regulation performed by the Federal Trade Commission, Federal Radio Commission, and Interstate Commerce Commission was supportive of the goals of large units in the affected industries. From his post as secretary of commerce, Herbert Hoover encouraged the trade association movement and worked to bring standardization and efficiency to the operations of American business. Federal policy throughout the 1920s was hospitable to industrial and financial mergers, unfriendly to organized labor, and oblivious to the consumer. "Never before, here or anywhere else," the *Wall Street Journal* was proud to state, "has a government been so completely fused with business."

The public mood after World War I was so militantly isolationist that U.S. membership in the League of Nations was never again seriously discussed. An American diplomat, Joseph C. Grew, even asked a newsman from the *Chicago Tribune* not to report that he had encountered Grew in front of league headquarters in Geneva. Each Republican president in the 1920s recommended that the United States join the World Court, but isolationists in the Senate were able to prevent a move for which few had much enthusiasm. It is not true, however, that the United States adopted an isolationist policy in the 1920s. It would be more accurate to say that the vast majority of citizens wanted nothing to do with the rest of the world and

Withdrawal from Europe

that the national government basically understood the necessity for American involvement in world politics but lacked both the courage and the wisdom to assume an enlightened role.

American isolationism had always applied chiefly to Europe—that tired, botched civilization from which white Americans had fled—not to Latin America or Asia, to which the American imagination reached out most naturally. European ties were to be avoided, such as by shunning membership in world governments or courts, or by turning a cold shoulder to France when it sought an alliance against Germany. There was also a disposition in Washington to ignore Europe's economic situation as well. Woodrow Wilson (also Lloyd George and Clemenceau) had been "not much interested in the economic questions" at Versailles, and the settlement had been focused on territorial issues, avoiding matters of trade, currencies, and raw materials. But continuing U.S. economic involvement with Europe was too substantial to ignore. The Allies hoped to extract thirty-three billion dollars in reparations from an exhausted Germany; they owed the United States ten billion. When Germany could not meet scheduled deadlines, the Allies slid toward default on the debt owed America. Britain, which had canceled debts owed it after the Napoleonic wars, suggested that the United States do the same. Washington would have none of it. "They hired the money, didn't they?" asked an irritated Coolidge.

Yet the interconnection of debts and reparations was compelling, and Secretary of State Charles Evans Hughes sent the Chicago banker Charles G. Dawes to Europe to arrange an international loan in 1924 to help Germany stabilize its currency and resume reparations payments. Four years later a New York financier, Owen D. Young, went on a similiar mission and scaled down the total reparation bill once again. Unfortunately America's willingness to assume some responsibility was not based on a sound grasp of the problem. The United States, as a result of the war, had become the world's creditor nation. World trade would eventually be paralyzed if that nation did not, as the British had done in the nineteenth century, run an "unfavorable" balance of trade. Allied debts could be paid and world exchange facilitated only if America allowed substantial imports and/or spent money abroad on investments or military facilities. All inter-Allied debts should have been forgiven, and American tariff barriers reduced to permit imports. But these policies would have required an unprecedented degree of vision, and this was especially lacking in all world capitals in the 1920s. World trade limped ahead on extensions of American loans, with the structure of international trade and finance weakened with unsuspected but fatal flaws.

The government was aggressively involved in the affairs of nations touching the Caribbean and the Pacific in the 1920s. Latin America had long been an exception to any isolationist doctrine. U.S. Marines controlled the political life of Nicaragua when Harding began his term, and the navy managed financial affairs in Santo Domingo and Haiti. By 1924 the United States was directing the fiscal and monetary policies of no fewer than ten Latin Ameri-

Latin America and the Pacific

can countries. To be sure, Harding withdrew American troops from the Dominican Republic, and Coolidge recalled the marines from Nicaragua. In 1927, however, when liberals in Nicaragua (backed by the Mexican government) threatened the conservative regime (backed by the United States), Coolidge did not hesitate to send in the marines once again. The United States, he announced, could not "fail to view with deep concern any serious threat to stability and constitutional government in Nicaragua tending toward anarchy and jeopardizing American interests."

A different set of problems confronted the United States in the Pacific. Americans were disturbed by the Anglo-Japanese alliance, by the swift growth of Japanese power in the Far East, and by the threat of a naval armaments race. Yet, when an international disarmament conference was convened in Washington in 1921, few of the delegates expected more than the customary rhetorical flourishes. Secretary of State Charles Evans Hughes startled the audience—and won enormous acclaim—by calling for specific and drastic arms reductions. "In thirty-five minutes," a British observer commented, "Secretary Hughes sank more ships than all the admirals of the world have sunk in a cycle of centuries." Five nations signed the Naval Limitation Treaty of 1922, which provided for a reduction of capital warships at a ratio of 5:5:3:1.75:1.75, respectively, for the United States, Great Britain, Japan, France, and Italy. In collateral treaties, both the United States and Japan joined various other nations in agreeing to respect each other's Pacific possessions and to maintain the "Open Door" in China. But promises of this sort, especially the limitation on naval tonnage, did little to adjust the realities of Pacific diplomacy to the inexorable rise of Japanese power. They were helpful first steps at checking the arms race, leaving more fundamental decisions to the leaders of the 1930s.

The optimism so characteristic of the 1920s was based upon real economic progress and international peace. Yet at times, as in the "booster" culture of novelist Sinclair Lewis's midwestern businessman George F. Babbitt, it took on a forced quality as if designed to overcome foreboding. Could the prosperity last? American Protestantism, after all, taught that humankind was sinful and retribution sure. Americans appeared to have entered a new era in which, as Herbert Hoover said in 1928, "we shall soon . . . be in sight of the day when poverty will be banished from this nation." This official optimism was widely held, but a strong undercurrent of dissent ran through the entire decade.

Undercurrents of Dissent

Since a long recession had settled in among the wheat, corn, and cotton staple sectors, it was not surprising that farmers were active in political protest. The farm bloc in Congress managed to push through several laws designed to benefit farmers: regulation of stockyard practices and trading in grain futures in 1921, aid to cooperatives in 1922, expanded rural credit in 1923. These scarcely brushed the surface of the problem, which was overproduction in the shrunken world markets of the 1920s. A scheme to have the government purchase agricultural surpluses for sale abroad (the

McNary-Haugen bill) twice passed Congress, but Coolidge vetoed it each time. Finding themselves unable to solve their economic problems through the two major parties, many farmers turned to more radical alternatives. The Non-Partisan League expanded from the base it had established in the Dakotas in 1915, and farmer-labor coalitions were formed through the upper Midwest to agitate for Federal aid and social reform. These coalesced in 1924, along with socialists, railroad brotherhoods, and elements of the prewar International Workers of the World (IWW) to found the Progressive party, which ran silver-haired "Old Bob" La Follette against the two major party candidates.

The extent of dissatisfaction with the social order was not adequately measured by the presidential vote of 1924; the reformist La Follette claimed five million votes, and two extremely conservative candidates took twenty-three million between them (fifteen million for Coolidge, eight million for Davis). Many intellectuals were deeply alienated from American life after the war, some expressing it in the decision to live abroad in Paris or London, others by writing a literature tinged with social criticism. Sinclair Lewis produced a devastating caricature of small-town life in *Main Street* (1927), and the same sentiments were echoed in the short stories of Sherwood Anderson and Edgar Lee Masters. H. L. Mencken, the Baltimore journalist, pursued the bigoted, fundamentalist "booboisie" whom he found in every rural hamlet, then denounced democracy itself. It was a time to debunk, to puncture idols. "Love," wrote Mencken, "is the delusion that one woman differs from another." And Ernest Hemingway, in *A Farewell to Arms* (1929), said, "I was always embarrassed by the words sacred, glorious, and sacrifice and the expression 'in vain'. We had heard them . . . now for a long time, and I had seen nothing sacred." This was a postwar sentiment shared by F. Scott Fitzgerald's character Amory Blaine in *This Side of Paradise* (1925), who had "grown up to find all Gods dead, all wars fought, all faiths in man shaken." This great negativism about the American culture nevertheless produced an artistic renaissance in American letters especially. Intellectuals in the 1920s were in full revolt against Victorian morality, the vulgarity of contemporary business culture, the machine age, religion, patriotism. They flourished in the same era as the sanctimonious Calvin Coolidge, and the paradox is perhaps best explained by recalling that intellectuals of that time were not interested in politics. "The great problems of the world—social, political, economic and theological—do not concern me in the slightest," wrote drama critic George Jean Nathan. They were cultural critics, but not reformers; America seemed to many of them quite hopeless. "What should a young man do?" asked the essayist Harold Stearns, and then answered: "There was nothing to do here, nothing at all. Get out of the country."

In retrospect it is clear that dissent in America during the 1920s was not confined to the complaints of a minority of impoverished farmers, or the social criticism of the intellectuals. Despite the low turnout of voters in 1924 and the virtually unchallenged hold on national political power enjoyed by a conservative Republican party, there were social problems that troubled the public deeply. The political life of the nation might present a placid exterior, as colorless men used positions of authority for banal speeches and there seemed no pressing public business to transact, but beneath this exterior the 1920s were turbulent. Economic issues receded somewhat after 1923, but cultural issues came to preoccupy millions of citizens. Rural and small-town America in the 1920s became alarmed by the urban challenge to traditional mores and values and began to agitate for reform. The prohibition movement, immigration restriction, the antievolution campaigns, and the Ku Klux Klan were the principal manifestations of the deep anxieties that perplexed the "jazz age."

Immigration Restriction

The red scare had spent itself by early summer 1920, but currents of nativism still ran strongly in postwar society, even if no longer in hysterical channels. The human tide of immigration from Europe resumed after 1918, and the drive for restriction developed irresistible pressure. A 1921 law ended unrestricted entry of aliens (recall that Chinese entry had been restricted in 1882, Japanese in 1907), and the National Origins Act of 1924 established a permanent system of quotas to achieve the goals of nativists. Under the law,

The trial (1920–1921) and execution (1927) of Nicola Sacco and Bartolomeo Vanzetti, two Italian-born anarchists, for the murder of a paymaster in a shoe factory robbery became a leading political and social controversy in the 1920s. Scholars still debate the two defendants' guilt or innocence, but no one can doubt that anti-immigrant feeling prevented a fair trial. (United Press International)

the number of aliens allowed to enter the United States from any nation was not to exceed 2 percent of those of that nationality who lived in America in 1890, with the total not to exceed one hundred fifty thousand annually. The nation now had an immigration policy, and it reflected the desire of Anglo-Saxons to ensure their numerical and cultural hegemony. Since the Western Hemisphere was exempted from the law of 1924, Mexican immigration continued through the 1920s. This flow of aliens, too, was soon shut off. By the mid-1930s the combined effects of economic depression, a stricter border patrol, and the organized repatriation drives of federal and local officials had actually reversed the movement of Mexicans. Thus, between 1921 and 1935, the great age of unrestricted migration to the United States came to an end.

The termination of unrestricted immigration was not the only product of a strong nativist current in the 1920s. After the ratification of the Eighteenth (prohibition) Amendment in 1919, Congress passed the Volstead Act, outlawing the manufacture and sale of alcoholic beverages. Support for prohibition came not only from those who thought drinking a sin against health and morals but also from rural nativists who associated drinking with the urban immigrant and who hoped through prohibition to reinforce the cultural ideals of Anglo-Saxon America. Another threat to traditional habits appeared to be the secularizing influence of modern science, in particular the theories of Darwinian biology, which conflicted with a literal interpretation of the Old Testament. Protestant fundamentalists in the 1920s mounted several state-level campaigns to outlaw the teaching of evolution in the public schools and were moderately successful in the South and Southwest. The antievolution crusade became a national issue when a young biology teacher, John T. Scopes, deliberately broke the Tennessee law in the little town of Dayton in east Tennessee. His trial in 1925 attracted to his defense the celebrated attorney Clarence Darrow, while William Jennings Bryan came to prosecute for the state under the "monkey law," which prohibited teaching that man descended from the apes. Bryan was defending not only a literal interpretation of the Bible, but an entire culture against an urban-modernist challenge. Bryan's difficulties with Darrow's sharp questions exposed the fundamentalist position to ridicule and even hilarity, yet the antievolutionist cause was not defeated either in law or in rural public opinion. Scopes was convicted and fined, the law's constitutionality was not successfully challenged, and the sentiment of rural America remained sympathetic to the suppression of the teachings of biological science. The gulf between urban and rural cultures had never appeared more vast.

The prohibition and antievolution crusades may have been misguided, but they were among the more benign forms of nativism in the 1920s. The anti-Negro feeling that had become so intense around the turn of the century showed no signs of abating after World War I. The riots of 1919 were exceptional and were not repeated, and the crime of lynching gradually

Prohibition and Antievolution Campaigns

declined (there were seventy-six reported lynchings in 1910, sixty-one in 1920, seventeen in 1925, and twenty-one in 1930). Yet the subordinate economic, social, and political position of blacks remained substantially unaltered. Anti-Semitism seemed to come more frequently into the open as the century went on, as with the lynching of the Jew Leo Frank by a Georgia mob in 1915, the battle over Louis Brandeis's nomination to the Supreme Court in 1916, the establishment of Jewish quotas at leading universities, and the publication of anti-Semitic material in Henry Ford's *The Dearborn Independent*. These animosities toward minorities were not shared by all Americans, but many felt them, and it was not long before they found an organizational outlet.

The Ku Klux Klan

That organization was the Ku Klux Klan. Revived in 1915, the Klan stagnated until about 1920, when in the climate of the red scare its membership began to climb toward a 1925 peak of four to five million. Limited to white Protestant males, the Klan was strongest in the Southwest, Midwest, and West, in cities as well as small towns, wherever white Americans from traditional rural backgrounds encountered the disturbing ethnic and cultural diversity of urban life. This "second KKK" adopted the white regalia, secrecy, and bizarre titles of the Reconstruction Klan but was somewhat less prone to acts of violence and somewhat more inclined toward political action, mass meetings, and marches. Klansmen were elected governor in Oregon and Indiana and controlled the legislature for short periods in Oregon, Oklahoma, Alabama, Texas, and other states. Once in office, Klan members sponsored sumptuary laws to reinforce the traditional mores— Sunday closing laws, the prohibition of boxing and gambling, and movie censorship. In explaining the Klan appeal, Imperial Wizard Hiram Wesley Evans wrote:

> We are a movement of the plain people, . . . demanding a return of power into the hands of the everyday, not highly cultured, not overly intellectualized, but entirely unspoiled and non de-Americanized, average citizen of the old stock. . . . These Nordic Americans for the last generation have found themselves increasingly uncomfortable, and finally deeply distressed. There appeared at first confusion in thought and opinion, a groping and hesitancy about national affairs and private life alike, in sharp contrast to the clear, straightforward purposes of our earlier years. . . . Finally came the moral breakdown that has been going on for two decades. . . . So the Nordic American today . . . decided that the melting pot was a ghastly failure . . . that an alien usually remains an alien no matter what is done to him, . . . that alien ideas are just as dangerous to us as the aliens themselves. . . . As they learned all this the Nordic Americans have been gradually arousing themselves to defend their homes and their own kind of civilization.

Election of 1928

In 1928 these cultural conflicts broke through into national politics more clearly than in 1924, when the Democrats had wrangled so long between protemperance and antitemperance candidates. Although the Republican dominance was not upset, the themes and personalities in this election provide a glimpse of the social tensions that agitated the prosperity decade.

The GOP nominated Herbert Hoover, who during eight years as secretary of commerce had built a solid reputation for efficiency and intelligence. Hoover also happened to be a perfect representative of Anglo-Saxon, rural America. He was born on a farm, college educated (Stanford), a successful businessman, married, white, "dry," and a Protestant. When the Democrats nominated New York's Governor Al Smith the stage was set for a confrontation of two Americas, the rural-traditional versus the urban-immigrant. Smith was an Irish-American, a Catholic, "wet," and a man whose speech clearly established his origins as being from the "sidewalks of New York." The men had somewhat different ideas about the functions of government, Smith being more inclined to liberalism. But the campaign did not turn on the economic or political views of the candidates; rather it was centered on cultural issues. As a Boston woman wrote in her diary, it was a contest "between two levels of civilization—the Evangelical, middle-class America and the Big City Tammany masses. . . . It is the old American, Puritan-based ideals against the new Latin ideals. . . .It is old stock agin the loose, fluctuating masses of the Big Cities. It is dry agin wet. It is Protestant against Catholic."

When the issues were stated in these terms, the outcome could not have been in doubt. Hoover cracked the solid South, taking forty of the forty-eight states with a popular majority of over six million votes. The identification of the Republicans with prosperity made a vital difference, but Hoover's election also meant that those identifying with the traditional society still outnumbered those who had been drawn into a more urban, pluralistic culture. Smith's defeat carried important portents, however. He captured most of the cities, including New York, Boston, Milwaukee, St. Louis, and San Francisco, and where the Democratic nominee of 1924 (John W. Davis) had polled eight million votes, Smith polled fifteen million. The Democratic party by nominating Smith had taken on an urban image, and the political power of urban America was growing stronger. Should a break in prosperity bring economic hardship to the less-substantial classes in rural and small-town America, they they might leave the Republican party for a union with the restless urban masses who were ready for change on social as well as economic grounds.

Stock Market Collapse

In retrospect, Smith was fortunate to lose. Americans were prepared to enjoy the millennium of prosperity that their political and economic leaders had guaranteed. "I am firm in my belief," said John J. Raskob of DuPont in August 1929, "that anyone not only can be rich, but ought to be rich." The shortest route to riches was by speculation in stock. As Herbert Hoover took the oath of office, the prices of shares were climbing far out of proportion to their normal value. By September, when the market first broke and prices started to tumble, American Can had reached 181, General Electric 396, and

"Ours is a land rich in resources," Herbert Hoover had said in his 1929 inaugural address: "In no nation are the fruits of accomplishment more secure." Seven months later came the stock market crash, and this puzzled gentleman found his sign of accomplishment very insecure. (United Press International)

Anaconda 162; two months later American Can was at 86, General Electric at 168, and Anaconda at 70. Nor was the panic over.

The stock market collapse triggered a depression for which Herbert Hoover bore the brunt of public blame, although he hardly deserved it. If Hoover erred, it was in maintaining that the depression was a temporary cyclical adjustment and that economic conditions were "fundamentally sound." By the end of 1929 more than three million were out of work. A year later that figure had doubled and a thousand banks had closed. By 1932 as factory production plummeted to 46 percent of 1929 levels, wages had shrunk from twelve billion dollars to seven billion. "How I wish," Secretary of State Henry L. Stimson noted in his diary, "I could cheer up the poor old President."

The stock market boom and bust was a symptom rather than a cause of the catastrophe. At fault was the American economic structure which, while appearing vigorous, contained fundamental weaknesses.

Causes of the Depression

1. Large parts of the American population had never shared in prosperity. No fewer than two million had remained unemployed throughout the 1920s. Farming had remained sick and neglected. Coal miners in Pennsylvania and West Virginia company towns, sharecroppers throughout the South, shoe-factory workers in New England, blacks in northern slums, all lived in poverty.
2. Industrial earnings were inequitably distributed. Too much was taken in profits—for high management salaries or stock dividends—and too little allocated for wages, which lagged behind the substantially improved productivity of workers. Some twenty-four thousand families at the top of the economic pyramid received an average income six hundred forty times greater than that of six million families at the bottom. Consumer purchasing power was therefore not great enough to absorb the goods pouring out of America's factories. In 1929 only one family in six owned an automobile, only one in ten a telephone.
3. The overextension of credit in particular areas of the American economy had been abused. Banks and other financial institutions made risky loans. One and a half million people played the stock market, many with margin (credit) accounts requiring little or no cash. The stock market crash burst the credit balloon, causing a rapid deflation.

These structural defects added up to an imbalance between productive capacity and purchasing power, reflecting a maldistribution of income. The resultant inadequate consumer demand would probably have led to a recession toward the end of the 1920s in any case because consumer credit could not forever expand to close the gap. With the collapse on Wall Street and the closing of many banks, more purchasing power was erased. A serious recession was in order unless some sector of the economy became revitalized. Agriculture was gripped by a long-range slump, and foreign trade continued to decline as a result of inadequate European recovery from the ravages of World War I. The new industries of the 1920s, especially radio and autos, had expanded to the limit of the consumer's ability to buy. A steep recession therefore set in by late 1929, with unemployment climbing from 3 percent to 9 percent of the work force in the twelve months following the crash.

Errors in Public Policy

Many of the structural flaws in the economy were perhaps beyond the remedy of responsible officials. This is particularly true of the decline of agriculture and the inherent weakness of postwar Europe. But much of the blame for the vulnerability of the American economy falls upon those who made public policy in the 1920s. First, the government failed to regulate the stock exchanges or limit excessive borrowing. Nor did the Federal Reserve system act as an effective check. "Banks," one writer has noted, "provided everything for their customers but a roulette wheel." Second, the tax structure had compounded the problem of gross inequities in the incomes of rich and poor. The Revenue Act of 1926 did lower the tax rate on small incomes, but it also halved inheritance taxes and set the maximum surtax at 20 percent. Third, while Americans sold and invested abroad, high tariff policies reduced the imports of foreign goods, and invited retaliation by other countries. In 1930, despite a protest registered by thirty-four nations and by a thousand American economists, Hoover signed the Hawley-Smoot bill, which raised the tariff to prohibitive levels. The withdrawal of American funds from overseas, and the Hawley-Smoot Tariff, hastened the financial collapse of Europe.

These policies exaggerated the structural flaws both in the American economy and in its international trade relations. One source of these policy mistakes was economic ignorance (the Democrats would have probably behaved in roughly the same way), but another was the predominant Republican view that the economy was nearly perfect in its essential outlines and that there was little for public officials to do other than shout encouragement to bankers and industrialists from the sidelines. In any event, governmental errors in economic policy were not at an end. Some economists—the "monetarists"—believe that the slump that began in 1929 would have corrected itself naturally by 1931, and the Great Depression would have been a two-year affair. In this view, the nation's economic flaws were not sufficient to account for the depth and longevity of the subsequent catastrophe. A monetary contraction from 1929 to 1931, which erased one-quarter of the money supply, was largely produced by unwise policies of national officials in the Federal Reserve system. This contraction, the argument goes, turned recession into depression.

Thus historians now disagree only over the question whether the public policies of the Roaring Twenties were more misguided than those formulated later on. The debate gives little comfort either to those who wish to believe in the soundness of the American economic system or to those who have faith in the remedial powers either of capitalists or government officials once economic breakdown begins.

COMMENTARY

"Now once more the belt is tight and we summon the proper expression of horror as we look back at our wasted youth," wrote F. Scott Fitzgerald as the Jazz Age gave way to depression. More had come crashing down in 1929 than stock prices. The collapse of a business civilization would for years discredit some of the basic assumptions of the 1920s—that the unregulated search for private gain led invariably to material prosperity for all,

that business leaders and government officials knew what they were doing, that the American system was nearly prefect. All of these ideas would revive in time, so deeply rooted were they in the national past. But for more than a decade the capitalist system would be on the defensive, and the relatively carefree hedonism of the 1920s would give way to a mood of serious introspection and receptivity to social reforms.

FREDERICK LEWIS ALLEN, *Only Yesterday* (1941)

THOMAS A. BAILEY, *Woodrow Wilson and the Lost Peace* (1944)

————, *Woodrow Wilson and the Great Betrayal* (1945)

LOIS BANNER, *Women in Modern America* (1974)

IRVING BERNSTEIN, *The Lean Years* (1960)

JOHN BRAEMAN, ed., *Change and Continuity in 20th Century America: The 1920s* (1968)

DAVID BURNER, *The Politics of Provincialism* (1968)

JOHN M. COOPER, *The Vanity of Power: American Isolationism and the First World War, 1914–1917* (1969)

E. DAVID CRONON, *Black Moses* (1955)

ROBERT D. CUFF, *The War Industries Board* (1973)

JOHN KENNETH GALBRAITH, *The Great Crash* (1955)

JOHN D. HICKS, *Republican Ascendancy, 1921–1933* (1960)

JOHN HIGHAM, *Strangers in the Land* (1955)

KENNETH JACKSON, *The Ku Klux Klan in the City, 1915–1930* (1967)

WILLIAM E. LEUCHTENBURG, *The Perils of Prosperity, 1914–1932* (1958)

N. GORDON LEVIN, *Woodrow Wilson and World Politics* (1968)

ARTHUR S. LINK, *Wilson the Diplomatist* (1957)

ERNEST R. MAY, *The World War and American Isolation, 1914–1917* (1959)

ARNO J. MAYER, *Political Origins of the New Diplomacy, 1917–1918* (1959)

ROBERT K. MURRAY, *The Red Scare* (1955)

————, *The Harding Era* (1969)

RODERIC C. NASH, *The Nervous Generation* (1971)

ROBERT E. OSGOOD, *Ideals and Self Interest in America's Foreign Relations* (1953)

H. C. PETERSON, and G. C. FITE, *Opponents of War, 1917–1918* (1957)

ANDREW SINCLAIR, *Prohibition: The Era of Excess* (1962)

GEORGE SOULE, *Prosperity Decade: From War to Depression, 1917–1929* (1947)

RUSSELL WEIGLEY, *The American Way of War* (1973)

13

Depression and New Deal, 1929–1940

Hoover and the Depression

President Hoover made his own analysis of the economic problems that were thrust upon him in late 1929 and spent three years in strenuous efforts to discover a solution that would be both effective and not in violation of his own principles. He was not successful, partially because his analysis was wrong and partially because his principles prevented him from taking important remedial measures. In Hoover's view the economy was basically sound, the depression came to America from Europe, and recovery would come only when businessmen regained confidence and began to expand their production. There was no place in this analysis for boosts in consumer purchasing power through federal fiscal policies or for the other internal reforms that economists now think were required. Hoover did not, however, believe in passively waiting for recovery. He called a series of conferences in 1930–31 to encourage investment and to plead with businessmen to refrain from laying off workers. When this did not work, he agreed to the creation of the Federal Farm Board (1929) to buy up surplus cotton and wheat, hoping to ease the farmer's problems. Without production controls the five hundred million dollars appropriated for these purchases was quickly exhausted, and agriculture remained prostrate.

The depression deepened in 1931—eight million were unemployed—and by 1932 the total out of work had reached fifteen million. Hoover agreed to a federal agency (the Reconstruction Finance Corporation) to lend money to insolvent banks, insurance companies, and railroads, but still the business community would not invest and bring recovery. Hoover was criticized for his opposition to federal relief funds to rescue the hard-pressed unemployed, but he insisted that relief would not only ruin the character of the recipients but also unbalance the federal budget, a step that would frighten the investment community. Doggedly, courageously, and probably wrongheadedly, Hoover held the line against proposals for federal relief and deficit spending. In establishing the Farm Board and the RFC and in earnestly encouraging private investment and private philanthropy, he had gone as far as he would go. Bolder measures would involve deficit financing and perhaps social reform. In Hoover's view, that would frighten the investment community, which held the key to recovery.

"Prosperity," he proclaimed, "cannot be restored by raids on the public Treasury." He was concerned about the homeless, the jobless, and the indigent, but he was committed to the idea that federal funds would harm individual initiative. "If we start appropriations of this character," he said, "we have not only impaired something infinitely valuable in the life of the American people but have struck at the roots of self-government." His decision to rely on private and local charity thus rested upon principle, but it seemed an inhuman principle to the unemployed when virtually all local relief agencies ran out of funds in 1931 and 1932.

Hoover's stubborn position on federal relief combined with his solemn, even leaden, personal temperament cast a pall of defeatism over his final months in office. The Great Engineer had tested his ideas against the depression and met abject defeat. What was not sufficiently noticed was how far Hoover had gone—reluctantly—toward the positive state: federal price supports in agriculture, a lending institution to rescue failing industry (the RFC), accelerated public works. Hoover, rather than his successor, had begun the tradition of federal responsibility for economic management. But at the end of his term all that mattered was the futility of his efforts. More people would probably have forgiven Hoover his inability to reverse such a worldwide and massive economic decline had he provided at least some spiritual inspiration. Yet he was a disciplined rather than a radiant person. "I have," he admitted, "no Wilsonian qualities." In late 1932, as the fourth winter of the depression settled in, Hoover best expressed the intellectual and political bankruptcy of his administration: "We are at the end of our tether."

The Great Depression

By the winter of 1932, at least thirteen million workers had lost their jobs. Their dependents, perhaps thirty million people, existed on vanishing savings, the dwindling reserves of private and public charity, or nothing at all. The economy spiraled down to a 1932 national income of forty-two billion dollars, just over half of the wealth produced in 1929. Factories were shut down or ran at reduced capacity. Banks failed, and foreclosures evicted Americans from homes and farms when payments could not be met. Homeless men wandered the city streets or camped out in cardboard and packing-crate shantytowns dubbed "Hoovervilles." Empty railroad boxcars carried thousands of hoboes and even children from town to town in an aimless wandering in search of something better.

Oddly enough, the general temper of the country on the eve of the 1932 election was one of hopelessness rather than revolt. There were a few exceptions to the reign of apathy and resignation. Farmers in the Midwest had formed the Farm Holiday Association in the summer, threatened a farmers' strike, and organized mass interference with farm foreclosures. The bonus army, a group of World War I veterans, had encamped near the national capitol at Anacostia Flats, Maryland, to pressure the government for early payment of a veterans' bonus, and rumors claimed that communists hoped to lead the veterans in violent demonstrations. There was indeed violence at Anacostia Flats, but only when Hoover orderd army troops under

General Douglas MacArthur to burn the camps. Scattered food riots erupted in Seattle, Detroit, Des Moines, and elsewhere, but these were isolated occasions. The overwhelming impression was one of hopelessness and despair. Business leaders paraded before congressional committees and admitted that they had no solution. "I have not," said the president of the First National City Bank of New York, "and I do not believe anybody else has."

The Election of 1932

No presidential election has ever been held amid such disastrous economic conditions, and everyone conceded that Hoover could not be reelected. The Socialists nominated the gifted orator Norman Thomas, but even three years of depression had not put the electorate in a radical mood. Thomas would poll about one million votes, a smaller percentage than Debs claimed in 1912. The alternative to Hoover was the Democratic nominee, New York Governor Franklin D. Roosevelt.

Roosevelt was something of an unknown quantity. His name, of course, was familiar and reassuring, and he had run unsuccessfully as vice-presidential candidate with James Cox in 1920. His service as governor of a large eastern state from 1928 to 1932 had proven him an able politician and administrator, a friend of public electric power, conservation, and unemployment relief. But his campaign against Hoover produced a mixture of

Defeated President Hoover joins President-elect Roosevelt for the ride to the latter's inauguration in March, 1933. Similarly dressed, they thought themselves vastly different, their transfer of power the fissure between two eras. Roosevelt, the winner, was cordial; Hoover, the loser, hardly spoke during their ride.   (Historical Pictures Service, Inc.)

themes and much evasiveness. He promised a balanced budget but talked of planning and active government. Personally he was warm, outgoing, capable of entertaining contradictory ideas at the same time, as difficult to pin down as he was to dislike. Journalist Walter Lippmann called him "a pleasant man who, without any important qualifications for the job, would very much like to be President." A bout with polio in 1923 had forced him to a wheelchair, a fact that his vitality obscured in the public mind and that may have toughened the character of this pampered only son of a wealthy Hudson River family.

Roosevelt hinted at stronger presidential leadership in the depression crisis, made no mistakes, and was easily elected by a popular margin of seven million votes and an electoral tally of 472 to 59. He spent the four months of the interregnum (until 1937, presidents were inaugurated in March) selecting a cabinet and avoiding Hoover's occasional efforts to draw him into cooperative ventures prior to his assumption of power. The winter of 1932–33 was one of the bitterest in memory, and an economically prostrate nation patiently waited through the long months of inaction that their political system placed between new public leadership and the old.

Roosevelt entered office in March 1933 without a detailed plan for economic rehabilitation. The new president did not believe in ironclad theories or immutable economic truths. Problems had to be solved or at least alleviated, and evils had to be reformed or at least mitigated by any effective democratic means. If people were hungry they must be fed. If men were unemployed jobs must be created. If industrial production was stagnant it must be stimulated. If bank failures were mounting financial aid must be extended. If agricultural prices had collapsed farming must be resuscitated. If mortgages were being foreclosed, homes must be saved. Federal action was to be the means, although Roosevelt was no socialist, and he intended government policies to heal rather than fundamentally alter the capitalist system. In his inaugural address, delivered on a cold Saturday when all the nation's banks were closed by an unprecedented collapse of the banking system, FDR avoided programmatic specifics in favor of a powerful message of action and confidence. "We have nothing to fear," he said in a memorable even if opaque sentence, "but fear itself. . . . We shall act, and act quickly. . . . I shall ask Congress for the one remaining instrument to meet the crisis—broad executive power to wage a war against the emergency . . . as if we were in fact invaded by a foreign foe."

The New Deal

Roosevelt fought the depression as if it were a war: on all fronts and with a wide range of weapons. At first his decisions tended to be cautious, traditional, deflationary, rooted in orthodox economic beliefs. Gradually, however, his strategy became more flexible, the experiments more radical, the effects more inflationary. But the New Deal was not a series of edicts rubber-stamped by a timid legislature. On the contrary, Congress often took the lead. Compromises between the executive and the legislature were

The Spectrum of New Deal Legislation

frequently necessary. Yet Roosevelt's spirit was decisive, and Congress as well as the nation followed his lead. "It is common sense to take a method and try it," said Roosevelt. "If it fails, admit it frankly and try another. But above all, try something."

Two days after his inauguration Roosevelt declared all banks closed (a bank "holiday") and placed an embargo on gold exports, a proclamation that Congress—meeting in special session—immediately approved. The Emergency Banking Act was passed forbidding the hoarding of gold, permitting the Federal Reserve system to issue notes against their assets, authorizing the Reconstruction Finance Corporation to extend loans to banks, and requiring the inspection and licensing of banks before they could reopen. "I can assure you," said Roosevelt in a fireside chat broadcast to the nation, "that it is safer to keep your money in a reopened bank than under the mattress." Within three days, seventy-five percent of the banks in the Federal Reserve system were operating. With banks' solvency assured, runs on them ceased. The stock market rose. The flow of gold from the treasury stopped. A federal bond issue was oversubscribed the day it was issued.

The Banking Act restored the confidence of bankers and businessmen, but there were other pressing problems that demanded action. Within a few months a remarkable array of relief, reform, and recovery measures began to

This man in a San Francisco breadline in 1933 projects the defeat that engulfed unemployed men with neither skills, youth, nor savings. Liberal thinkers in the 1930s broadened the idea of "waste" to include the loss of the productive energies of men such as these. (Dorothea Lange Collection, The Oakland Museum)

issue from Congress. The Federal Emergency Relief Administration was established, headed by Harry Hopkins, to extend direct relief to the unemployed. The Civilian Conservation Corps enrolled two hundred fifty thousand young men to work in the national forests. The Home Owners' Loan Corporation rescued householders from foreclosures by enabling them to refinance their mortgages. A similar law helped farmers pay their debts. The Tennessee Valley Authority was empowered to construct dams to generate hydroelectric power and to control floods. Designed to bring about the comprehensive development of the Tennessee River and valley, the TVA was authorized to market power, manufacture fertilizer, encourage soil conservation, and even build recreation facilities. By the Glass-Steagall law, investment and commercial banking operations were separated. Bank deposits were insured to five thousand dollars—a step Roosevelt did not initially favor—through the creation of the Federal Deposit Insurance Corporation. But of all legislation passed in the first one hundred days, two New Deal acts stand out as the most ambitious efforts toward national recovery: the AAA for agriculture and the NRA for labor and industry.

A perverse problem had long plagued the American farmer: the land produced too much. In Asia and Africa and parts of Europe, land was intensively cultivated and still did not yield enough to feed the people. But the American experience was different. While people elsewhere starved because of scarcity, in the United States starvation occurred in the midst of abundance. Too many hogs, too much wheat and corn and milk and cotton, resulted in rock-bottom market prices. Some crops were left to rot in the fields because they were not worth the expense of harvesting.

The Agricultural Adjustment Act

Farm leaders, meeting with Secretary of Agriculture Henry Wallace and his advisors, worked out a program that within two months became law: the Agricultural Adjustment Act. Basically the law sought to raise the purchasing power of farmers by paying them to limit specified crops. There were various methods of limiting crops, the selection left largely to the discretion of the secretary of agriculture. The one that became most common as the program developed was that of making "benefit payments" directly to the farmer for voluntarily reducing his acreage. Thus, a farmer who contracted with the government received a check in proportion to the amount of land he agreed not to plant. Payments for the program were to derive from a tax on processors of agricultural goods.

The act was riddled with ambiguities and inequities. The AAA administrators favored owners of large cotton plantations at the expense of tenant farmers and sharecroppers. Liberals and leftists in the Department of Agriculture who would not condone this bias were dismissed. The most caustic criticisms came from Norman Thomas, a much respected Socialist party leader. He believed it sheer, even criminal, idiocy to encourage scarcity in the midst of a depression. Surely, he felt, if the collective political intelligence of the United States could not conceive of a better solution, then America was intellectually bankrupt. Economists have continued to disagree on the merits of the AAA. Some have pointed to the marked rise in farm prices and farmer cash-income levels between 1933 and 1936. Many farmers prospered and the increase of their purchasing power stimulated sales of manufactured products, which in turn benefited industrial workers. Economists of the Keynesian school, however, dissented. The billion and a half dollars pumped into the farmers' pockets derived in the first instance from the processing tax. But the processor raised his prices to the middleman, who passed the increase on to the consumer. In sum, Keynesians argue, the AAA decreased the purchasing power of the general public and made no real contribution to recovery. It helped bring stability to one sector—agriculture—and installed a system of federally enforced crop controls that has lasted with minor changes to the present day. The New Deal taught farmers how to act collectively—most of them—to keep their own prices high enough to return a profit. Moving sector by sector, it attempted to do the same thing for industry.

When Roosevelt signed the National Industrial Recovery Act (NIRA) in June 1933, he called it "the most important and far-reaching legislation ever enacted by the American people." For four years, while industrial markets dwindled, and production far exceeded demand, manufacturers had felt they had no option but to cut wages. Unless workers had more to spend, however, demand could not expand. Yet individual manufacturers, faced with cutthroat competition, could hardly be expected to increase their costs unilaterally. The National Recovery Administration, a complex and imaginative agency, was designed to unravel these economic knots. By national planning and by encouraging cooperation of labor and capital, it hoped to effect a balance between industrial production and consumer demand. Each industry, according to the law, would be regulated by its own "code of fair competition," which would stipulate minimum wages and maximum hours for workers, and would set limits to production. Many of the codes would also, in effect, fix prices or at least put a floor under them. Labor would benefit by higher salaries; industry would in turn benefit by increased consumption.

National Industrial Recovery Act

General Hugh Johnson, a tough and colorful ex-cavalry officer, was chosen to administer the program. He made the Blue Eagle its symbol and, by pageantry and persuasion, attempted to arouse popular allegiance. The Blue Eagle was seen everywhere—on billboards and fences, on trees, in store windows, pasted on cars, printed on newspaper mastheads. A quarter of a million people marched down New York's Fifth Avenue in a Blue Eagle parade. But the NRA proved to be the most serious blunder of the New Deal. The Blue Eagle signs faded; their torn and dusty remnants became a mocking reminder that prosperity could not be gained by faith and ballyhoo.

The NRA never balanced production and demand. Unemployment continued to mount, and workers simply did not possess the purchasing power to stimulate the economy. Prices increased faster than wages, probably the most crucial reason for the failure of the NRA. Further, the NRA was based

TVA's Fontana Dam, on the Little Tennessee River, was completed in time to contribute its 200,000 kilowatts to the war effort. TVA represented a major national investment in a lagging region, the South, called by Roosevelt "the nation's number one economic problem." (Tennessee Valley Authority)

largely on faith rather than on coercion. Had the administration relied less on business leaders in composing the "codes of fair competition," restricted the codes to key industries, and provided adequate enforcement machinery, perhaps the NRA might have succeeded. But such was not the case. Consumer interests were hardly represented on the committees charged with drafting the codes. Moreover, the mania for regulation was carried to comical extremes. There was even a burlesque industry code containing a stipulation that no show could have more than four stripteasers. Finally, although General Johnson appealed for cooperation based on patriotism, there was widespread chiseling. Over one hundred fifty thousand violations were noted, but less than one of every four hundred was prosecuted.

Critics of the NRA were more vocal than its defenders. Labor was dissatisfied with the results of the act. Section 7A of the act guaranteed the right of collective bargaining, a right also specified in every code. Yet industrialists resented this provision and attempted to evade it. Trade unions grew amid the discontent. A rash of bitter strikes swept the nation. Progressives assailed the administration for its encouragement of monopoly and its postponement of antitrust prosecutions. Small businessmen were bitter about the higher wages they were forced to pay. The Public Works Administration, created by the act, was directed so cautiously by Secretary of the Interior Harold Ickes that its significant results were not immediately apparent. By 1935 the NRA was disparagingly referred to as the "National Run-Around." Roosevelt seemed curiously oblivious to these criticisms. He continued to preach class harmony and a team alliance of banking, agriculture, industry, labor, and capital—with himself as the quarterback. He was genuinely shocked when the Supreme Court unanimously declared the NRA unconstitutional (*Schechter Poultry Co.* v. *United States*). The *London Daily Express* announced the results in a headline: "AMERICA STUNNED; ROOSEVELT'S TWO YEARS' WORK KILLED IN TWENTY MINUTES." Actually the NRA was then beyond salvation. The Supreme Court decision was its coup de grâce.

With the New Deal stalled and the national economy still in the doldrums, other leaders began to attract audiences of respectable size. Three men in particular became nationally prominent, powerful enough to challenge Roosevelt's political hegemony.

Other Mass Leaders

Dr. Francis E. Townsend of California proposed a federal pension of two hundred dollars a month to people over the age of sixty. To qualify the pensioner had to fulfill two conditions: he could not engage in remunerative work, and he had to promise to spend the entire sum each month in the United States. Townsend attracted over five million staunch supporters, mainly elderly people who were convinced that his prescription would immediately and miraculously bring about national prosperity. Some commentators ridiculed the Townsendites as dreamers and quacks. But the fact remained that Dr. Townsend had organized older people into a potent political force. Many politicians of both parties had to cooperate with them or risk defeat. Not until 1936, as a result of corruption in their movement and the passage of the Social Security Act the year before, did the power of Townsend wane.

Father Charles Coughlin of Royal Oak, Michigan, was the only person who had more radio listeners and fan mail than the president. At first he supported Roosevelt. "The New Deal," he proclaimed, "is Christ's Deal." This alliance between God and Roosevelt did not last very long in Coughlin's mind. He, too, was emboldened to break with the administration when economic recovery was disappointing in Roosevelt's first two years. There had been too few reforms for Coughlin's taste—no effort to redistribute wealth, no attempts to break up the large corporations who subsequently dominated the NRA, almost nothing for labor, and only the limited Securities and Exchange Act (1933) to control the power of Wall Street. It was money and banking that especially obsessed Coughlin, who suspected an international conspiracy of bankers behind the world's economic woes. He touched old populist themes, calling for the monetization of silver ("the gentile money") and hinting broadly that Jewish financial interests had captured the New Deal. In 1934 he organized the National Union for Social Justice around a twelve-point platform that blended liberal and semifascist ideas in a confused mix. He attacked Roosevelt openly in his radio broadcasts and seemed eager to lead a political counteroffensive.

But among these potential mass leaders, Senator Huey Long, the Louisiana "Kingfish," was the most substantial threat to FDR and the routines of the American political system. The Louisiana governor (1928–32) had made a reputation as a clownish but determined Robin Hood, denouncing corporation control of his state and producing a record number of new roads, schools, hospitals, and public services for the poor. Elevated to the Senate in 1932 by a state legislature he had dominated by ruthless tactics, Long first seemed friendly to the New Deal. Then in 1934 he decided that its failure to attack big business and end the depression by a massive redistribution of wealth had left him an opportunity. In that year he founded the Share Our Wealth Society and emerged as a national figure. His program, like Coughlin's, was both vague and shifting, but it always included heavy taxation of the rich and a minimum income, decent housing, and free public education for all. Long was brilliant, unscrupulous, and driven by a sense of destiny. He was also successful at presenting himself as a folksy sort of man without elitist pretensions and deflated the mighty with a biting wit. (He referred to the president as "a scrootch owl," the secretary of agriculture as "Lord Corn-Wallace," and said of a high Ku Klux Klan official that "when I call him a son-of-a-bitch I am not using profanity but am referring to the circumstances of his birth.") Long demonstrated his political appeal in visits to Iowa and New York City and claimed five million members in the SOW clubs. A Democratic poll estimated that he could carry four million votes in 1936 if he led a third party effort. He was a leading part of the "Thunder on the Left" of 1934–35. His assassination in September 1935 somewhat diminished the administration's fear of a demagogue-led mass movement, but Roosevelt knew that the southern poor whites, western farmers, and urban workers who rallied to Long could be mobilized by others if the New Deal could not bring recovery.

Townsend, Coughlin, and Long were not the only forces opposed to Roosevelt. Bankers and industrialists buffeted him from another direction. They claimed that the New Deal was ruining American morale and eroding American initiative, that federal programs made people lazy, shiftless, and overdependent upon the government. They pointed to the TVA as an example of "sovietization" in the United States. Under the guise of saving capitalism, they believed, Roosevelt was introducing a creeping socialism. The American Liberty League was formed to alert citizens to the peril. Its pamphlets emphasized the need for economy and a balanced budget, states' rights, individualism, and free enterprise. Attacked from the left and right, with the economy listless and colorful competitors threatening, Roosevelt decided in 1935 that the best policy was a renewed offensive on the depression—a "second New Deal."

The American Liberty League

The early New Deal had attempted a "concert of all interests," offering something for all economic groups and avoiding undue stress upon the need for reform or redistribution. Its strategy revolved around national planning, and its style was to seek harmony among contending interests. By 1935 it was clear that the first New Deal had been promising but inadequate. Recovery had been very gradual; eleven million were still out of work, and the GNP was up only to fifty-seven billion dollars. The electorate, judging by

The Second New Deal

the burgeoning movements on left and right, seemed to be moving away from the New Deal toward both extremes. Without explicitly rejecting any of the early New Deal, Roosevelt in early summer 1935 decided to move sharply to the left. Industrialists might consider him too radical, but the workers and farmers—who had the votes—apparently thought he was too conservative.

The president led another burst of activity, this time strongly supporting measures formerly kept at arms' length—a 1935 wealth tax bill to counter Long's strength, another reform of the banking system, antitrust action against the public utility holding companies, a large ($4.8 billion) relief appropriation, a labor relations act, and the establishment of a system of old age and unemployment insurance (to counter Townsend's appeal). Conservatives might be outraged, but Roosevelt concluded that he had already lost them. While politically more radical in this second New Deal, the administration was economically more modest in its guiding strategy. Where planning had seemed the path out of depression in 1933, now the New Deal would attempt to redistribute power and wealth from the business classes toward consumers with its program of taxation and antitrust action. "The First New Deal characteristically told business what it must do," historian Arthur M. Schlesinger, Jr., has commented. "The Second New Deal told business what it must *not* do."

Of the laws enacted by the Democratically controlled Congress in 1935, three deserve special comment.

THE EMERGENCY RELIEF APPROPRIATIONS ACT   The President was empowered to spend almost five billion dollars on relief measured by this act—the single greatest appropriation in history to that date. Harold Ickes, who favored huge capital undertakings judiciously selected and rigidly supervised, wanted to control the major part of these funds. But Roosevelt chose Harry Hopkins, who favored faster spending on smaller projects. Hopkins' Works Progress Administration (WPA) put three million people to work, including artists, writers, musicians, and scientists, as well as skilled and unskilled laborers. There was some inevitable boondoggling, which made the WPA the butt of anti–New Deal jokes. The program's substantial contributions, however, could be measured by the numbers of hospitals, schools, playgrounds, and airports erected and by the enthusiastic response of Americans who felt useful after years of inactivity.

THE SOCIAL SECURITY ACT   This act provided for old-age insurance through a system of compulsory contributions by both employer and employee; a cooperative federal-state program for unemployment compensation; and a grant of federal matching funds to the states for the care of dependent mothers and children, the destitute blind and crippled. Some advocates of social insurance protested the decision to finance the system with payroll taxes, insisting that it would be regressive in its impact and a drag on recovery. They were essentially correct, but Roosevelt decided to fund social security out of special payroll taxes rather than the treasury so that workers, seeing their stake more clearly, would resist conservative attempts to repeal the law. In 1935, fear of a conservative counterattack against social security was not unfounded. One congressman reflected the near hysteria in the business community by saying that "never in the history of the world has any measure . . . been so insidiously designed . . . to enslave workers." Another predicted that "the lash of the dictator will be felt and 25 million free American citizens will for the first time submit themselves to the fingerprint test." When Roosevelt won the 1936 election, social security was safe, and time was to wrap it in the protection of popular acceptance, despite the real flaws in financing and inadequate coverage.

THE WAGNER ACT Championed by Robert Wagner of New York and belatedly endorsed by Roosevelt, this act became the legal basis for industrial unionization. The law recognized the right of workers to unionize without interference or intimidation; it specified the rules by which unions and management were to bargain collectively; and it defined a number of unfair practices. The National Labor Relations Board was created to supervise adherence to these regulations. For a long time the NLRB was regarded with suspicion, if not outright hostility, by employers. Today its supervisory value is appreciated by all parties.

Election of 1936

The political sagacity of Roosevelt's second New Deal was confirmed by the 1936 election. Roosevelt was renominated by acclamation at the Democratic convention and reelected by one of the greatest majorities in American history. Socialists and Communists had chastised him for feeding the nation aspirin tablets when surgery was called for. Their respective candidates together polled an insignificant number of votes, far less than 1 percent of the total. Townsend and Coughlin supported a third-party candidate, William Lemke of North Dakota. His "Union" ticket obtained less than 2 percent of the total. The Republicans nominated Alf Landon, the "Sunflower" from Kansas, on a platform that attacked the New Deal's "shameful waste and financial irresponsibility." Landon received less than 40 percent of the total. In fact, he carried only two states, Maine and Vermont. "As Maine goes," the Democrat, James A. Farley, gleefully wisecracked, "so goes Vermont."

Roosevelt's campaign speeches had not been as equivocal as in 1932. He lacerated the "economic royalists" and selfish forces of "organized money." He reminded audiences of the "better, happier America" created by the New Deal. He recited the list of administration reforms and promised more. John L. Lewis, director of the Congress of Industrial Organizations, helped swing a heavy labor vote to Roosevelt. The Democrats were victorious in every region, but their main and most loyal adherents came from the big cities of the North.

Blacks and the New Deal

In northern cities the black vote, which had been traditionally Republican, shifted en bloc to the Democrats. The party might contain southern racists—Senator Theodore Bilbo of Mississippi, who wished to send twelve

John L. Lewis, head of the United Mine Workers, spearheaded the formation of the Congress of Industrial Organizations (CIO) in 1935–1936, when the American Federation of Labor (AFL) proved resistant to industrial unionism.   (Wide World)

million black American citizens back to Africa, was a prime example—but no other administration had ever honored black men as did that of Franklin D. Roosevelt. Other presidents had, on occasion, invited a few select blacks to White House social functions. Roosevelt courted a large number, solicited their political advice, appointed more of them to governmental positions. The "black brain trust" and "black cabinet" were derided by some critics as nothing more than clever political strategy on Roosevelt's part. Nor did Roosevelt attempt to break the patterns of discrimination in the South. The Civilian Conservation Corps maintained a policy of strict segregation. The Agricultural Adjustment Act, as administered, victimized black sharecroppers and tenant farmers. The Social Security Act, by excluding agricultural and domestic workers from its provisions, failed to benefit huge numbers of blacks. Works Progress Administration aid was applied so unevenly, according to historian John Hope Franklin, "as to make impossible any general statement with regard to the treatment of Negroes."

Nevertheless, none could deny that the New Deal was immensely important to black people. One-third of all low-cost federal housing was built for black families; two-fifths (two hundred thousand) of the young men working in CCC camps were black; one-tenth (sixty-four thousand) of those participating in the student-work program of the National Youth Administration

Eleanor Roosevelt made a point of her sympathy for the Negro community, frequently visiting black schools and meeting with black political leaders. For this she was both loved and intensely disliked, polarizing national opinion even more than her husband, who avoided the race issue whenever possible. (The Franklin D. Roosevelt Library)

were black. Moreover, in ten years, a million blacks were employed by the WPA. Eleanor Roosevelt would have preferred her husband to be more aggressive in the field of civil rights, particularly in the removal of poll taxes and the support of antilynching legislation. But, Roosevelt told her, "First things come first, and I can't alienate certain votes I need for measures that are more important at the moment by pushing any measure that would entail a fight." The majority of blacks felt that Roosevelt was doing what he could for them, and they expressed their appreciation politically. In October 1936, when he campaigned in New York City, according to Secretary of the Interior Harold Ickes: "It was especially interesting to see the turnout of Negroes. Senator [Robert F.] Wagner remarked to me afterward that in former times Negroes would not turn out to see any Democratic candidate. There were thousands of them and they displayed great enthusiasm."

By 1936, then, Roosevelt and his party had reached the apogee of political power. The problem was to sustain it.

One obstacle seriously hindered Roosevelt's chances of continuing his program of reform. The Supreme Court of the United States had struck down the NRA, the AAA, and other New Deal laws concerning railroad workers' pensions, bankruptcy, farm mortgages, and the bituminous coal industry. The Court had even declared unconstitutional a New York state law that established minimum wages for women in certain occupations. Roosevelt feared that the Social Security Act and Wagner Act would suffer a similar fate and that further reform legislation might also be declared invalid. He was convinced that some measure to counteract the obstructionism of the Court was both imperative and justified.

Certainly Roosevelt had ample precedent for an attack upon the federal judiciary. America's strongest presidents—Jefferson, Jackson, Lincoln, and Theodore Roosevelt—had quarreled with or resented the power of the Supreme Court. Two senators recommended that the Court's historic authority be altered or destroyed. Senator Burton K. Wheeler of Montana proposed a constitutional amendment to provide that any national law held unconstitutional by the Supreme Court would be valid if reenacted by a two-thirds vote of Congress. Senator Joseph O'Mahoney of Wyoming introduced an amendment to require that a two-thirds vote of the Court, instead of a simple majority, be necessary to declare any law unconstitutional.

Supreme Court Obstacle

Roosevelt rejected the Wheeler and O'Mahoney formulas as too radical. As he well knew, the Court was an inviolable institution to many Americans, an attitude the business interests had helped to foster in the 1920s. Roosevelt did not wish to alienate a major segment of public opinion. Besides, his problem was not the Court or the Constitution but four or five old and reactionary justices who consistently voted against New Deal laws. The plan Roosevelt suggested to Congress in February 1937 was by comparison a most conservative scheme. In essence, it stated that for every federal judge who refused to retire at age seventy, Roosevelt would be permitted to appoint another—to a maximum of six new judges on the Supreme Court and forty-four in the lower courts. According to this strategy, either the reactionary justices would be frightened into resigning or the new appointees would outvote them. In either case the New Deal would be rescued.

For all Roosevelt's vaunted political acumen, court packing proved to be a tactical blunder. Neither Congress nor the country was prepared for it. Roosevelt had anticipated Republican opposition, but he had not foreseen the dissension it would cause in Democratic ranks. Progressives like Wheeler and O'Mahoney and conservatives like Senator Carter Glass of Virginia feared the precedent Roosevelt's plan might establish. Future presidents, they felt, might also decide to pack the Court. The independence of the judiciary would be seriously compromised, if not destroyed. The problem was compounded by the fact that one of the oldest judges, Louis Brandeis, was also the most liberal and respected. Obviously, the justices' age was not really the problem. The issue consumed 168 days of acrimonious congressional controversy before Roosevelt reluctantly conceded defeat.

The Court-Packing Plan

The Supreme Court did not demolish the New Deal. Before Roosevelt had submitted his plan to Congress, one of the justices, Owen J. Roberts, switched to the liberal side in a key decision. The Social Security and Wagner acts were later sustained. As old judges gradually dropped from the Court, Roosevelt filled the vacancies with appointees who were more sympathetic toward New Deal experiments. These new justices—Hugo Black, Stanley Reed, Felix Frankfurter, William O. Douglas, and Frank Murphy—dominated the Court for the next two decades. Roosevelt later claimed that his plan had frightened the judges into compliance. Perhaps this was so. But the cost in party harmony and public confidence was great.

The New Deal Court

Roosevelt never regained the degree of national loyalty and party unity he had possessed in 1936. During his second administration he had as much trouble with recalcitrant Democrats as with Republicans. His attempt to purge a dissident bloc within his party failed. A wave of violent strikes swept the automobile and steel industries. Ten strikers were killed by the police at a steel plant in South Chicago. John L. Lewis later deserted Roosevelt and advised workers to vote Republican—advice they firmly rejected—in the next presidential election. To climax these worries an economic recession took place in 1937, which, many people felt, discredited the entire New Deal.

The basic facts of the collapse are simple. By the summer of 1937 industrial production had risen 77 percent over 1932 levels; during the same period national income increased from forty to seventy-two billion dollars. Although extensive unemployment was still a problem, the nation was obviously on the path to recovery. The time had come, Secretary of the Treasury Henry Morgenthau, Jr., advised, "to strip off the bandages, throw away the crutches," and see if the economy "could stand on its own feet." Roosevelt agreed. He had never conceived of pump-priming as a permanent feature of the New Deal. Moreover, he was concerned about the national debt, which had reached thirty billion dollars. He wanted to balance the budget. Thus, in the fall of 1937 Roosevelt slashed PWA funds and cut WPA spending in half. A policy of credit contraction was also invoked. The results were disheartening. An immediate economic relapse occurred. Industrial production plummeted and unemployment skyrocketed. Five years of gradual recovery were eradicated in a few months. The national emergency seemed a replica of the 1932 crisis.

The Recession of 1937

For several months Roosevelt did little. He seemed to be waiting for the economy to recuperate naturally. Instead it steadily worsened. Roosevelt's only option was to resume large-scale government spending. He requested, and Congress appropriated, billions more for public works, work relief, low-cost housing, agricultural parity payments, and a variety of other projects. By 1938 the economic indicators began to ascend, but with discouraging slowness. Thus nagging questions remained: Was the cure real or fallacious? Was the New Deal a success or a failure?

Conservative Americans, shocked at the expansion of governmental influence in American life during the 1930s and certain that the principal impact of the New Deal had been to weaken the free market incentive system, saw in Franklin Roosevelt's tenure a deplorable revolution. Liberal friends of the New Deal accepted the term "revolution" but insisted that the changes had been reasonable, gradual, practical, and had produced in the end an economic system capable of self-correction through wise public intervention.

Time has brought perspective, calming both the fears of the enemies of the New Deal and moderating the enthusiasm of its friends. The changes brought by the New Deal did not constitute a "revolution" by any acceptable meaning of that slippery word. If one looks beneath contemporary rhetoric and the forest of alphabetical agencies and laws, one must concede the argument advanced by the "Old Left" socialists of the 1930s and the "New Left" scholars of today. The New Deal was never socialistic, even in the misunderstood TVA experiment; it did not noticeably redistribute income or wealth; it did not cripple capitalism, but stabilized it, at the price of small concessions such as the recognition of unionization and collective bargaining. The New Deal's strength among the poor, the black, the disadvantaged, was honestly earned by its intentions but hardly by its concrete results. Changes in the distribution of economic power were minor. Organized farmers and workers were helped to join the middle class and gain a stake in the system.

To these observations, often stated as criticisms, the New Dealers would for the most part have assented. They were neither socialists nor radicals, with few exceptions. Roosevelt and his liberal team intended to find a middle way between laissez-faire capitalism and socialism; they found it—a "managed capitalism" that was closer to the old system than to any revolutionary new model. To those who claim that the New Dealers failed to secure fundamental social reforms, they would answer that the obstacles were too great—economic ignorance, entrenched rural-conservative power in a southern-Democratic Congress, inadequate time. Given the obstacles, a halfway revolution, in the words of historian William Leuchtenburg, may have been all that was possible.

These are judgments based upon the main thrust of the New Deal. One must not forget certain tendencies it either set in motion or encouraged, some of them bright, some dark. The conservation record of the New Dealers was superior. It was rooted in FDR's love for the land and was expressed in the tamed rivers of the Tennessee valley, the reclaimed soils under the hoes of CCC or Soil Conservation Service workers, the shelterbelts of trees planted to resist storms of dust. Another contribution of the New Deal, which is too easily neglected, was the encouragement to cultural pluralism, to a more diverse and tolerant democracy. New Dealers guided the changeover to a more enlightened Indian policy, expressed in Indian Commissioner John Collier's administration of the Indian Reorganization Act of 1934. The New Deal's receptivity to Jews, blacks, and women was

George Gillette (left), chairman of the Fort Berthold Indian Tribal Business Council, weeps as Secretary of the Interior J. A. Krug signs a treaty selling 155,000 acres of reservation land in North Dakota to the government for use as a reservoir. "The members of the tribal council sign this contract with heavy hearts. . . . Right now the future does not look good to us." Despite the increased sympathy for Indians in the 1930s and the improved policies of Commissioner John Collier of the Indian Bureau in the 1930s, the Indian continued to lose his land and the distinctiveness of his culture. (Courtesy of Wide World Photos)

markedly warmer than that of any preceding administration. Franklin Roosevelt himself, while a classic representative of the wealthy white social elite, was a man of genuinely democratic sympathies—and so was his wife, Eleanor. In 1938 he said to an audience of the Daughters of the American Revolution: "Remember, remember always that all of us, and you and I especially, are descended from immigrants and revolutionaries." The 1930s was the decade when the American government began to shift its sympathies, to respond to previously forgotten groups in American society, and to open its ranks slowly to a more diverse sampling of American democracy.

On the other side, the imperial presidency that came to full flower in the 1970s was nurtured, if not actually born, in the 1930s. It was a crisis time—first the struggle against a crippling depression and then the war against fascism. The New Dealers responded to that era of suffering and turmoil by creating the modern interventionist state and active presidency.

Power was centralized for reasons overwhelmingly humanitarian. But history has demonstrated the ambiguities of such power, that it may be utilized in ways that threaten democracy as well as vitalize it.

The year 1940 found America poised on the eve of a great war that would *America in 1940* bring world upheaval and usher in an atomic age with boundless possibilities and dangers. The first four decades of the century had transformed the country more decisively than all but the most imaginative social prophets had foreseen. The country was now inhabited by 132 million people, producing a GNP of $100 billion (a share per capita of $761). The average American now lived to be sixty-three years of age (whites lived to be sixty-four, nonwhites, fifty-three). The rate of illiteracy had dropped to 3 percent. Most of the population lived in urban areas; five cities now counted over a million people within their limits. The farm work force had declined to 23 percent, the farm and rural population to 43 percent of the total. About a third of the farms now had electricity, the average urban white family now owned a radio and an automobile, and eighty million people attended movies—with sound and often in color—each week. After ten years of depression, the country resumed its advance into an era of material progress and men began to talk of an end to poverty.

COMMENTARY

In 1939, the future stirred in American laboratories: Harvard and IBM technicians began to construct the Mark I computer, and scientist Niels Bohr announced to a group of startled physicists that the atom had been split in a controlled experiment, releasing a potentially awesome source of power. And in that year in Europe, a former corporal named Adolf Hitler launched his German armies eastward against Poland, igniting a second world war that would fundamentally challenge and alter the American republic.

SUGGESTED READING

DAVID H. BENNETT, *Demagogues in the Depression* (1969)
CAROLINE BIRD, *The Invisible Scar* (1965)
JAMES M. BURNS, *Roosevelt: The Lion and the Fox* (1956)
PAUL CONKIN, *The New Deal* (1967)
MILTON DERBER , and EDWARD YOUNG, *Labor and the New Deal* (1958)
FRANK FREIDEL, *Franklin D. Roosevelt: The Triumph* (1956)
———, *Franklin D. Roosevelt: Launching the New Deal* (1973)
MILTON FRIEDMAN, and ANNA J. SCHWARTZ, *The Great Contraction, 1929–1933* (1965)
OTIS L. GRAHAM, *The New Deal: The Critical Issues* (1973)
DONALD H. GRUBBS, *Cry from the Cotton* (1971)
ELLIS W. HAWLEY, *The New Deal and the Problem of Monopoly* (1967)
CHARLES P. KINDELBERGER, *The World in Depression, 1929–1939* (1973)

JOSEPH P. LASH, *Eleanor and Franklin* (1971)

WILLIAM E. LEUCHTENBURG , *Franklin D. Roosevelt and the New Deal, 1932–1940* (1963)

BROADDUS MITCHELL, *Depression Decade: From New Era Through the New Deal, 1929–1941* (1947)

RAYMOND MOLEY, *After Seven Years* (1939)

JAMES T. PATTERSON, *The New Deal and the States* (1969)

ALBERT ROMASCO, *The Poverty of Abundance* (1965)

ARTHUR M. SCHLESINGER, JR., *The Age of Roosevelt: The Coming of the New Deal* (1959)

————, *The Age of Roosevelt: The Politics of Upheaval* (1960)

HERBERT STEIN, *The Fiscal Revolution in America* (1969)

ROBERT SHERWOOD, *Roosevelt and Hopkins* (1948)

BERNARD STERNSHER, ed., *The Negro in Depression and War* (1969)

REXFORD G. TUGWELL, *The Democratic Roosevelt* (1957)

T. HARRY WILLIAMS, *Huey Long* (1969)

14

War Again–Hot and Cold, 1940–1950

By the close of the 1930s, contemporaries could sense that international events were building toward a crisis that would supplant the domestic preoccupations of the depression decade. While the United States had sought democratic solutions to economic problems and largely ignored developments abroad, many other countries had turned to totalitarianism and then made preparations for aggressive war.

March of Aggression

In 1931 Japan attacked and seized Manchuria, thereby becoming the first nation to upset forcibly the uneasy status quo established at Versailles. The international community protested but could not agree upon any effective action to discourage Japan's resort to force. The fascist dictator of Italy, Benito Mussolini, sent troops to attack defenseless Ethiopia in 1935 and spoke of a new Italian empire. Adolf Hitler came to power in Germany in 1933 and stirred the German people with promises of national glory, territorial expansion, and revenge for the humiliations of 1919. In 1936 his Nazi forces occupied the Rhineland in violation of the Versailles treaty. That year civil war began in Spain when General Francisco Franco rebelled against a weak Republican government. Hitler and Mussolini supplied Franco with troops, planes, and military supplies. The Americans, like the British and French, had no intention of becoming involved, and the elected Spanish government fell to fascists who had been helped from abroad. The Spanish war did not spread, but in 1937 came the Japanese attack upon China after an incident along the Manchurian border. The war between those countries was to last until 1945 and eventually would embroil every major nation.

The Soviet government suggested joint action to force Japan to withdraw from China, but Britain, France, and the United States, meeting in conference in Brussels, declined to risk involvement. Adolf Hitler was quick to sense the weakness of Germany's democratic neighbors. In 1938 he seized Austria, then forced Czechoslovakia to yield up the Sudetenland. At a meeting in Munich in September 1938, British Prime Minister Neville Chamberlain sought to appease the German dictator's appetites by agreeing to the Czech partition. Hitler promised to make no more demands, but he was privately con-

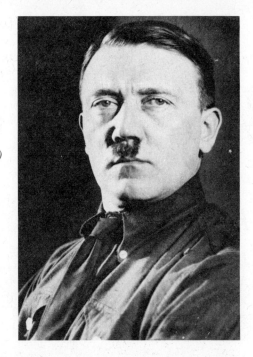

The German Fuhrer Adolph Hitler was elected to office in the same year as Franklin Roosevelt. He was to lead Germany into World War II. "What is America," Hitler was reported to have said, "but millionaires, beauty queens, stupid records, and Hollywood? A decayed country, . . . half Judaized and half negrified, with everything built on the dollar." (United Press International)

vinced that the western democracies were so afraid of war that they would not resist German expansion to the east, however brazen. He planned a move against Poland, and Winston Churchill, sensing the insatiable thirst of Nazi ambition, warned the British people:

> Do not suppose that this is the end. This is only the beginning of the reckoning. This is only the first sip, the first foretaste of a bitter cup which will be proffered to us year by year unless, by a supreme recovery of moral health and martial vigor, we arise again and take our stand for freedom as in the olden time.

American Neutrality

To many Americans the "olden time" meant World War I; they considered participation in it a monstrous error that they did not intend to repeat. Europeans, they felt, had deceived the United States by clever but specious propaganda, and they swore it would not happen again. The "faithless foreigners" had not even paid their wartime debts to Uncle Sam. Senator Gerald Nye of North Dakota conducted a congressional investigation in 1934 that exposed the unconscionable profits made by armament manufacturers and their allegedly decisive influence upon the 1917 vote for war. Woodrow Wilson's reputation was denigrated; his idealism, long repudiated, was again abused. Congress was determined to fashion a wall of neutrality legislation behind which the United States could live in peace.

The neutrality acts passed between 1935 and 1937 seriously restricted Roosevelt's flexibility in the conduct of foreign affairs. The "permanent" law of 1937 specified that the following stipulations would go into effect when the president recognized a state of war outside the Americas:

1. There would be a mandatory embargo on the export of all war supplies to belligerent powers.
2. No loans could be made to the belligerents.
3. American citizens could not travel on belligerent ships.
4. Belligerents could purchase designated goods in the United States, but only for cash, and such goods could not be transported in American vessels.

Critics protested that the neutrality acts constituted an abandonment of freedom of the seas. More important, they said, by failing to distinguish between aggressor and victim, the neutrality acts encouraged totalitarian conquests. Roosevelt's famous "quarantine speech" of October 1937 warned Americans "that the epidemic of world lawlessness is spreading," that the United States was vulnerable to attack, and that "there is no escape through mere isolation or neutrality." But critics of the neutrality acts were in a distinct minority. Isolationist strength could be gauged by the widespread public support for Congressman Louis Ludlow's proposed constitutional amendment in 1938. Except in the case of an invasion of American territory, the amendment declared, the United States could not enter a war unless a majority of the people favored it in a national referendum. Roosevelt complained that, while the Ludlow amendment might appear to be democratic and reasonable, its effect would be pernicious. He exerted considerable pressure upon Congress to defeat it. But even with the president's strong opposition the amendment failed by only twenty-one votes, 209 to 188.

Isolationism, deeply ingrained in the American mind, was not monopolized by any region, economic interest, class, or ethnic group. It rested upon traditional American assumptions—that European civilization was essentially corrupt, that the new world was both materially and intellectually self-sufficient, that the two oceans provided adequate security. World War I and its aftermath had reinforced the desire for separation from world problems, since intervention had produced so little gain and so much disappointment.

The Isolationist Position

Isolationists differed in their views but certain dominant ideas united them. They assumed that wars were usually not fought over matters of principle but to please certain ruling groups and were in any event invariably a mistake; that extensive armaments usually led to war rather than ensuring security; that Germany was either not a threat to American vital interests or could not be defeated if the United States joined in another war against the German nation. European squabbles threatened to engulf America, the typical isolationist reasoned, because of the influence of the munitions industry and international bankers upon American policy and the meddlesome instincts of some presidents. As Wilson had talked the nation into war in 1917, so Franklin Roosevelt was suspected of the same intentions in the 1930s. "The three most important groups which have been pressing this country toward war," said the aviation hero, Colonel Charles Lindbergh, a leading spokesman for the isolationist America First Committee, "are the

Wake up! Wake up, Uncle!
A contemporary cartoon reflects the president's frustration in 1940–1941 as the country reached an impasse, deeply divided between those who supported and those who opposed American involvement in the European war. (Bishop/St. Louis Star-Times)

British, the Jewish, and the Roosevelt administration." Other isolationists would have added to this list the armor plate and munitions manufacturers. The isolationist thought that the general public was firmly opposed to meddling in foreign wars, and only the manipulation of events by interventionist elites could subvert the majority will.

Lindbergh's comment reflects a tinge of anti-Semitism that was sometimes present in isolationist discussion, though it was far from characteristic. A tendency to assert conspiracy theories also cast some discredit upon the isolationist argument. When isolationists insisted that Roosevelt wanted a war so that he could become a dictator, or that Nazi Germany was invincible and perhaps "the wave of the future," or that American diplomacy in the twentieth century could still be based upon no entanglements and no obligations, the isolationists were uttering sentiments that time was to reveal as both ridiculous and tragic.

But the isolationist position was not without its insights. Some historians point out that since Hitler had no concrete and immediate plans to threaten the Western Hemisphere and since the Japanese had limited ambitions, war in both theaters may not have been necessarily the best solution available to U.S. policy makers. Certainly the isolationists were right that President Roosevelt had deceived the public on several occasions; for example, he concealed the aggressive use of American warships in helping the British to locate German submarines in the north Atlantic. And war, as the isolationists often pointed out, would greatly strengthen the presidency and encourage secrecy in government activities, developments that contained some threat to American constitutional democracy. Yet on the whole the judgment of historians upon isolationists in the 1930s has been harsh: they mis-read the nature of fascist aggression, and encouraged German and Japanese appetites by crippling the Roosevelt administration's few and admittedly tardy efforts to prepare for a deterrent role.

The Internationalist Position

Internationalists argued that America's safety depended upon Britain's survival. "It is not the water that bars the way," Secretary of State Cordell Hull warned. "It is the resolute determination of British arms. Were the control of the seas by Britain lost, the Atlantic would no longer be an obstacle—rather, it would become a broad highway for a conqueror moving westward." The internationalists maintained that isolationism was no longer a wise or tenable policy in the mid-twentieth century, when distances had contracted, strategy was global, and freedom everywhere could be endangered. They pointed out that the three militaristic regimes—the Germans, Italians, and Japanese—had signed a treaty in September 1940, which parceled the world into areas each would ultimately control. If the Nazis subjugated Britain, most of Europe, and North Africa, Hitler would next obtain footholds in South America. The fundamental issue was thus the preservation of liberty, which internationalists felt could only be preserved through collective security. The vast majority of them agreed with the organization, headed by William Allen White, called "the Committee to Defend America by Aiding the Allies." A minority advocated an immediate declaration of war upon Germany.

World War II

As conditions in Europe continued to deteriorate Roosevelt tried to persuade congressional leaders to modify the neutrality laws—to no avail. The isolationists remained unconvinced. "Well, Captain," Vice-President John Garner told Roosevelt, "we may as well face the facts. You haven't got the votes, and that's all there is to it." Where Roosevelt failed to sway Congress, Adolf Hitler succeeded. The second European war of the twentieth century started on September 1, 1939, when Nazi legions poured into Poland in a terrifying display of military might. Britain and France had previously proclaimed their determination to fight if Poland were invaded. Now both countries declared war upon Germany. Both needed munitions in order to compete with Hitler's vast military resources. "If we let this nutty Nye embargo stand as it is," wrote one senator, "Hitler, who has built up a tremendous air force and who has the most powerful army in Europe, has a chance to overrun all of Europe."

A special session of Congress debated the issue for six weeks, with considerable rancor, before rescinding the embargo on arms. The new legislation of 1939 permitted belligerents to purchase munitions from the United States on a "cash-and-carry" basis. Isolationists predicted that it was a step toward American involvement. Roosevelt maintained that there was not "the remotest possibility of sending the boys of American mothers to fight on the battlefields of Europe."

Election of 1940

Neither those who wanted war nor those who favored isolation had a real choice in the election of 1940—though the former generally voted Democratic and the latter Republican. The Democratic party renominated Roosevelt for an unprecedented third term on a platform that espoused continued aid to Britain. The Republicans sensed the changed mood of the country, rejected front-runners Thomas Dewey and Robert Taft, and selected a dark horse candidate who endorsed Roosevelt's internationalism—Wendell Willkie of Indiana.

At the outset Willkie seemed to possess the qualities necessary for victory, but one by one they turned into liabilities. He was a novice in politics, and his freshness and exuberance generated considerable enthusiasm among grass-roots Republicans. But the party professionals were openly hostile. "Willkie is slipping badly," a Democrat reported in September 1940. "This is acknowledged by Republican Senators. They laugh and joke about him." Willkie's attempt to capitalize upon the unwritten tradition that no president should serve more than two terms was less effective than had been expected. Most people did not seem to care. Particularly during a period of international crisis, the Democrats rebutted, an experienced hand was preferable to that of a rank amateur. The New Deal was no longer an issue in American politics. In fact, although Willkie outdid Roosevelt in promises of social reform legislation, the workers remained unconvinced. Polls indicated that they would remain steadfastly Democratic. Finally, in a desperate effort to win votes, Willkie predicted that Roosevelt would embroil the United States in war. "On the basis of his past performances with pledges to the people," declared Willkie, "if you re-elect him you may expect war in April, 1941." Roosevelt was forced to reply categorically—in words his detractors neither forgot nor forgave—"I have said this before, but I shall say it again and again and again: Your boys are not going to be sent into any foreign wars." Roosevelt triumphed by five million votes, the smallest plurality since 1916 when Woodrow Wilson had defeated Charles Evans Hughes under similar circumstances.

Neutral to Nonbelligerent

Within a year of the war's outbreak, Britain stood alone. Denmark, Norway, Holland, Belgium, and France fell in remarkably short order before Germany's blitzkrieg. British troops experienced a tragic defeat before their heroic evacuation at Dunkirk. When the new prime minister of England, Winston Churchill, addressed Parliament on June 4, 1940, his words were meant to be heard by Americans as well:

> Even though large tracts of Europe and many old and famous States have fallen or may fall into the grip of the Gestapo and all the odious apparatus of Nazi rule, we shall not flag or fail. We shall go on to the end, we shall fight in France, we shall fight in the seas and oceans, we shall fight with growing confidence and growing strength in the air, we shall defend our island, whatever the cost may be, we shall fight on the beaches, we shall fight on the landing-grounds, we shall fight in the fields and in the streets, we shall fight in the hills; we shall never surrender, and even if, which I do not for a moment believe, this island or a large part of it were subjugated and starving, then our Empire beyond the seas, armed and guarded by the British Fleet, would carry on the struggle, until, in God's good time, the New World, with all its power and might, steps forth to the rescue and the liberation of the Old.

The events in Europe weakened the isolationist position, and emboldened the Roosevelt administration to shift toward nonbelligerent but active involvement. Even before the fall election the president had directed a flow of military supplies toward Britain, bolstering its ability to withstand the German siege but also depleting its financial reserves. In September Roosevelt arranged to supply Britain with fifty old but desperately needed destroyers in exchange for ninety-nine-year leases on a series of naval bases in the British West Indies. Congress enacted a peacetime draft and appropriated sixteen billion dollars for rearmament. While still determined to stay out of the war, a majority of the American public had sensed the inescapable necessity to begin preparing for the worst. As journalist Walter Lippmann put it, "Before the snow flies again we may stand alone and isolated, the last great Democracy on earth."

His reelection secured, Roosevelt took his boldest step. Britain's funds were exhausted, but its need was greater than ever. Proclaiming in late December 1940 that "we must be the great arsenal of democracy," the president sent to Congress (one week later) a request for a step far beyond the "cash-and-carry" supply of arms to Britain. This was the ingenious Lend Lease idea. The United States would provide arms to Britain, which it would return after the war; thus no money would change hands. Over vigorous opposition the relatively large sum of seven billion dollars was appropriated for Lend Lease—an amount equal to all loans to the Allies in World War I and larger than the federal budget in the year Roosevelt had come into office. It was, in Winston Churchill's phrase, "the most unsordid act in the history of any nation." As Lend Lease material began to flow to the British Isles, top American and British military personnel joined to design a plan of common strategy (the ABC-1 Staff Agreement) to be used in the event of America's entry into the war.

This condition of active, pro-British nonbelligerency lasted for six agonizing months. As the battle of Britain raged in the skies over the English Channel and the city of London, the U.S. Navy aided the British fleet in protecting convoys from German submarines. In July 1941 American troops relieved British forces in Iceland. In August Roosevelt and Churchill jointly signed and issued the Atlantic Charter after a dramatic meeting off the coast of Newfoundland. One of the charter's eight principles called for "the final destruction of the Nazi tyranny." Roosevelt ordered the American navy to convoy British ships, and weeks later the U. S. S. *Kearney* and the U. S. S. *Reuben James* were torpedoed by German submarines. A state of virtual war existed between the United States and the Axis nations, but Hitler pointedly ignored the American role while President Roosevelt knew that public opinion would not permit the final step—a declaration of war. The tense autumn weeks dragged on, with World War II in a critical suspension. Then while Hitler pondered his final blow against Britain and Roosevelt watched helplessly from Washington, the Japanese took the decisive step.

The energy and industrial proficiency of the Japanese people had begun to destabilize the Pacific balance of power as early as 1904–05 when the Japanese had quickly defeated the Russians in a struggle over control of Manchuria. Its vigorous population pressing hard against limited island resources, Japan found its expansionist hopes blocked by Western colonial powers at the Versailles conference in 1919, at the London Naval Conference in 1922, during the Manchurian incident in 1931, and again when war broke out with China in 1937. To the Japanese, their ambitions for a "Greater East Asia Co-Prosperity Sphere" under Japanese hegemony were the legitimate and well-deserved aspirations of a people fated for world leadership. They regarded the opposition of the white colonial powers as cynical and hypocritical, considering their nineteenth-century record of conquest and imperialism. But to the British, French, Dutch, and Americans whose interests in the Pacific were substantial, Japanese expansionism represented naked military aggression and threatened an end of the Open Door to China and the vast potential of southeast Asia.

With France under German domination and England desperately rallying to defend its own shores, the Japanese recognized a historic opportunity. They pressed the war against China and sent armed forces to probe southward along the Indochinese coast. Only the United States had the means or the will to resist. In the summer of 1940 Roosevelt ordered the economic noose tightened in an effort to stop Japanese expansion. An embargo prohibited the export to Japan of oil, aviation gasoline, scrap metal, and other military materiel. Japanese funds in the United States were frozen. The Panama Canal was closed to Japanese traffic. Few Americans wanted war, but the majority agreed that economic sanctions against Japan were warranted.

America's coercive action forced Japan to choose among three distasteful options: to submit and abandon its conquests in Asia, to continue military expansion at the risk of economic strangulation, or to resort to an all-out offensive against the United States. While Japanese moderates cautioned restraint, their militarists advocated war; the latter view prevailed. American cryptographers had broken the Japanese diplomatic code. By late November

Pearl Harbor

1941, through intercepted messages, the United States government knew that Japan planned a large-scale military operation. American commanders in the Pacific were alerted, more than once, as a matter of routine. Nevertheless, very few believed that Japan would be audacious enough to attack American ground. The onslaught was expected to come against the British or Dutch at Singapore or somewhere in the Netherlands Indies. Then on the morning of December 7, 1941, a Japanese fleet that had been marshaled off the Kuriles broke out of the fog northwest of Oahu in the Hawaiian Islands and launched waves of air strikes against the naval base at Pearl Harbor. The brilliantly timed surprise attack caught aircraft on the ground and the American battleship fleet moored helplessly in the small harbor north of Honolulu. Some 2,335 American servicemen were killed, five battleships were sunk, and other vessels were crippled or damaged. Another Japanese force struck the American air base near Manila, destroying much of General Douglas MacArthur's air force as it sat in convenient rows on the airstrip. Monday, December 8, Congress heard President Roosevelt declare: ''Yesterday, December 7, 1941—a date which will live in infamy—the United States of America was suddenly and deliberately attacked by the naval and air forces of the Empire of Japan.'' The Senate voted unanimously, the House 388 to 1, for war with Japan. On December 11, honoring their tripartite pact with the Japanese, the Germans and Italians declared war upon the United States. The war was now global, and for four more years it would produce its harvest of death, destruction, toppled empires, and a new weapon that would bring global annihilation within the reach of man.

Within two hours after their surprise attack on Pearl Harbor on the morning of December 7, 1941, the Japanese had succeeded in damaging or destroying eight battleships, three cruisers, three destroyers and 170 airplanes, as well as important shore installations. Here the battleship California *burns after torpedo hits.*

The Japanese attack was a profound psychological blunder. Japan's war leaders had not planned to invade or defeat the United States but hoped that, beleaguered on two fronts, the Americans would eventually accept a peace granting all of Japan's demands in the Far East. But the Pearl Harbor attack united the American people as never before in a world war and created a steady determination to fight until complete victory was assured. The cost would be high. Of the sixteen million Americans who served in the armed forces, two hundred fifty-four thousand died and sixty-six thousand were missing in action. Dollar costs were estimated at three hundred twenty-one billion dollars, a sum twice as large as the total spent by the federal government from 1789 to Pearl Harbor, ten times as much as the cost of World War I. The government raised about one hundred forty billion of the cost of war from taxation and borrowed the rest, raising the national debt from forty-nine billion dollars in 1941 to two hundred fifty-nine billion at war's end.

Mobilization

To make this staggering effort, the national government quickly designed new techniques and institutions for mobilizing social energies. The revenue structure was altered to reach the incomes of more Americans and to bite more deeply into higher incomes and corporate profits. For the first time, the impact of federal taxes was sufficiently powerful, at progressive rates, to change the distribution of income in the country. The top 5 percent of income earners saw their share of disposable income drop from 26 percent in 1940 to 16 percent in 1944, an achievement that New Dealers would have envied. Roosevelt wanted Congress to confiscate all income over twenty-five thousand dollars, but few wished to impose that degree of sacrifice, and the measure was shelved. The financial resources required beyond what the revenue system brought in were raised by bond sales to banks and the public, and these were invariably oversubscribed by a public united behind the war effort and stimulated to patriotism by the publicity efforts of the Treasury Department and the Office of War Information.

Defense contracts began to lift the American economy out of depression in late 1940, and a year later unemployment had shrunk virtually to zero. The problem in wartime was not so much to achieve the required volume of defense-related production but to coordinate the complex economy to minimize bottlenecks and shortages. President Roosevelt experimented with a series of coordinating boards in a search for some central direction of the economy: the War Resources Board of 1939, the Advisory Commission of the Council of National Defense of 1940, the Office of Production Management of 1941, the War Production Board of 1942. Lines of authority were never entirely clear, there was conflict between civilian and military purchasing procedures, and Roosevelt reluctantly made the decision in 1942 to vest coordinating power in one individual, despite his concern that "the industrial czar" would come to rival the presidency. Sears, Roebuck executive Donald Nelson made some headway against the chaos of industrial mobilization as head of the WPB in 1942–43, and Roosevelt's decision to reorganize economic management under Supreme Court Justice James

Planning Production

Byrnes and an Office of War Mobilization in 1943 finally brought a reasonable degree of order.

The government's performance as industrial planner was just barely satisfactory; the production sustained by the American economy was more a reflection of the inherent strength of the nation than of any managerial genius in Washington. Depite severe labor shortages, hoarding of scarce materials, tie-ups in transportation, and mountains of governmental red tape, some three hundred thousand military planes, eighty-seven thousand tanks, sixty-five thousand landing craft and two million six hundred thousand machine guns rolled off American assembly lines. Axis and Allies alike had underestimated the speed of United States' conversion to war production, and even Americans were astonished when innovative techniques and sheer energy allowed the shipyards of Henry J. Kaiser to cut the production time for merchant ships from 105 days to 14, with one "Liberty Ship" actually turned out in just 4 days, 15.5 hours. Despite diversion to military purposes and the deliberate curtailment of civilian products such as automobiles and heavy appliances, the American economy was able to supply not only the armed forces but a growing civilian population. Living standards at home actually went up during the war, even in the face of inflation. In order to keep inflation down to the enviable four-year rate of 35 percent, the government went beyond high taxes and bond sales to extend wage and price controls throughout the economy. For some scarce commodities—rubber, gasoline, meat, coffee, sugar, and other items—a system of rationing was administered by the Office of Price Administration under advertising executive Chester Bowles.

With the government exacting sacrifices from every citizen, social and political conflict was inevitable. Average wages in manufacturing went up from $25.20 in 1940 to $43.39 in 1945, a net gain despite inflation and the slightly lengthened work week. But American workers, aware that industrial profits were high and that farmers had won from Congress a promise of price controls at 110 percent of prewar parity, felt that labor was carrying too large a share of the burden of war. The AFL-CIO had made no-strike pledges after Pearl Harbor, but rising prices drove organized labor to frequent strikes from 1943 to 1945. Small businessmen pointed out—correctly—that the lion's share of defense contracts went to the large corporations. Amid the crosscurrents of anxiety and interest-group maneuvering, the Roosevelt administration attracted mounting criticism from both its friends and its enemies. Conservatives managed to vote an end to the WPA, the National Resources Planning Board, and the Farm Security Administration by the end of 1943. Wartime controls seemed to breed a dislike of New Deal social measures. Roosevelt, sensing the shift of the public mood to the right, declared at a press conference in 1943 that "Dr. New Deal" would give way to "Dr. Win-the-War." Many liberals were dissatisfied with any moratorium on progressive legislation, arguing that the struggle against fascism abroad required an unremitting attack upon social inequalities at home. But the center of public opinion did unmistakably shift toward the conservative pole during the war years.

An American citizen, who happened to be of Japanese ancestry, waits for evacuation to a camp in the Owens Valley in 1942. *(Library of Congress)*

Evacuation of the Japanese-Americans

Compared to World War I, the war years from 1941 to 1945 were remarkable for the general absence of repression directed against internal enemies. Vigilantism against spies or disloyal persons was minimal, and Americans of German or Italian descent were not harassed. The government rounded up some spies, as well as some American Nazis and others suspected of being agents of European fascism. But socialists and other radicals were essentially unmolested, and conscientious objectors were allowed a variety of noncombatant options. Roosevelt himself had a strong respect for civil liberties, and his attorney general, Francis Biddle, was a lawyer with a scrupulous respect for citizens' constitutional rights.

This general record of moderation was deeply marred by the handling of resident citizens of Japanese ancestry and Japanese immigrants. The West Coast was swept by fears of invasion after Pearl Harbor. Its anxieties were based mostly upon rumor but occasionally were punctuated by reports of submarines sighted off the coast and the shelling of an oil refinery by a lone submarine off Santa Barbara, California. The Rose Bowl was played in Durham, North Carolina, on January 1, 1942, but by the end of that month it was clear to responsible officials that the Japanese armed forces had neither the capacity nor the will to strike the American mainland. Nonetheless, newspapers and citizens' groups created a frenzied atmosphere of distrust of the Japanese-Americans in California, Oregon, and Washington, accusing them of sabotage and treason. No case of sabotage has ever been proved. The hysteria was motivated by racism, economic resentments, and the anxieties of the worst winter for American armed forces in the Pacific. Few prominent citizens objected to the proposal of Major General John DeWitt, in charge of the Western Defense Command, to evacuate the one hundred twelve thousand alien and American citizens of Japanese ancestry. President Roosevelt, citing military advice, signed the order for wholesale removal, and army trucks rolled at once to tear the Japanese-Americans from their homes and possessions and transfer them to several hastily arranged camps located all the way from inland California to Arkansas. The Supreme Court in 1944 (*Korematsu v. United States*) decided that removal on the grounds of race was justified by the military emergency, though Justice Frank Murphy wrote a blistering dissent.

Black leaders let it be known quite early, and quite forcefully, that they would not passively endure racism at home while America fought racism abroad. A. Philip Randolph, president of the Pullman porters union, threatened a black march on Washington—a significant prelude of things to come—to demonstrate against discrimination in industry. Secretary of the Interior Harold Ickes agreed with him. "Here are ten percent of our people who are not even considered for defense jobs," noted Ickes, "while, at the same time, the color line is pretty rigidly drawn by the Army. I do not see what enthusiasm the Negroes could be expected to show in helping us defend ourselves against Hitler." The pressures worked. In June 1941 the Fair Employment Practices Committee was established to eliminate "discrimination in the employment of workers in defense industries because of race, creed, color, or national origin." By 1944 more than two million blacks were employed in defense-related manufactures, and more than a million served in the armed forces. The military remained segregated, but even here the first breaches in the color line were effected.

Black Americans and the War

In general, excepting the harsh treatment of the Japanese-Americans, there was no official vindictiveness toward any minority group as there had been in World War I. On the contrary, the Roosevelt administration attempted—by statute and by propaganda—to foster the concept of human brotherhood. Some Americans found it hard to swallow the government's message. When millions of southern blacks and impoverished whites moved to northern cities to work in war plants, several ugly incidents occurred. A race riot flashed through Detroit in June 1943, leaving thirty-four dead. The event was deplorable. It was a sign of social change and upheaval that would become even more pronounced in the decades following the war.

Despite his critics Roosevelt still seemed indispensable to most Americans in 1944. The Democrats renominated him for a fourth term, although conservative members of the party forced Roosevelt to reject Henry Wallace and accept another running mate, Senator Harry Truman of Missouri. The Republicans selected New York's Governor Thomas Dewey, a youthful, handsome, aggressive, and moderate politician of no great distinction. Dewey promised to maintain New Deal reforms and yet save the free enterprise system. Roosevelt responded that "no performing elephant could turn a hand-spring without falling flat on his back." Dewey censured Demo-

Election of 1944

cratic waste and inefficiency, which undoubtedly existed, but virtually full employment at home and approaching victory abroad counted heavily against him. Compared to the president Dewey appeared colorless and inexperienced. The peace settlements, Democrats emphasized, would require a practiced hand. Once again Roosevelt won, this time by 3.6 million popular votes and an electoral majority of 333.

Like Abraham Lincoln in 1864, Roosevelt was undoubtedly helped, in his effort to retain power, by American military successes. At first, in the months after Pearl Harbor, there had been a string of reverses. The Japanese had taken Wake Island and the Philippines from the United States and Singapore, Hong Kong, Burma, and the East Indies from the British and Dutch. Then the battle of Coral Sea in May 1942 weakened the Japanese carrier force and turned back their threat to Port Moresby in New Guinea. American forces began the long and bitter series of island assaults that brought U.S. air forces within range of Tokyo—Guadalcanal and Tarawa in 1943, Iwo Jima in 1944, Okinawa in early 1945. The Pacific became thoroughly familiar to a generation of Americans, who knew intimately the location of the scattered island chains leading northwestward to Japan—the Solomons, the Gilberts, the Marshalls, the Marianas, the Bonins, the Ryukyus. Anglo-American forces under General "Vinegar Joe" Stilwell penetrated from northern Burma into the Yunnan province of China, and in late 1944 General Douglas MacArthur landed on Leyte Island in the Philippine chain from which he had been driven in the early weeks of the war.

Campaigns in the Pacific and Europe

   The war had begun and the first reverses were suffered in the Pacific. President Roosevelt and the Joint Chiefs of Staff made the decision to concentrate American power against Hitler, however, who was considered the most dangerous enemy. Russia, reeling before German panzer divisions which had struck deep into the Caucasus, pleaded for an Anglo-American invasion of France in 1942. Churchill convinced Roosevelt instead to land in Algiers and Morroco, eventually trapping a large German force operating against the British in North Africa. Through 1943 the Western Allies chose to marshal their strength in England for a cross-channel invasion, and the Russians had to be content with the smaller Allied invasion of Sicily and Italy, where German troops put up fierce resistance. The winter of 1942–43 was Hitler's high tide, for the Russians were to drive him back from Stalingrad in the Ukraine and to inflict heavy losses. Allied planes were able to establish sufficient air superiority and bombardment techniques to rain bombs on German cities from late 1942 onward, sending one thousand planes against Cologne in one night, boldly moving to daytime raids in 1943, and eventually dropping a million and a half tons of explosives upon the soil of Germany. On June 6, 1944, came D-Day, the Overlord invasion of Normandy that involved four thousand American and British naval vessels. The Germans were driven steadily backward, fighting now on two fronts. In December Hitler launched a desperate counterattack in the Ardennes Forest, driving a "bulge" into Allied lines, which the Americans con-

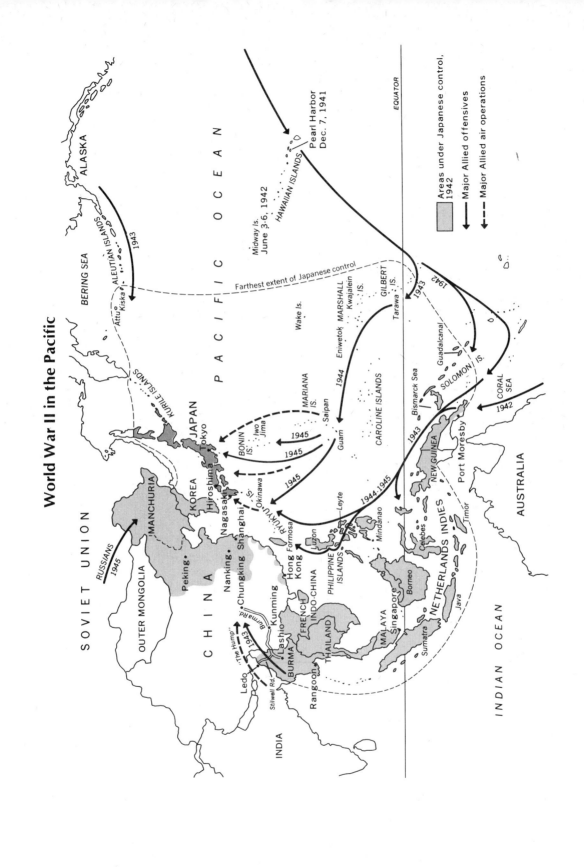

World War II in the Pacific

ALASKA

BERING SEA

ALEUTIAN ISLANDS
Attu Kiska
1943

Farthest extent of Japanese control

P A C I F I C   O C E A N

Midway Is.
June 3-6, 1942

Pearl Harbor
Dec. 7, 1941

HAWAIIAN ISLANDS

EQUATOR

Areas under Japanese control, 1942

Major Allied offensives

Major Allied air operations

Wake Is.

Eniwetok MARSHALL
Kwajalein IS.

GILBERT
IS.
Tarawa
1943

1942

MARIANA
IS.
Saipan
Guam
1944

CAROLINE ISLANDS

1945

BONIN
IS. Iwo
Jima
1945

Guadalcanal
SOLOMON IS.

1943

Bismarck Sea

CORAL
SEA
1942

NEW GUINEA
Port Moresby

AUSTRALIA

KURILE ISLANDS

JAPAN
Tokyo
KOREA
Hiroshima
Nagasaki
Shanghai
RYUKYU
Okinawa
Is.

SOVIET UNION

MANCHURIA
Peking
Nanking
Chungking
Kunming
Hong Kong
Formosa
Luzon
Leyte
Mindanao
PHILIPPINE
ISLANDS
1944-1945

OUTER MONGOLIA

RUSSIANS
1945

CHINA

BURMA
Rangoon
Lashio
Burma Rd.
1943
"The Hump"
Stilwell Rd.
Ledo

FRENCH
INDO-CHINA
THAILAND

MALAYA
Singapore
Borneo
Celebes
Timor

NETHERLANDS INDIES
Sumatra
Java

INDIA

INDIAN OCEAN

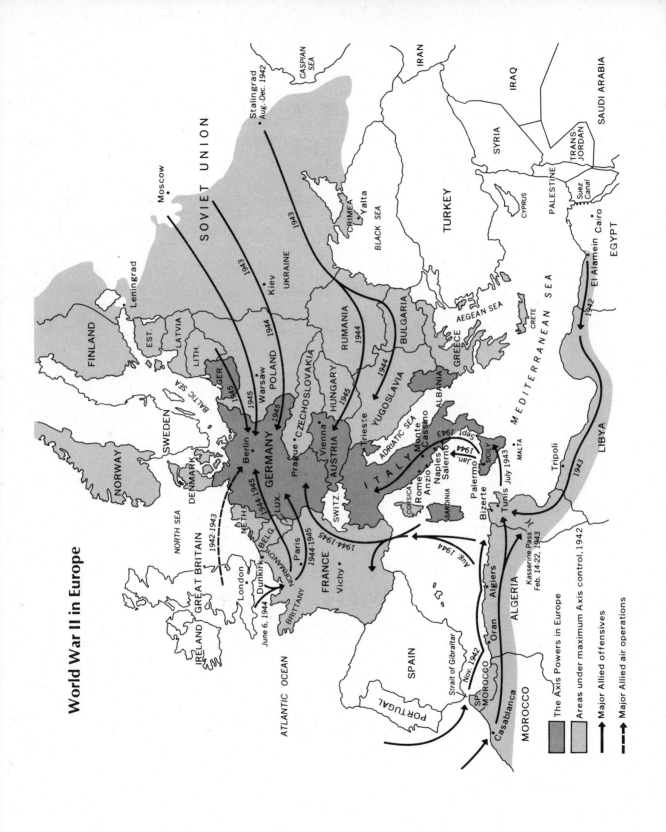

World War II in Europe

The Axis Powers in Europe

Areas under maximum Axis control, 1942

Major Allied offensives

Major Allied air operations

SOVIET UNION

Moscow

Stalingrad
Aug.-Dec. 1942

CASPIAN SEA

IRAN

IRAQ

SAUDI ARABIA

TRANS-JORDAN

SYRIA

PALESTINE

Suez Canal

CYPRUS

El Alamein Cairo

EGYPT

1942

LIBYA

Tripoli

1943

MEDITERRANEAN SEA

CRETE

MALTA

TURKEY

AEGEAN SEA

GREECE

BLACK SEA

CRIMEA

Yalta

Leningrad

FINLAND

NORWAY

SWEDEN

BALTIC SEA

EST.

LATVIA

LITH.

GER.

1945

Berlin

1945

Warsaw

POLAND

1944

1945

Kiev

UKRAINE

1943

1943

RUMANIA

1944

BULGARIA

1944

YUGOSLAVIA

1945

ALBANIA

Trieste

ADRIATIC SEA

Monte
Cassino

Sept. 1943

Jan. 1944

SICILY

Tunis July 1943

Bizerte

Palermo

Naples

Salerno

Anzio

Rome

CORSICA

SARDINIA

Aug. 1944

HUNGARY

AUSTRIA

Vienna

Prague

CZECHOSLOVAKIA

SWITZ.

GERMANY

1944-1945

LUX.

NETH.

BELG.

Paris

1944-1945

1944-1945

FRANCE

Vichy

I T A L Y

DENMARK

NORTH SEA

IRELAND

GREAT BRITAIN

London

1942-1943

Dunkirk

NORMANDY

June 6, 1944

BRITTANY

ATLANTIC OCEAN

SPAIN

PORTUGAL

Strait of Gibraltar

Nov. 1942

SP. MOROCCO

Casablanca

MOROCCO

Oran Algiers

ALGERIA

Kasserine Pass
Feb. 14-22, 1943

tained by stubborn resistance near Antwerp, Belgium. The Russians struck in January with 150 divisions, and by March the Anglo-American forces had resumed broad momentum and reached the Rhine. A few hours after Adolf Hitler committed suicide in his bunker near Berlin, Germany surrendered to the Americans. V-E Day was May 8, 1945.

Close observers thought the president looked ill during the campaign of 1944, but only a few knew that he had been suffering from cardiovascular disease for several years. By an effort of will he displayed enough physical vigor to reassure the electorate, but his doctors and friends knew that his health was rapidly declining. With the containment of Nazi Germany's last counterattack at the Battle of the Bulge in December 1944 and January 1945, Roosevelt found himself facing a set of decisions affecting the postwar world, decisions he had delayed as long as possible. One had to do with the new weapon being prepared under the army's Manhattan Project. Roosevelt had committed two billion dollars to a secret research project designed to produce an atomic weapon; if the project succeeded, the weapon promised to revolutionize both warfare and international politics. Roosevelt received advice from scientist Leo Szilard and others to share the news of the progress with our ally, the U.S.S.R., but in the autumn of 1944 the president accepted Winston Churchill's counsel to continue the policy of secrecy for the time being.

Other matters required immediate discussion with the Russians, and both Roosevelt and Churchill traveled in February to the Black Sea resort at Yalta

Roosevelt's Last Months

In February 1945 the "Big Three," Prime Minister Winston Churchill, President Roosevelt, and Premier Stalin, met at Yalta on the Black Sea. The ambiguous language of the Yalta accords masked deep disagreements among the wartime allies, especially over the future of Poland and other liberated areas in Eastern Europe. (Ewing Galloway)

to meet with Marshal Joseph Stalin. The agenda at Yalta held questions that had been glossed over or avoided at the earlier "Big Three" meeting at Teheran: Russian participation in the war against Japan, the future of Germany, the formation of a postwar organization of nations, and, above all, the territorial and political future of nations and peoples liberated from Nazi occupation. The Soviets readily agreed to join the war against Japan and cooperate in a United Nations organization. Their intentions toward liberated countries, some thought, were more ominous. Churchill expected conflict with the Soviets and at Yalta pressed for strong Anglo-American support for a Declaration on Liberated Peoples, which would commit Russia to allow complete self-determination in eastern and central Europe. As the three men met, reports came of political oppression behind the Soviet armies as they swept through Rumania, Bulgaria, and Poland. Roosevelt chose to delay a confrontation with the Soviets. On the one hand, as he had told Stalin, he "did not intend to go to war" over Soviet handling of Eastern Europe. On the other, he faced potential political difficulties at home if postwar settlements allowed a cynical Soviet domination of formerly independent nations. Stalin produced an ambiguous promise to allow democracy in Poland, and a weary Roosevelt accepted it. The Yalta conference ended in displays of goodwill. "We really believed that this was the dawn of the new day we had all been praying for and talking about for so many years," said FDR's friend and advisor Harry Hopkins. Later, when the Soviets prevented free elections anywhere in the occupied territories, it would be said that Roosevelt had given away the fruits of victory. Certainly he was a tired and sick man at Yalta. But with Russian troops in control of Poland, Roosevelt had chosen to rely upon his own diplomatic skills to ease Stalin's fears of an independent Eastern Europe and arrange an acceptable if not perfect relationship between postwar victors. Exhausted from his thirteen years in the center of decision, he traveled to Warm Springs, Georgia, in April. On April 12, while sitting for a portrait, he slumped forward with a cerebral hemorrhage and died.

Vice-President Harry S Truman of Missouri, according to the custom of the day, had been picked for the position largely because he offended no important group and while in the position had been told almost nothing and been allowed to do even less. He took the oath of office with Eleanor Roosevelt and the cabinet standing helpfully by, a humble and unpretentious man with an unexpected supply of determination. Fortunately, the war in Europe required little attention as it approached the end, and the Japanese resistance on Okinawa was broken through after bitter fighting in April and May. From Okinawa and Saipan the United States Air Force could intensify the bombing of Japanese cities by the B-29s of General Curtis LeMay's Strategic Air Command. An invasion of the main islands was planned for November 1945, and military strategists anticipated the loss of one million American lives against desperate Japanese resistance. Then on July 16 an atomic weapon was detonated on a New Mexico desert by a team of

A New President—and Victory in the Pacific

The first detonation of an atomic bomb was on July 16, 1945, at Alamogordo, New Mexico. "Now we're all sons of bitches" said one physicist to another seconds after the blast. A scientist at the University of Pittsburgh recently estimated that 400,000 infant and fetal deaths have been caused since 1951 by fallout from atmospheric nuclear tests. A typical nuclear explosion in the Pacific proving grounds is shown here. (Los Alamos Scientific Laboratory)

American scientists who witnessed its mushroom cloud with mixed feelings of elation and dread. President Truman's committee of top officials and scientists recommended that one or two bombs be used on Japan at once. Like Roosevelt before him, Truman and his advisors assumed that the bomb was built to be used and seriously considered only the most appropriate place, timing, and the issue of prior warning. Truman sailed to Europe in July to attend the Potsdam Conference; he told Marshal Stalin offhandedly that the United States had developed a new weapon but supplied no further details. He then ordered its use against Japan. Hiroshima was devastated on August 6, Nagasaki on August 9. A hundred thousand people died, and thousands more suffered dreadful burns. After an intense struggle inside the Japanese government, Hirohito forced his military officials to submit to surrender terms on August 14. The costliest war in history was over—but the peace that followed would be partial and incomplete.

War against fascism had brought the United States and the Soviet Union together in a warm but relatively short friendship. Lend Lease aid and wartime cooperation seemed to promise postwar cooperation. Yet conflict had a longer history. The United States had not welcomed the bolshevik revolution, and American troops had been sent to overturn it in 1919–20. Washington refused to recognize the U.S.S.R. until 1933, and relations even

Breakdown of the United States–Soviet Alliance

after that did not become warm between two societies of such divergent economic and political systems. Thus Soviet-American relations were a mixture of friendliness and suspicion as World War II came to its end. Roosevelt had bequeathed to his successor, Harry Truman, the broad promises made at Yalta and the delicate task of creating from them an acceptable postwar international order. He could not leave Truman his experience or his charm, but in the circumstances the value of these qualities is easily overestimated. The two nations were on a collision course and lacked a tradition of friendship and understanding. The prospects that any one man could resolve their differences were dim at best.

Relations became strained even as Germany collapsed. Invaded by the West twice in thirty years, the U.S.S.R. was determined to achieve security. Security meant a cordon of friendly states between itself and the West, along with the permanent occupation or division of Germany. That the states in Eastern Europe proposed as buffers had a deep desire for independence and were largely anti-Communist meant little to the Soviets. The Red army was master of the area, and Russian security demanded that anti-Communist elements be crushed and "friendly" governments installed. These arrangements became the center of Soviet policy as the Soviets swept westward. There is no firm evidence that in 1945 Soviet territorial ambitions extended beyond a belt of states running from Finland southward to Rumania on the Black Sea. Where those ambitions extended, however, the U.S.S.R. acted with ruthless speed and military force.

Postwar Russian Actions

American interest in Eastern Europe was recent but surprisingly strong. Not only did Americans sympathize with all national aspirations to independence, but substantial ethnic groups pressured Washington to exert its influence on behalf of their European homelands as the Soviets overran them. At Yalta Roosevelt and Churchill urged Stalin to allow elections in Poland, but Stalin, fearful that the Poles would install an anti-Soviet government, refused to give anything but vague promises. Since Soviet troops had occupied the area, a weary Roosevelt accepted the promises and hoped for the best. Yet almost at once there were reports of Soviet interference in Polish political and economic affairs. Such actions, along with Soviet hostility to suggestions that the West be allowed to send observers to Poland, led President Truman to deliver an angry rebuke to Ambassador Molotov in April 1945.

Presidential rebukes had no effect on the future of Poland. There the Soviet army, in control, helped Polish communists tighten their grip over liberated Poland. The cold war thus began in the twelve months between the spring of 1945 and the spring of 1946, as the Soviets reduced a belt of Eastern European states to subservience in the interests of Russian security, and its former allies refused to condone what was being done.

America, the U.S.S.R., and Eastern Europe

The deteriorating relations were evident at the interminable meetings of the Council of Foreign Ministers, which began in London after the Potsdam

Conference of heads of state had produced no real agreement and ran on fruitlessly for eighteen months. Treaties had to be written with the former Axis states, most of which—Hungary, Rumania, Bulgaria, and large parts of Austria and Germany—were actually under Soviet occupation. Shorn of details, the pattern was simple: the British and Americans pressed for free elections with Western observers, early removal of Soviet troops, and free access for Western economic and cultural influences. The Soviets stalled and wrangled, using the delays to ship portable wealth eastward and to hamper or eliminate non-Communist political elements. The more the Western allies urged ''open'' societies, the stronger became the Soviet determination to close them.

The future of Germany was crucial, but it was the failure to reach agreement over Eastern Europe that blocked a German settlement, not the other way around. While the United States and the U.S.S.R. had earlier agreed that Germany should be not only demilitarized but fragmented, the situation in Eastern Europe led Americans to favor restoring Germany industrially and politically to serve as a balance against the Soviets. This the Russians rejected, and a deadlock on Germany further complicated Russo-American relations. To the United States it appeared that the Soviets were deliberately obstructing the postwar settlement in order to solidify their ideological hold over the occupied territories, perhaps as a preliminary to further expansion. The Soviets, observing that the United States excluded them from participation in the reconstruction of Japan and Italy, resented U.S. protests regarding their rule in Eastern Europe, believing them to be motivated by ill will rather than altruism.

Thus almost nothing could be agreed upon in the endless discussions of reparations, territorial concessions, dispositions of colonies, and other details. Every proposal was interpreted as stemming from the worst motives. By mistake an inexperienced Truman signed the order cutting off Lend Lease aid to Russia in May 1945 when the need for it was still great. The Soviets thought it a move calculated to weaken and to intimidate them. An American offer to share atomic secrets, presented in early 1946, fell afoul of suspicions on both sides. An earlier draft drawn up by Dean Acheson and David Lilienthal was modified by a wary Truman and Bernard Baruch (who had been chosen to introduce the plan in the United Nations) to contain extra safeguards, which had the effect of permitting extensive American surveillance of the Soviet economy. The Russians, less interested in avoiding a nuclear arms race than in preventing Western interference in their internal affairs, rejected the plan.

The Cold War

Scholars are only now untangling the record of affront and counteraffront that broke apart the wartime alliance in the first year after the war, and it is far from clear that the Soviets, who suffered most from the war, had the edge in suspicion and self-assertion. By the spring of 1946 leaders on both sides began to speak openly of irreconcilable animosities. Stalin returned to the hard line in a series of speeches calling on the Soviet people for the sacrifices necessary to prepare for conflict with the West. In Fulton, Missouri, in March 1946 Winston Churchill delivered his famed "iron curtain" speech, in which he spoke of the "expansionist tendencies" of Russia and of "an iron curtain which has descended across the continent."

Truman's Response

Having become convinced that the U.S.S.R. intended to replace the German threat with its own expansion, the Truman government groped for a policy. It might conceivably have decided to grant the Soviets their sphere of influence and ignore the result, hoping that trust would not be rewarded by further demands. But the heavy Republican fire aimed at the administration because of Secretary of State James Byrnes's agreement in December 1945 to recognize Soviet-installed governments in Rumania and Bulgaria had alerted Truman to the political risk of negotiating agreements confirming a sovietization of Eastern Europe. Further, Truman and most of his advisors had themselves concluded that Soviet absorption of Eastern Europe was not a limited policy but was akin to Hitler's unlimited ambitions in the late 1930s. If anything had been learned from Munich, they reasoned, it was that such pressures must be met with prompt American resistance.

The decision to regard Soviet ambitions as unlimited was largely Truman's, and, right or wrong, it required some courage. It was another matter to back up the decision with an intelligent and successful American policy. Truman had tried firm words, beginning with Molotov, but these had produced little result beyond a feeling that he was standing for the right. More positive policies would require an awakened nation. Yet the American public in 1946 seemed in no mood for suggestions that victory had not brought the opportunity to relax. Popular pressures had forced the administration to remove wartime economic controls and demobilize the armed forces with excessive haste. Public response to Churchill's Fulton speech was generally critical, as the speech seemed to suggest a future full of sacrifices by a people weary of tension and exertion. Throughout 1946 the administration, preoccupied with problems at home and aware of its military and political weaknesses, sought a policy course more effective than rhetoric.

Truman Doctrine

A crisis in Greece in the spring of 1947 brought matters to a head. Communist insurgents in that country seriously threatened the British-supported monarchist government, and Britain informed Washington that England could afford no longer to play a supervisory role in the area. The extension of communism to Greece would menace the entire Mediterranean, and was unthinkable to the West. On March 12, Truman went before a joint session of Congress to request four hundred million dollars for military and economic aid to the governments of Greece and Turkey. He emphasized that such action was not a temporary expedient to save Greece, as important as that might be, but the beginnning of a new Truman doctrine of global application: "I believe that it must be the policy of the United States," he said, "to support free peoples who are resisting attempted subjugation by armed minorites or by outside pressures." Truman had declared himself

332   [14] WAR AGAIN—HOT AND COLD, 1940–1950

ready to apply the lessons of the Hitler era. While such a foreign policy was a break with the past, the war had so undercut the isolationist argument that the appropriation passed quickly through Congress, helped not only by the president's dramatic speech but also by the hard work of a leading Republican and converted isolationist, Senator Arthur Vandenberg.

By 1949 American assistance had enabled the Greek government to put down the insurrection. American action had been swift and successful, but many were worried by certain aspects of the doctrine. The Greek government was not popular. Was the United States to give money and arms to any government under internal pressure from communism, however incompetent, corrupt, or authoritarian that government might be? Moreover, it seemed to some critics that an essentially military response did not touch the economic backwardness and social injustice that lay at the root of political instability. They wanted the United States to come up with a policy that was directed at causes, not merely symptoms.

An answer came from a group of foreign policy experts in the state department, the Policy Planning Staff, headed by career diplomat George F. Kennan. In a memo written early in 1947, Kennan argued that Soviet territorial ambitions were indeed limitless and that negotiations with the U.S.S.R. could not at that time lead to stabilization. Yet Kennan believed that the Soviets were eager to avoid war, and he therefore urged a policy of "long-term, patient, yet firm and vigilant containment," to confine the Soviet threat until time had moderated its leadership. Such containment would necessarily be military, utilizing American strength augmented by alliances, but the analysis did not stop there. Kennan went on to urge that containment be supplemented by an attempt to cure the basic causes of totalitarianism, the economic and political breakdown resulting from war and depression.

Policy Planning Staff Analysis

The Truman doctrine had been an expression of the defensive, military side of the Policy Planning Staff's recommendations. To give form to the non-military, curative side, Secretary of State George Marshall in a speech at Harvard University announced the administration's plan for a program of economic aid to all European nations, the U.S.S.R. included. The word "communism" did not appear in the speech. The enemy was poverty and the unrest it engendered. The Marshall plan, as it was soon called, would make available to Europe a sum as large as twenty billion dollars to be administered by Europeans for their own economic reconstruction. The American Congress, alarmed by the Communist seizure of Czechoslovakia and relieved that a suspicious U.S.S.R. and its satellites refused to participate, passed the Marshall plan in early 1948 and eventually appropriated twelve billion dollars. The non-Communist countries of Europe quickly formed a Committee of European Economic Cooperation, worked out plans for the effective use of the funds, and used them to stimulate a remarkable recovery. By 1950 European economic activity was above prewar levels, a recovery which was crucial in reducing Communist voting strength in the West.

The Marshall Plan

The Berlin airlift was a strategic and psychological masterstroke, avoiding both war and a diplomatic defeat. But the drama of this Cold War incident obscured the fact that Allied plans to unify and arm an anti-communist West Germany was of deep and legitimate concern to the Soviet Union, and would continue to trouble East-West relations.   (Fenno Jacobs/Black Star)

Berlin and NATO

The American response to the problem of communism had gone beyond verbal objections to a twofold policy of military resistance and economic aid. Although the cold war was destined to intensify, the United States now possessed a policy and a bipartisan understanding of the need to make sacrifices to implement it. At times the Truman doctrine predominated. When the West moved to establish a strong West German government in June 1948, the Soviets retaliated by hampering and finally shutting off all land traffic to isolated Berlin. But Truman would neither yield nor provoke war by an armed convoy. Instead, he ordered the famed airlift of supplies to the Allied sector of Berlin, bringing in over two and a half million tons of food during the next nine months. In the spring of 1949 the Russians ended the blockade. The incident awakened Europe to the need for a military alliance to deter the Soviets, and in 1949 the United States took the lead in forming the North Atlantic Treaty Organization, a defensive military alliance of twelve nations. Congress appropriated a billion dollars for armaments to go to the signatories, thus extending to Western Europe the response Truman had made to Greece two years earlier.

At other times the Marshall plan emphasis was primary. In his inaugural address on January 20, 1949, Truman appealed to Americans to come to the aid of "the more than half the people of the world living in conditions approaching misery." This was the fourth point in his program, and "Point Four" aid in the form of technical assistance to foster economic growth in the underdeveloped countries commenced in 1950 and eventually reached a total of four hundred million dollars in American contributions.

Point Four

The containment policy did not seek to win a quick victory over the Soviet Union but to convince it to live in peace with its neighbors. It sought to make time work to Western advantage. Such a policy, promising only slow progress and requiring great patience and restraint, would never have been received with enthusiasm in a country accustomed to quick solutions. Yet Truman's foreign policy in some cases failed to produce progress at any speed.

Revolution in China

The Chinese Nationalist government had been given military and economic aid during and after the war, as it struggled first with Japanese invaders and then with Communist armies in the north. The Communists seemed to be succeeding after the war, and Chiang Kai-shek's hold on China weakened. After fact-finding missions by Generals Marshall and Wedemeyer, the Truman government judged the Nationalists' faults so great and the situation so irretrievable that it rejected an eleventh-hour proposal from Wedemeyer for the commitment of ten thousand American servicemen. Instead, it decided to continue a limited (one billion dollars) aid program and allow the Chinese to settle the future of China. The Nationalists steadily lost ground, and fled to Formosa in early 1949, leaving the mainland to the victorious Communists under Mao Tse-tung. Making the doubtful assumption that more American involvement could have rescued Chiang Kai-shek's regime without drawing the United States into an Asian ground war, Truman's critics attacked a containment policy that did not contain. But the administration held firm against pressures to prevent the Communist conquest of China and in early 1950 took some hesitant steps toward normalization of relations with the government of Mao Tse-tung. Although Korea was divided and tense, with an American-supported government in the south and a communist regime in the north, in early 1950 the cold war in Asia was much less intense than in Europe. There were even some signs of a disposition to seek accommodation. The war in Korea would shatter this prospect and decisively polarize world politics.

The end of World War II brought domestic problems as difficult as those abroad. It was impossible simply to stack the guns and resume normal activities. The government had mobilized men and women and industry and purchasing power, and it was responsible for the delicate task of reconverting these people and resources to a peacetime economy. While all Americans wanted to return to civilian pursuits, bitter and protracted disputes began over the details of reconversion, disputes that centered in Washington where the decisions would be made.

Postwar Domestic Problems

At first it seemed that nothing more was at issue than the release of controls. *Wartime Controls*
Each economic group wanted the controls on it lifted first: farmers wished
price ceilings lifted on food but not on manufactured goods, workers wished
wage but not price controls scrapped, employers reversed these priorities,
owners of rental property wanted rent control lifted. Each group expected
the government, while releasing it from restraints, to hold the line on the
other groups to prevent a rampant inflation that would wipe out all gains.

Behind the issue of economic controls lay the basic question of the role of
government in the economy. The fighting over reconversion exposed the
New Deal to new debate and attack. To its proponents, the New Deal meant
the use of government as a compensating mechanism in an economy that
chronically developed imbalances. It meant government efforts, through
taxing and spending, to balance purchasing power with productive capacity.
It meant legislation to protect the least powerful (the workers and farmers)
from the most powerful (bankers and industrialists). It meant a federal
guarantee that no American would starve or go without necessities, whether
the economy needed his services or not. When Franklin D. Roosevelt died in
1945, he left New Deal liberalism leaderless and incomplete. Future administrations might either enact the remainder or repeal it all.

To its enemies, the New Deal had always been an unnecessary interference *Postwar Conservatism*
with a free enterprise system that functioned best when left alone. They
wished to repeal not only the wartime controls on industry but the entire
New Deal structure: enforced collective bargaining, compulsory social security, minimum wages, and steep progressive taxes. They were disappointed
when in September 1945 Truman revealed himself a liberal, asking Congress
for an extension of social security, broader coverage for the minimum wage,
a health insurance program, and more river developments like the TVA.
Despite Truman's emergence as a liberal, conservatives sensed the public's
desire to be free of wartime controls, and they hoped to utilize that desire to
bring about elimination of the government programs enacted between 1933
and 1938.

This was the theme of postwar domestic politics, intricate in details but *Postwar Political
Struggles*
simple in essentials. It was soon clear that Congress would not enact Truman's program, and all of his proposals were either defeated or ignored. A
liberal bill to ensure full employment was emasculated by conservatives,
becoming the Employment Act of 1946, a measure that stated a mild federal
commitment to maintain the health of the economy. With Truman's proposals out of the way, the battle then shifted to reconversion and to fashioning a
workable compromise between inflation and controls. Truman felt that the
pent-up purchasing power of the war years—when wages and salaries had
been high, and rationing and savings bonds had kept a vast amount of
income from being spent—posed a potential inflationary threat if the price
and rent controls of the war were dropped too quickly. Congress refused to
give the president the powers he wished, passing a weak price control bill,
which he vetoed. As a result, serious inflation began in the summer of 1946,

for which the parties blamed each other. The elections that year strengthened conservatives of both parties, especially Republicans, who gained control of both houses of Congress. In June 1947 they were able to push through, over Truman's veto, the Taft-Hartley bill, canceling some of the New Deal gains of organized labor. A stalemate had been reached. The conservatives were not able to dismantle the New Deal, but neither was Truman able to extend it. Harassed on all sides by demands for relief from taxes and inflation, wrestling with crises in Berlin and China, Truman entered the election year of 1948 with little prestige and slim chances.

Election of 1948

Truman sensed, as the Republicans did not, that the country wished to retain the New Deal gains, and he ran on a strong liberal platform. Not only did he call again for strengthened welfare legislation, but he added a strong plea for federal protection of civil rights in the areas of voting, employment, and racial violence. He suffered defections on the left where Henry Wallace's Progressive party thought his foreign policy too anti-Soviet and on the right where Strom Thurmond's Dixiecrat party thought his domestic policy too pro-black. But Truman defeated his confident Republican opponent, Thomas E. Dewey, by a vote of twenty-four to twenty-one million, a verdict that was less a compliment to a spunky underdog than it was a sign that the public did not wish the New Deal endangered.

Truman's Second Term

Encouraged by the results, Truman sought after 1948 to extend the New Deal—now termed the Fair Deal—by calling for federal health insurance, assistance to blacks in search of jobs, repeal of the Taft-Hartley Act, federal aid to education and middle-income housing, and broader social security provisions. But Truman was not thought to have received any mandate in the 1948 election, and congressional committees were in conservative hands. No major part of the Fair Deal was enacted. Truman had to be content with measures that essentially extended or continued the New Deal—a major Housing Act in 1949, an extension of social security coverage, establishment of the National Science Foundation. Congressional approval was not required to integrate the armed services, which Truman set in motion with an executive order in 1948. Historians cannot agree whether the 1949 stalemate resulted from Truman's ineptitude and lack of commitment to his announced goals or to the obstacles he faced in Congress. Either way the president refused to go on the defensive. His State of the Union message in January 1950 renewed his requests for all the familiar Fair Deal measures, and he announced a new Brannan plan to shift agricultural policy toward greater benefits for small farmers and consumers. Perhaps the November 1950 elections would favor the liberals and strengthen the president's hand. "I hope," Truman remarked in early 1950, "that by next January, some of the obstructionists will be removed." As in foreign policy, the Truman administration in 1950 hoped for an opening to the left, toward renewal social reform at home and a more flexible approach to the problem of international communism. But the Korean War ended these hopes and divided the 1940s decisively from the 1950s.

Harry Truman stands with two successive secretaries of state, on his left George C. Marshall (1947–1949) and on his right Dean G. Acheson (1949–1953). One reason for Truman's stature among historians was his ability to make use of such men, whose talents exceeded his own.   (Wide World)

COMMENTARY

Journalist William L. Shirer, looking back from the year 1950, wrote that it was "a time of unparalleled violence, revolution, war, bloodshed, tyranny, confusion, and strife. My own generation had known little else. . . . One felt one was living in, as the poets and psychologists said, an Age of Anxiety, with the threat of a new war, a new revolution, a new bomb, another aggression, another crisis frightening the frenzied mind and exacerbating nerves already frayed." * It seemed that the crisis which arrived in 1929 had never eased, but merely intensified and changed its form from internal breakdown to external threat. The public life of the 1940s was overshadowed by an awareness of mortal danger. Yet things were to get worse, in June of 1950, when conflict broke out in faraway Korea. The 1950s, too, would be an Age of Anxiety.

*William L. Shirer, Midcentury Journey (Farrar, Straus and Young), 1952, p. 4.

BARTON J. BERNSTEIN, ed., *Politics and Policies of the Truman Administration* (1970)

JOHN M. BLUM, *V Was for Victory* (1976)

A. RUSSELL BUCHANAN, *The United States and World War II* (1964)

DIANE S. CLEMENS, *Yalta* (1970)

ROBERT A. DIVINE, *The Illusion of Neutrality* (1962)

HERBERT FEIS, *The Road to Pearl Harbor* (1959)

————, *The Atomic Bomb and the End of World War II,* rev. ed. (1966)

JOHN L. GADDIS, *The United States and the Origins of the Cold War* (1972)

LLOYD C. GARDNER, et al., *The Origins of the Cold War* (1970)

AUDRIE GIRDNER and ANNE LOFTIS, *The Great Betrayal: The Evacuation of the Japanese-Americans During World War II* (1969)

ALONZO HAMBY, *Beyond the New Deal: Harry S Truman and American Liberalism* (1973)

JOHN HERSEY, *Hiroshima* (1946)

GEORGE F. KENNAN, *Memoirs, 1925–1950* (1967)

GABRIEL KOLKO, *The Politics of War, 1943–1945* (1969)

WALTER LAFEBER, *America, Russia and the Cold War, 1945–1966* (1967)

RICHARD LINGEMAN, *Don't You Know There's a War on: The American Home Front, 1941–1945* (1974)

WALTER LIPPMANN, *The Cold War* (1947)

SAMUEL LUBELL, *The Future of American Politics* (1952)

DONALD R. and RUETTEN MCCOY, *Quest and Response: Minority Rights and the Truman Administration* (1973)

MARTIN J. SHERWIN, *A World Destroyed: The Atomic Bomb and the Grand Alliance* (1975)

GADDIS SMITH, *American Diplomacy During the Second World War* (1965)

HENRY L. STIMSON and MCGEORGE BUNDY, *On Active Service in Peace and War* (1948)

15

Troubled Giant, 1950–1960

The Great Divide: War in Korea

At the start of 1950 the Truman administration had some grounds for hope that its domestic policies would begin to move through Congress that year or the next. The president continued to press for his Fair Deal reforms, and the autumn elections might strengthen his party. In foreign affairs, the Marshall plan and NATO had apparently begun to restore the strength and confidence of the Western democracies, and the administration privately planned to move toward an accommodation with the Red Chinese as one way of containing Russian communism. Then misfortune struck; in June the North Koreans suddenly attacked the forces of Syngman Rhee's South Korean government. In a speech earlier that year Secretary of State Dean Acheson had described Korea as lying outside the perimeter of vital American interests, but the attack altered the administration's thinking. Acting quickly, President Truman committed United States troops just five days after the outbreak of the conflict, without asking Congress for a declaration of war. The U.S. also secured United Nations condemnation of the North Korean action.

For a time the South Korean–American forces were driven rapidly toward the tip of the peninsula and apparent defeat, but General Douglas MacArthur broke out of the perimeter at Pusan by executing a daring amphibious landing on the east coast near Inchon. As MacArthur's forces drove the enemy northward, Truman was faced with a difficult decision. His intention from the beginning was to prevent the alteration of the world balance of power through force. It had been no part of American thinking to reunite Korea or to achieve military victory for its own sake. To deny the fruits of aggression had been the central purpose. The limits within which Truman intended to operate became clearer in November 1950. MacArthur was weeks away from conquering all North Korea, when the Chinese intervened in overwhelming numbers and brought the United Nations force close to disaster. Truman refused to sanction the use of nuclear weapons or bombing north of the Yalu River into China (once he was certain the U.N. force would not be driven into the sea), although MacArthur openly demanded such action. A truce finally ended the war without victory for either side, and troops withdrew along a truce line approximating the original border

...oving in single file through a soggy ... paddy field in South Korea, a ...m carrying gun ammunitions ...wly advances toward the front ...es.   (Acme photo by Ed Hoffman, ...ff photographer)

between North and South Korea. Truman's decision rested upon a judgment that the European theater was primary and that the U.S. buildup there was hampered by diverting men and arms to Asia. The joint chiefs of staff supported the president, agreeing with General Omar Bradley that an enlarged war with China would be "the wrong war, in the wrong place, at the wrong time." The decision to subordinate Korea to global concerns and to accept a stalemate brought home to Americans the many frustrations of the containment policy.

The president's chief critic was General MacArthur himself, who made no secret of his objection to Truman's political restraints. Faced with virtual insubordination, Truman removed MacArthur from command, bringing on himself a storm of denunciation. For weeks, until cooler heads prevailed, the general (who returned to tour the country and address Congress) was spectacularly popular and the president was in disrepute. Truman bore the criticism in silence, learning how great were the psychological costs of a policy of limited counterforce. His foreign policy continued to generate enemies, to the right and the left, who sought to alter it or seize the presidency. On the left, Henry A. Wallace, a New Dealer who had been close to Roosevelt, broke with Truman in 1946 when he felt that the president was making unreasonable demands on the Soviet Union, and ran unsuccessfully for president in 1948 on a platform calling for reduced cold war tensions and accommodation with Russia. More numerous were critics on the right, who felt that the United States should use its overwhelming military power to defeat communist movements everywhere, including some who would like to eliminate communism at its source by a "preventive" nuclear strike on Moscow. These hard-line critics, some of them prominent Republicans like Senators Taft, McCarthy, and Jenner, stepped up their attacks as the administration's Far Eastern policy "lost" in China and "tied" in Korea. The administration seemed to have few supporters as Truman's second term came to an end.

Truman's Critics

The outbreak of a war in Asia that required great sacrifices (including the lives of fifty-five thousand Americans) without the satisfaction of victory served to dash the administration's hopes for domestic reforms and to harden the lines of cold war politics. Shortly after the North Korean attack, Truman ordered the Seventh Fleet to protect the Nationalist Chinese remnant on Formosa by patroling the strait between the island and the mainland. Any thought of normalization of relations with Red China was shattered by the Chinese entry into the war in November. For more than twenty years the United States would build its Far Eastern diplomacy upon the theory that the legitimate China was on Taiwan, not in Peking, and upon the assumption that world communism was monolithic and must be dealt with similarly everywhere. The war required wage and price controls and, more important, large defense expenditures that reversed the gradual shrinkage of defense spending Truman had struggled to achieve in 1948–49. The administration

Impact of the Korean War

now accepted without reserve the argument of an influential National Security Council memo (NSC-68) that United States spending on defense ought to be vastly increased—perhaps as high as 20 percent of the gross national product. The cold war had heated up and its alignments had hardened. And the arms race had broken through the few barriers that contained it before the Korean War erupted.

Perhaps because World War II had not been fought with the same sense of exaggerated hopes and fears as World War I, it had not been immediately followed by an orgy of repression and vigilantism against domestic dissidents. The postwar mood may have been conservative, but it was not irrational, and the Truman administration had no interest in fanning the flames of nativism or superpatriotism. Yet postwar developments placed a great strain upon the public's basic optimism and sense of tolerance. Inflation followed the lifting of wartime controls, taxes did not seem to return to prewar levels, government regulation did not disappear. But far more important, the postwar years saw a series of stunning gains for communism—a resurgent and expansionist U.S.S.R., the addition of one-quarter of the world's population to "the communist side" when the Chinese revolution succeeded in 1949. The tiny but active Communist party of the United States worried many people, whose anxieties were heightened by the trials for espionage of Ethel and Julius Rosenberg (arrested in 1946) and Alger Hiss (arrested in 1948).

Yet in the twentieth-century American experience, red scares do not arise spontaneously out of an anxious population. They are catalyzed and guided by elected and appointed public officials, who have careers to build, and by the news media, who have a product to sell. *Life* magazine told the public as early as 1945 that "the 'fellow traveler' is everywhere," a message frequently repeated by other parts of the press and from pulpit and platform. The Truman administration did not long remain aloof from the concern about subversion. Shaken by charges that its foreign policies were "soft on communism" and its attitude toward internal radicalism and espionage was lax, the administration in 1947 instituted a new loyalty program for government employees. Attorney General Thomas Clark conducted the program with more zeal for results than respect for civil liberties, and many employees were dismissed without a fair hearing. Clark and Truman launched the program partly to head off a congressional witch hunt but also because they shared a deep alarm about domestic communist infiltration. Truman's foreign policy rhetoric describing a world polarized between "free" and "captive" nations contributed to the feeling that a person who was not a fierce anticommunist must probably be a communist. The internal threat was magnified by FBI director J. Edgar Hoover in a series of speeches and articles in the late 1940s, but no administration official went beyond Attorney General J. Howard McGrath in 1950, when he declared, "There are today many communists in America. They are everywhere—in factories, offices, butcher shops, on street corners, in private business—and each

Postwar Red Scare

carries with him the germs of death for society." Such statements contributed to a mood that was soon to be recklessly exploited by others who had less restraint and no other business to occupy their time.

Such a person was the junior senator from Wisconsin, Joseph R. McCarthy. Hoping to repair his lackluster record in the Senate (to which he had been elected in 1946), McCarthy suddenly claimed, in a speech in Wheeling, West Virginia (February 5, 1950), to have a list of 205 communists who were currently employed by the State Department. If true, this would neatly explain the foreign policy reverses of 1945–50. McCarthy found that he had struck a responsive chord in the national emotions. The press dutifully reported McCarthy's charges in headlines, while finding little news value of the subsequent failure of his evidence to withstand scrutiny. From a base in a subcommittee of the Government Operations Committee and protected by the Senate's code of deference toward its members, McCarthy launched a series of investigations of internal subversion that were well covered by the news media. These produced headlines, polls reporting great public support for McCarthy, an intimidated State Department—but no communist spies. Spurred by McCarthy, an antisubversive campaign spread to industry, schools and colleges, and even churches, where people were intimidated and fired if their beliefs were not found appropriately "American."

Senator Joseph McCarthy

Senator Joseph McCarthy at the height of his power in the early 1950s. No one has ever satisfactorily measured the damage done by his demagogic anti-communism, but it is now clear that he narrowed the bounds of permissible political discussion considerably, making American foreign policy dangerously inflexible well into the late 1960s. (United Press International)

General "Ike" Eisenhower was surely the most popular political figure of his era, and, unlike other presidents, was as popular at the end of his term of office as at the beginning. His hold upon popular affections did not reflect his political philosophy, which was vague and largely inarticulate, or his political achievements, which consisted chiefly of preserving things as they were. He was idolized because of personal qualities—warmth, simplicity, candor, and a somewhat misleading air of being ill at ease in the world of politics. (Wide World)

Election of 1952

Discontented, energetic groups who overestimated their own numbers turned to the elections of 1952 as an opportunity to break the deadlock and set America on a new (or back on the old) path. Those who wished a liberal reform era supported the eloquent Democratic candidate, Adlai Stevenson; those who wished to get back to the old ways voted for the Republican candidate and military hero, General Dwight D. Eisenhower. The results of the voting, an Eisenhower victory and a Republican Congress, seemed to indicate to the latter group that the way was clear for conservative reform.

Eisenhower as a Conservative

The signs were at first encouraging to anti–New and Fair Dealers. Eisenhower filled his cabinet with wealthy and presumably conservative businessmen like Charles Wilson of General Motors and George Humphrey of the Mark Hanna Corporation and made clear that his philosophy of government assumed a minimal federal role in the "natural" workings of the economy. The administration moved at once to slash federal expenditures by approximately 10 percent in order to balance the budget, allowed an old New Deal agency—the Reconstruction Finance Corporation—to die, and ended federal controls adopted during the Korean War.

It was not long before reality intervened to spoil conservative hopes for sweeping changes. Ideally conservatives wished to reduce federal aid to special groups and balance the budget, but in reality a balanced budget sent the economy into a slump. Groups whose federal assistance had been slashed became angry at the responsible politicians. And it soon appeared that certain public functions ranging from defense to transportation languished when left alone. Faced with a recession in 1954 and increasing political complaints, Eisenhower proved himself flexible, and for the remainder of the decade pursued as best he could a moderately active federal policy that resembled the New Deal in some of its less exuberant years. He assumed federal responsibility for the health of the economy and fought the recession of 1954 with the usual Keynesian methods of easy money and a deliberately unbalanced budget. He was forced into expansionary measures again after the recession of 1957–58 and left office with a record of five years of deficit and three of small surplus. Federal spending, the Republicans learned, not only staved off economic slumps but was good politics, since groups that had come to depend on New Deal programs were not interested in economy at their expense. The Eisenhower government therefore extended social security coverage and benefits three times, continued federal housing programs amounting to twenty-five thousand low-income units a year, and inaugurated a new program of federal aid for interstate highways. The secretary of agriculture, Ezra Taft Benson, who hoped to return agriculture to free market conditions, found that he could whittle only a small amount from federal support and had to content himself with storing the mounting surpluses or distributing them to schoolchildren and the needy, as had New Dealers Wallace and Hopkins twenty years earlier.

In some areas the administration found itself going even beyond the New Deal–Fair Deal agenda. When Russia sent up the Sputnik satellite in 1957, federal aid to the nation's hard-pressed schools became a matter of high national priority, and in 1958 the National Defense Education Act was passed, authorizing federal loans to students and grants for science facilities. As a final irony, it was Eisenhower, for all his belief that laws could not improve human behavior, who signed the first federal legislation since Reconstruction to aid the black in gaining full citizenship.

Eisenhower as a New Dealer

The assumption that black Americans were experiencing social gains was reinforced by the knowledge that the federal government had begun to throw its weight on the side of equal rights. Of the three branches of government the Supreme Court had been most active on behalf of blacks. Segregated education had come under judicial attack in a series of cases beginning in the late 1930s: in 1938 the decision of the Court in *Missouri ex rel. Gaines* v. *Canada* required the state of Missouri to admit a black to its publicly supported law school; in 1949 the state of Texas was told in *Sweatt*

The Federal Government and the Black

The admission of twelve black students to all-white Central High School in Little Rock, Arkansas, in 1957 provoked white mobs to protest and violence. President Eisenhower very reluctantly sent National Guard troops to restore order—a step he might have avoided by early support for court-ordered integration. (Wide World)

v. *Painter* that its hastily created black law school was inferior and that blacks must be admitted to the all-white law school of the University of Texas; in 1950, in *McLaurin* v. *Oklahoma State Regents,* the University of Oklahoma was enjoined from requiring a black student to eat at a separate table. These cases showed that the Court was moving toward the position that separate education was unequal and therefore a violation of the "equal protection of the laws" clause of the Fourteenth Amendment. The Court took the final step in 1954 in the famous *Brown* v. *Topeka Board of Education* case, ruling in a unanimous vote that "separate education was inherently unequal" and that all public educational facilities in the nation must now be desegregated.

The executive and legislative branches of government had also taken part in the recommitment of federal power to the cause of black rights. President Truman in 1946 had appointed the Committee on Civil Rights, which produced a critical report on the nation's race relations, *To Secure These Rights* (1947), and Truman had drawn from that report the proposals for antilynching legislation, a fair employment practices commission to fight discrimination in hiring, and the abolition of the poll tax, which he urged on the Congress in 1948. Truman secured none of these measures during his seven years in office, but he needed no congressional permission to order the integration of the armed forces, which he accomplished by executive order in 1948. President Eisenhower showed less interest in federal efforts to aid the black, but he did commit troops to enforce an integration order at Little Rock, Arkansas, in 1957, after violence had broken out against black children, and his administration had a hand in the shaping of the Civil Rights Acts of 1957 and 1960—the first since Reconstruction. The 1957 law empowered the attorney general to seek court injunctions against local infringements of the right to vote and created the Civil Rights Division in the Department of Justice; the 1960 law made bombing a federal crime and provided that if the attorney general could prove that a pattern of voting discrimination existed in some locality, the courts could order the registration of blacks by a federal referee. These laws were cumbersome and extended only to voting discrimination, but, taken with the *Brown* decision and the integration of the armed services, they seemed to many whites to constitute substantial gains for the American black.

In reality, by the end of the 1950s there was growing evidence that despite a strong economy and recent federal protection of civil rights, the American black was making torturously slow progress toward equality. Segregation was still the rule in all areas of life and in all parts of the country. Of the occupations in which Americans made their livelihood, only in entertainment and in organized sport were there any signs of equal opportunity, and these were painfully limited. In professional baseball, for example, brilliant athletes such as Satchel Paige, Josh Gibson, and Martin Dihigo had played out their careers in the black minor leagues, and the Baltimore Orioles once passed off a black second baseman as an Indian nicknamed Chief Tokohomah; the 1948 breakthrough made by Jackie Robinson of the Brooklyn Dodgers was only very slowly extended to others.

Scant Progress for Blacks

Even in education, where the Court had intervened, there had been little real integration. Ten years after the *Brown* decision only 2 percent of southern blacks attended school with whites. In 1960 only 14 percent of the blacks in the South were registered to vote; in Mississippi, as few as 6 percent. Southern resistance to reform in race relations was firm, and northern whites were demonstrating little more willingness than southerners to accept blacks as fellow workers and neighbors. Perhaps most important, blacks had not shared equally in the economic advance of the country since the war. Urban blacks experienced some slight economic gains, but whites gained faster, and rural blacks actually seem to have lost ground economically from 1950 to 1960.

Blacks soon proved that they were very much aware of the differential economic progress of the races and the limited extent of actual integration. In December 1955 in Montgomery, Alabama, a black woman named Rosa Parks refused to give up her seat on a bus to a white man, for which she was arrested. The massive bus boycott by Montgomery blacks that followed her arrest showed that her attitude was widely shared. The country had entered a new era in race relations. Black protest, formerly conducted by an elite of NAACP lawyers whose arena was the courts, began after Montgomery to transform itself into a mass movement that exerted direct pressure in public places. The spontaneous drugstore lunch counter sit-ins by black college

Greater Militancy Among Blacks

students in Greensboro, North Carolina, in 1960 demonstrated the extent to which a new spirit of direct action had permeated the younger generation of blacks. Under the leadership of the Reverend Martin Luther King, Jr., who headed the Montgomery boycott, the new tactics of mass protest were conducted in a spirit of Christian and Gandhian nonviolence. The willingness of large numbers of southern blacks to accept the physical risks of marches and sit-ins was a sign of the extent of the frustration that marked the life of the black American. As the temper of the black movement changed and blacks with their white allies intensified their pressure upon the mass of whites who had not shed their prejudices and did not plan to, it was clear that political leaders had less time than they thought if they were to avert violence and more bitterness.

The chief national problem, however, seemed to be the foreign threat, and the American people in 1952 had elected an expert to deal with it. They were hopeful that Eisenhower might end the chain of disasters of the Truman period—the "loss" of China, the Korean stalemate, the "loss" of Eastern Europe. Eisenhower and his secretary of state, John Foster Dulles, promised a new look in foreign policy and wasted no time in speaking very differently from how Truman had spoken. Dulles especially was a phrasemaker of the new diplomacy. He announced in early 1954 that America would no longer be drawn into little wars that would sap its strength but would rely upon "massive retaliation" by its nuclear-armed air force. The policy not only promised to avoid devastating wars against Asian numbers but also promised to be cheaper (a few bombers were less expensive than large conventional armies). Accordingly the administration began to reduce spending on the army, navy, and marine corps.

Eisenhower and Foreign Affairs

No one can be sure whether the massive retaliation policy was responsible for preventing another world war or whether, as its critics (like Harvard's Henry Kissinger or Chief of Staff Maxwell D. Taylor) charged, it invited limited Communist attacks because the U.S. conventional ground forces were weakened. Certainly the verbal and strategic reliance upon instant nuclear retaliation kept the American people on a war footing emotionally and ensured that the Soviets would press forward in the arms race. Under the policy, each foreign crisis carried with it the threat of a general atomic war, taking the country "to the brink," as Dulles candidly admitted having done at least three times in his first four years in office.

With the shift to massive retaliation went a determination to replace Truman's containment policy—which the GOP platform in 1952 called "negative, futile and immoral"—with a positive "moral" policy of "rollback" or "liberation." Such language had a strong appeal for many Americans, and especially for the William Knowland–John Bricker conservatives in the Republican party. But the government found it hard to go beyond speeches to the actual rollback of Soviet power. The Soviets removed troops from Austria, as did the Allies, but not under threat. The U.S. government's

"Liberation"

restraint during the Hungarian revolt against Soviet rule in 1956 demonstrated both to those living behind the iron curtain and to American policy makers that the United States could only talk of "liberation." With hydrogen weapons held by both sides (the Soviets detonated the bomb in 1953, and the United States did so nine months later, in 1954), America could not risk sending more than encouragement to rebelling people near the Soviet border.

This it did, keeping the nation militarily strong, taking no risks either of credulity or of arrogance. As under Truman, the results were solid but not spectacular. Europe continued its economic recovery and there were no more territorial losses to the U.S.S.R.; but the administration found no way to end the smoldering, expensive conflict. Germany remained divided, its status uncertain and worrisome. Incessant talks concerning nuclear disarmament produced no agreement, although both sides professed a strong desire to institute some restraints. Mutual suspicion continued unabated, and a hard line on both sides dominated the military and political councils and annually diverted large sums to weapons.

Eisenhower made valiant efforts to take advantage of the signs after Stalin's *Summitry* death in 1953 that Soviet leadership was becoming more moderate. His Geneva summit meeting with Premier Bulganin in 1956 produced a promising spirit of friendliness, but this was erased by the tensions of the Hungarian revolt and the Anglo-French invasion of Egypt after the Suez incident. The president pursued his peace explorations with Nikita Khrushchev, who accepted an invitation to visit the United States in 1959 and concluded the trip with a cordial meeting with Eisenhower at Camp David, Maryland. But

As a climax to the temporary "era of good feeling" toward the end of Eisenhower's presidency, Soviet Premier Nikita Khrushchev visited the U.S. in the autumn of 1959, touring farms and factories and meeting the press. But resultant easing of tensions was reversed when a U.S. pilot was shot down over Russia during an espionage flight in May 1960, and Khrushchev broke off the summit talks planned for September. (United Press International)

"the spirit of Camp David" evaporated on the eve of the Paris summit conference of 1960, when an American plane was downed while flying over the U.S.S.R. on reconnaissance. Khrushchev chose to publicize the affront to break up the conference. Despite strenuous personal efforts to reach a better footing with the Soviet Union, Eisenhower was unable to shape the policies that would accomplish his desire for a better world.

Even as American policy held steady in the Truman mold under his Republican successor, the world was changing. One of the chief results of the war was the impetus it gave to the breakup of the old colonial empires and the emergence of third world nationalism. Britain in the years after the war withdrew from India, Burma, and Egypt; France from Indochina; the Netherlands from Indonesia. New states appeared almost yearly in Africa, molded out of crumbling empires. The drive toward independence was not orderly; nationalism bred violence. But since the United States had little empire, this need not have threatened it. What complicated the American position was the occasional union of nationalism with communism. Marxism possessed certain advantages over democracy in the emerging areas. A creed emphasizing social discipline rather than individual liberties, it seemed admirably designed to serve nationalistic elites seeking to regiment their societies for the swift, difficult passage into economic modernization. *Anticolonialism*

The proliferation of new states in the third world, nationalistic and noncapitalist, if not anticapitalist, was a fact of life with which American policy increasingly had to deal. Many observers, among them George Kennan, believed that such developments made the military-oriented containment policy obsolete. Kennan felt that underdeveloped nations experimenting with Marxism were not necessarily a threat to the United States and might be split off from the Soviet bloc by a flexible American policy. Such splitting, or "polycentrism," he felt, could be accomplished by establishing working political and economic relations with some Communist states in order to detach them from others.

But American policy was made by John Foster Dulles, not Kennan, and it continued to treat all Communist states as part of a monolith dedicated to the destruction of the West. American leaders instinctively regarded revolutionaries like Vietnam's Ho Chi-minh, Cuba's Fidel Castro, and Egypt's Gamal Nasser with suspicion and intervened with force on at least two occasions (Guatemala in 1954, Lebanon in 1958) to prevent new Communist regimes from coming to power. While believing in economic development, the administration spent most of its money and energy on the construction of military alliances, such as the Southeast Asia Treaty Organization of 1954. Frequently such alliances were with staunch anti-Communists who were also reactionary dictators, like Spain's Franco, Portugal's Salazar, or South Korea's Rhee. While the administration saw little alternative to such alliances and such priorities, the United States increasingly seemed to be set against the aspirations of a large part of the emerging world. The Soviets and the Chinese, on the other hand, appeared to be aligning themselves with popular aspirations. When Vice-President Nixon was spat upon in Venezuela in 1958, Americans learned with dismay of America's great unpopularity in a country whose government was officially friendly.

In defense of the United States it was said that, as the country fated to uphold the Western cause just as emerging nations were revolting against centuries of imperialism, we would simply have to expect to be the target of resentments that should have been directed to London, Paris, and Lisbon. Nonetheless, a vocal segment of American opinion was critical of the government for rigidly conforming to a military-oriented containment policy, which, whatever its merits in the European theater, was proving unsuccessful in the underdeveloped world. Cold war costs, financial and psychological, were heavy, and many yearned for a more effective policy. Eisenhower himself left office disturbed that the years of global cold war might have made it an institution. In his farewell address delivered in January 1961, the president spoke of "the conjunction of an immense military establishment and a large arms industry," which was "new in American experience" and whose "total influence is felt in every city." "We must guard against the acquisition of unwarranted influence by the military-industrial complex," Eisenhower warned, a complex the cold war had created and that now had a vested interest in its continuance.

Cold War Costs

The power complex that Eisenhower warned of showed its full influence only after his administration ended. In the 1950s a more apparent price of the cold war was the continued dominance of the shallow and repressive form of anticommunism nurtured by Senator McCarthy. For four years, McCarthy used his Senate position to search for subversives in the State Department, the army, and other federal agencies, never finding a single communist spy but hounding several people out of the civil service and encouraging a repressive atmosphere in the country. The senator was censured by the Senate in 1954 for his abusive treatment of witnesses and even his senatorial colleagues; the red scare began to wane. Yet the four to five years of panic over subversives had made their mark. No known communists had been ferreted out of the federal service, but the country was now committed to the intensive scrutiny of the political beliefs of federal and state employees, teachers, union leaders, and many workers in private industry, including Hollywood writers. As of 1955, the FBI and other federal security agencies maintained surveillance of the political loyalties of eleven million people. In this atmosphere of suspicion and anxiety, not only communists but all types of nonconformists were in disfavor, and vigorous social criticism from loyal Americans was greatly stifled. The American people were in no mood for risks. School boards were encouraged to ban all controversial material from textbooks. The State Department purged its overseas libraries of books thought too critical of America and discontinued the services of several academic advisors tainted by McCarthy's freeswinging criticisms, men such as Philip Jessup of Columbia and Owen Lattimore of Johns Hopkins. Ignoring the First Amendment, 45 percent of those polled in 1954 felt that socialists should not be allowed to publish newspapers in the United States. In the defense of freedom, the traditional liberties of Americans were being greatly narrowed.

Although the fear of internal subversion eased somewhat after 1954, the entire decade of the 1950s was characterized by a strongly conservative mood. Church leaders hailed a "return to religion," citing rising membership trends that sent church membership from 50 percent of the population in 1945 to 61 percent in 1957. Religious themes appeared prominently in contemporary novels and plays, and carried popular songs such as Frankie Laine's "I Believe" and Les Paul and Mary Ford's "Vaya Con Dios" to enormous commercial success. In 1954 Congress reflected the prevailing sentiment when it added "under God" to the Pledge of Allegiance. The word "conservative," formerly a label most Americans shunned, was rehabilitated by the school of new conservatives. Men like William F. Buckley, Russell Kirk, and Wilmoore Kendall founded avowedly conservative journals such as *The National Review* and *Modern Age*. On the campuses, young people were reported as interested in secure jobs with large corporations, early marriages, and the comforts of suburban affluence; few were attracted to risky personal adventures, nonconformity, or social reform. Some observers called the young in the 1950s "the silent generation" and lamented (in the words of a Nebraska professor) that "they are politically comatose . . . they are listeners. Are they really listening? Their minds are as quiet as mice."

According to several social critics, adults displayed the same urge to conformity as the young. David Riesman in *The Lonely Crowd* (1950) discerned a historic shift in the national character from an "inner-directed" to an "other-directed" personality, forever adjusting his or her behavior to accommodate the signals of approval or censure sent out by the peer group. William S. Whyte, Jr., in *The Organization Man* (1957) found American males being transformed by their roles in the bureaucracies of large corporations into faceless and unfeeling automatons who preferred security to the risks of individualism. By these and other reports, Americans in the 1950s had lost the pioneer spirit of rebelliousness and independence in the affluent, anaesthetizing surroundings of bureaucratic occupations and suburban living.

A strain of conservatism also appeared in the world of scholarship. Historians wrote of the ideological consensus that had united the American people since colonial times and displayed little interest in economic or racial conflict. Economists, taking for granted that income and wealth had become much more equitably distributed since the 1930s (which was not true), turned to building models of how the economy worked and might be "finely tuned" by public officials. Social scientists were interested in the functioning of major institutions and did not often raise basic normative issues. As sociologist Daniel Bell summed up in 1960, there had been an "end to ideology" in America after the war, and conflict over fundamental ethical or ideological issues had given way to restrained discussions of how to administer the existing social machinery scientifically. In their own way, scholars were reflecting the national mood of caution and pragmatism. Like other Americans in the early years of the cold war, they took their major institutions for granted and examined their workings rather than raising questions about their very existence.

One can always say of the American people that there are more of them than there used to be. The population increase of the 1930s had been a low 7.2 percent, bringing the total by 1940 to one hundred thirty-one million people. But a postwar baby boom raised the birth rate from nineteen per thousand in 1940 to twenty-five per thousand by 1950, and the rate did not begin a significant decline until the 1960s. As a result of the higher birth rate (immigration played no real part in the growth) and better medical care the population climbed to one hundred fifty million in 1950, one hundred seventy-eight million in 1960, and crossed the two hundred million mark in 1967 (the projected population in 2000 A.D.: three hundred twenty million). Overcrowding in schools was a widespread result of this population boom.

Midcentury Population Changes

"Well, Here We Are Back in School, Sort-Of."
(*From* The Herblock Book [*Beacon Press,* 1952])

Not only did the American people increase, but they also moved. There was an accelerated flow from farms to cities, reducing the rural part of the population from 23 percent in 1940 to 7 percent in the mid-1960s; yet there was also a surge of movement from cities to suburbs, which grew twice as fast as the core urban areas.

Most spectacular was the rearrangement of the population from region to region. People moved southward and to the coasts, both because defense industries had located there during World War II and the cold war and for the benefits of warmer, sunnier weather. Between 1940 and 1960, New Mexico's population increased 80 percent, Arizona and Florida grew by 160 percent, and by 1963 California's growth of some 140 percent had made it the nation's most populous state with twenty million people and thousands moving in daily. An important aspect of this regional shifting was the continuing migration of blacks out of the South to the cities of the Northeast, Great Lakes–Ohio Valley region, and the Far West. While 80 percent of the Afro-American population still lived in the South prior to World War II, they left the region in large numbers during the war, and by 1960 more blacks lived outside the South than within it. These population flows steadily moved the mythical population center westward from the Indiana-Illinois border (1940) to a farm just thirty miles east of the Mississippi River in 1970. Reflecting this westward shift of people, the New York (baseball) Giants moved to San Francisco, the Philadelphia Athletics to Kansas City and then to Oakland, and the Brooklyn Dodgers to Los Angeles.

This growth and movement of population came against a background of stunning economic expansion. No elected official or no governmental program approached the power the American economy exercised over the lives of the American people. Using the leading technology of the world it created new products and new desires, drew people out of old occupations into new, shifted populations from region to region with a careless hand, unified the continent with innovations in transportation and communication. The GNP grew from $206 billion to over $500 billion (in 1954 dollars), in the 20 years following 1940, representing a per capital increase of $919. By 1955, with 6 percent of the world's population, the United States produced and consumed one-third of the world's entire annual product. Several growth industries led the way: automobiles, aircraft and aerospace, chemical synthetics, electric appliances, and lightweight metals.

And certainly the most visible expansion came in the leisure industries. Where once the middle and lower classes had little money to expend on recreational purchases, postwar affluence both expanded leisure time and permitted more imaginative uses of it. By 1963, the average industrial worker had eight paid holidays a year plus a two-week vacation and worked a forty-hour week. And the proportion of families with annual incomes of ten thousand dollars or more crept gradually up, from 9 percent of the total in 1947 to 33 percent in 1968. With more time and money, Americans now spent billions on boating, bowling, golf, cameras, second cars, motorbikes,

Postwar Economic Growth

radio equipment, music, and television sets. Adolescents alone spent twenty-two billion dollars in 1963, some of it on food and clothes and much of it on recreation—records, movies, guitars, and basketballs. Television seemed the symbol of the new prosperity. An experimental device in 1940 and a novel product of a puny industry producing six thousand sets in 1946, the television quickly became a necessity rather than a luxury. Seven million sets were sold in 1953, fifty-four million were in operation by 1960, and ninety million by 1971 (twenty-four million of these were the more expensive color sets). Forests of antennas sprouted over suburbs, television personalities became better known than senators and scientists, and the snappy phrases of television commercials entered the language.

Critics were not long in pointing out the dangers of affluence. John Kenneth Galbraith in *The Affluent Society* (1958) criticized the overemphasis upon consumer pleasures as against the need for clean air, parks, and traffic-free transportation, and Vance Packard in *The Waste Makers* (1955) condemned both manufacturers and consumers for indulging in the wasteful habit of yearly changes in car and clothing styles. Cartoonists and other satirists lampooned a culture in which golfers rode about on electric carts, people slept under electric blankets, opened cans with electric can openers, and brushed their teeth with electric brushes. These were telling points and could be met only with assertions that such frivolities were the price of consumer "freedom of choice," or that a good part of the new affluence also went toward schooling, music, books, and the international tastes of a people familiar with foreign cars, Danish furniture, African art, Scotch whisky, French wines, Dutch beer, and pizza.

The Affluent Society

By 1960 it was clear that the economy, while expanding at a rate of 2 to 3 percent a year, was not developing as fast as that of other industrial nations (the Soviet rate of 1950–58 was 7.1 percent), or at the 4 to 5 percent rate economists thought possible. Billions of dollars worth of goods were "lost" each year as machines and men sat idle, unused because consumer buying power did not match capacity. The sluggishness of the economy could be seen in the unemployment figures, which mounted to 6.8 percent of the work force in 1958 and climbed toward 8 percent in 1960. Population continued to increase, jumping by twenty-eight million between 1950 and 1960, and the employment problem became more acute as twenty-five thousand young Americans entered the work force every week. The reasons for the unemployment of men and machines varied, but they were principally a combination of inadequate demand (compared to productive capacity), a population growth that produced too many job applicants, and technological unemployment caused by automation. Economists disagree about the number of jobs lost because of automation, but it is clear that the people who were replaced by machines often lacked the geographical mobility and skills necessary to find employment elsewhere. Not only was industrial automation responsible for an undetermined number of lost jobs,

Unemployment

but agricultural automation also cut farm employment and generated a migration to the cities. Farm population dropped from 23 percent of all Americans to 7 percent in the period 1940–60, and many of these migrants continued to encounter employment problems.

The first Republican administration since Hoover either preserved the outlines of the New Deal or modestly enlarged them. The opposition of the Democrats who controlled Congress after 1954; the presence of organized groups who lobbied against budget cutting in programs affecting themselves; the continued need for military expenditures; all of these factors limited Eisenhower's conservative impulses. The nation remained on dead center despite the new faces in and around the White House, with the electorate apparently contented to see little change in the world Ike inherited in 1952. The eight years of relative calm and absence of politically induced change, either forward or backward, may have been psychologically necessary to a nation whose exertions in the 1930s and 1940s had been enormous. They certainly proved that the Republicans could govern after twenty years out of power, and brought both parties generally into agreement about the mixed capitalist order. Only in politics, however, was there relative stability. While politicians crowded the middle of the road, dynamic forces were at work reshaping the American landscape and creating a host of problems that could not wait forever for public attention.

The Eisenhower Consensus

COMMENTARY

America came to the end of the Eisenhower years having escaped serious internal conflicts but facing growing areas of public and private neglect. Federal expenditure in the public sector was held steady by a conservative administration. Given the increase in population and GNP, this meant a relative decline in federal attention to the national estate. Many wondered how long the country could ignore the evidence of problems that were not taking care of themselves.

SUGGESTED READING

CHARLES C. ALEXANDER, *Holding the Line* (1975)
SEYOM BROWN, *The Faces of Power* (1968)
WILLIAM CHAFE, *The American Woman: Her Changing Economic and Political Roles, 1920–1970* (1972)
DWIGHT D. EISENHOWER, *Mandate for Change* (1963)
———, *Waging Peace* (1965)
JOHN K. GALBRAITH, *American Capitalism* (1952)
———, *The Affluent Society* (1958)
ROBERT GRIFFITH, *The Politics of Fear: Joseph McCarthy and the Senate* (1970)
ALAN D. HARPER, *The Politics of Loyalty* (1969)
TOWNSEND HOOPES, *The Devil and John Foster Dulles* (1973)
MARTIN LUTHER KING, JR., *Stride Toward Freedom* (1958)

JOHN T. MCALISTER, *Vietnam: The Origins of Revolution* (1969)
JOHN B. MARTIN, *Adlai Stevenson of Illinois* (1976)
WILLIAM L. MILLER, *Piety Along the Potomac* (1964)
C. WRIGHT MILLS, *The Power Elite* (1956)
HERBERT PARMET, *Eisenhower: The Necessary President* (1972)
JAMES T. PATTERSON, *Mr. Republican: A Biography of Robert A. Taft* (1972)
JOHN B. RAE, *The Road and the Car in American Life* (1971)
DAVID REES, *Korea: The Limited War* (1964)
DAVID RIESMAN et al., *The Lonely Crowd* (1952)
RICHARD ROVERE, *Senator Joe McCarthy (1959)*
———, and A. M. SCHLESINGER, JR., *The MacArthur Controversy* (1965)
GADDIS SMITH, *Dean Acheson* (1972)
WILLIAM H. WHYTE, JR., *The Organization Man* (1956)

16

Affluence and Crisis, 1960–1977

The Election of 1960

The Democratic nomination went to the energetic forty-two-year-old senator from Massachusetts, John F. Kennedy. He won it through hard work, good organization, and a growing reputation for intelligence and judgment, but his political opinions were not clear. The son of a rich financier, Senator Kennedy's voting record had been neither liberal nor conservative with any consistency, and he headed a party of diverse political components. But during the primaries, Kennedy sensed that the country was eager for change, and he accepted the arguments of an aide, historian Arthur Schlesinger, Jr., that the conservative cycle had run its course and that a new period of liberal reform was in the making. Kennedy's opponent, Vice President Richard M. Nixon, was also a young man, but his identification with the previous eight years and his basic conservatism restrained him from offering the electorate an equal sense of new vistas. Kennedy's New Frontier somewhat vaguely promised liberal reforms and invigorated governmental leadership. These themes mobilized support along old New Deal lines, combining labor, blacks, intellectuals, and urbanites. Although his majority (a bare 112,881) was limited by fears of his Catholicism and his "lack of experience," Kennedy nevertheless seemed to enter the White House in 1961 with a slim but enthusiastic mandate for new departures.

Kennedy's New Frontier

The New Frontier was largely an attempt to set a mood, to draw the citizenry away from their private pursuits to a spirit of national discipline and self-sacrifice so that the nation might attack its internal and external problems with renewed energy and imagination. As a search for a spirit of dedication, especially among the young, the New Frontier was an instant success. Kennedy drew into government service great numbers of young men and women who were glad to forsake conventional careers for an opportunity to pit themselves directly against public problems. New blood and a new spirit invaded Washington, filling old agencies like the departments of justice and labor and new ones like the Peace Corps. Yet the country was large, and Washington only its capital. Whether the new spirit reached out into the country was hard to determine.

John F. Kennedy, 35th president of the United States, 1961–1963. From his inaugural address: "Let the word go forth from this time and place, to friend and foe alike, that the torch has been passed to a new generation of Americans, born in this century, tempered by war, disciplined by a hard and bitter peace, proud of our ancient heritage, and unwilling to witness or permit the slow undoing of those human rights to which this nation has always been committed . . . ." (Henri Dauman/Magnum)

If the New Frontier was primarily a mood, it was also a set of proposals for national action. The clearest commitment was to an invigorated economy. Kennedy's promise "to get the country moving again" was understood to be a condemnation of the 8 percent unemployment rate and sluggish economy that characterized the end of the Eisenhower years. Kennedy conveyed in general terms a reformer's dissatisfaction with the condition of American cities, the situation of minorities, the overall torpor of the national cultural life. Immediately after his election he set task forces to work preparing plans to deal with unemployment, area redevelopment, regulatory reform, health care, housing, and other domestic issues. An important part of the New Frontier was to be the reassertion of American influence abroad, the "closing of the missile gap," and the recapture of the initiative in the cold war.

There were no barriers to Kennedy's new mood save apathy, but his legislative program met determined resistance in a Congress, which felt it had received no mandate for new and expensive programs. A series of Kennedy measures, designed to redistribute American purchases from the private to the public sector through taxing and federal spending, made their slow and discouraging way through the legislature. A bill providing over five billion dollars in federal aid to public schools was defeated in the House. The

Kennedy and Congress

celebrated Medicare bill, providing medical insurance to those over sixty-five who were covered by social security, died in the Senate by four votes. Legislation calling for the establishment at the cabinet level of a department of housing and urban affairs to direct and initiate federal urban programs was defeated. The president received authorization to spend nine hundred million dollars on public works in depressed areas, succeeded in raising the minimum wage from one dollar to one twenty-five, and won the passage of a housing bill appropriating nearly five billion dollars for urban redevelopment. But the Congress either rejected or weakened most of his efforts to redirect national resources into areas of growing public need.

Although interested in programs to improve individual security, health, and education, Kennedy believed that inducing a faster-growing economy by creating jobs would go far toward remedying most domestic problems. Economists differed as to the path to fuller employment. Some saw unemployment as structural, a product of automation or of shifts in buying habits. They pointed to the coal mining regions of the Appalachians and the textile towns of New England. The answer these economists usually offered was federal retraining to help people alter their skills to match new job opportunities. But other economists saw unemployment as a product of inadequate demand, and urged a general expansion using the Keynesian tools now employed by all Western countries to increase buying power.

Kennedy and the Economy

At first Kennedy seemed to favor the structural approach, asking Congress in 1961 for a federal retraining program for depressed areas. But in time he came to doubt that this approach alone would achieve the growth he wanted, and under the tutelage of economist Walter Heller, he began to espouse the expansionary New Economics. Heller felt that a deliberate federal deficit created early in the year would produce the needed economic stimulus, and that by the end of the year federal revenues would have been so increased by the growing GNP that the budget would soon come into balance. In January 1963 Kennedy sent the Congress his proposal for an expansionary fiscal policy, a budget that created a deliberate deficit, because of a tax cut of ten billion dollars and no reduction of expenditures. Federal deficits were not new, but to plan a large deficit and claim that the result would be both economic growth and an eventually balanced budget was a dramatic departure from traditional methods of influencing the economy.

The New Economics

Congressmen, especially those from districts with large unemployment, could understand retraining programs, and the Area Redevelopment Act of 1961 appropriated four hundred million dollars for 675 regions of economic stagnation. But the New Economics was greeted with suspicion, and Kennedy's 1963 tax cut was shelved. Congress also defeated the president's proposals for tax reforms, which would have shifted the burden of taxation slightly toward the upper brackets. The administration therefore approached the end of 1963 with its basic economic legislation stalled. However, increased defense expenditures did throw the budget out of balance to some extent, providing an economic stimulus that ended the recession of 1960–61. But in 1963 unemployment was still over 5 percent, and the economic growth rate was about 3.5 percent as compared to the 5 percent Kennedy wanted.

Critics of the president argued that his leadership left America pretty much where he found it, with decaying cities, too many poor, a worsening race situation, and an economy producing much less than it might. In his defense it was justly pointed out that he inherited a conservative Congress, that his own election was so close as to provide no mandate for clear action, and that the process of voter education was slow. Nowhere were these limitations more apparent than in Kennedy's difficulties in fashioning a policy to cope with the country's racial troubles.

Kennedy was a racial liberal but thought himself trapped on the issue between a hostile southern bloc in Congress and the fact that 49.9 percent of the voters had preferred his opponent. He therefore sought a path between dramatic federal action on the one hand and complete inaction on the other. Although he knew the 1957 and 1960 civil rights laws were inadequate, the president at first tried to use the powers he had rather than ask for new ones. His brother, Attorney General Robert Kennedy, increased the staff of the Civil Rights Division and brought pressure through the courts to reduce discrimination in transportation facilities and in voting. The president established the Committee on Equal Employment Opportunity on March 6, 1961, to combat job discrimination by corporations holding government contracts. He announced his intention to nominate a black, Robert Weaver, as head of the cabinet-level Department of Urban Affairs. He issued an executive order in November 1962 banning segregation in federally assisted housing.

Kennedy and the Blacks

These steps were quite limited in their effect, but nonetheless the president, largely because of his brother's image as a strong advocate of civil rights, declined in popularity among white southerners. When black James Meredith's attempts to attend the University of Mississippi in the fall of 1962 produced rioting by white students and townspeople, Kennedy committed federal marshals and then units of the National Guard. Thirty thousand troops were used to quell riots that took two lives and injured 375. The president, who had never encouraged the integration of any university, was simply carrying out his constitutional responsibilities, but the events at "Ole Miss" earned John Kennedy the hatred of many southerners, who saw him as a relentless champion of racial integration.

Yet the truth was that as of the early spring 1963 Kennedy had not pressed hard against the nation's biracial system and habits. For those who were more impressed with the urgency of the situation than with Kennedy's political difficulties, he was much too cautious. Critics pointed out that Kennedy had waited almost two years before issuing his housing order and that it affected only 18 percent of the new housing units built annually. And they added that in his first two years Kennedy had refused to endorse a

One of the great emotional moments in the history of the civil rights movement was Reverend Martin Luther King, Jr. leading 100,000 people in a peaceful march on Washington in the summer of 1963. King addressed his famous "We Shall Overcome" speech to a crowd stretching between the Lincoln Memorial and the Washington Monument. *(United Press International)*

strong congressional bill to remedy the defects of the voting laws of 1957 and 1960. But more effective than these criticisms in moving the president to action was the mounting racial violence. Crimes of violence against blacks increased, but the latter only intensified their nonviolent tactics, staging more than eight hundred demonstrations in 1963 alone. On May 3, 1963, a peaceful march of blacks and whites in Birmingham, Alabama, was broken up by fire hoses and police dogs in full view of a horrified national television audience, creating the sense of urgency that Kennedy needed for further legislation.

In June the president addressed the nation demanding action, saying that "we face a moral crisis as a country and as a people." The bill that he sent to Congress gave the government power to institute suits to desegregate schools (formerly such suits had to be brought by private individuals), but its heart was a section guaranteeing equal access to public accommodations. A "March on Washington" by two hundred thousand people added enormous moral impetus to the drive for legislation, but two southerners, James Eastland of Mississippi in the Senate and Howard Smith of Virginia in the House, held the bill in committee as the president enplaned for Dallas in November.

While Kennedy could implement little of his domestic program, Congress was less willing to refuse when he asked for changes in the conduct of foreign affairs. Blocked in many of his plans for larger federal expenditures for domestic programs, the president asked for a 15 percent increase in defense spending and with the aid of a crisis in Berlin in 1962 it was largely granted. He decided that the country should race the Soviets to put a man on the moon, despite estimates that the effort would cost approximately twenty billion dollars (a sum he could well have used rebuilding American cities). Congress responded favorably, cutting his request only slightly.

Kennedy and Foreign Affairs

Kennedy's promise of an improved foreign policy involved not only increased spending but also new approaches. As he saw it, military preparedness alone was not enough to ensure national security; America must address itself to the roots of war—poverty, disease, ignorance. Kennedy asked for and received in 1961 the most comprehensive aid program since the Marshall plan, this one—the Alliance for Progress—providing American and international funds up to twenty billion dollars for Latin America. In the same year Congress established the Peace Corps for young Americans who wished to go abroad and serve as technicians and ambassadors of goodwill. In 1962 Kennedy secured the Trade Expansion Act, designed to lower United States tariff barriers and encourage world trade.

These efforts to make American foreign policy more flexible and creative did not end the tensions and crises of the cold war. When Kennedy permitted an American-supported Cuban exile force to invade Cuba at the Bay of Pigs on April 17, 1961, the landing was crushed by the Communist government of Fidel Castro with damage to the American reputation for candor and judgment that could hardly be estimated. Almost immediately Khrushchev chose to increase the pressure on the Allied outpost in Berlin. He tested the American president again in October 1962 by placing Soviet missiles in Cuba. Kennedy told the nation that aerial reconnaissance had detected the missiles and that an American naval blockade would go into effect at once. There commenced the most dangerous week in American history, as Soviet ships bearing more missiles steamed toward a confrontation that might easily have become a general nuclear war. Only the Soviet leader's decision to recall the ships and withdraw the missiles already in Cuba secured Kennedy's promise not to invade the island and averted conflict between the two nuclear powers. As Khrushchev later said, "the smell of burning was in the air."

A Series of Crises

People on both sides were appalled at the narrowness of the escape (Kennedy himself had resisted pressure to bomb or invade)—and it was the missile crisis, not the election of 1960, that brought a deep change in United States–Soviet relations. Almost at once a thaw occurred between the two states. At American University on June 10, 1963, Kennedy made a historic speech in which he spoke of the dangers of nuclear war and the necessity of relaxing tensions and working for a peace in which people could "live

Détente with the U.S.S.R.?

together in mutual tolerance.'' The Soviet Union, affected by October's narrow escape and its widening disagreements with China, seemed genuinely interested in an easing of tensions. The two states concluded a historic atmospheric test ban treaty in July 1963, and installed a ''hot line'' between the two heads of state to lessen the danger of nuclear accident. It began to appear that it might be John F. Kennedy who would lead the United States toward the end of the cold war with Russia, the same Kennedy who only months before had carried the nation, under circumstances not of his choosing, so close to the nuclear termination of both civilizations.

Kennedy was assassinated in Dallas, Texas, on November 22, 1963, an act that shocked and saddened the entire world. His successor, Lyndon B. Johnson, inherited the problems Kennedy had wrestled with so inconclusively. The assassination, however, seemed to create a national mood favorable to decisive action to resolve the domestic crisis. Johnson, a Texan who had been unusually effective as Senate majority leader in the 1950s, moved with his usual political skill to exploit this mood. His strength was legislation rather than administration, and his presidency would be known for a legislative explosion rivaling the Hundred Days of Franklin Roosevelt.

Assassination of John F. Kennedy

Lyndon Baines Johnson takes the presidential oath after John Kennedy's assassination in Dallas, Texas, on November 22, 1963. Kennedy's widow, Jacqueline, stands at Johnson's left. Johnson's presidency will be difficult to appraise. Not only did he lead an imaginative, vigorous attack upon domestic problems, but he also took the country into the worst foreign policy disaster in American history—in Vietnam. (United Press International)

Johnson retained most of Kennedy's advisors and took from them one of his first major programs, the war on poverty, which the president declared in his State of the Union address in 1964: "This administration, here and now," he insisted, "declared unconditional war on poverty in America." It was a novel turn in social policy, but Johnson intended a very minor war. Congress appropriated just under a billion dollars for a variety of retraining and public employment programs in the first year. Poverty would also be reduced by the economic expansion triggered when Johnson pushed through Congress the tax cut of February 1964, providing a stimulus that propelled economic growth until the end of the decade.

Johnson's legislative momentum increased with these achievements. The Senate, for the first time in its history, voted to cut off a southern filibuster and passed the Civil Rights Act of 1964, best known for its protection of access to public accommodations. In that year, a determined conservative challenge was beaten down when Johnson was elected over Republican Barry M. Goldwater by an electoral vote of 486 to 52, Goldwater carrying only six states. With such an apparent mandate and a strongly liberal Congress, the president called for action on a broad front to achieve the Great Society, in which none would be shut out of the fullest enjoyment of the benefits of American economic success.

The attack on urban problems was stepped up with the creation of the Housing and Urban Development Department to which Johnson appointed Robert Weaver secretary, as Kennedy had intended. In 1965 Congress passed the Medicare plan, establishing a system of health insurance for those over sixty-five under Social Security. The Voting Rights Act of 1965 authorized the appointment of federal registrars in counties showing evidence of voter discrimination. These were landmark enactments, but the characteristic activity of the federal government during the Great Society years was the "categorical" grant program in which money was provided to state and local governments to attack social problems. Of the ninety-five areas in which federal grants were available in late 1968—areas such as transportation, education, housing, law enforcement, and water treatment—thirty-nine had been added under Lyndon Johnson. Federal grant programs almost doubled—the most often cited figures are 225 separate programs in 1964 to 438 in 1968—and officials admitted that a precise count was impossible.

In Johnson's view, the legislative successes of his administration represented enormous strides toward a "Great Society: a society of success without squalor, beauty without barrenness, works of genius without the wretchedness of poverty." Critics, noting the administrative confusion and proliferation of Great Society programs, insisted that Johnson and the Democrats were merely "throwing money at problems." Republican Senator Everett Dirksen parodied the strategy of the Great Society saying: "A million here, a million there—in time that adds up to real money."

Once again war intervened to divert national resources and energies away from domestic reform. Relations with the U.S.S.R. continued to improve, but in Asia the costs of the cold war were mounting. After twenty years of

Lyndon B. Johnson and the Great Society

Johnson and Foreign Affairs

American policy, China was if anything more embittered; and now that it was a nuclear power, predictions of war were heard in both countries. Of more immediate concern was the conflict in Vietnam. When the French had been driven from that country by the Communist forces of Ho Chi-minh in 1954, the United States had established a non-Communist government in the South at Saigon in the hope of confining communism to the northern half of Vietnam. When insurrection in the South threatened that government in the late 1950s, Presidents Eisenhower and Kennedy supported the Saigon regime by stepping up American arms, aid, and military advice. The weakness of the Saigon government and the military success of the Vietcong, as the South Vietnamese guerrillas were called, brought a crisis in 1965. Rather than see the country unified under a Communist government, President Johnson made the decision to commit American combat forces and to begin bombing the North as well as the South. By 1967 the American force had reached five hundred fifty thousand, and heavy fighting raged through most of South Vietnam.

Refugees in South Vietnam were helpless victims of domestic revolution—and the American decision to shape the outcome of that revolution through military intervention. (Hiroji Kubota/Magnum)

As the war claimed more and more of the American budget, costing roughly twenty-four billion dollars in 1966 with 1967 sure to bring higher figures, it became the center of a great controversy. The administration argued that Communist subversion must not be allowed to topple the South Vietnamese government lest all Southeast Asia fall, as Eisenhower had earlier said, like dominoes. But as the president escalated the war, and as the costs and the casualties mounted, criticism reached a level unknown in any other American military engagement in the twentieth century. Protests were heard in the Senate, the universities, the press, and the pulpit. Critics marched, staged teach-ins, organized peace pickets at every political level, and worked to deny the Democratic nomination to the president in 1968.

The Vietnam Controversy

Leading this effort was an early opponent of the war, Senator Eugene McCarthy, Democrat of Minnesota, who began what appeared to be a forlorn effort to defeat the incumbent president in the fall of 1967. The war was unpopular, not only among those who saw it as an overextension of American power, but also among those who resented its length, indecisiveness, and its human and material costs. President Johnson's popularity ratings dipped steadily through the fall and into the winter, as the public seemed to lose confidence in the candor of an administration which had so long promised success in Southeast Asia. A Communist offensive in Vietnam during the Tet holidays in February 1968 brought high American casualties and threatened every major city in South Vietnam. Against this background of military and political difficulties, Senator McCarthy almost defeated President Johnson in the New Hampshire Democratic primary in March, and Senator Robert Kennedy of New York also entered the race for the Democratic nomination as an outspoken critic of the president's foreign policies. On the night of March 31, 1968, President Johnson announced a bombing halt north of the Thirty-eighth Parallel, and then stunned the country by adding that he would not be a candidate for another term in office.

The year, which had begun with mounting bloodshed in South Vietnam, soon turned into an ordeal for the American people, as political assassination carried away two of the nation's greatest leaders. On April 4, 1968, Martin Luther King, Jr., was shot and killed in Memphis, Tennessee, an event that brought riots in 125 cities with forty-six deaths and a widespread outpouring of national grief. Then two months later, on June 5 in Los Angeles, following a victory in the California Democratic primary, Senator Robert Kennedy was shot and killed by an assassin in the Ambassador Hotel.

Assassinations of King and Kennedy

The loss of two of America's most popular and visionary leaders helped create a national mood of confusion, apprehension, and drift. Former Vice-President Richard M. Nixon took the Republican nomination in July and went on to defeat Vice-President Hubert H. Humphrey in the November presidential elections. Nixon ran a cautious, moderate campaign, and, when Humphrey declined to satisfy the McCarthy wing of his party by decisively

Election of 1968

breaking with the president's Vietnam policy, the campaign resolved itself into a contest between individuals and parties, without a sharp division over issues. Of all the problems facing the American people in 1968—war and peace, environmental pollution, urban violence, poverty—the campaign demonstrated that political leaders were sure of the public's sentiments on only one, and that was physical violence. Both candidates stressed "law and order," and a third, former Alabama Governor George Wallace, entered the campaign almost solely on that issue. Behind the sudden importance of such a meaningless phrase lay five summers of urban rioting, the confrontation politics that had spread through the college campuses, and the shocking skirmishes between police and demonstrators—along with innocent bystanders—that had disrupted the Democratic National Convention in Chicago in August. The American people were not sure why the level of violence and disruption had risen to almost uncontrollable heights in the 1960s (President Johnson appointed a commission on violence to find out), but they clearly wanted it condemned. Nixon, who made slightly more of the need for order than Humphrey, defeated his opponent with 43 percent of the popular vote to Humphrey's 42 percent and an electoral vote of 301 to 191.

TABLE 16–1
**Characteristics of Major Types of Civil Strife
in the United States, June 1963–May 1968[a]**

Type of event	Number of events identified	Estimated number of participants	Reported number of casualties	Reported arrests
Civil rights demonstrations	369	1,117,600	389	15,379
Antiwar demonstrations	104	680,000	400	3,258
Student protests on campus issues	91	102,035	122	1,914
Anti-school integration demonstrations	24	34,720	0	164
Segregationist clashes and counter-demonstrations	54	31,200	163	643
Negro riots and disturbances	239	(200,000)	8,133	49,607
White terrorism against Negroes and rights workers	213	(2,000)	112	97

Source: Hugh Davis Graham and Ted Robert Gurr, *Violence in America: Historical and Comparative Perspectives,* a report submitted to the National Commission on the Causes and Prevention of Violence (New York: Bantam Books, 1969), p. 576.

[a] The data in the table include many estimates, all imprecise. Figures in parentheses are especially tentative.

If the 1950s could be described as a decade of America's preoccupation with its enemies without, the 1960s were a time for the discovery of its problems within—problems that had existed all along but that had been ignored by most people in the cautious, defensive atmosphere of the early cold war. Indeed, so many flaws were discovered in American society and so many voices of protest were raised that historian William O'Neill entitled his history of the 1960s *Coming Apart* (1971).

Most of the social malfunctions uncovered in the 1960s seemed to be associated in one way or another with the city. The cities had been growing rapidly since the nineteenth century, and successive crusades by urban reformers had attempted to deal with urban growing pains through governmental reform, public housing, better sanitation, and the like. These valiant efforts undoubtedly made America's cities somewhat cleaner and better administered, but since nothing was done to halt the movement from farms to cities, the urban areas faced unrelenting pressure upon their public services and their living space. By 1970, 70 percent of the population in the country was urban, and, while individual cities were no longer growing within their municipal limits, an urban sprawl now connected city to suburb and suburb to city in a virtually unbroken megalopolis from Boston to Norfolk, from Chicago to Pittsburgh, from Jacksonville to Miami, and across the entire Los Angeles basin. Within the center cities especially, transportation facilities were strained and traffic congestion was a constant irritant. One could cross the continent in a comfortable jet airplane in less than five hours and then spend another tedious hour getting into New York, Boston, or Baltimore through the afternoon traffic jam. Rivers and lakes near every large city were polluted by effluent, both industrial and human. Lake Erie, absorbing the waste from Detroit, Toledo, Cleveland, and Buffalo, became what many experts called the most polluted large body of water in the world, and one day in the 1960s a small river flowing through Cleveland actually caught fire.

While the sources of the urban crisis were many, the factor of race unfailingly appeared as a crucial variable. Beginning in the early 1950s, the flow of whites into center cities dropped off, and the ratio of whites to blacks began to move toward unity in the large metropolitan areas. Blacks continued to migrate to cities, but whites were engaged in a postwar movement to the suburbs so massive as to rival the great waves of immigration at the turn of the century. Between 1950 and 1970 the number of people living in suburbs (thirty-seven million in 1950) actually doubled, and virtually all of these people were white. Blacks, meanwhile, continued to move from the rural South to cities, and the two flows of population transformed the demography of urban areas and deeply affected urban life. By 1961, Washington, D.C., was predominantly black; by 1970, so were Newark, Gary, and Atlanta, and seven other major cities were 40 percent black. Whites were escaping urban problems by a flight to the suburbs and literally abandoning the cities to the growing Afro-American majorities. "Unless something is done to halt the trend," said an official of a population research institute, "America's cities will become almost exclusively black, and the surrounding suburbs almost exclusively white by the end of the century."

The flight of the white population to the suburbs siphoned off the more energetic and affluent citizens, many retail stores, and some light industry, thereby reducing the economic and human resources available to cope with the city's pressing problems. City governments, burdened by strained transportation and sanitation systems, were also caught by rising welfare costs. Since blacks were "the first fired and the last hired," they were twice as likely to be unemployed as whites and were forced on the welfare rolls. In 1968, ten million people were receiving public aid of some sort, and by 1970 the figure had reached thirteen and a half million, at an annual cost of fifteen billion dollars. Some of these welfare recipients were rural, but most were urban. In Boston one of every five people received public assistance; in New York and San Francisco, one in seven. More people were on welfare in New York City than the entire population of Baltimore.

Congestion, crowding, and high unemployment rates undoubtedly were major causes of the steady rise in urban crime that was reflected in the FBI's Uniform Crime Reports. FBI director J. Edgar Hoover in the late 1950s had begun to sound the alarm about a national crime wave, but until about 1967 criminologists and statisticians tended to discount his claims. America had experienced higher crime rates in the late nineteenth century, they pointed out, and much of Hoover's alarming data could be explained by better police reporting methods and by Hoover's desire to gain larger appropriations for his agency. But whether there had been a crime wave in the late 1950s and early 1960s, there was agreement among the experts that sometime in the mid-1960s crimes of violence began increasing at an alarming rate. Between 1960 and 1967, bank robberies increased 248 percent, assault with a deadly weapon increased 84 percent, and the FBI announced that a woman was raped every twelve minutes and a house burglarized every twenty-seven seconds. It did not reassure the public to be told that the average person was five times as likely to meet death in his own automobile than at the hand of a criminal (in an average year in the 1960s, there were 13,650 reported homicides and 55,200 auto deaths). Fearful citizens refused to venture out at night, bought guns and sturdier door locks, and demanded of public officials that "law and order" be restored at whatever price.

The racial dimension of urban crime could not be ignored. According to FBI figures released in 1968, the Negro crime rate was twelve times that of whites. It was correctly pointed out that the high black crime rate was a product of centuries of discrimination and exploitation, and was not a racial characteristic. Criminologists further argued that the black arrest rate for crimes of violence was only three per thousand members of the black population, solid evidence that the vast majority of Afro-Americans were law-abiding citizens. It was also pointed out that police were more likely to interrogate and arrest blacks than whites and that many crimes committed

Urban Crime

generally only by whites—"white-collar" crimes such as tax evasion—were not reflected in the FBI figures. But, while these observations helped place the problem in perspective, there was no disputing the fact that the cities were not only crowded, unsightly, and dirty, but they were also increasingly dangerous to blacks and whites alike.

For a time in the middle 1960s it had seemed that the nation was on the threshhold of a solution to the racial problems that had marred its history for over three centuries. A powerful, nonviolent movement had grown up among blacks that had been strong enough, with its white allies, to push aside desperate southern resistance in Congress in order to secure federal laws guaranteeing equal access to public accommodations in 1964 and a strong voting law in 1965. Conservative Senator Everett M. Dirksen, of Illinois, who brought Republican support to the public accommodations bill, had remarked aptly that "no army is stronger than an idea whose time has come." But even as these victories were being won, new currents within the black community signaled that freedom for the black American was still distant, and would not be so easily bought as presidents and legislators hoped when they gathered to enact new laws.

Black and White in America

The civil rights movement, despite the shift from the early NAACP legal tactics toward Martin Luther King's direct but nonviolent action, had been optimistic, reasonably patient, and dedicated to the integration of blacks into the white world. But deep frustrations were tearing apart the old civil rights movement as early as 1964–65, years that most whites would have called the best ones for blacks at the end of their best decade. Increasing numbers of blacks began to turn away from the old civil rights organizations, leaders, and tactics, toward new and (to whites) disturbing ones.

The new element was the growth of black nationalism. Actually, black nationalism, meaning racial pride and a desire for an independent ethnic existence, had a long history among American blacks. The West Indian black Marcus Garvey, had rallied a small group of followers in the urban Northeast in the 1920s with a program of black separatism. For many reasons Garvey's movement was never strong outside his Harlem base. Black nationalism was kept alive in the 1930s and 1940s by a group of Black Muslims under Georgia-born Elijah Poole (Elijah Muhammad), who adopted African dress and a North African religion (Islam) and advocated economic and cultural separatism. The Nation of Islam was a tiny and obscure minority until the 1960s, when it produced a leader of tremendous oratorical power and personal magnetism—Malcolm X. Malcolm spoke of the need for racial pride and solidarity, criticized integration, and seemed strongly antiwhite. Urban blacks in significant numbers joined the Nation of Islam, rejecting white culture and taking on with their new Muslim names a new demeanor of pride and militancy. The famous professional football player Jim Brown became an adherent to the Muslim faith, and the world heavyweight boxing champion Cassius Clay changed his name to Muhammad Ali. Malcolm was

Black Nationalism

Born Malcolm Little in Omaha in 1925, Malcolm X was the son of a Baptist minister who helped organize Marcus Garvey's back-to-Africa movement of the 1920s. In his autobiography Malcolm wrote: "If I can die having brought any light, having exposed any meaningful truth that will help destroy the racist cancer that is malignant in the body of America—then, all of the credit is due to Allah. Only the mistakes have been mine." (Eve Arnold/Magnum)

assassinated in 1965, but he left a movement that had taken root among the lower-class urban blacks whom the NAACP and the Urban League had never reached.

If there had been any doubts that the problems of the city were inextricably bound up with America's racial difficulties, they disappeared in the four "bloody summers" of urban rioting, 1965–68. Five days after the signing of the 1965 Voting Rights Act, a riot broke out in Watts, California, a black ghetto within Los Angeles, ultimately claiming thirty-four lives and destroying property valued at thirty-five million dollars. Thereafter, during four successive summers when the cities sweltered with heat, there were outbreaks of violence as blacks erupted out of ghettoes, burning stores and assaulting whites who happened to be in the area. There were forty-three separate outbreaks in 1966, with eight major riots in 1967. In the two worst periods of violence in 1967, in Newark and Detroit, sixty-nine people were killed. Then the assassination of Martin Luther King in April 1968 triggered riots all across the country, the most severe occurring in Washington, D.C. Some seven thousand fires were set in the capital during two days of rioting, and the pall of smoke, combined with the sight of army tanks and National Guard bayonets, appeared to bring the aspect of war to the very edge of the White House.

Riots of 1965–1968

The riots were denounced by black and white leaders alike as unjustified and criminal acts, but they were also understood to be a communication from blacks to whites, a cry of rage and frustration that the lives of Afro-Americans were little changed by the rhetoric and legislation of the past decade. As Negro novelist Claude Brown said of the Harlem riots of 1966 in his *Manchild in the Promised Land:* "There were too many people full of hate and bitterness crowded into a dirty, stinky, uncared-for closet-size section of a great city."

What had happened to the civil rights movement which had seemed so close to a resolution of America's racial problems in 1963? One thing at least was clear: Americans had not appreciated how hard it would be to eliminate the disadvantages of the black after centuries of slavery and second-class citizenship. Legal barriers to integrated education, exercise of the suffrage, and access to public accommodations had finally been removed, after great exertions by both blacks and whites. Yet the actual conditions of life for black Americans continued to be deplorable.

President Johnson understood how much needed to be done on the racial front after the laws and their enforcement had been made color-blind. "Freedom is not enough," he said in a remarkable speech at Howard University in 1966: "It is not enough just to open the gates of opportunity. All our citizens must have the ability to walk through those gates." By many important measures, blacks began to translate their new legal equality into a great social equality during the 1960s. An expanding economy was a contributing cause, as were diminishing racial discrimination, the social programs of the Great Society, and sustained black efforts. In the summary of two noted scholars, Sar Levitan and Robert Taggart, blacks in the ten years after 1960 "doubled their real income; they moved into preferred status occupations and higher paying jobs; they graduated from high school more frequently and went on to college more often; their health improved in areas clearly related to deficient care; substandard housing declined and owner-ship increased." And in the crucial category of income, nonwhite males closed the income gap between themselves and white males from 56 percent in 1959 to 69 percent in 1973, and black females reached 92 percent of the mean income of white females in that period. These gains could be guessed at from the well-publicized successes of a number of talented Afro-Americans in various fields after 1960: the athlete who finally broke Babe Ruth's home run record, Henry Aaron, the peerless heavyweight boxing champion Muhammad Ali, Mayors Richard Hatcher of Gary, Indiana, and Tom Bradley of Los Angeles, Congresswomen Barbara Jordan of Texas and Yvonne Burke of California, Senator Edward Brooke of Massachusetts, Supreme Court Justice Thurgood Marshall.

But these individual careers and the socioeconomic progress they heralded did not tell the whole story. In some critical areas the condition of blacks in America declined during the civil rights era. The black family structure apparently deteriorated, judging by the measures of illegitimacy,

Measurements of Black Progress

female-headed households, divorce and desertion rates. The proportion of births out of wedlock among blacks rose from 22 percent in 1960 to 37 percent in 1971, and by the early 1970s the proportion of black women who were divorced had climbed to 42 percent (among whites it was 23 percent). Residential segregation worsened; whites fleeing from the center city enlarged the number of all-black neighborhoods while the suburbs stubbornly retained their overwhelming white preponderance. Black crime rates caused widespread concern; by 1972 blacks were twenty times more likely than whites to be arrested for robbery.

Behind these persistent indications of social disorganization was the knotty problem of poverty. Blacks had made some income gains, but they started so far behind that the grip of poverty was tenacious. Most of America's poor were white, but the proportion of blacks among the poor had always been very high. Four out of ten black families were poor in 1960, and the decade of economic expansion lifted at most one of these four families from poor to "near poor." This was progress, but it was painfully slow. Unemployment was twice as high for black than for white Americans, and black teenage unemployment ran as high as 40 percent in some cities. Here was the crux of the matter—not whether blacks had the legal right to buy lunch at formerly segregated restaurants or ride in the front of the bus, but whether they could earn the purchasing power to attain tangible social equality. Oddly enough, the years of the most rapid economic progress for minorities—the middle and late 1960s—were also the years of the most intense and sometimes even despairing protest. Census data show that the recession of 1970–71 arrested black economic gains and in some areas even slightly reversed them, but the 1970s saw the racial issue blunted in American politics and the tactics of black leaders shift toward moderation. Both races seemed to sense that to make good on America's promises of not only legal but full social equality would be a very expensive, difficult, and time-consuming process.

Black Poverty

One thing at least was clear: a fundamental and irreversible transformation had taken place in the years after World War II. The black's problems had become America's problem. Once the ward of the South, the black had migrated north and west until by 1968, 45 percent of all blacks lived outside the South and 69 percent of them were urban dwellers; in so doing blacks had forced their problem upon a reluctant nation. If the black was miserable he was now miserable in the midst of the great cities, America's nerve centers. Long before urban riots transferred some of the social costs of poverty to other economic groups, skyrocketing welfare costs had taught city officials in places like New York, Chicago, Detroit, and Los Angeles that the bill for years of neglect in the rural South might have to be paid by other parts of the nation. It was a lesson in the interrelatedness of all parts of American society. The ills of any substantial part of it were easily transferred to the whole. The elevation of the black to full equality was not only commanded by morality but by considerations of national order, prosperity,

Black Problem as National Problem

and even survival. Because of black leaders like Malcolm X and Eldridge Cleaver, who identified with the plight of the world's nonwhite peoples in underdeveloped countries, it was harder to ignore the isolation of white, affluent America in a world that was largely nonwhite and that was not solving its economic problems. Awakening to this situation was the first step toward a constructive response to it, and for this initial step the country may one day thank a group of men whose social background, and strident tone did not mark them as educators in the usual meaning of the term.

The riots of 1965–68 were but one form of protest from groups with rising grievances and diminishing patience. Mexican-Americans, confined for years to the barrios of western and southwestern cities, or shuttled between the shabby migratory labor camps of California's Imperial and San Joaquin valleys, turned increasingly to militant protest in the 1960s. Frequently calling themselves *Chicanos* to assert pride in a once-despised heritage, they found a brilliant leader in Cesar Chavez who successfully organized migratory farm labor in the grape and lettuce industries. In Los Angeles and other cities, "Brown Berets" provided a somewhat less effective institutional focus for Chicano nationalism and economic protest. In New York and elsewhere, younger Puerto Ricans joined the "Young Lords," a group patterned on the Black Panthers and Brown Berets. And among American Indians there were a series of spontaneous protests against the encompassing white political and cultural domination. A group of Indians seized Alcatraz Island in San Francisco Bay and held it for twenty months in 1969–71, and on Thanksgiving Day, 1970, two hundred Indians appeared at Plymouth Rock to proclaim a day of national mourning. "That damned rock," said a young Mohawk, "I'd like to blow it up. It was the start of everything bad to the American Indian." Dee Brown's sad history of the white armed conquest of the last surviving plains Indians, *Bury My Heart at Wounded Knee,* was a best-seller in 1971, and cars carried bumper stickers announcing that "Custer Died for Your Sins."

> *Other Ethnic Protests*

By the late 1960s "the revolt of the minorities" was an accepted part of the contemporary scene. A majority of Anglo-Saxons now answered to public opinion poll questions that nonwhite groups had indeed been barred by prejudice from full participation in American life. The white majority had granted their critics' case in principle and were gradually, if somewhat grudgingly, yielding to demands for preferment for nonwhites in hiring, admission to institutions of higher education, and for fairer treatment of non-Anglo Saxon Americans in schoolbooks and the mass media. But the demand for equality had spread to another minority that was potentially a majority—the feminists in the new women's movement.

The first women's movement had essentially ended in 1920 when females were granted the vote. Yet women's suffrage had neither reformed the society nor altered the situation of women. The number of women in professional fields such as law, medicine, and teaching had increased

> *The New Feminism*

Feminists march in support of the Equal Rights Amendment in New York City. (Elizabeth Hamlin/Dietz Hamlin)

gradually from the 1890s through the 1920s, and then the curve flattened out. Women made few occupational gains after the onset of the Great Depression, and in some areas their opportunities narrowed. Women received 16 percent of the Ph.D. degrees granted in the 1920s, for example, but by 1960 their share had declined to only 11 percent. Long after the Nineteenth Amendment, there were few women in the more desirable positions in business, the professions, or government.

Yet significant change was underway in the roles, and following that in the aspirations, of American women. World War II expanded employment opportunities and began to break down the informal bars to the hiring of females to do skilled, technical work. When the wartime labor crisis came to an end the prewar patterns were never fully restored. The labor force participation of women continued to increase, climbing from the 25 percent rate of 1940 (of females over sixteen) to over fifty percent by 1970. But unlike the prewar years, when the typical working woman was young and single, the postwar trend saw the working wife and mother become an institution. By 1972 more than half of the women with school-age children were in the labor force.

Inexorably this economic participation began to erode traditional views of women's role in society. In the years immediately after World War II the dominant stereotypes did not seem in jeopardy. The female was seen as more passive and "sensitive" than the male, fitted by God for a supporting, domestic role. A college president in the Midwest told the graduating class of a woman's college in 1955 that "the college years must be a rehearsal period for the major performance of marriage," and Adlai Stevenson told the graduates of Smith College to influence American males through their "humble role of housewife." Women's magazines reinforced a domestic orientation, carrying articles on cooking, sewing, and natural childbirth.

This traditional emphasis was to change in the 1960s. Betty Friedan's influential book of 1963, *The Feminine Mystique*, described modern women as not fulfilled by their domestic role but trapped in it. The culture told women to aspire to marriage, motherhood, and suburban consumerism, and most women accepted these goals only to experience, in Friedan's view, high levels of boredom, fatigue, and neurosis. Friedan urged women to free themselves from the "comfortable concentration camp of the home" and to insist upon access to opportunities that males had always denied them.

In the 1960s, many women, especially the younger and better educated, shared Friedan's analysis. By the middle of the decade, a female revolt against the predominant cultural role for women was in full swing. Women held rallies, confronted college presidents, television executives, and even their husbands, demanding access to prestigious jobs, child care centers, more liberal abortion laws, shared housework, and an end to the stereotypes of sheltered helplessness. In 1966 Friedan joined with others to found the National Organization for Women (NOW), whose main focus was an equal rights amendment to guarantee that "equal rights under the law shall not be denied or abridged by the United States on account of sex." Congress approved the amendment in 1970, and by 1976 it had been ratified by thirty-four states.

The impression of deep social discontent was heightened by the role played by young Americans, especially college students, after 1964. Prior to World War II, the college population had been an insignificant portion of the nation's young people. In 1900, only 3.9 percent of the group from eighteen to twenty-one years old was enrolled in a college or university, and by 1940 the slow expansion of higher education brought the proportion only to 14.5 percent. Yet a dynamic period of growth in higher education followed World War II, as federal and local government funds supported a burgeoning of public colleges, and more young people sought the occupational advantages of a college degree. By 1970, 47 percent of the group aged eighteen to twenty-one was attending college, a total of 6.3 million Americans.

Until about 1964, it was assumed that college students were more numerous but no different than before, continuing to pursue athletics, sex, and academic studies in the isolation of college communities. In December 1964 the "free speech" movement at the University of California, Berkeley, shattered the calm, and it was apparent that a new spirit was stirring among the young. The Berkeley protest was against university rules and officialdom, but close attention to the rhetoric af Mario Savio and other student leaders revealed that the university was being attacked on grounds that potentially threatened economic and political institutions as well. What students claimed most to dislike about the "multiversity" was its huge size, inflexible administration, and impersonal routine, relentlessly suppressing both individuality and idealism.

Rebellion on the Campuses

Conceivably this campus unrest might not have gone beyond occasional disputes at the larger universities where impersonality was most endemic. But the American military intervention in Vietnam in 1965 fanned student unrest to a peak. Hundreds of campuses surged with rallies and marches from 1966 through 1970, the most violent uprisings taking place at Columbia University in the spring of 1968, at Harvard, Yale, Cornell, and the University of California, Santa Barbara, in 1969. The decision to invade Cambodia in the spring of 1969 provoked unparalleled resistance across the country. Many campuses shut down before the end of the term, and at least six students were killed either by the National Guard (at Kent State University, where four were killed) or the police (at Jackson State College, where two were killed). The protests had broadened from a criticism of universities to include American racial patterns and foreign policy, and the violence spilled over to mar the Chicago convention of the Democratic party in 1968, as police and students clashed repeatedly. Most of this turmoil was spontaneous, but several radical youth organizations sprang up in an attempt to provide a national focus for protest. Students for a Democratic Society (SDS) was established at Port Huron, Michigan, in 1962, just as the student mood began to change. By the late 1960s, SDS had been joined by many organizations, among them the Progressive Labor party and, in the desperate atmosphere of 1968–69, the Weatherman faction of SDS with its dedication to insurrectionary violence.

The campus mood became somewhat less tense in 1971 and 1972, allowing Americans to realize that most college students were still politically inactive or moderate in their views, that most women continued to aspire to marriage and motherhood, that most blacks, browns, and reds not only rejected violence but also did not demand instant changes in old traditions and institutions. Yet there was no question that at the beginning of the 1970s more aggrieved groups were active and stirring in the country and more basic challenges were being pressed against American institutions than at any time in the past. Mingled with the signs of an affluent, disciplined, and technologically oriented society were the jarring notes of angry, romantic, and radical social protest. "Power to the People," young people shouted after political speeches, or pasted bumper stickers upon their Volkswagen buses calling for "Revolution for the hell of it." Conflict, both physical and ideological, encroached deeply upon the American consensus, and the country entered the 1970s much more anxious and less confident than it had been a decade before.

Upon his election in 1968, Richard M. Nixon said that the objective of his administration would be "to bring the American people together." It was hard to see how any single individual, however powerful, could accomplish this task in the 1970s, given the deep divisions that had opened between the races, age groups, and contending economic interests. Yet Nixon's performance was energetic and inventive, even if it was not entirely successful. During twenty years in public life he had been a staunch economic conservative and a devoted anti-Communist, but as president he abandoned these old

The Nixon Presidency

positions and meshed conservative and liberal ideas in a resourceful if inconsistent blend designed to appeal to as many groups as possible.

Conservative citizens expected Nixon to fulfill his promises to strengthen "law and order," to cut federal spending, and to terminate the active support for minority rights that had characterized the Kennedy-Johnson era. In some respects the new president did not disappoint them. His top-level appointments to the Justice Department, beginning with Attorney General John Mitchell, were men who preferred prosecuting criminals and political radicals rather than antitrust suits, and who showed little interest in civil rights. Nixon appointed four conservative judges to the Supreme Court—Warren E. Burger, Henry Blackmun, Lewis Powell, and William Rehnquist—and nominated two others so unsympathetic to the cause of equal rights (and so intellectually mediocre) that the Senate refused to confirm them. By 1971 the new Nixon Court had begun to shift the advantage in pretrial criminal procedures back toward the police and away from the rights of the accused. In September 1969, the administration eased the pressure on southern school districts to achieve immediate integration, and later opposed busing for the purpose of achieving racial balance in the schools. Nixon also quietly ended Johnson's war on poverty, phasing out the Office of Economic Opportunity.

Nixon the Reformer and Planner

Nixon irritated the liberal community with some of his policies, and he kept them off balance with others. He proposed a reform of the welfare system that contained work incentives but was built around a "guaranteed annual income" concept, which would provide a minimum payment of sixteen hundred dollars to a family of four. His "new federalism" program seemed cut from a more traditional conservative fabric, as it promised to return decision making in many program areas to state and local governments. Yet the central proposal carrying the new federalism thrust was revenue sharing, an innovative idea originally conceived by liberal economists in Johnson's administration. While he talked of decentralization, Nixon centralized power in a streamlined White House, with a growing staff and a new Domestic Council for policy coordination. In other areas Nixon seemed the activist: he supported a national land-use planning system, a national growth policy, and executive branch reorganization.

Nixonomics

Of the president's major policies, all but general revenue sharing were blocked by a Democratic Congress. Economic management, however, was a standing assignment of the modern presidency, and here Nixon made few friends either to his right or his left. When inflation cut the value of the dollar by 6 percent for two years in a row (1969 and 1970), the president in August 1971 clamped a ninety-day wage and price freeze on the economy and followed it with a complicated system of federal controls. This was an interference with the "free market," which conservatives had traditionally abhorred. To add discomfort to the business community, the Nixon government, while it held down spending on domestic programs, continued to accept deficits as defense spending soared beyond revenues. Largely because of the costs of the war in Vietnam, a military pay raise, the antiballistic missile defense system, and a huge defense budget (the administration requested $75.9 billion in defense spending for 1972–73, the highest sum in history), the administration ran a $58 billion deficit in the two-year period 1970–72, a sum greater than the entire national debt ($46 billion) at the end of FDR's New Deal. Deficits of this size alarmed liberals as well as conservatives, but even with this stimulus the economy struggled with undiagnosed maladies. The recession that set in toward the end of 1969 had ended by 1972, but the rise in economic activity did not reduce unemployment below a stubborn 5.5 percent. Despite the network of controls the inflationary surge continued, rising from an annual rate of 6 percent in 1970 to 11 percent in 1974.

Détente

In foreign policy, the Nixon administration also displayed an ideological flexibility that irritated conservatives who had hoped for an uncompromising anti-Communist posture. The administration was continuously engaged in peace talks with the North Vietnamese that dated back to 1968 and in arms limitations talks with the Soviets after November 1969. In Vietnam, the president moved slowly toward "winding down the war." In June 1969, he withdrew the first (twenty-five thousand) of a series of contingents of American troops, without explicitly altering the commitment to the survival of the Thieu regime in South Vietnam. The gradual troop reductions appeared to have defused the antiwar movement until, on April 30, 1970, the president launched a joint United States–South Vietnamese invasion of neutral Cambodia to eliminate Communist sanctuaries. Massive protests probably hastened the end of this military adventure by June, and the troop withdrawals continued until only one hundred fifty thousand Americans remained in Vietnam in mid-1972. The president did not admit that the Vietnam intervention had been a mistake, and it was not clear that he would continue the troop withdrawal even if a Communist victory appeared imminent. But these unanswered questions seemed less important in the election year 1972 than the fact that the administration had reduced American troop strength in Asia, lowered American casualties (Vietnamese casualties probably mounted under Nixon as the bombing of North Vietnam and Laos was intensified), and seemed cautiously headed toward a liquidation of the entire affair.

This pragmatic course may have disappointed some conservatives, but they were even more shocked by Nixon's five-day visit to mainland China in February 1972. Nixon held talks with Communist leaders Mao Tse-tung and Chou En-lai, and the meetings appeared to have lowered tensions between the two hostile powers. In late May the president flew to Moscow for talks with Soviet leaders, looking toward arms limitation and expanded trade and cultural relations. By the fall of 1972, Richard M. Nixon, one of the most vociferous anti-Communists of the early 1950s, seemed to have almost singlehandedly brought the cold war to an end.

President Nixon stands at the Great Wall of China in 1972, an event that was covered by American television. The trip not only contributed greatly to Nixon's re-election in November but also symbolized a new era in world diplomacy. (United Press International)

The Election of 1972

Democrats knew that the odds were heavily against unseating any incumbent president at the end of one term, especially one who had just completed a spectacular round of diplomacy with major adversaries. The opposition party proved to be in the same mood in 1972 as the Republicans had been in 1964: Let us have a choice, not an echo, a clear challenge to the Nixon government rather than a candidate who would crowd toward the moderate center (Hubert Humphrey, Edmund Muskie) or even the right (George Wallace). And so the Democrats nominated South Dakota Senator George McGovern, a liberal and long-time opponent of the Vietnam War. McGovern was a plain-spoken man of great moral earnestness. He advocated an immediate withdrawal from the war, a cut of some thirty billion dollars in the defense budget (the money to be used in urban and environmental programs), a generous minimum income plan, and tax reform.

This indeed was a sharp alternative to the Richard Nixon–Spiro Agnew ticket offered by the GOP. Surrendering to the impulse to seek a majority on the moral ground away from the pragmatic center had brought defeat to the Republicans in 1964, and it had the same effect on the Democrats in 1972—although in both years the opposition faced an incumbent president with his enormous advantages. On election day President Nixon polled 61 percent of the vote to McGovern's 38 percent, 45.9 million votes to 28.4 million, 521 electoral votes to 17. It was a landslide of historic proportions, but the president's popularity did not transfer to all Republicans. The Democrats gained two Senate seats and retained control of the House.

Watergate

Even before Nixon's landslide returned him to office, a series of events was underway that would drive him to an unprecedented resignation in 1974. On June 17, 1972, a security guard in the Watergate apartment complex in Washington, D.C., surprised and arrested five intruders in the offices of the Democratic National Committee. They were found to be employees of Nixon's campaign committee. Relentless investigation, spurred largely by two *Washington Post* reporters, disclosed that the break-in had been part of a broad campaign of political sabotage and ''dirty tricks'' directed against ''enemies'' of the administration. Each time the story seemed about to end, a new revelation would expand its damaging significance. While the administration denied that any official was involved in any wrongdoing, investigation revealed an ascending linkage of plans, payoffs, and cover-ups leading from the Watergate burglars up through a series of White House officials and the attorney general to the president's highest ranking staff. Critical testimony implicating chief of staff Robert Haldeman and domestic counselor John Ehrlichman came from the president's lawyer, John Dean, and these men resigned under fire on April 30, 1973. The administration was crippled by revelations of perjury and cover-up in high places, especially after the discovery that a tape recording system had preserved every conversation in the oval office. Nixon refused to turn over the tapes to the special prosecutor, Archibald Cox of the Harvard Law School, and to a committee of the Senate under Senator Sam Ervin that was investigating the affair. Then, as public suspicion mounted, an edited version of the tapes was released in April 1974, with critical conversations deleted. A Supreme Court order forced Nixon to release all tapes in late July, and the House Judiciary Committee voted three articles of impeachment. On August 8, 1974, Richard Nixon resigned his office rather than endure certain impeachment. The Watergate incident had brought a president down, and in his wake some fifty-six men, many of them top administration officials, were convicted of Watergate-related crimes.

The Imperial Presidency

In his last hours in the White House, Richard Nixon was reported to have pounded the floor in anguish, asking ''Why?'' The answer, of course, must go far beyond an attempted burglary and its cover-up. Nixon's administration had established a pattern of abuses of presidential power that had deeply alarmed the Congress, the media, and the public. He used government funds to equip his two villas (one in Florida, one in California) lavishly and took illegal advantage of the tax laws to claim a huge write-off for donation of his public papers. As the tapes revealed, he and his aides had aggressively sought to ''use the government to screw our enemies,'' directing the Internal Revenue Service to audit the tax returns of opposition politicians and reporters, exerting pressure upon radio and television stations through the Federal Communications Commission licensing process. In his 1972 reelection campaign, aides extorted huge contributions from corporations and other interest groups, receiving much of it after the legal deadline. He carried his disagreements with Congress to the extreme of refusing to administer certain laws and impounded funds on a scale no other president had ever dared.

These actions created a constitutional crisis that Watergate then precipitated. Yet it was obvious that the sources of these presidential abuses ran deeper than the character and judgment of Richard Nixon. It is true that the tapes revealed him as a frequently vindictive, profane, and mean-spirited man, whose judgment was impaired by the extreme isolation that his aides rigidly enforced against the media and public. But as historian Arthur M. Schlesinger, Jr., traced in his book *The Imperial Presidency* (1973), the sustained era of national crisis that began in 1939 had systematically led every president since Franklin Roosevelt to aggrandize power from the other branches, to stretch constitutional limits upon executive authority, to resort to secrecy and to justify even illegal actions with the claim of defending national security. The presidency had indeed become imperial, isolating its occupant from the realities of life through a swarm of courtiers, lavish appointments, and an unhealthy atmosphere of near-reverence. Nixon's misfortune was to bring to a disastrous fulfillment many of the dangerous tendencies that had afflicted the modern American presidency since total war, hot and then cold, came to distort American life at the end of the Great Depression.

Nixon's vice president, Maryland's Spiro Agnew, resigned in late 1973 after pleading nolo contendere (no contest) to well-documented charges of income tax evasion (from income on bribes). Nixon named as his replacement Congressman Gerald Ford of Michigan, a lackluster but well-liked Republican. Suddenly, in August 1974, the choice took on critical significance, as Ford was sworn in as the first president who had never been elected to any national office.

Ford saw himself as a caretaker and promised honesty, openness, and a healing time. He lived up to his promises, charting a two and one-half year presidency in which the traumas of Watergate gradually receded. This was an achievement for which Ford's successor was to thank him in the first sentence of his inaugural address. But beyond fashioning a steady and taint-free administration, Ford could offer little leadership. In part this stemmed from his personal qualities, in part from his long background as a minority-party legislator whose main concern was resistance, and in part it derived from the division of powers inherent in the Democratic control of Congress. No major domestic program came from the Ford White House, and probably none could have been enacted had it been proposed. In economic management the Ford administration—staffed by many of Nixon's appointees—faced a formidable combination of inflation and high unem-

The Presidency of Gerald Ford

ployment. The president chose to regard inflation as the major enemy. Since his deeply conservative instincts prohibited any thought of economic controls, his administration relied upon fiscal restraint and tight monetary policies. Ford used the veto frequently, opposing legislation to expand public employment, education, and conservation programs on the grounds of their expense in an inflation-prone economy. He talked of a drastic reduction in federal economic regulation. These positions alienated labor unions, conservationists, lower-income groups, and liberals in general. Ford's economic policies must be judged a success, however, in one important respect—they helped bring the annual inflation rate down from 11 percent in mid-1974 to 5 percent by 1976. But the cost was high unemployment—joblessness ranged from 8 percent to 10 percent of the work force during Ford's two and one-half years in office—and a virtual cessation of economic growth. "I am a Ford, not a Lincoln," the president remarked, and he managed to combine essentially Nixonian social policies with a refreshing candor and lack of pretense. He entered the 1976 election an underdog, the polls reporting that the public saw the president as "a nice guy" whose policies and capacity for executive leadership were widely doubted.

The Election of 1976

The presidential primaries of 1976 were financed for the first time by public funds, and there was intense competition for both major party nominations. President Ford narrowly survived a challenge from the Republican right wing led by California ex-Governor Ronald Reagan. A series of primary victories gave an insurmountable delegate majority to a Democrat who had been virtually unknown as 1976 opened—former Georgia Governor Jimmy (James Earl) Carter. Carter, a farmer, businessman, and ex-navy submarine commander, made an appeal to labor unionists and party moderates that George McGovern had not generated in 1972. He promised an active presidency in pursuit of full employment and liberal social goals, while reassuring centrists with demands for governmental reorganization, budget balancing, and improved management. A series of television debates between the candidates appeared to confirm Carter's judgment and grasp of details, although Ford challenged him strongly and eliminated the Democrat's early lead in the polls. Carter unseated the incumbent president with a narrow but solid victory; he compiled 40.8 million votes to Ford's 39.1, with an electoral edge of 297 to 241. The electorate had decided to end the eight years of divided government as it prepared for its third century; it placed an activist president again in the White House and gave the Democratic party control of both executive and legislative branches of government.

The last months of the Ford administration coincided with the coldest winter in America since the mid-nineteenth century. Yet while the weather brought a time of severity, the political cycle seemed to have moved toward hope. The newly elected president's preparations for office during the transition were the most orderly in the history of such shifts of power, with task forces working on every element of the Carter program. The inauguration on January 20 of Carter and his vicepresident, Walter F. Mondale, was made

President Jimmy Carter stands beside the man he defeated, Gerald R. Ford. Carter's election represented a significant reconciliation of North and South, black and white. Carter promised an intriguing blend of populism, sound management, and planning.   (Mark Godfrey/Magnum)

an occasion of graciousness toward the defeated Ford and his party, and some of the trappings of the imperial presidency were shed when Carter shunned the bullet-proof limousine and, with his wife and daughter, walked the length of Pennsylvania Avenue from the Capitol to the White House. In his first months in office the president forwarded to Congress far-reaching proposals for reform: a national energy plan, executive-branch reorganization, simplification of the tax system, and welfare reform. In foreign policy he stressed human rights, improved hemispheric relations through a gradual yielding of control over the Panama Canal, and stronger efforts to limit the spread of both nuclear and conventional arms. Carter's pace was deliberate; he expected results to come only after months and even years of patient work with Congress. Only time would tell whether the Georgia peanut farmer, now president, could mobilize the resources of government against national problems with better success than the activist predecessors of his own party—Johnson, Kennedy, Truman, Roosevelt. Yet his very election as a white southerner who had received 91 percent of the southern black vote symbolized the great social reconciliation that closed a decade of racial and ideological strife. The duration of this "honeymoon" between parties and interest groups was left for the future to reveal.

From the very beginning, American civilization had been based upon an assumption shared by the entire Western world: economic and population growth were the certain path to human progress. No more revolutionary turn in Western intellectual history may be imagined than a reversal of this faith in growth. Yet this was to take place in the 1970s. One influential book was an example of this rethinking of the global growth economy. In 1972 the Club of Rome published *The Limits to Growth,* one of the most pessimistic books ever to become a best-seller. It foretold a "collapse" of the world system by the mid-twenty-first century if the exponential growth of human population and attendant environmental pollution were not controlled. The book appeared (and sold two million copies in twenty-six languages) in a year of climatic disasters—a Saharan drought, failure of the Russian wheat and potato crop, a late Asian monsoon, a drop in the Pacific fish harvest resulting from a shift in the Humboldt current—that brought the first drop in world food production in thirty years, the exhaustion of world food reserves, and the intensification of world famine.

Many people disagreed with the Club of Rome's pessimistic analysis, but no one denied the reality of the cluster of interrelated problems (the "problématique) that threatened human progress. Most alarming were trends in world population. It took the human race thousands of years to reach the number of one billion (1830), one hundred years to add the second billion, thirty years to add the third (reached by 1960), and sixteen to reach four billion (March 1976). A peak in the human growth rate was reached in 1970 when an annual rate of 1.9 percent was estimated by United Nations sources. At this rate the global population would double in thirty-five years. Fortunately the rate of population growth began a gradual decline in 1970, dropping to 1.64 percent by 1975. This trend reflected death rates raised by famine but also the influence of economic development, changed attitudes toward fertility, family planning effort, and greater reliance upon abortion. Six industrialized nations (all of them in Europe) had achieved population stabilization by 1974, the year of the United Nations population conference in Bucharest, Rumania. Yet in the less-developed world where the vast majority of humankind lived, a population explosion continued, and demographers projected a leveling-off somewhere between eight and fifteen billion people, with famine and disease inevitably a part of the process of population control.

Of the six most populous nations in the world, only two—the United States and the Soviet Union—had no population policies, and both continued to add human numbers. In the United States the fertility rate declined steadily to a subreplacement level of 1.8 percent in 1976, yet the population continued to grow at approximately 1.6 million a year. This growth reflected the large number of young women who were of child-bearing age, a longer life expectancy, and the massive impact of immigration. Legal immigration added four hundred thousand people a year, and illegal immigration in the 1970s went "out of control" in the words of Immigration and Naturalization

The World Problématique: Population, Resources, Environment

Population Trends in the United States

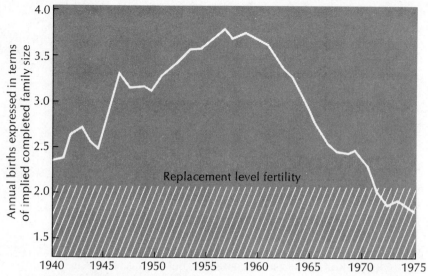

Total Fertility Rate: 1940 to 1975

In the early 1970s the U.S. total fertility rate dipped to below the replacement level of 2.1. This widely-reported trend convinced many people that the U.S. now had no "population problem." But the 1972 Report of the Presidential Commission on Population and the American Future *pointed out that, even at replacement level fertility, the American population would continue to grow for 30 to 50 more years, and with legal immigration running at 400,000 annually, it would never stop growing. When it is remembered that illegal immigration in the 1970s had reached an estimated total of 800,000–1,000,000 a year, the problem of population control in the U.S. remains acute.*
(Source: Bureau of the Census, *Current Population Reports,* Series P-25, No. 545; and unpublished data.)

Service officials, adding between eight hundred thousand and a million and a half people a year. The presidential Commission on Population Growth and the American Future in 1972 recommended that "the nation welcome and plan for a stable population," but neither President Nixon nor congressional leaders responded to the commission's fifty-two recommendations for population control.

The idea that American resources might be finite was not a new one. It lay at the basis of the conservation movement that had emerged at the beginning of the twentieth century. Yet the 1970s brought this idea home with impressive force. An important shift of values was symbolized in the passage of the National Environmental Protection Act of 1970, requiring environmental impact statements for all major federal projects. Americans could no longer build without careful prior consideration of potential environmental damage. Many states followed suit, requiring impact statements for all major private developments. A premonition of raw materials shortages led to the appointment of the second national commission on materials policy in 1970 (the first had been appointed by Harry Truman in 1950 and had reported in

The Era of Limits

1952), but the commission's report in 1973 made much less news than the shortages of that year. A Russian purchase of 25 percent of the American wheat crop brought a realization that the staff of life was in limited supply. Then came the 1972–73 embargo on oil sales by a new Arab cartel, propelling an escalation of petroleum prices and shortages of both oil and natural gas. Having taken cheap energy for granted since the discovery of petroleum and its uses, Americans found themselves urgently required to reevaluate their traditional methods of providing shelter, transportation, employment, and recreation.

Population Redistribution

Higher energy costs emerged as one of the major forces at work in reshaping American civilization. If oil reserves would last no more than twenty-five to forty years, as most experts predicted, a civilization built around the gasoline-powered automobile, the freeway, universal air-conditioning, and oil-heated swimming pools would have many adjustments to make. Alternate energy sources either carried a high environmental price tag—such as coal—or were yet in the experimental stages, as with solar, geothermal, and wind energy. But if the rapid rise in energy costs in the 1970s did not immediately produce revolutionary changes in the American life-style, they did appear to lend a major impetus to substantial shifts in economic and population growth patterns.

The president's biennial National Growth Report of 1976 revealed that the "sunbelt" of southern and western states was rapidly drawing population away from the older northeastern states. Between 1970 and 1975, Florida grew by 23 percent and Arizona by 25 percent, while Pennsylvania added only 0.2 percent to its population and New York actually lost residents. These population shifts reflected a greater social preference for warmer climes, and energy costs were at least one dimension of this preference.

This map reflects the striking population growth experienced in the so-called "sun belt" in the 1970s. Close examination shows that the most rapid growth took place not only in sunny climes but in small- to medium-sized cities or in their surrounding suburbs.

Metropolitan Areas with Population Increases of 12 Percent or More: 1970 to 1975

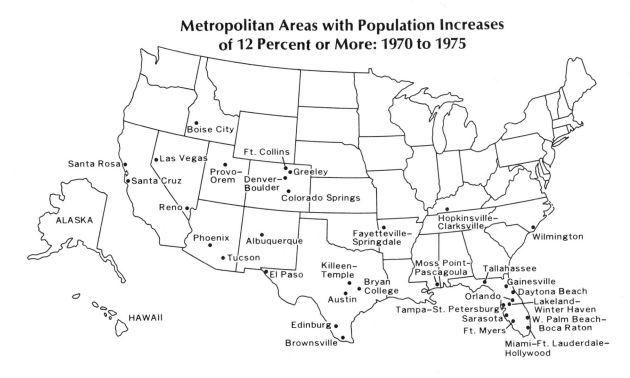

The same governmental report also noted that the historic and at least century-old flow of population from rural to metropolitan areas had been arrested in the 1970s. The surplus agricultural population had finally been relocated through the decades of painful migration to the North and West. Now many rural areas were experiencing an economic rejuvenation built not upon agriculture but upon recreation, retirement communities, and service industries. Even more striking than this development in population distribution patterns was the apparent end of the migration of population from the South. In the early 1970s the net white migration into the South was larger than the exodus, and the black outmigration not only was balanced by returning blacks, but there was slight evidence that more blacks were entering the region than were leaving. These demographic figures signified the end of an era in American life and reflected deep changes in the society.

COMMENTARY

If America's first century had been taken up with national survival, and the second concentrated mostly upon expansion, the agenda of the third seemed once again dominated by survival issues. At some point in the third century, the United States—along with other nations—would be required to reach some form of equilibrium between human population pressures and the viability of the ecosystem itself. This would be an assignment of staggering difficulty, implying social changes that could only be guessed at. And while the design of a stable-state economy was beset with every difficulty, an escalating conventional and nuclear armaments race threatened to ignite a war at any moment that would deny humanity the opportunity to evolve new institutions and habits for the era of limits. Thus Americans began their third century with an unaccustomed sense that time itself might be in the shortest supply—time to arrest uncontrolled growth before ecological crisis overwhelmed the world or a nuclear holocaust cut short efforts to sustain the progress of the human race.

SUGGESTED READING

ELIE ABEL, *The Missile Crisis* (1966)
RICHARD J. BARNET, *Roots of War* (1972)
RONALD BERMAN, *America in the Sixties* (1968)
JIMMY CARTER, *Why Not the Best?* (1975)
BARRY COMMONER, *The Closing Circle* (1971)
THEODORE DRAPER, *The Abuse of Power* (1967)
PAUL EHRLICH, *The Population Bomb* (1968)
ROWLAND EVANS and ROBERT NOVAK, *Nixon in the White House* (1971)
BETTY FRIEDAN, *The Feminine Mystique* (1963)
ELIE GINZBERG and ROBERT SOLOW, eds., *The Great Society* (1974)
HUGH GRAHAM and TED GURR eds., *Violence in America* (1969)
OTIS L. GRAHAM, JR., *Toward a Planned Society: From Roosevelt to Nixon* (1976)
DAVID HALBERSTAM, *The Best and the Brightest* (1972)
MICHAEL HARRINGTON, *The Other America* (1963)

Roger Hilsman, *To Move a Nation* (1967)

Norris Hundley ed., *The Chicano* (1975)

Doris Kearns, *Lyndon Johnson and the American Dream* (1976)

Stuart Levine and Nancy Lurie eds., *The American Indian Today,* rev. ed. (1968)

Carey MacWilliams, *North from Mexico* (1948)

Peter Matthiessen, *Sal Si Puedes* (1969)

Malcolm X, *Autobiography* (1965)

August Meier and Elliott Rudwick, *CORE* (1973)

Herman P. Miller, *Rich Man, Poor Man* (1964)

Herb Parmet, *The Democrats: The Years After FDR* (1976)

William Safire, *Before the Fall* (1975)

Jonathan Schell, *The Time of Illusion* (1976)

Arthur M. Schlesinger, Jr., *The Imperial Presidency* (1973)

Irwin Unger, *The Movement* (1974)

Richard J. Walton, *Cold War and Counter-Revolution* (1972)

INDEX